Manual for the Strong Interest Inventory

Jo-Ida C. Hansen & David P. Campbell

MANUAL FOR THE
Strong Interest Inventory

Form T325 of the
Strong Vocational Interest Blanks®

FOURTH EDITION

Distributed by
Consulting Psychologists Press, Inc.
3803 E. Bayshore Road
Palo Alto, CA 94303

Published by Stanford University Press
Stanford, California 94305

Distributed by Consulting Psychologists Press, Inc.
3803 E. Bayshore Road
Palo Alto, CA 94303

Printed in the United States of America.

ISBN 0-89106-026-X   LC 84-40413

97 96 95 94   13 12 11

Preface

As the 1981 revision of the Strong Vocational Interest Blank (the Strong-Campbell Interest Inventory, SVIB-SCII) was being published, plans for the 1985 revision of the SVIB-SCII were already being developed at the Center for Interest Measurement Research (CIMR) at the University of Minnesota, following discussions with the publisher. Within six months another full-fledged revision project had been set in motion. Thus, the Strong Interest Inventory has been under almost continuous revision and development since 1977, and the completion of the 1985 revision marks the end of the most intense and most productive period of research in the inventory's history. Most likely the instrument will never again see such a high level of activity sustained over so long a period.

To a large extent this active period of research on the Strong, which began in 1971 with David Campbell's development of the initial edition of the SCII, was a result of the women's movement. Prior to the 1974 publication of the SCII, the Strong was published in two forms—one for women and one for men. As the women's movement turned its attention to inequities in the job market and the limited employment options available to women, interest inventories also were scrutinized for inequities. And they all—the Strong Vocational Interest Blank included—were found wanting. With growing outside pressure, the publisher of the SVIB was encouraged to make the financial commitment necessary to produce dramatic changes and improvements in the inventory.

The sex-equalization process that began in 1971 has continued throughout 15 years, with each revision representing a fairer, more balanced instrument. With the completion of the 1981 revision, 162 Occupational Scales were included on the profile; half of those were normed on female occupational groups, half on male occupational groups. In mid-1981, 10 years after the effort to merge the previous women's and men's forms into one inventory had begun, I had the luxury for the first time of contemplating improvements in the inventory that would go beyond those related to sex equalization.

The plan for the 1985 revision included two important proposals. The first was to extend the breadth of the Strong to include more nonprofessional and vocational/technical Occupational Scales. The second was to develop new Women- and Men-in-General Samples to use in the renorming of the General Occupational Themes and the Basic Interest Scales and in the reconstruction of all 1981 Occupational Scales.

The proposal to expand the occupational offerings of the Strong addressed the concern of users that the instrument had come to be oriented toward exploration of career opportunities only in occupations requiring a college degree. This was not a deliberate effort on the part of the authors and, in fact, the Strong profile always has included several nonprofessional Occupational Scales (e.g., FARMER, POLICE OFFICER, BEAUTICIAN, EXECUTIVE HOUSEKEEPER). However, the majority of the Occupational Scales added to the profile in 1974 and 1981 represented professional occupations.

On the 1985 profile, 32 percent of the Occupational Scales represent occupations with educational requirements less than a college degree and include such additions as BUS DRIVER, CARPENTER, ELECTRICIAN, EMERGENCY MEDICAL TECHNICIAN, HORTICULTURAL WORKER, MEDICAL TECHNICIAN, RESPIRATORY THERAPIST, CHEF, FLORIST, FUNERAL DIRECTOR, OPTICIAN, TRAVEL AGENT, and FOOD SERVICE MANAGER. Each of the new nonprofessional or vocational/technical occupations is represented by both female- and male-normed Occupational Scales, and all of them have an average or above-average employment outlook for the future. These new scales should make the Strong useful with a broader range of clients than has been the case in the past. And when the profile is used in conjunction with Appendixes A and B to generalize to occupations not on the profile, its utility should be greatly increased.

The proposal to develop new Women-in-General (WIG) and Men-in-General (MIG) samples addressed the concern that the societal changes of the 1970's and early 1980's outdated the extant WIG and MIG samples. The 300 women and 300 men in the 1985 WIG and MIG samples were drawn from 93 occupations. And for the first time, the female and male subjects in the WIG and MIG are matched on occupational title. For example, if the MIG sample contained five carpenters, so did the WIG sample; if the WIG sample included two beauticians, so did the MIG sample. The development of these new samples, particularly at this time in the history of interest measurement, represents a tremendous step forward in the effort to do comparative studies on the interests of women and men and is critical to the validity of the inventory.

The Fourth Edition of the *Manual for the SVIB-SCII* contains all of the data needed to describe the samples, the scales, the reliability, and the validity of the 1985 inventory. Two hundred and two occupational samples containing 48,238 people (24,179 females and 24,059 males) were used for Occupational Scale construction. The bulk of the testing was done in the late 1970's and the 1980's, and 81 of the samples were collected specifically for this revision.

Of the 207 Occupational Scales now included on the profile, 202 are matched-sex, meaning that there are 101 occupations represented by female-normed Occupational Scales (such as CARPENTER, GEOGRAPHER, MEDICAL ILLUSTRATOR, SCHOOL ADMINISTRATOR, REALTOR, and BANKER) that also are represented by male-normed Occupational Scales. In addition, there are four occupations represented only by female-normed scales (DENTAL ASSISTANT, DENTAL HYGIENIST, HOME ECONOMICS TEACHER, and SECRETARY) and one occupation represented only by a male-normed scale (AGRIBUSINESS MANAGER).

Each sample represents experienced, satisfied workers who are performing their jobs within their occupation in a typical way. The 48,238 sample members were drawn from a total of 142,610 people, from across the country, who were tested in the course of the research.

The samples range in age from the relatively youthful female foresters (mean age 26.6 years) and male carpenters (mean age 27.3 years) to the middle-aged female college professors (mean age 49.0 years) and male elected public officials (mean age 46.3 years). The overall mean age (mean of the means of the samples) is 38.1 years.

Each person surveyed was asked to report her or his level of education and number of years of experience in the occupation being studied. In educational level the samples range from female licensed practical nurses (11.4 years of education) and male Marine Corps enlisted personnel (12.7 years) up to female physicians (21.9 years of education) and male biologists (21.6 years). The average level of education over all samples (the mean of the means of the samples) is 16.8 years.

In terms of experience, the samples range from the relatively junior female foresters (3.4 years of experience) and male flight attendants (4.0 years) to the well-established female medical technicians (21.1 years of experience) and male farmers (24.3 years). The average length of experience over all samples is 11.8 years.

The *Manual for the SVIB-SCII* serves as the primary technical resource for the Strong. The *Manual* frequently refers the reader to the *User's Guide for the SVIB-SCII* for interpretive guidelines, theoretical possibilities, and clinical information. A grasp of the contents of both the *Manual* and the *Guide* is recommended for thoroughly understanding the SVIB-SCII.

The cadre of people working on the 1985 revision was unusual in that several of the key players in the 1981

revision returned to work on the 1985 revision. And for the first time in the history of the Center for Interest Measurement Research (CIMR) the operation had more than one full-time employee.

Dana Benassi Leach, one of the most industrious undergraduates to work on the 1981 revision, returned as a University of Minnesota alumna to fill the role of Assistant Administrator at CIMR. She was responsible for everything from hiring personnel to budget preparation to the critical task of obtaining sample sources. She was the glue that held our large (26 people) and very diverse group together—no easy management task, since the majority of the staff was part-time undergraduate student employees without a psychology major among them.

Tamara Nelson, Graduate Research Assistant, took a supporting role in the 1981 revision; on this revision, she worked with Dana to ensure an uninterrupted flow of work by everyone. She was the manager for all of the data collection—a tremendous responsibility that involved supervising the preparation and mailing of over 200,000 testing packets, the organization of all the returns from subjects, and the selection and screening of the subjects to be included in the criterion samples.

Jean Forsberg, Senior Secretary, has been at CIMR through three revisions of the Strong. During that time, I have never heard a grouchy word from her; she provides the even keel for our exacting production schedules and deadlines. During the course of this revision, she became a word-processing expert and probably can quote the *Manual* in her sleep after completing so many drafts.

Jane Swanson, Graduate Research Assistant, validated her SVIB-SCII Academic Comfort score first by completing her M.A. during the 1981 revision and then by returning to work on her Ph.D. Jane was in charge of CIMR's computer operations during the final critical phases of the revision; she represents counseling psychology's scientist-practitioner model at its best. She worked with Jim Wick, who started his career at CIMR as an undergraduate in computer science and completed it as an M.B.A. graduate; Jim provided invaluable initiative and creativity updating our computer software. Jane also worked with Tom Dohm and Derek Bolan, Graduate Research Assistants, to process data for thousands of subjects—usually after midnight—the only hour that electronic scanning equipment was available to us.

Others who made special contributions to the project were Sony Hideki Sano, Graduate Research Assistant, who tabulated all of the data presented in Appendix A to describe the Occupational Criterion Samples, and Bev Retzlaff, Secretary, who typed thousands of mailing labels and letters of inquiry. The Undergraduate Research Assistants who stuffed the packets, recorded the returns, prepared the answer sheets for data analysis, and assisted with computer operations and typing responsibilites included Barb Anderson, Caroline Anderson, Sue Davey, Joe Dawis, Steven Durben, Sharon Gayle, Lonnie Hartley, Sandi Jelley, Craig Kemp, Wendy Kolberg-Aho, Kristen Mengelkoch, Mary Kay Putchel, Paul Read, Chandrika Seshadri, Ava Slemrod, and Ivy Wong. As I reflect on each of the undergrads who worked on the project, what strikes me as most notable—other than their contribution to the work of the revision—is their 90 percent graduation rate; they were a truly remarkable group of young adults.

The completion of the 1985 SVIB-SCII revision marks the end of the last phase in the project, first designed in 1974 by David Campbell, to merge E. K. Strong, Jr.'s Women's and Men's forms of the inventory. The major innovations, other than the merger itself, include the incorporation of a theory with the inventory's basic empiricism, the tremendous expansion in Occupational Scales for both women and men in professional as well as nonprofessional and vocational/technical occupations, and the development of matched Women- and Men-in-General samples. During each revision an effort was made to make the inventory more useful to practitioners and their clients while maintaining its scientific integrity. My hope is that in the future the publisher will continue to impose on the instrument the rigorous psychometric standards upon which Strong, Campbell, and I always have insisted.

Minneapolis   Jo-Ida C. Hansen
May 1985

Contents

Figures and Tables

Manual for the Strong Interest Inventory

CHAPTER ONE

Making Use of the Strong

The Strong-Campbell Interest Inventory (SCII), the current edition of the Strong Vocational Interest Blank, is a carefully constructed questionnaire (SVIB-SCII, Form T325) that employs 325 items to inquire about a respondent's interest in a wide range of occupations, occupational activities, hobbies, leisure activities, school subjects, and types of people. The respondent is asked to indicate "Like," "Indifferent," or "Dislike" in response to the items; the answers then are analyzed by computer (the SCII cannot be scored by hand) to derive scores on 264 *scales*. The results are reported on a sheet called a *profile*, which presents the scale scores in an organized format and offers interpretive information. Although the profile is largely self-explanatory, it is helpful to have a counselor guide the respondent to an understanding of the scales and an interpretation of the scores. The *Manual for the SVIB-SCII* provides counselors with the detailed technical information about the development and validation of the scales that is necessary for a thorough understanding and evaluation of the inventory. The *User's Guide for the SVIB-SCII* (Hansen, 1984), which blends theoretical possibilities, research findings, clinical knowledge, case studies, occupational data, and a modicum of technical information, was written as a training resource for professionals who administer the Strong on a routine basis.

The SVIB-SCII uses a person's responses to *familiar* items to provide information about her or his probable interest in activities he or she finds *unfamiliar*. The basic assumptions in the development of the Strong were:

1. That the interest factors underlying familiar activities are the same as those underlying unfamiliar activities.

2. That responses to familiar activities (items), therefore, can be used to identify unfamiliar occupational interests.

3. That even though a person may not be knowledgeable about all jobs or occupations, she or he can give informed responses (such as like, indifferent, or dislike) to items about familiar activities that reflect the work patterns of various jobs and occupations.

The Strong gives the respondent five main types of information: first, scores on six General Occupational Themes, which reflect the respondent's overall occupational orientation; second, scores on 23 Basic Interest Scales, which report consistency of interests or aversions in 23 specific areas, such as art, science, or public speaking; third, scores on 207 Occupational Scales, which indicate degree of similarity between the respondent's interests and the characteristic interests of women and men in a wide range of occupations; fourth, scores on two Special Scales that measure introversion-extroversion and degree of comfort in an academic environment; and fifth, 26 Administrative Indexes that help to identify invalid or unusual profiles.

Scores are arranged on the profile in a format that encourages the respondent to note overall trends, to see how these trends are related to the world of work, and to employ these findings in a program of career exploration. The emphasis is on organizing the information to help the respondent develop a general strategy toward approaching career decisions.

Using Psychological Testing in Career Counseling

Typically, the self-exploration phase in career counseling includes obtaining information on interests, needs, and abilities. Psychological testing is one technique used to assist self-exploration; other techniques include biographical interviews, recollection of previous experiences, and direct observation of others. But because psychological testing offers several advantages over other methods of data gathering, it is incorporated into all major approaches to career counseling as an integral component of self-exploration (Crites, 1974). Among these advantages are the following:

1. People can be taught to use tests more easily than they can be trained to use other methods of observation, such as rating scales or interviews.

2. Tests are subject to less bias than other methods of observation; that is not to say that tests cannot be influenced by the prejudices or beliefs of the test constructors, but with tests the biases can be controlled to a greater extent.

3. Observations made through tests are more easily communicated than observations made through other means.

4. Tests reduce the time necessary for information gathering; in other words, they provide a shortcut to the information.

5. Tests provide a standard of comparison against

which a person can judge herself or himself and thus improve self-evaluation.

6. Tests provide people with a sample of their psychological traits to use in developing hypotheses about themselves.

Thus, interest inventories can be used effectively for a variety of purposes. This chapter reviews the more common applications.

Counseling the Individual Student or Employee

Interest inventories should perform one or both of two principal functions in career counseling. First, they should provide people with information about themselves and their relationship to the working world, information that will lead them to greater self-understanding and to better decisions about the course of their lives. Second, interest inventories should provide people who must make decisions about others—counselors, teachers, administrators, personnel managers, supervisors—with comparable information as well as strategies for interpreting it, so that their decisions can consider the unique qualities of each individual.

Interest inventories can be used in many ways to serve these functions. The following does not exhaust the possibilities; it does list the applications that have been found to be the most effective.

As an aid in making educational and occupational choices. This is by far the most common use. People must make decisions about the course of their lives, and because their choices of educational major and eventual occupation may have more impact on their lives than any other decisions they make, those choices should be well informed.

When people make these decisions, they should have access to good occupational information, to professional advice, and to the best possible data about themselves. The Strong was designed specifically for these situations, and the information it provides about a person's pattern of interests is directly applicable to making educational and occupational choices. Of course, other information, such as experiences and abilities, also should be considered in making these choices; the SCII profile offers only a measure of interests.

Some counselors use interest inventories only with people who are uncertain about what they want to do, but many people who already have made firm decisions are reassured in seeing their choices confirmed. One common reaction to the profile is, "Yes, my scores look reasonable: that's about what I figured. This information is reassuring."

The Strong is used by a variety of institutions to assess interests—high schools, colleges and universities, social-service agencies, community organizations, corporations, consulting firms, and employment agencies; it can be used with a variety of age groups—high school and college students as well as adults; and it can be used in career counseling that leads to decisions such as selecting a major, choosing an occupation, making a mid-career change, or preparing for retirement (Hansen, 1984).

As a stimulus for the exploration of lifestyles. Scores on the SCII also may be used to identify preferences for non-work activities, such as interests in avocational or recreational activities, or in living or work environments, or interests reflecting preferences for types of people. Using the Strong to organize interests in all areas of life helps a person learn to integrate various life roles and to maximally satisfy her or his interests.

As a vehicle in discussions between client and counselor. Many people who are seeking vocational guidance feel more comfortable in counseling sessions if the initial discussion is structured, and they are grateful for an organized assessment of their interest patterns. Test scores provide a focus that moves conversation quickly to areas of concern to the client. Many counselors, especially inexperienced ones, also appreciate the focusing qualities of the profile scores. Tests, of course, should not be used as a crutch, but that is seldom a problem once the counselor has accumulated some experience.

As a catalyst in discussions between student and parent. Although experienced teachers and counselors can guide discussions with students quite adroitly without the aid of tests, many parents do not have the same facility. Again, interest-test scores can stimulate discussion of topics such as career choice and personal development. These scores present the parent with specific information about the student's interests—information that may not have surfaced in earlier discussions—and they give the student an opportunity to explain personal feelings in ways not usually possible. In such settings, useful decisions often can be reached. For example, several years ago, a university student reported, with considerable relief, that his results on the inventory had helped him convince his parents that he had good reason for not wanting to go to medical school. He was from a family with a long history of physicians—a parent, two siblings, a grandparent, and two other relatives had all gone to medical school—but he had never wanted to be a doctor. Whenever he said this to his family, they always responded, "Sure, we all felt that way when we were your age. After you get into it, you'll like it." Years of protest on his part had not availed, but the evidence provided by the interest profile—that his interests were quite different from those of physicians—finally convinced them that he was not destined to follow in the family tradition. With no further protest on their part, he took his degree in architecture and today is contentedly designing schools and industrial facilities.

In a similar situation, a student whose parents were advising her to enter nursing training had set her sights higher—she wanted to go to medical school—and she used her profile (and tests of ability) to demonstrate to them that her interests (and aptitudes) were similar to those of physicians and other biological scientists. Shown this evidence, the parents supported her plans.

As a selection device for those who must make employment decisions. Precisely how test scores should be used in employee selection will vary with the situation and with the training of the person who is doing the hiring. Employment decisions are important for all concerned, and they should be made by people with professional training. Using the inventory simply as a "go/no go" employee-selection device, and making each decision on the basis of a fixed cutoff score, is not recommended, though such a strategy is better than basing the decision on whether or not the applicant is friendly and has a good handshake.

For employee-selection purposes, the inventory is most effective when it is part of a general screening process developed by someone with professional training. Similarly, using an inventory to make placement decisions about people already on the payroll is handled best by a trained personnel worker who can study the respondent's scores, then discuss them with her/him along with other considerations dictated by the practical setting.

As a tool in helping people understand their job dissatisfaction. Some people are dissatisfied with their jobs because they are in positions that fail to allow them outlets for their dominant interests, or because they are in settings in which they have little in common with their colleagues. Many times an interest profile can identify the problem by showing the individual how she/he is different. When an accountant is shown that her interests lean more toward the artistic than those of most executives, she has information that can help her contend with the routine of her job. Even if she cannot change careers, she can take steps to improve her situation, perhaps by becoming active in the local art institute during her off-hours or by seeking employment as an accountant in some art-related firm, such as an advertising agency. What plan she develops depends on her imagination and energy, but the inventory can give her some direction.

Conducting Research on Groups

Most of the practical, day-to-day applications of the Strong have been discussed. But the instrument need not be confined to the individual; researchers studying groups should consider the following possibilities. This list, like the first, is incomplete; an imaginative scientist can find many more novel uses for good measuring instruments.

Studying characteristic interests of particular occupations. Data on a new scale, such as its item-reponse percentages, scale means, and intercorrelations with existing scales, provide information about the dominant interests of people in a given occupation. For example, interest-inventory data from a sample of women geologists showed that their likes were concentrated in academic areas such as science and mathematics, as well as in nature, outdoor, and mechanical activities. Their aversions focused on social service and religious activities, and on traditional home and family activities. They also showed an aversion to enterprising endeavors such as merchandising and sales.

Detailed information about an occupation is useful for many purposes, such as helping people decide if they would like employment in the occupation, planning recruiting efforts to attract to the occupation those people who would be most likely to remain, or identifying people already in the occupation who might be more happily and more effectively assigned elsewhere.

Studying change in groups. Interest inventories have been used to test groups at one point in time and then to retest them at some later time to see how they have changed. In a study by the American Association of Medical Colleges, 2,800 medical school students were tested as entering freshmen and retested four years later upon graduation (Hutchins, 1964). The results, discussed in more detail in Chapter 5 and in the *Handbook for the SVIB-SCII* (Campbell, 1971), indicated that these students showed a decline in both scientific and social-service interests, areas in which they had scored very high as freshmen, and a mild increase in adventuresome interests. These findings run counter to expectations, and afford an interesting basis for psychometric research and speculation.

Interest inventories are not precise enough, however, to detect small, subtle, short-term changes in groups. Because the items for the inventory were selected for long-term stability and validity, small day-to-day shifts are not reflected in the scores. For example, teachers who test students before and after a specific course to determine the impact of the course usually will find that the Strong scores show little, if any, change. Most people's interests, as measured by the SCII, are quite stable over the short range.

Over a longer period, such as two or three years, changes may occur in some people—especially young people—and the inventory scores should reflect those changes.

Studying change in institutions. Interest inventories can be used to compare different classes, different pools of applicants, or different recruit or volunteer groups at various times. One study that examined the characteristics of freshman classes at Dartmouth College over a 20-year period (Campbell, 1969) showed that the more recent classes were much more academically oriented—with stronger interests in science and the arts—than their predecessors, who were more attracted to business endeavors.

Studying general societal trends. When samples tested in the 1930's and 1940's are compared with analogous samples tested in the 1960's, 1970's, and 1980's, estimates of general change within society can be drawn. The results of such studies (Campbell, 1966b; Hansen, 1981; Hansen, 1982) show that vocational-interest patterns are much more stable over long time spans than the average person (or psychologist, for that matter) might think.

Studying change within an individual. Interest inventories can be used in case studies of change over time, or lack of change, with a single person representing some generalized societal phenomenon. Several examples of this application are given in the *Handbook*.

Studying cross-cultural influences. Several projects have used the inventory to study occupations in other countries. For some of these, the form has been translated into another language; for others—studies in Ireland and Pakistan, for example—the English-language version was used. Examples include Lonner's work with German-speaking psychologists and accountants (Lonner, 1968, 1969); Shah's work with Pakistani physicians and engineers (Shah, 1971); Hanlon's study of Irish students (Hanlon, 1971); Stauffer's work with the German and French translations of the Strong (Stauffer, 1973); and Fouad's work with the Spanish translation (Fouad, 1984; Fouad, Cudeck, and Hansen, 1984). The results of these studies show considerable similarity of interest, across several countries, among people in the same occupation; generally, American norms are usable in other countries as representations of the interests of specific occupations there.

One problem in using earlier editions of the Strong cross-culturally was that a few items—such as *Be a cheerleader* or *Work with Democrats*—were peculiarly American. These items bemused or irritated foreign respondents. Though the number of items was too small to have an appreciable effect on scoring, the loss of goodwill was substantial. This problem was addressed in the development of the Strong in 1974, and many troublesome items were eliminated. Consequently, problems have been minimal with recent translations into other languages (Hansen & Fouad, 1984); most items (for example, *Operating machinery*, *Writing reports*, *Watching an open-heart operation*) translate easily into other languages, eliciting the same responses as they do in English. Chapter 2 discusses in more detail the translation and validation of the Strong in several languages.

Some Potential Research Uses

The foregoing covers the usual research applications of interest inventories. Because of the improvements being made in the SCII, other applications may become common. Here are some likely possibilities.

Identifying homogeneous types on which to do further research. Dimensions of interests can be used in the same way that we have learned to use measures of general intelligence or socioeconomic status. The General Occupational Themes (discussed in later chapters) may be especially useful. People can be grouped into Realistic types, Artistic types, Social types, and so forth as a prelude to other investigations. Almost certainly, people of these types will behave differently in various environments, and researchers could use this typology as a classifying variable. For example, investigators studying the reactions of people to crowding might first separate their subjects into predominantly social and predominantly artistic samples, since these groups are likely to have different reactions to crowds.

Selecting counseling interventions. Recent work in matching people with different types of interests to different types of counseling indicate that such matches improve counseling outcomes (Kivlighan, Hageseth, Tipton & McGovern, 1981). The SVIB-SCII's General Occupational Themes can be used to identify an individual's global interests and, then, to select counseling techniques that will improve the counseling process whether in one-to-one or group sessions.

Understanding influences on career development. Strange as it may seem, almost nothing is known about the way patterns of interest develop. Virtually all previous research has concentrated on the technology of measuring interests, describing group characteristics, determining the degree of predictability of vocational behavior by inventoried interests, or studying other correlates of interests. Little has been done to learn how different patterns of interest form in the first place. To a large extent, this neglect has persisted because the measuring instruments have not lent themselves to this type of research. The bulky empiricism of traditional approaches—dealing with dozens of scales—has restricted the range of applicability of the inventories, leaving no easy way to study early determinants of various patterns of scores. Now that the profile has a more definite theoretical framework, research of a more theoretical nature can be organized.

Identifying the origin of interests. Just as there is no definitive knowledge of how interests develop, little conclusive information exists on the origin of interests. Hopefully, the behavior genetic method of studying the heritability of interests may someday offer us some insights into the question. The Minnesota Study of Twins Reared Apart (Bouchard, Heston, Eckert, Keyes, and Resnick, 1981), which began in 1979 and is continuing at the University of Minnesota, is the most comprehensive study ever conducted on twins reared apart. The study controls for the potential inflation of similarity as a function of environmental similarities. To date, the results of the Minnesota Study suggest that the interest similarities between twins in the reported case studies are greater than could be expected on the basis of coincidence, and that the correlation between the interests of twins is greater than that between the interests of other familial pairs (Bouchard, Hansen, Scarr, and Weinberg, 1983).

Carrying out a census of interest patterns. How many people in a given society have scientific interests? How many have artistic interests? Are cultures with many enterprising individuals more progressive than cultures with few? Interest inventories can help research such questions.

Studying interpersonal relationships. Marriages between people of similar interests might be more successful than others. Parents and children with different patterns of interest might need more help in communicating with each other than do those with similar interests.

Studying the behavior-type composition of groups. Groups exhibiting heterogeneous interest patterns may be more or less efficient than homogeneous groups. The characteristics of the individuals within any group have an impact on overall group behavior, and interest inventories can help in studying such issues.

Designing jobs around the interests of people. Interest inventories are a systematic means of asking people what they like and dislike. Such information should be useful—indeed, crucial—in designing work environments that people will find appealing. Given the current level of knowledge, this may be, at the moment, a grandiose goal. Still, if we know for example that psychologists have strong artistic interests, perhaps departments of psychology and psychological clinics would do well to allocate some portion of their supply budgets to making their environments more artistically exciting. If we know that people in sales have high levels of adventuresome interests, perhaps we should design sales incentives that capitalize on that knowledge. And perhaps we should design clerical work out of the technician's job, since we know that these people abhor those activities.

Similar, but more subtle, modifications of working environments have been made by the workers themselves, often through decades of gradual change, but we should learn to shape environments more systematically, to create a greater impact sooner. Such an approach could lead to greater diversity in work environments. In the absence of forces to the contrary, conformity, not diversity, is the rule in most contemporary work settings. The better we can document that different people, or different subgroups of people, like different things, the more successfully we can adapt their work environments.

This chapter has discussed the major uses of interest inventories and has suggested several applications for future research. The chapters that follow examine the development of the SVIB-SCII in detail and report data on its statistical characteristics.

CHAPTER TWO

Testing and Scoring Materials

The materials for the SVIB-SCII include the inventory booklet (Form T325), an answer sheet, and a profile form that reports the respondent's scores. An alternative to the profile form is an interpretive report that offers an interpretation tailored to the respondent's results in addition to the scores and generalized interpretation of the basic profile. The SCII also is available in Spanish (Form T325S), French Canadian (Form T325FC), and Hebrew (T325H) translations, and the wording has been adapted for use in Great Britain (T325B). All of these materials are discussed in this chapter.

The Inventory Booklet

The core of the SVIB-SCII system is the inventory booklet (Fig. 2.1). This form lists 325 items, to most of which the person responds by filling in either "Like," "Indifferent," or "Dislike" on the answer sheet.

Types of items in the inventory. The test booklet has seven parts:

Part I. Occupations (131 items). These items are all names of occupations, and this is the inventory's best part in terms of measurement power; that is, these items elicit more variability in response from one occupation to the next than any other part. People respond to the stereotypic nature of occupational titles, and their responses signal their own occupational orientation.

Part II. School Subjects (36 items). The school subjects cover a wide range of educational situations, including academic and other areas. Most people, even students as young as 13 or 14, have little trouble in deciding how they feel about a given subject, even though they may never have studied it.

Part III. Activities (51 items). This section contains a diverse collection of activities, such as *Repairing electrical wiring*, *Making statistical charts*, and *Interviewing clients*. This is another powerful section; occupations differ widely in the percentage of people answering "Like" or "Dislike" to these items.

Part IV. Leisure Activities (39 items). These items cover spare-time activities, hobbies, games, and a variety of entertainments. Some examples are *Poker*, *Symphony concerts*, and *Preparing dinner for guests*. Many of the items in this section provoke striking differences in the characteristic responses of occupational groups.

Part V. Types of People (24 items). This section asks whether the respondent would enjoy working day-to-day with various types of people such as *Highway construction workers*, *High school students*, and *Babies*.

Part VI. Preference Between Two Activities (30 items). This section asks the respondent to contrast two activities or circumstances, such as *Taking a chance* versus *Playing it safe*, or *Having a few close friends* versus *Having many acquaintances*, and to decide which is the more appealing, or whether the two should be marked as equally attractive or unattractive.

Part VII. Your Characteristics (14 items). The respondent is asked to read a statement such as *Usually start activities of my group*, and to respond either "Yes," "?," or "No" to indicate if the statement is an apt self-description. Almost everyone appears to answer this section honestly, and these responses furnish another type of information about the respondent's occupational orientation.

Chapters 9 and 10 and the *User's Guide* discuss ways in which the client's response rate to each of the parts can be used in counseling.

The value of a varied item format. Variation in item content and format from section to section is helpful in two ways; first, the variety provides some redundancy and subtlety in the scales (a person's interests can thus be tapped from several approaches and at several levels); second, it presents a more interesting task to the person filling in the inventory (to respond to several hundred items of the same format can be boring).

Selecting items for the booklet. There are two paramount concerns in selecting items for interest inventories: first, the items must collectively produce valid, reliable scales; and second, the items should not irritate, offend, or embarrass the respondent in any way, if the inventory is to be effective in a variety of situations.

The items in the 1985 SVIB-SCII booklet are identical to those in the 1974 and 1981 forms of the SCII. However, seven of the items related to religious activities have been modified; where the original wording of these items primarily used Christian terms, the new wording is more generic and should elicit more reliable answers from respondents.

With two exceptions, all of the items on Form T325 were taken from the earlier Strong booklets, either the men's form, published in 1966, or the women's, published in 1969. Excellent item statistics are available on these items, and the best of them were selected for

Fig. 2.1. SII inventory booklet, Form T325.

inclusion in the SCII booklet. The following guidelines or criteria were used in selecting items from the two booklets:

1. Each item should elicit a wide range of response among occupations. Specifically, the range of "Like" and "Dislike" percentages across occupations should be large; if people in most occupational samples gave the same response to an item, the item would not add much to the scales. Examples of items eliminated because of restricted range of response were *Funeral director*, to which virtually everyone answered "Dislike," and *Geography*, to which most people in every occupation answered "Like." Examples of items eliciting a wide range of response are *College professor*, where the range of "Like" responses runs from 5 percent among farmers, people in the skilled crafts, and some lower-level business occupations, to 99 percent among psychologists, political scientists, and anthropologists; and *Operating machinery*, where the range is from 5 percent among artists and writers to 97 percent among farmers and machinists.

This empirical criterion of response range—essentially a measure of item validity—was the single most important factor in deciding whether an item was to be retained; if the distribution over several hundred occupational samples was narrow, the item was discarded; if the distribution was broad, the item then faced the other criteria below. A more extensive discussion of this criterion appears in Chapter 3.

2. Items should cover a wide range of occupational content. Evaluating items on this criterion calls for some judgment in defining the universe of vocational interests across all occupations. How do we know what breadth of content that universe contains, and whether or not the items selected address all of its more important components? We cannot be sure, but the general goal was to seek diversity in items. Combining the men's and women's booklets helped considerably: the items in the merged booklet cover far more interest areas than did the items in either of the original booklets.

3. Items should be free of sex-role bias. Because one of the primary motivations for merging the two forms in 1974 was the elimination of sex-role bias, considerable attention was given to this factor in the selection and wording of items. Wherever possible, existing items were modified to eliminate gender: for example, *Policeman* became *Police officer*, *Salesman* became *Salesperson*. And where gender was an integral part of an item, versions for both sexes were included: for example, *Actor/Actress*, *Dressmaker/Tailor*, *YMCA/YWCA staff member*.

The words "man, men, woman, women" were eradicated. Thus, *Prominent businessmen* became *Prominent business leaders*, *Athletic women* became *Athletic people*, and *Advertising man* became *Advertising executive*.

No item was eliminated simply because of a large male-female difference in response. Although discarding such items might solve a few technical problems—such an expedient was followed in the early days of intelligence testing—its effect would be misleading. About one-third of the items in the inventory show large differences in the responses of men and women; our task is to learn how to work with differences in ways that do not disadvantage either sex, not to ignore the differences. Chapters 6 and 7 discuss these issues further.

4. Items should not be culture-bound. Items need to be judged against this criterion for two reasons. First, psychologists and educators in other countries are interested in adapting proven American techniques to their own needs; if items can be translated easily, the adaptation will be more successful. Second, and equally important, items that are easily adapted for a variety of foreign cultures are more appropriate for the wide range of subcultures in the United States.

Examples of culture-bound items in earlier editions of the SVIB-SCII were those related to religious activities that were worded with Christian or Judean terms. The extent to which the items had meaning for people with other religious convictions or beliefs depended on the flexibility of the respondent. For the 1985 SCII revision, therefore, these items were modified to have a more generic meaning. For example, *Church worker* is now *Worker in a religious vocation*; *Church young people's group* is *Young people's religious group*; and *Reading the Bible* is *Reading the Bible or other sacred writings*.

5. Items should be up to date. Even one or two dated items out of several hundred are sufficient to create a loss of confidence in an inventory. Because the Strong Interest Inventory, which originally was published in the 1920's and 1930's, was revised in the 1940's and 1960's and again in 1974 and 1981, most of the obviously dated items have been removed. A few borderline items remain, however, because they offer good validity statistics. For example, one obviously dated item, *Pursuing bandits in a sheriff's posse*, was retained because the validity statistics are good, with "Like" responses ranging from 5 percent among ministers, school superintendents, and physicians to 80 percent among police officers and highway patrol officers.

6. Items should be unambiguous; everyone who reads them should interpret them the same way. This is seldom a problem with items that are occupational titles or activities, but problems do occur occasionally. For example, the item *City or state employee* is not as precise as some respondents would like, but it was retained because the validity statistics are good.

Another example is the item *Interviewing men for a job*. This item was occasionally interpreted as taking the role of interviewee rather than interviewer. The problem was solved by rewording the item to *Interviewing job applicants*, which also eliminated its male orientation.

A third case, *Have good judgment in appraising values*, clearly demonstrates the problem of ambiguity. The highest percentage of "Yes" responses was, in men, among accountants (98 percent) and psychologists (92 percent), and in women, among buyers (86 percent) and physicians (77 percent). Obviously, not everyone was interpreting the word "value" in the same way. This item was discarded.

7. Items should be in good taste. People should not be

asked to respond to items that offend them; questionnaires with offensive items continually create problems for users.

The items in the Strong booklet were screened closely on the criterion of good taste, and few of them will offend anyone. However, it is impossible to eliminate every item that may make a few people wince. For example, some people think that all references to religious activities should be eliminated; others believe that all military occupations should be expunged. In general, however, the items fit well with most people's criteria of good taste.

8. Items should have predictive as well as concurrent validity. Concurrent validity is the power to discriminate between individuals who are, at the same point in time, in different occupations; predictive validity is the power to discriminate between those who will, at some future time, enter different occupations. Because interest inventories generally are used to help people make long-range plans, the emphasis should be on predictive validity.

Some items, however, offer only concurrent validity. An extreme example, to make the point, would be the item *I am an engineer*, which would have perfect concurrent validity but little value in a predictive sense, especially when used with students. No such extreme items have ever appeared in the Strong booklets, but other, more subtly limited items have. The vast array of statistics available on each SVIB item made it possible to identify these items and to eliminate them. Some examples of eliminated items are: *Do my best work late at night*, answered "Yes" most often by nightclub entertainers and highway patrol officers; *My advice is asked for often*, answered "Yes" most often by psychiatrists, lawyers, and high-level executives; and *Worry a good deal about mistakes*, answered "Yes" most often by surgeons and musicians. Though one could argue that these items have potential predictive power, the pattern of responses in the SVIB archives suggests strongly that people learn to give these answers after entering their occupations and being exposed to particular job activities, and that similar responses among young people therefore would not necessarily be predictive of a tendency to enter these occupations.

Cleaning out the more manifest of these items improved the psychometric quality of the inventory, but the effect was not substantial, since only a dozen or so items were affected. Predictive validity, however, is an important element in test construction; one could, by stacking up items deficient in that respect, build an interest inventory with excellent concurrent-validity statistics but one that would be useless in any predictive sense. Thus longitudinal research is crucial in test development; without long-range studies, predictive or nonpredictive items could not be identified.

9. Items should be easy to read. The reading level of the items, the instructions, and the profile should be kept as low as possible. For the SCII, the reading level is at about the sixth-grade level, although it usually is not administered before the eighth or ninth grade. Most students in a typical eigth-grade class can handle the inventory, although they occasionally will inquire about the precise meaning of some items, especially some of the advanced school subjects like *Calculus* or *Physiology*.

10. Responding to the items should be interesting, perhaps even entertaining. No empirical data are available concerning what makes tests fun to take; but if people are to enjoy the experience of answering a psychological test or inventory, the booklet and answer sheet must be free of various irritants, such as fuzzy instructions, illogical layouts, glib assertions, coarse typography or printing, or inadequate space for writing one's name.

Moreover, the item content of the inventory must make sense to the respondent; if vocational interests are being surveyed, then the items should be perceived as having direct relevance to that issue, and should not inquire into such topics as sex, family relationships, or personal finances.

Answer Sheets

The SVIB-SCII test booklet (Fig. 2.1) is designed to be used with either a separate answer sheet (Fig. 2.2) or in a format that combines the booklet and answer sheet. Machines called optical scanners read the answers from the answer sheets, and the computer then calculates scores on scales and administrative indexes, and prints out the results on profile forms. Since each scoring agency uses its own scoring machine, and each machine works from its own adaptation of the SCII answer sheet, the sheet used depends on which agency is scoring the inventory. Thus each agency provides its own answer sheets, under license from the publisher.

It is important that answer sheets ask for sex of respondent. Although everyone is scored on all scales, regardless of sex, men and women—even those in the same occupation—often respond differently to the same item or scale. Thus the interpretive comments—which compare the respondent's scores to the scores of a sample of her or his own sex, rather than to a combined-sex sample—supply much valuable information, but only when sex of respondent is known. If sex has not been indicated on the answer sheet, a statement such as "Because sex indication was omitted, some interpretive comments cannot be included on this profile" will be printed.

Profile Forms

The respondent's SCII scores are reported on a specially designed form called a "profile" (Figs. 2.3 through 2.6).

The layout of the profile has been guided by the occupational taxonomy devised by John Holland, a scheme that organizes the world of work into six basic types of occupational interest—realistic, investigative, artistic, social, enterprising, and conventional. These types, or General Occupational Themes, are quite similar to the scale groupings that appeared on pre-SCII editions of the profile, but they have the advantage of being more precisely defined, more inclusive, and ex-

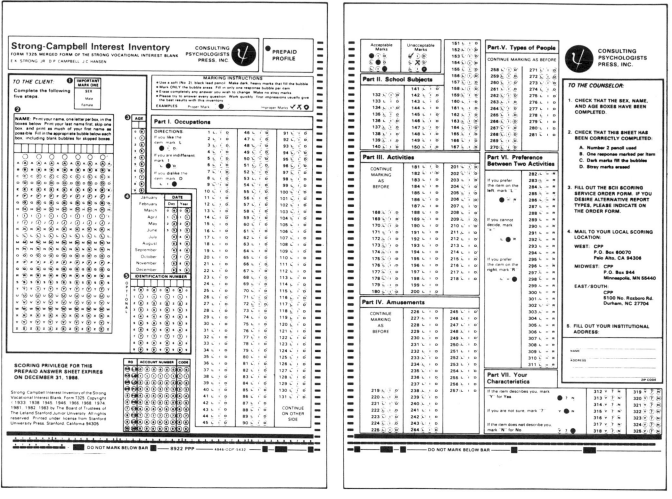

Fig. 2.2. SVIB-SCII answer sheet.

haustive. Further, because Holland has developed and explicitly stated the theoretical structure underlying these categories, many useful inferences can be drawn from both the theory and the test results. Chapter 4 discusses Holland's theory and the General Occupational Themes in detail, and the reverse side of the profile (see the discussion immediately following) gives useful general information on the Themes and on other aspects of the profile.

Profile layout. One form for the SCII profile is shown in Figs. 2.3 through 2.6; a variant of that format is shown in Fig. 2.7. Each scoring agency produces its own adaptation of the profile form under license from the publisher. Details of computer programming and profile format may differ from one scoring agency to another, but the results printed out on the various agencies' adaptations are invariant in substantive detail.

Two copies of the profile form are returned to the customer (that is, to the institution administering the inventory) by the scoring agency—one for the person who completed the inventory, the other for the insti-

tution's counseling service, to use in counseling the person and perhaps to retain on file. The two copies are identical on the front (scoring) side; and both carry the entire printout of scores. The reverse side (see Figs. 2.5 and 2.6) of at least one copy of the profile carries explanatory material that will help the client to understand her or his scores on the SCII.

The name of the person who completed the inventory, the date the form was administered, and the date the inventory was scored are printed at the top of the profile. Although the profile-form adaptations used by the different scoring agencies differ slightly, the following comments apply, in all important particulars, to all versions.

General Occupational Themes. The scales for the six General Occupational Themes begin the six main groupings of scales on the profile. The respondent's standard scores are printed next to the scale names by the computer, and interpretive comments, based on the level of score with respect to that of a norm group of the person's own sex, are printed in the column to the right of the standard scores. Each score also is plotted visually, in the form of an asterisk or similar mark printed at the appropriate point along the scale range. On each scale, the average score and scoring range for the Women- and Men-in-General samples (see pp. 30–31) are given in the form of preprinted bars. See the reverse side of the profile (Figs. 2.5 and 2.6) for a good general discussion of these Themes; and see Chapter 4 for more detailed information.

Basic Interest Scales. Below the scales for the General Occupational Themes are the 23 Basic Interest Scales, grouped into six categories corresponding to their relationships to the General Occupational Themes. Scores are reported in the same format as are scores on the General Occupational Themes (see above). See the reverse side of the profile for an explanation of the scoring ranges; and see Chapter 5 for more detailed information.

Occupational Scales. The 207 Occupational Scales conclude the six scale blocks on the profile. Like the Basic Interest Scales, they are assembled into groups corresponding to the six General Occupational Themes, depending on that occupation's mean scores on the Theme scales; the method used to code the scales is described in Chapter 6.

Scores for the Occupational Scales are printed to the right of the scale names. The standard score is printed under the heading "Standard Score"; scores on the female-normed and male-normed Occupational Scales appear in the columns labeled f and m, respectively. Where female- and male-normed scales for the same occupation have identical codes, scores for the two scales appear on the same line of the profile, after a single scale name, for example:

F	M	Scale	F	M
R	R	AIR FORCE OFFICER	32	56

Where the two scales for the same occupation fall within the same primary Theme but have different codes, two different lines are used, and the codes assigned to the opposite-sex scale is printed in the (otherwise) empty column.

F	M	Scale	F	M
IR	[I]	BIOLOGIST	15	(I)
I	[IR]	BIOLOGIST	(IR)	25

For those scales with dissimilar primary codes, the scale name appears twice on the profile—once in each General Theme area. In these cases, the code for the opposite-sex scale assists the counselor and client in locating the other scale:

F	M	Scale	F	M
[IR]	RI	VETERINARIAN	(IR)	7
[RI]	IR	VETERINARIAN	35	(RI)

In the few cases where an opposite-sex scale is not on the profile, the empty column is filled with "NA."

F	M	Scale	F	M
SCI	N/A	DENTAL HYGIENIST	10	N/A

An asterisk is plotted on the scale range at the point corresponding to the client's own-sex score, graphically representing the degree of similarity with the scores of people in that occupation. Scores of 10 and below are plotted on the lowest point on the scale range; scores of 59 and above are plotted on the highest point. The highest scores are plotted as "Very Similar," the lowest as "Very Dissimilar," with respect to scores of people working in those occupations, and intermediate scores are plotted accordingly within the central portion of the "Mid-Range" category.

Although all scales are scored, regardless of the respondent's sex or the sex norms of the scales, only those scores on scales normed on the same sex as the respondent are plotted graphically (that is, with an asterisk, on the scale range). This approach resolves the dilemma of providing the maximum number of scores to each individual while at the same time emphasizing those scores that are normed in the most technically accurate manner. Scores on other-sex scales are given only in the "Standard Score" column. Chapter 7 discusses these points at length.

Administrative Indexes and Special Scales. The lower right corner of the profile presents scores for the Administrative Indexes and Special Scales. The Special Scales, which include INTROVERSION-EXTROVERSION and ACADEMIC COMFORT, are discussed in detail in Chapter 8, the Administrative Indexes in Chapter 9.

Interpretive Reports

A second type of profile, called an interpretive report, is offered as an option (a portion of a sample report is shown in Fig. 2.7). The interpretive report is produced completely by computer and a great wealth of information, including scores and interpretations of scores, is provided expressly for the individual respondent. The printed interpretive statements vary according to the responses made by that person to the inventory. Computer-produced interpretive reports are more convenient in many contexts, especially group interpretations. Comparisons of various technological modes for presenting inventory results (e.g., slides, videotape, computer-assisted, and computer-written interpretive information) suggest similar levels of client satisfaction (Johnson, Korn, and Dunn, 1975; Maola and Kane, 1976; Miller and Cochran, 1979; Oliver, 1977). The *User's Guide* (Chapter 20) provides a sequence of steps to follow in conducting individual or group interpretations.

Administering the Inventory

The SVIB-SCII is simple to administer; and it can be given individually or in groups, in person or by mail. The respondent needs only a place to write, a test booklet and answer sheet, and a dark lead pencil.

Time required. Fast readers can complete the in-

STRONG-CAMPBELL INTEREST INVENTORY OF THE
STRONG VOCATIONAL INTEREST BLANK

PAGE 1 PROFILE REPORT FOR: DATE TESTED:

ID: DATE SCORED:
AGE: SEX:

SPECIAL SCALES: ACADEMIC COMFORT
INTROVERSION-EXTROVERSION

TOTAL RESPONSES: INFREQUENT RESPONSES:

OCCUPATIONAL SCALES

| | STANDARD SCORES | | | VERY DISSIMILAR | DISSIMILAR | MODERATELY DISSIMILAR | MID-RANGE | MODERATELY SIMILAR | SIMILAR | VERY SIMILAR |

REALISTIC

GENERAL OCCUPATIONAL THEME - R 30 40 50 60 70 F M

BASIC INTEREST SCALES (STANDARD SCORE)

AGRICULTURE — F / M

NATURE — F / M

ADVENTURE — F / M

MILITARY ACTIVITIES — F / M

MECHANICAL ACTIVITIES — F / M

F	M	Occupation	F	M
[CRS]	RC	Marine Corps enlisted personnel	(CRS)	
RC	RC	Navy enlisted personnel		
RC	RC	Army officer		
RI	RIC	Navy officer		
R	R	Air Force officer		
[C]	R	Air Force enlisted personnel	(C)	
R	R	Police officer		
R	R	Bus driver		
R	R	Horticultural worker		
RC	R	Farmer		
R	RCS	Vocational agriculture teacher		
RI	R	Forester		
[IR]	RI	Veterinarian	(IR)	
RIS	[SR]	Athletic trainer		(SR)
RS	R	Emergency medical technician		
RI	RI	Radiologic technologist		
RI	R	Carpenter		
RI	R	Electrician		
RIA	[ARI]	Architect		(ARI)
RI	RI	Engineer		

INVESTIGATIVE

GENERAL OCCUPATIONAL THEME - I 30 40 50 60 70 F M

BASIC INTEREST SCALES (STANDARD SCORE)

SCIENCE — F / M

MATHEMATICS — F / M

MEDICAL SCIENCE — F / M

MEDICAL SERVICE — F / M

F	M	Occupation	F	M
IRC	IRC	Computer programmer		
IRC	IRC	Systems analyst		
IRC	IR	Medical technologist		
IR	IR	R & D manager		
IR	IR	Geologist		
IR	[I]	Biologist		(I)
IR	IR	Chemist		
IR	IR	Physicist		
IR	[RI]	Veterinarian		(RI)
IRS	IR	Science teacher		
IRS	IRS	Physical therapist		
IR	IRS	Respiratory therapist		
IC	IR	Medical technician		
IC	IE	Pharmacist		
ISR	[CSE]	Dietitian		(CSE)
[SI]	ISR	Nurse, RN	(SI)	
IR	I	Chiropractor		
IR	IR	Optometrist		
IR	IR	Dentist		
I	IA	Physician		
[IR]	I	Biologist	(IR)	
I	I	Mathematician		
IR	I	Geographer		
I	I	College professor		
IA	IA	Psychologist		
IA	IA	Sociologist		

ARTISTIC

GENERAL OCCUPATIONAL THEME - A 30 40 50 60 70 F M

BASIC INTEREST SCALES (STANDARD SCORE)

MUSIC/DRAMATICS — F / M

ART — F / M

WRITING — F / M

CONSULTING PSYCHOLOGISTS PRESS

F	M	Occupation	F	M
AI	AI	Medical illustrator		
A	A	Art teacher		
A	A	Artist, fine		
A	A	Artist, commercial		
AE	A	Interior decorator		
[RIA]	ARI	Architect	(RIA)	
A	A	Photographer		
A	A	Musician		
AR	[EA]	Chef		(EA)
[E]	AE	Beautician	(E)	
AE	A	Flight attendant		
A	A	Advertising executive		
A	A	Broadcaster		
A	A	Public relations director		
A	A	Lawyer		
A	AE	Public administrator		
A	A	Reporter		
A	A	Librarian		
AS	AS	English teacher		
[SA]	AS	Foreign language teacher	(SA)	

Fig. 2.3. SVIB-SCII profile form, upper half.

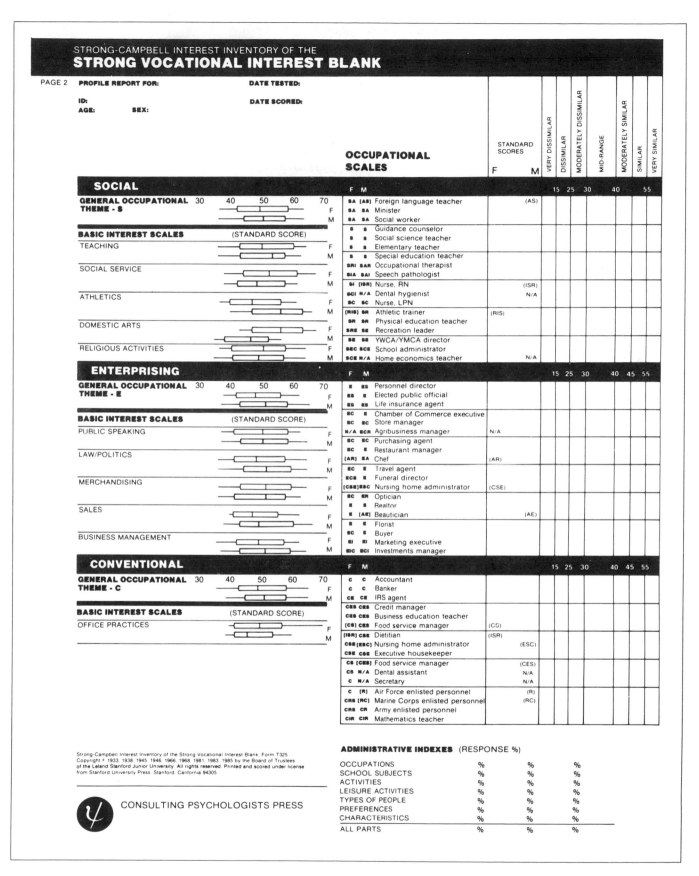

Fig. 2.4. SVIB-SCII profile form, lower half.

Understanding Your Results on the Strong

Your answers to the test booklet were used to determine your scores; your results are based on what you said you liked or disliked. The results can give you some useful systematic information about yourself, but you should not expect miracles.

Please note that this test does not measure your abilities; it can tell you something about the patterns in your interests, and how these compare with those of successful people in many occupations, but the results are based on your *interests,* not your abilities. The results may tell you, for example, that you like the way engineers spend their day; they do *not* tell you whether you have an aptitude for the mathematics involved.

Although most of us know something of our own interests, we're not sure how we compare with people actively engaged in various occupations. We don't know "what it would be like" to be a writer, or receptionist, or scientist, for example. People using these results are frequently guided to considering occupations to which they had never given a thought before. In particular, this inventory may suggest occupations that you might find interesting but had not considered simply because you have not been exposed to them. Or the inventory may suggest occupations that you ignored because you thought they were open only to members of the opposite sex. Sexual barriers are now falling, and virtually all occupations are open to qualified people of either sex — so don't let imagined barriers rule out your consideration of any occupation.

Men and women, even those in the same occupation, tend to answer some items on the test differently. Research has shown that these differences should not be ignored — that separate scales for men and women provide more meaningful results. Generally, the scales for your sex — those marked in the "Standard Scores" column corresponding to your sex — are more likely to be better predictors for you than scales for the other sex would be.

Your answers have been analyzed in three main ways: first, under "General Occupational Themes," for similarity to six important overall patterns; second, under "Basic Interest Scales," for similarity to clusters of specific activities; third, under "Occupational Scales," for similarity to the interests of men and women in 106 occupations. The other two groups of data on the profile — labeled "Administrative Indexes" and "Special Scales" — are of interest mainly to your counselor. The first are checks to make certain that you made your marks on the sheet clearly and that your answers were processed correctly. The second are scales that have been developed for use in particular settings and require special interpretation; your counselor will discuss them with you.

■ The Six General Occupational Themes

Psychological research has shown that vocational interests can be described in a general way by six overall occupational-interest Themes. Your scores for these six Themes were calculated from the answers you gave to the test questions. The range of these scores is roughly from 30 to 70, with the average person scoring 50.

Men and women score somewhat differently on some of these Themes, and this is taken into account by the printed statement for each score; this statement, which might be, for example, "Very High," is based on a comparison between your score and the average score for your sex. Thus, you can compare your score either with the scores of a combined male-female sample, by noting your numerical score, or with the scores of only members of your own sex, by noting the phrasing of the printed comment.

The differences between the sexes on these Themes also are shown on the profile; the open bars indicate the middle 50 percent of female scores, the shaded bars show the middle 50 percent of male scores. The extending, thinner lines cover the middle 80 percent of the scores, and the mark in the middle is the average.

Following are descriptions of the "pure," or extreme, types for the six General Occupational Themes. These descriptions are only generalizations; none will fit any one person exactly. In fact, most people's interests combine several Themes to some degree or other.

R-Theme: People scoring high here usually are rugged, robust, practical, physically strong; they usually have good physical skills, but sometimes have trouble expressing themselves or in communicating their feelings to others. They like to work outdoors and to work with tools, especially large, powerful machines. They prefer to deal with things rather than with ideas or people. They enjoy creating things with their hands and prefer occupations such as mechanic, construction work, fish and wildlife management, radiologic technologist, some engineering specialties, some military jobs, agriculture, or the skilled trades. Although no single word can capture the broad meaning of the entire Theme, the word REALISTIC has been used here, thus the term R-Theme.

I-Theme: This Theme centers around science and scientific activities. Extremes of this type are task-oriented; they are not particularly interested in working around other people. They enjoy solving abstract problems, and they have a great need to understand the physical world. They prefer to think through problems rather than act them out. Such people enjoy ambiguous challenges and do not like highly structured situations with many rules. They frequently are original and creative, especially in scientific areas. They prefer occupations such as design engineer, biologist, social scientist, research laboratory worker, physicist, technical writer, or meteorologist. The word INVESTIGATIVE characterizes this Theme, thus I-Theme.

A-Theme: The extreme type here is artistically oriented, and likes to work in artistic settings that offer many opportunities for self-expression. Such people have little interest in problems that are highly structured or require gross physical strength, preferring those that can be solved through self-expression in artistic media. They resemble I-Theme types in preferring to work alone, but have a greater need for individualistic expression, and usually are less assertive about their own opinions and capabilities. They describe themselves as independent, original, unconventional, expressive, and intense. Vocational choices include artist, author, cartoonist, composer, singer, dramatic coach, poet, actor or actress, and symphony conductor. This is the ARTISTIC Theme, or A-Theme.

S-Theme: The pure type here is sociable, responsible, humanistic, and concerned with the welfare of others. These people usually express themselves well and get along well with others; they like attention and seek situations that allow them to be near the center of the group. They prefer to solve problems by discussions with others, or by arranging or rearranging relationships between others; they have little interest in situations requiring physical exertion or working with machinery. Such people describe themselves as cheerful, popular, and achieving, and as good leaders. They prefer occupations such as school superintendent, social worker, high school teacher, marriage counselor, playground director, speech therapist, or vocational counselor. This is the SOCIAL Theme, or S-Theme.

E-Theme: The extreme type of this Theme has a great facility with words, especially in selling, dominating, and leading; frequently these people are in sales work. They see themselves as energetic, enthusiastic, adventurous, self-confident, and dominant, and they prefer social tasks where they can assume leadership. They enjoy persuading others to their viewpoints. They are impatient with precise work or work involving long periods of intellectual effort. They like power, status, and material wealth, and enjoy working in expensive settings. Vocational preferences include business executive, buyer, hotel manager, industrial relations consultant, political campaigner, realtor, sales work, and sports promoter. The word ENTERPRISING summarizes this pattern, thus E-Theme.

(Continued on page 2 back)

Fig. 2.5. SVIB-SCII profile form, reverse side, upper half.

(Continued from back of page 1)

C-Theme: Extremes of this type prefer the highly ordered activities, both verbal and numerical, that characterize office work. People scoring high fit well into large organizations but do not seek leadership; they respond to power and are comfortable working in a well-established chain of command. They dislike ambiguous situations, preferring to know precisely what is expected of them. Such people describe themselves as conventional, stable, well-controlled, and dependable. They have little interest in problems requiring physical skills or intense relationships with others, and are most effective at well-defined tasks. Like the E-Theme type, they value material possessions and status. Vocational preferences are mostly within the business world, and include bank examiner, bank teller, bookkeeper, some accounting jobs, mathematics teacher, computer operator, inventory controller, tax expert, credit manager, and traffic manager. The word CONVENTIONAL more or less summarizes the pattern, hence C-Theme.

These six Themes can be arranged in a hexagon with the types most similar to each other falling *next* to each other, and those most dissimilar falling directly *across* the hexagon from each other.

REALISTIC	R ⌐‾‾‾‾⌐ I	INVESTIGATIVE
CONVENTIONAL	C ⟨ ⟩ A	ARTISTIC
ENTERPRISING	E ⌐___⌐ S	SOCIAL

Few people are "pure" types, scoring high on one and only one Theme. Most score high on two, three, or even four, which means they share some characteristics with each of these; for their career planning, such people should look for an occupational setting that combines these patterns.

A few people score low on all six Themes; this probably means they have no consistent occupational orientation and would probably be equally comfortable in any of several working environments. Some young people score this way because they haven't had the opportunity to become familiar with a variety of occupational activities.

The Basic Interest Scales

These scales are intermediate between the General Occupational Themes and the Occupational Scales. Each is concerned with one specific area of activity. The 23 scales are arranged in groups corresponding to the strength of their relationship to the six General Themes.

On these scales, the average adult scores about 50, with most people scoring between 30 and 70. If your score is substantially higher than 50, then you have shown more consistent preferences for these activities than the average adult does, and you should look upon that area of activity as an important focus of your

interests. The opposite is true for low scores. Your scores are given both numerically and graphically, and an interpretive comment, based on a comparison between your scores and the average score for your sex, also is provided.

Your scores on some of the Basic Interest Scales might appear to be inconsistent with scores on the corresponding Occupational Scales. You might, for example, score high on the Mathematics scale and low on the Mathematician scale. These scores are not errors; they are in fact a useful finding. What they usually mean is that although you have an interest in the subject matter of an occupation (mathematics), you share with people in that occupation (mathematicians) very few of their other likes or dislikes, and you probably would not enjoy the day-to-day life of their working world.

The Occupational Scales

Your score on an Occupational Scale shows how similar your interests are to the interests of people in that occupation. If you reported the same likes and dislikes as they do, your score will be high and you would probably enjoy working in that occupation or a closely related one. If your likes and dislikes are different from those of the people in the occupation, your score will be low and you might not be happy in that kind of work. Remember that the scales of your sex — marked in the "Standard Scores" column with the sex corresponding to yours — are more likely to be good predictors for you than scales for the other sex.

Your score for each scale is printed in numerals — for those scales normed for your sex — and also plotted graphically. Members of an occupation score about 50 on their own scale — that is, female dentists score about 50 on the Dentist F scale, male fine artists score about 50 on the Fine Artist M scale, and so forth. If you score high on a particular scale — say 45 or 50 — you have many interests in common with the workers in that occupation. The higher your score, the more common interests you have. *But note that on these scales your scores are being compared with those of people working in those occupations;* in the scoring of the General Themes and the Basic Interest Scales you were being compared with "people-in-general."

The Occupational Scales differ from the other scales also in considering your dislikes as well as your likes. If you share in the same *dislikes* with the workers in an occupation, you may score moderately high on their scale, even if you don't agree with their *likes*. But a higher score — 50 — reflects an agreement on likes *and* dislikes.

To the left of each Occupational Scale name are one to three letters indicating the General Themes characteristic of that occupation. These will help you to understand the interest patterns found among the workers in that occupation, and to focus on occupations that might be interesting to you. If you score high on two Themes, for example, you should scan the list of Occupational Scales and find any that have the same two Theme letters, in any order. If your scores there are also high — as they are likely to be — you should find out more about those occupations, and about related occupations not given on the profile. Your counselor can help you.

Academic Comfort and Introversion-Extroversion

There are two Special Scales derived from your Strong responses that may give you additional insight into your interests and expectations.

The Academic Comfort Scale differentiates between people who enjoy being in an academic setting and those who do not. Remember, however, that the Academic Comfort Scale *does not measure ability*. About 2/3rds of all people who take the Strong score in the range of 32 to 60. People with low scores (below 40) often are inclined to view education as a necessary hurdle for entry into a career. People with high scores (above 50) typically seek out courses that allow them to explore theory and research in their chosen field.

The Introversion-Extroversion Scale is associated with a preference for working with things or ideas (high scores, say, above 55) or with people (low scores, say, below 45). Scores between 45 and 55 indicate a combination of interests that include working with people and ideas or things in the same occupation.

Using Your Scores

Your scores can be used in two main ways: first, to help you understand how your likes and dislikes fit into the world of work; and second, to help you identify possible problems by pointing out areas where your interests differ substantially from those of people working in occupations that you might be considering. Suppose, for example, that you have selected some field of science, but the results show that you have only a moderate interest in the daily practice of the mathematical skills necessary to that setting. Although this is discouraging to learn, you at least are prepared for the choice among (1) abandoning that field of science as a career objective, (2) trying to increase your enthusiasm for mathematics, or (3) finding some branch of the field that requires less mathematics.

In the world of work there are many hundreds of specialties and professions. Using these results and your scores on other tests as guides, you should search out as much information as you can *about those occupational areas where your interests and aptitudes are focused.* Ask your librarian for information on these jobs and talk to people working in these fields. Talk with your counselor, who is trained to help you, about your results on this test and other tests, and about your future plans. Keep in mind that choosing an occupation is not a single decision, but a series of decisions that will go on for many years. Your scores on this inventory should help.

Fig. 2.6. SVIB-SCII profile form, reverse side, lower half.

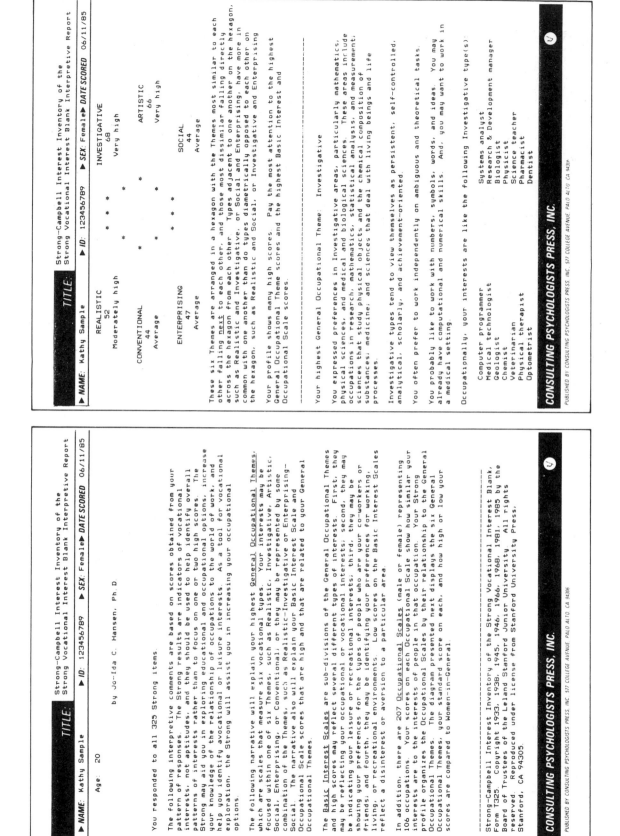

Fig. 2.7. SVIB-SCII interpretive report, portion of a sample report generated by computer.

ventory in about 20 minutes; slow readers may require an hour. The average adult takes about 30 minutes.

Reading level. The SCII booklet reads at about the sixth-grade level, though a few items (for example, *Physiology* and *Calculus*) are unfamiliar to some students at that level. Some people who read at the sixth-grade level do not have sufficiently long attention spans to complete the inventory in one sitting, and counselors have reported cases in which they successfully have allowed these clients to complete the inventory during several shorter sessions.

Appropriate age level for use. Most students in an average eighth- or ninth-grade class—students aged 13–15—can read and complete the inventory; above this age, virtually everyone can complete it successfully.

Whether eighth-grade students *should* complete the inventory, even though they *can*, is another question, and the answer depends on why the test is given, how the results are used, and the type of professional counseling available to the students. Under the proper circumstances, 13-, 14-, and 15-year-old students can benefit from the inventory, though they must be cautioned that their results are likely to be somewhat transitory. Counselors who wish to stimulate career planning can use the General Occupational Themes and Basic Interest Scales with students of this age as a vehicle for discussion, showing the students something about choices and about structure in the world of work.

Historically, the major use of the Strong has been with adults and 16-, 17-, and 18-year-olds. At 17 or 18, interests begin to solidify for most students, and the results begin to be useful for career-planning purposes. By age 21, interests have become even more established, and by 25, interest patterns have stabilized for nearly everyone. The *User's Guide for the SVIB-SCII* (Chapter 2) provides more detailed information on the administration of the SCII.

Faking. *The Handbook for the SVIB* (Campbell, 1971) includes a general review of the issues of faking on the Strong; what follows is a summary.

When instructed to do so, respondents can bias their scores substantially. For example, students who are asked to "Answer like the average engineer" raise their scores on the ENGINEER scale by 10 points or more, usually scoring higher than the average engineer. But when people respond to the items in customary fashion, in situations where they might be expected to bias their scores—such as when applying for a job or for admission to medical school—they usually answer truthfully. In studies of these situations, the detectable bias is seldom more than a few points. Although we should not naively suppose everyone always is truthful, most people appear to answer this inventory honestly, even in highly competitive selection environments.

Translations of the Strong

The Strong currently is available in four translated versions—Spanish, French Canadian, Hebrew, and British—and work is under way to provide a German translation and a French translation for use in Europe.

Spanish translation (T325S). The Strong was translated into Spanish by the publisher using a three-step process: first, a translation was prepared by a university professor of Spanish; second, the original translation was reviewed, corrected, and modified by a bilingual whose native language was Spanish; and third, the revised translation was forwarded to a professor of Spanish for a final review.

Validation of a translated test typically involves a back translation and field testing. The back translation of the Spanish SCII required a bilingual person to translate the Spanish version back into English. After the back translation was completed, the two English versions (i.e., original and back-translated) were compared for discrepancies. Only eight out of the 325 items did not have identical wording (e.g., *Social section of the newspaper* (Spanish) for *Family pages in a newspaper* (English) and *Debates* (Spanish) for *Arguments* (English). These eight items were modified for the 1985 revision to reflect more accurately the English meaning.

Field testing involved bilingual high school and community college students from 11 schools in the states of California, New Mexico, and Washington (Hansen & Fouad, 1984). Most of the subjects were of Mexican heritages; a small number were of Cuban, Puerto Rican, Central American, and South American descent. Each person completed both the Spanish and English versions of the SCII. Correlations between scale scores on the Spanish and English forms were high (median for GOT = .85, for BIS = .84, and for Occupational Scales = .83); the average student's Spanish and English Occupational Scale profiles correlated .92 with each other.

Another study (Fouad, Cudeck, and Hansen, 1984), which extended Hansen and Fouad's work on the accuracy of the T325S translation, provided evidence of the divergent and convergent validity of the English and Spanish General Occupational Themes as well as evidence that the psychological constructs of the two forms are similar. Confirmatory factor analysis showed that a model that postulated two method factors and six trait factors, with a hexagonal pattern hypothesized among the trait factors, appeared to fit the data. The method factors (two forms of the inventory) were very similar, producing a correlation of .79. The correlations among the trait factors (the six General Occupational Themes) formed a perfect circumplex supporting Holland's model of the structure of interests.

Other translations. The SCII also has been translated into French Canadian by J.-M. Chevrier (1979), of the Institute of Psychological Research in Montreal, Canada, for use in Canada. Two separate Hebrew translations were prepared and were then merged into one form by Pinchas Freedman, Director of the Israeli Center for Vocational Placement in Netanya, Israel; the merged form was back-translated to check the accuracy of the translation. The wording of the SCII items also was adapted for use in Great Britain (Cook, 1982, pers. comm.); for example:

SVIB-SCII (American English)	British English version
Art museum director	*Art gallery/ museum director*
Auto racer	*Racing driver*
Business teacher	*Commerce teacher*
City or state employee	*Civil servant*
City planner	*Town planner*
Realtor	*Estate agent*

Studies using samples from a variety of occupations (e.g., police officers, artists, psychologists, physicians, engineers, and lawyers) in several countries (e.g., Germany, Austria, Switzerland, Scotland, Australia, Canada, Great Britain, New Zealand, South Africa, Pakistan, and Mexico) support the conclusion that the interests of people in a particular occupation are extremely similar across cultures (Fouad, 1984; Lonner, 1968; Lonner and Adams, 1972; Shah, 1971; Strong, 1943). The use of the Strong with U.S. minorities is discussed in Chapter 6.

CHAPTER THREE

Item Technology

Interest inventories are effective because different people give different responses to the individual inventory items, and because people who have found satisfying work in an occupation tend to respond to particular inventory items in a characteristic way. These two facts, illustrated and documented in the following pages, are the foundation for the entire enterprise of interest measurement.

Item-Response Distributions

As examples of the different responses that people in different occupations give to particular items, item-response distributions for three SVIB-SCII items, *Artist*, *Farmer*, and *Night clubs*, are given in Figs. 3.1 to 3.3 (for another example, see Fig. 7.1). These three items were chosen to illustrate the variance in sample response distribution from one item to the next. Each increment of cross-hatching in the distributions represents one sample (male and female samples are cross-hatched distinctively); and each sample is plotted at the point corresponding to the percentage of its members answering "Like" to the item in question. The samples are the occupational samples stored in the archives of the Center for Interest Measurement Research at the University of Minnesota. Except for unusual groups like astronauts and famous football coaches, the samples range in size from 72 to 1,199. For the *Artist* and *Farmer* items, data from 523 samples are presented; for the *Night clubs* item, which did not appear in some previous editions of the inventory, data are presented for 385 samples. For each item, the five highest- and five lowest-ranking samples of each sex are identified above the distributions; these lists convey the essence of the distribution extremes and illustrate the occupational differences in responses to interest-inventory items.

Most of the samples included in these distributions are the adult criterion samples that have been tested over the years—from 1927 to 1984—to develop the Occupational Scales; the others are miscellaneous samples that have been tested for various research projects. Collectively, these samples represent an extremely diverse array of employed female and male adults.

Fig. 3.1 shows the distribution of item-response percentages for the *Artist* item. Psychometrically, this is an excellent item, because it produces a broad distribution of responses: in some occupations, almost everyone responded "Like" to this item; in others, almost no one did. In contrast are those items to which nearly everyone responds in the same manner; such items, which elicit minimal discrimination among people or among groups, contribute nothing to the purposes of the inventory, and in successive editions of the SVIB-SCII they gradually have been dropped. Most SCII items produce roughly the same spread that the *Artist* item does—over 90 percentage points from lowest- to highest-response sample—though the shapes of the distributions vary, as a comparison of Figs. 3.1 to 3.3 indicates (another item distribution is given in Fig. 7.1). The *Farmer* item (Fig. 3.2) is an example of an item with only a moderate variability of response; most of the samples, both female and male, fell within a 20 percent range. This item is useful chiefly because it separates agricultural occupations from the others; unlike the *Artist* item, it does not spread the other occupations across a broad response range.

The third item, *Night clubs* (Fig. 3.3), is included here to demonstrate the power of the items to elicit subtle differences between occupations. The ranking of the occupational responses to this item, too, is reasonable, but the high and low clusters are less obvious than those for the other two items illustrated. This ability to uncover characteristic, but less readily inferable, differences between occupations is one of the inventory's major strengths.

Item-response distributions such as those in Figs. 3.1 to 3.3 are available for all of the SCII items, in computer-accessible storage; collectively, they illustrate several important points:

1. The popularity of the individual item varies greatly from occupation to occupation. The distributions in Figs. 3.1 to 3.3 are typical, showing as they do a range of "Like" responses extending over 90 percent—from lows of 4 or 5 percent to highs of over 95 percent. Most of the SCII items show similar ranges. The power of the individual items to discriminate between occupations directly establishes the usefulness of the inventory. Valid scales can be constructed only from individually effective items.

2. The content of each item is related to the occupations endorsing or rejecting it. Occupational samples respond to the SCII items as one would expect: artists endorse artistic items; scientists, scientific items; and

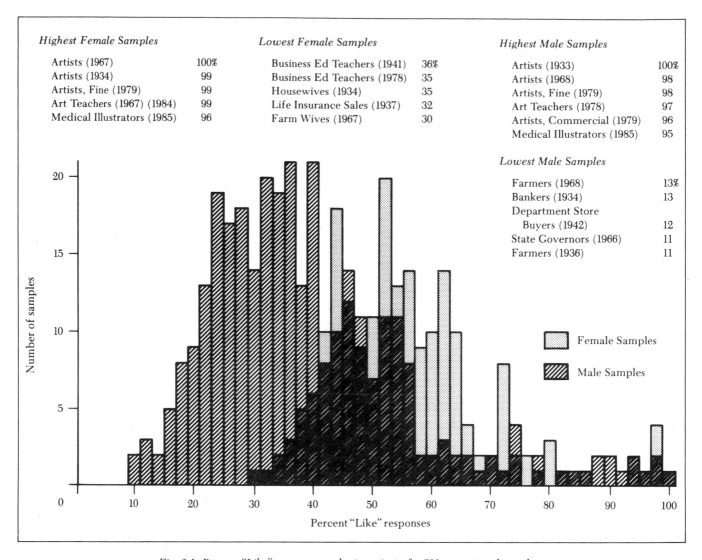

Fig. 3.1. Percent "Like" responses to the item *Artist* for 523 occupational samples.

mechanics, mechanical items. The rank ordering of the five highest- and five lowest-scoring male and female samples in Figs. 3.1 and 3.2 emphasizes the general reasonableness of the item responses. The point is worth stressing, for in some quarters psychological tests are viewed as highly adroit probers into a mysterious, otherwise inaccessible portion of the psyche. They are not. Although systematic arrangement of obvious data can lead us to subtle insights about individuals that we might otherwise overlook (as demonstrated by the distribution of percentages for the *Night clubs* item), psychological tests—or interest inventories at least—generally operate in a straightforward manner, having as their basis the systematic arrangement of empirically detectable differences between occupations.

This is not to imply that the measurement of interests is simple-minded; quite the contrary. The systematic use of empirical data, which incidentally happen to be reasonable, is probably the most effective way to proceed in measuring important psychological characteristics. But

because the information is generally so reasonable, it is sometimes seen as trivial; people often ask, "Why did you go to all that trouble to prove the obvious? Don't you already know that farmers will say they like to be farmers, and artists that they like to be artists?" The answer to this charge is that much of what seems so obvious becomes apparent *only after* the data have been organized.

Of course, the chief benefit of the systematic, empirical approach is that concepts can be quantified, then compared quantitatively *and* qualitatively.

3. Many items identify strong but subtle or unexpected differences in interests between occupations. The *Night clubs* item (see the item-response percentages in Fig. 3.3) is not occupationally obvious, yet like the *Artist* and *Farmer* items it spreads occupations over a wide response range, almost 80 percentage points. Again, when the percentages are rank-ordered, the data appear reasonable, with flight attendants, astronauts, sales managers, beauticians, broadcasters, and entertainers at the

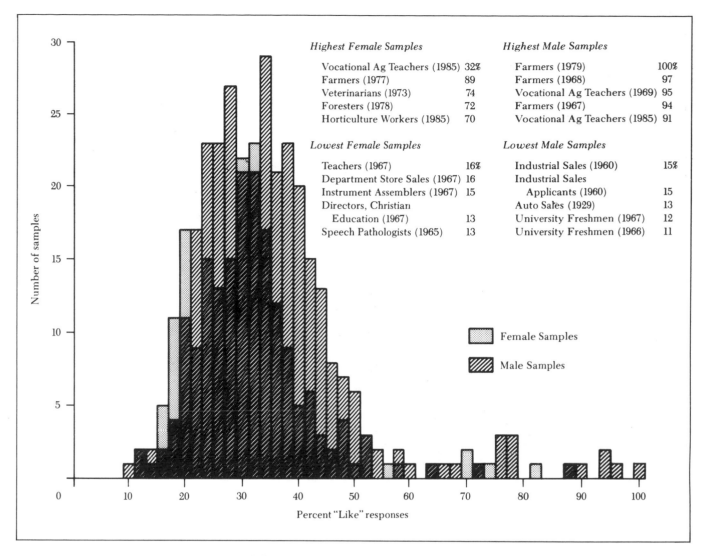

Highest Female Samples

Vocational Ag Teachers (1985)	32%
Farmers (1977)	89
Veterinarians (1973)	74
Foresters (1978)	72
Horticulture Workers (1985)	70

Lowest Female Samples

Teachers (1967)	16%
Department Store Sales (1967)	16
Instrument Assemblers (1967)	15
Directors, Christian Education (1967)	13
Speech Pathologists (1965)	13

Highest Male Samples

Farmers (1979)	100%
Farmers (1968)	97
Vocational Ag Teachers (1969)	95
Farmers (1967)	94
Vocational Ag Teachers (1985)	91

Lowest Male Samples

Industrial Sales (1960)	15%
Industrial Sales Applicants (1960)	15
Auto Sales (1929)	13
University Freshmen (1967)	12
University Freshmen (1966)	11

Fig. 3.2. Percent "Like" responses to the item *Farmer* for 523 occupational samples.

high end, and artists, scientists, ministers, mathematicians, and directors of Christian education at the low end. Even the low percentage among retired Army officers seems right; at an average age of 69 years, it is understandable that they might reject night life. But again, the reasonableness of the data becomes apparent only *after* the high- and low-percentage occupations are identified; few people, shown an unlabeled distribution, can list correctly any of the occupations at the high or low ends of the response range.

The inventory items do, then, capture subtle differences between occupations, and even identify a few surprising characteristics of some, all of which leads to a precision of measurement not possible with cruder assessments of interests.

4. The items vary in their characteristics, especially in average popularity and in the range of spread they create among the occupational samples. The graphic presentation of the *Artist, Farmer,* and *Night clubs* item distributions illustrates the two most important charac-

teristics of individual items: first, their overall popularity, represented by the mean of the distribution; and second, their popularity spread, represented by the standard deviation of the distribution. These two characteristics vary considerably, and independently, across the items in the inventory, and most of the scale-construction and scoring techniques that have been developed, such as the General Reference Sample (Women-or Men-in-General) and the establishment of base-rate norms, are intended to control for these item differences. If all of the items operated identically—that is, if all of them were equally popular and if all were equally effective in separating occupations—reference samples and norms would not be necessary.

5. For the most part, the items are stable over time. An occupational sample tested in one decade gives about the same responses as does another sample, from the same occupation, tested three or four decades later. Table 3.1 presents data on the stability of items over time. In 46 instances, three different samples of the same

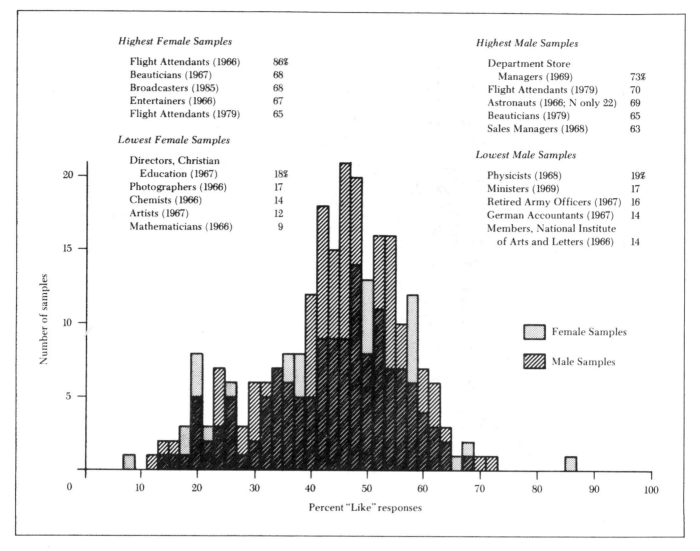

Fig. 3.3. Percent "Like" responses to the item *Night clubs* for 385 occupational samples.

sex in the same occupation were tested, each in different decades, one in the 1930's or 1940's, generally by Strong; a second in the 1960's, by Campbell; and a third in the 1970's or 1980's, by Hansen. The percentages responding "Like" to the *Farmer* and *Artist* items are given in Table 3.1; the table also gives the response differences, over three time intervals, between successive samples of the same occupation.

Some of the differences over time are undoubtedly due to sampling differences, not occupational shifts. The samples were seldom selected or tested in exactly the same way by the three investigators. Still, the differences over time are impressively small. As the summary statistics at the bottom of the table show, the average difference over time was modest, ranging from 1.2 percent to 10 percent. The data also indicate that the number of individual comparisons showing "substantial" differences is in no case more than 12 out of 46, and usually is smaller. (In the discussion of item-response percentage, below, a "substantial" difference is defined

essentially as one 16 percent or larger.) These data demonstrate that the item-response percentages from a given occupational sample can be used safely over many years to represent that occupation.

Of course, the finding that in some comparisons over 16 percent of the occupation shifted "substantially" on an item over a 30-year period argues that the occupational norms should be checked periodically. And, as data in the *Handbook* indicate, the items, too, can shift in popularity, some more than others. Criterion Samples and items alike need periodic monitoring.

Still, in these comparisons, as in most others in the area of vocational interest measurement, stability over time is the rule, not the exception.

6. Male and female samples, even in the same occupation, give different responses to many items. The distributions of the male and female samples in Figs. 3.1, 3.2, 3.3, and 7.1 demonstrate that the two sexes do not respond identically to SCII items. On the *Farmer* and *Night clubs* items, the two sex distributions are fairly

TABLE 3.1

Comparisons of Percent "Like" Responses to the Items *Farmer*
and *Artist* Between 1930/40's, 1960's, and 1970/80's for 46 Occupational Samples

| | | Farmer item | | | | | | Artist item | | | | | |
| | | Percent "Like" responses | | | Difference | | | Percent "Like" responses | | | Difference | | |
Occupational sample	Sex	1930/40's	1960's	1970/80's	30/40's vs. 60's	30/40's vs. 70/80's	60's vs. 70/80's	1930/40's	1960's	1970/80's	30/40's vs. 60's	30/40's vs. 70/80's	60's vs. 70/80'
Accountants	m	25	25	39	0	+14	+14	20	26	32	+6	+12	+6
Advertising executives	m	25	22	29	−3	+4	+7	56	68	70	+12	+14	+2
Architects	m	27	28	42	+1	+15	+14	87	88	82	+1	−5	−6
Artists	f	31	22	25	−9	−6	+3	99	100	99	+1	0	−1
Artists	m	29	28	34	−1	+5	+6	100	98	98	−2	−2	0
Bankers	m	41	30	41	−11	0	+11	13	26	34	+13	+21	+8
Business education teachers	f	22	17	26	−5	+4	+9	36	39	35	+3	−1	−4
Buyers	m	23	21	31	−2	+8	+10	24	34	31	+10	+7	−3
Chemists	m	36	27	37	−9	+1	+10	25	46	39	+21	+14	−7
Dentists	m	32	37	49	+5	+17	+12	41	55	48	+14	+7	−7
Dietitians	f	33	31	38	−2	+5	+7	39	57	42	+18	+3	−15
Engineers	m	26	30	51	+4	+25	+21	28	42	35	+14	+7	−7
English teachers	f	29	21	26	−8	−3	+5	53	65	58	+12	+5	−7
Farmers	m	88	97	100	+9	+12	+3	11	13	18	+2	+7	+5
Foresters	m	47	64	73	+17	+26	+9	21	37	34	+16	+13	−3
Funeral directors	m	33	26	34	−7	+1	+8	23	27	24	+4	+1	−3
Guidance counselors	m	30	41	38	+11	+8	−3	22	26	39	+4	+17	+13
Home economics teachers	f	24	31	36	+7	+12	+5	50	67	42	+17	−8	−25
Investments managers	m	27	23	29	−4	+2	+6	30	45	29	+15	−1	−16
Lawyers	f	31	22	32	−9	+1	+10	47	50	52	+3	+5	+2
Lawyers	m	26	35	45	+9	+19	+10	19	37	44	+18	+25	+7
Librarians	f	31	26	35	−5	+4	+9	57	64	60	+7	+3	−4
Life insurance agents	f	21	19	28	−2	+7	+9	32	53	57	+21	+25	+4
Life insurance agents	m	29	28	38	−1	+9	+10	21	22	28	+1	+7	+6
Mathematicians	m	27	23	28	−4	+1	+5	30	47	41	+17	+11	−6
Medical technicians	f	36	31	35	−5	−1	+4	45	56	41	+11	−4	−15
Ministers	m	43	38	51	−5	+8	+13	36	41	51	+5	+15	+10
Nurses	f	33	29	41	−4	+8	+12	53	54	55	+1	+2	+1
Personnel directors	m	27	32	36	+5	+9	+4	32	40	33	+8	+1	−7
Physical education teachers	f	21	32	51	+11	+30	+19	41	53	45	+12	+4	−8
Physicians	f	38	34	47	−4	+9	+13	54	63	52	+9	−2	−11
Physicians	m	36	41	46	+5	+10	+5	32	53	47	+21	+15	−6
Physicists	m	25	23	47	−2	+22	+24	37	53	43	+16	+6	−10
Police officers	m	27	32	44	+5	+17	+12	16	30	29	+14	+13	−1
Psychologists	f	32	24	29	−8	−3	+5	58	76	63	+18	+5	−13
Psychologists	m	29	23	27	−6	−2	+4	45	55	51	+10	+6	−4
Public administrators	m	45	28	38	−17	−7	+10	28	40	44	+12	+16	+4
Purchasing agents	m	26	35	34	+9	+8	−1	15	36	39	+21	+24	+3
Realtors	m	26	28	38	+2	+12	+10	18	26	37	+8	+19	+11
Reporters	f	35	24	35	−11	0	+11	72	73	62	+1	−10	−11
Reporters	m	28	23	40	−5	+12	+17	54	55	56	+1	+2	+1
School administrators	m	37	39	46	+2	+9	+7	16	26	30	+10	+14	+4
Secretaries	f	21	20	25	−1	+4	+5	48	55	36	+7	−12	−19
Social Science teachers	f	32	26	30	−6	−2	+4	47	49	48	+2	+1	−1
Social Science teachers	m	25	33	43	+8	+18	+10	18	32	37	+14	+19	+5
YWCA directors	f	31	23	33	−8	+2	+10	49	62	51	+13	+2	−11
Average difference					−1.2%	+7.7%	+8.9%				+10.0%	+7.0%	−3.0%
Number of differences larger than 15%					2	9	4				12	10	5

similar, with the male samples slightly more positive in their response; on the *Artist* item, the two distributions are quite dissimilar, with the women's mean considerably higher. Clearly, sex of respondent is an important factor in analyzing the responses to some items. This is a major concern in the development of the SCII scoring system; Chapter 7 is devoted entirely to this issue.

7. *The shape of the item-response distributions varies from one item to the next, but which distribution shape is best is not clear.* Obviously, items having narrow, peaked distributions are of little value; just as obviously, items with broad distributions are useful. What other attributes of the item distributions are desirable is impossible to say within present knowledge of psychometrics. The various functions of the instrument are probably served best by drawing upon a variety of distributions, and variety was a criterion in the selection of items for the SCII booklet.

8. *Drawing valid conclusions about item-response distributions requires that vast quantities of data be analyzed.* The foregoing has drawn on the extensive archives of item-response distributions in the files at the University of Minnesota's Center for Interest Measurement Research. These distributions, which are extraordinarily useful in understanding how individual items perform, have been available only since about 1970, and the 1974 edition of the Strong, the SCII, was the first that had the benefit of such data in item selection and scale construction. Although E. K. Strong's methodical care in preserving and storing his data made it possible for these distributions to be available today, Strong himself never saw them, for he conducted his research before the days of the electronic computer. Strong's data, along with those collected during the last 20 years at Minnesota, have been organized into a computer-accessible archive of vast utility.

The Use of Statistics and the Construction of Scales

Some of the earlier research on vocational interests suffered from the misuse of statistics, and future investigators will want to avoid the mistakes of the past. By far the most common misuse of statistics in vocational-interest research has centered around the concept of statistical significance: a statistic is tested to see if it could have occurred by chance. But many years of experience indicate that people do not give random (that is, chance) responses to psychological inventories, and testing their responses, or any combination of them, against chance is an almost useless pursuit. An investigator who tests two samples, compares their means, calculates *T*-tests, finds more differences than one would expect by chance, and then reports that the inventory has successfully differentiated the interests of the two samples has made virtually no contribution to understanding of the two samples or of the general nature of interests. If these questions are to be studied seriously, more substantial information about the *magnitude* and the *content* of the differences is needed.

In the following discussion of guidelines for the inter-

pretation of data collected with the SVIB or SCII, all of the minimum standards suggested are far beyond the levels of chance. These guidelines have come to be respected in part because statistical theory has given them sanction, but also because they produce valid and reliable scales. They are, of course, applicable only to three-choice items, that is, to items with response choices similar to the "Like," "Indifferent," "Dislike" categories; true-false items or items with five or more choices have different characteristics, and require different statistical guidelines.

Item-response percentages. One of the ways that interest-inventory data are most frequently used is in the comparison of item-response percentages between two or more samples. Each of the Occupational Scales, for example, is nothing more than a collection of items that have shown large differences in response percentage between a sample of people in that occupation and a reference sample. But to identify items that are suitable for that Occupational scale, there must be a basis for establishing what is meant by "large differences."

Item-percentage differences are calculated by systematically comparing the "Like" and "Dislike" response percentages of the two samples (the occupational and reference samples), one item at a time. (The difference on the "Indifferent" response, which is rarely if ever the largest difference of the three, is ignored at this step; as discussed in Chapter 6, it is sometimes used, if large enough, to refine the item weights.) This comparison yields, for each item, two percentage differences, one between the two "Like" percentages, one between the two "Dislike" percentages. The larger of the two differences then becomes the ranking of that item, with respect to other items, toward its possible selection for an Occupational Scale based on the responses of the Occupational Criterion Sample; that is, an item is called a "12-percent item," a "30-percent item," and so on, depending on the size of the larger difference.

Substantial experience has shown that differences of 10 percent and smaller should be ignored completely. Samples tested and retested over short periods typically yield about a dozen item-response differences of 10 percent or larger between test and retest. Consequently, ignoring differences of this size or smaller eliminates the risk of selecting items that reflect only the normal fluctuations within a sample. In general, 12-percent items are barely important (about four items will differ between test and retest at this level); and 16-percent items are important (usually no items will differ on short test and retest intervals at this level). Every extra point above that becomes more important, and 20-percent and larger items are extremely important. Thus "important" means that the item responses reflect a real difference between the samples, one that will replicate on repeated sampling, and one that will manifest itself in differential behavior of most of the individuals making up the two samples—they will, for example, choose different activities, not only on paper but in their actual behavior.

Just as important as the *size* of the item-response differences, in the construction of an Occupational Scale, is the *number* of items, across the full range of the inventory, that exhibit these large response differences. The average occupational sample provides about 60 items that have a 16-percent or larger difference vis-à-vis the general (reference) sample. That number of items (60) with that large a difference (16-percent) will produce a scale that separates the occupational sample from the general sample by about two standard deviations. Scales with more items or larger differences will discriminate even better. Table 6.1, which reports for each Occupational Scale the number of items used, the minimum percent differences scored, and the resultant overlap between score distributions for the criterion and reference samples, provides many illustrations of this point.

These guidelines for the use of item-response differences are based on the assumption that both samples contain at least 200 people. If the samples are smaller than that, the item-percentage differences should be increased, to at least 18–20 percent for samples as small as 50. But for samples containing more than 200 people, •the minimum-percentage guidelines should *not* be lowered; though smaller differences are *statistically significant* with larger samples, they are *in a practical sense insignificant.*

Differences between means. Once the selection of items for an Occupational Scale has been completed, the next step is to determine whether or not the scale clearly distinguishes the new sample from other samples—reference samples or otherwise.

When the mean scores of two samples on an Occupational Scale are compared, differences of 4 points or less should be ignored; 5-point differences, which represent half a standard deviation, are the minimum worth noting, and then only when the samples are large enough (at least 30 people) to ensure that the differences are stable. Obviously, greater differences—of 10 or 20 points—are much more impressive. Mean differences between occupational samples on the Occupational Scales range as high as 45 points, but such enormous differences are found only between occupations with patently different outlooks, such as psychologists and military officers, or scientists and salespeople.

The range of response differences on the Basic Interest Scales and the General Occupational Themes is smaller than that for the Occupational Scales because of their different purposes and psychometric characteristics. The next three chapters discuss these differences in detail. Briefly, an Occupational Scale (Chapter 6) contains all of the items that discriminate between an occupational sample and a reference sample, some items weighted positively and some negatively, depending on the direction of the difference; its purpose is to produce maximum discrimination between the occupational and reference samples (preferably also between its sample and other occupational samples). In contrast, the Basic Interest Scales (Chapter 5) are designed for maximum ease in interpretation, and the General Occupational Theme scales (Chapter 4) are designed specifically to represent the occupational types hypothesized by Holland; be-

TABLE 3.2

Median Test-Retest Correlations for the Men's SVIB Occupational Scales for Varying Ages and Test-Retest Intervals

Age at first testing	Test-retest interval					
	2 weeks	1 year	2–5 years	6–10 years	11–20 years	20+ years
17–18	—	.80	.70	.65	.64	—
19–21	.91	.80	.73	.67	.67	.64
22–25	—	—	.78	.69	.75	.72
26+	—	—	.77	.81	.80	—

cause their content is more homogeneous, that is, more focused on a single content area, these scales are shorter than the Occupational Scales. Consequently, the range of individual and mean scores is smaller, and smaller differences are worth noting. For the Basic Interest Scales and General Occupational Themes, 3-point differences are indicative of "real" differences between groups, that is, differences that will replicate and that will be reflected in the behavior of most members of the groups. Greater differences, of course, are more impressive.

Scores for individuals. When the scores for a particular person are considered, the minimum differences worth studying are much larger, but there is no good empirical method for specifying how different two scale scores must be on the same profile before the difference is worth noting; in general, acceptable minimums appear to be 5–8 points on the General Occupational Themes or the Basic Interest Scales and at least 10–15 points on the Occupational Scales. The same levels apply to comparisons across profiles; that is, person X should differ from person Y by at least 10 points on an Occupational Scale before one concludes that the two people differ with respect to that scale.

Item intercorrelations. A different type of statistical guideline for analyzing the SCII items grew out of the original research on the Basic Interest Scales. That project clustered together items with high intercorrelations to produce homogeneous scales; consequently, some definition of "high" was needed. To arrive at a practical definition for these purposes, all of the possible item intercorrelations between the 400 items of the old SVIB—80,000 correlations for the men's booklet and 80,000 more for the women's booklet—were calculated. Frequency distributions of these correlations were made for both booklets (see p. 90 of the *Handbook for the SVIB*); these showed that item intercorrelations above .30 are rare, occurring less than 5 percent of the time. Consequently, the items were clustered together with that figure as a guide; most of the items finally included on each Basic Interest Scale are intercorrelated .25 or above with the other items on that scale. Because these scales have proved valid and reliable, that figure of .30 is a useful guideline, one that can be adopted by other investigators working with three-choice (that is, L-I-D) items.

Test-retest statistics. The most common measure of

stability over time is test-retest reliability, which usually is represented by a Pearson product-moment correlation between the test and retest scores. However, no good test exists to evaluate this statistic. For example, a test-retest correlation of .97 over three days obviously is good; how much lower the figure goes before one concludes that it is "poor"—.90, .85, .80, .60, .30—is diffi- cult to say. No easy answer exists, but again we can use some typical findings as guidelines. Table 3.2, taken from Johansson and Campbell (1971), gives median cor- relations for various editions of the Strong. These figures can be used for comparisons with other samples. See also Table 6.3, which reports 3-year SCII test-retest data; stability over even longer periods remains high.

CHAPTER FOUR

The General Occupational Themes

In the development of the 1974 SCII, one type of analysis used was the search for general themes in people's responses to the test booklet, specifically those six themes represented by the occupational types hypothesized and identified by Holland (1966, 1973). This chapter discusses these types and their role in the construction and scoring of the General Occupational Theme scales.

The SVIB and Occupational Theory

From its inception in 1927, the Strong Vocational Interest Blank was an empirical, atheoretical instrument. Employing hard work and boundless energy, and without benefit of automatic data-processing equipment, E. K. Strong, Jr., learned to develop empirical scales that had impressive validity and reliability statistics and great utility. But his profile presented a person's scores with only the laconic statement that "This score represents the degree of similarity between your interests and [those of] workers in this occupation." The person was left to decide, with the aid of a counselor, what those interests were for each occupation. However, the empirical success of the Strong Blank obscured the lack of an organizing theory.

Profile groupings. Strong realized early, in the late 1930's, that systematic clustering of the scales was necessary. He was testing more and more occupations, and he wanted to arrange their scales in groupings that would make interpretations more fruitful. His first tentative step toward a theory was to gather the scales into groups on the profile; he formed the groups by using scale intercorrelations, and he was guided to some extent by factor analyses carried out by L. L. Thurstone.

Because these groupings of related occupations were a great aid in scale interpretation, they soon were used widely in both applied and research applications of the inventory. However, the groupings presented several problems; the most serious was the lack of a general theoretical structure—which led to a proliferation of irritating idiosyncrasies and aberrations. For example, several scales—those for PRODUCTION MANAGER, CPA OWNER, and PRESIDENT, MANUFACTURING CORPORATION—defied grouping with any others. They were an anomaly in the system, and counselors usually skipped over them quickly. Researchers working with the profile groups also ignored these scales.

What was needed was an organizing structure that would be at once global and parsimonious, one that would embrace all of Strong's scales and all scales to come.

Strong's Group Scales. Strong's next attempt in this direction was his development of Group Scales, each of which was based on a combination of the occupations in a single profile group. Not satisfied with these scales, partly because of their questionable psychometric qualities, Strong tried to evaluate them in the same way that he evaluated the Occupational Scales—by calculating percent overlap with Men-in-General. The results were not impressive, and rather than consider whether these scales might be evaluated in a different way, he dropped them.

The Basic Interest Scales. The next attempt to find a guiding theoretical structure was the development of the SVIB Basic Interest Scales (Campbell, Borgen, Eastes, Johansson, and Peterson, 1968). The objective of these scales was to identify homogeneous clusters of items that would be easy to interpret. The result was a set of scales (about 20) that was too large and unwieldy to serve as a theoretical structure, especially since most experts agree that a much smaller number of basic dimensions, probably not more than five to seven, underlies the structure of interests. Although the Basic Interest Scales are useful for other purposes, they do not provide a parsimonious organization for the domain of interests.

The General Occupational Themes. In an attempt to develop an occupational-classification system closely tied to psychometric research, Holland (1959) proposed six basic categories of occupational interests, categories closely resembling the dimensions usually seen in research on vocational interests with the Strong Blank. In succeeding years, Holland refined and expanded his classifications in a theory encompassing the broad area of educational and vocational behavior, retaining as its foundation the original six categories (Holland, 1965, 1973). As reported elsewhere in more detail (Campbell and Holland, 1972; Hansen and Johansson, 1972), scales using Strong Blank items were developed for these six categories and then applied to Strong's data; the results provide a structure that is helpful in understanding both the Basic Interest Scales and the Occupational Scales; and on the strength of this research, Holland's theory was used to organize the profile scores for the SCII.

Holland's Theory and Categories

Holland's theory, which he presented in *Making Vocational Choices: A Theory of Careers* (1973), is based on four main assumptions:

First, in our culture, most people can be categorized in terms of six types—realistic, investigative, artistic, social, enterprising, or conventional—and each person may be characterized by one, or some combination, of these types. The six types, which are described in detail below, correspond closely to the groupings on the earlier SVIB men's profile—one indication of the utility of the theory in working with the SCII.

Second, occupational environments can be divided into the same six types, and each environment will be found to be dominated by a particular type of person. Thus, the personality types of co-workers, as much as job requirements, establish the working tenor of a given occupation.

Third, people search for environments that let them exercise their skills and abilities, express their attitudes and values, take on problems and roles they find stimulating and satisfying, and avoid chores or responsibilities they find distasteful or formidable.

Fourth, behavior is determined by an interaction between a person's personality and the characteristics of his or her working environment. Factors such as job performance, satisfaction, and stability are influenced by this interaction.

Obviously, a classification system of only six types is insufficient for the wide diversity of human personalities or working environments, and Holland expanded his classification to incorporate combinations of the six types, using terms such as realistic-investigative, artistic-social, and enterprising-social-conventional, depending on the relative strength of each type in a given individual or a given working situation. In theory, using all possible combinations of the six types, 720 classifications can be established. In practice, the use of the most strongly manifested one, two, or three types seems sufficient for most purposes.

The core of Holland's system is his six basic occupational categories. He has described their genesis (1966, pp. 15, 10):

The formulation for the types grew out of my experience as a vocational counselor and a clinician, and out of my construction of a personality inventory from interest material. After reviewing the vocational literature—especially factor-analytic studies of personality and vocational interests—I concluded that it might be useful to categorize people into six types.

The present types are analogous in some ways to those proposed earlier by Adler, Fromm, Jung, Sheldon, and others. They differ from these earlier typologies in their origin—which is largely our vocational literature—and in their definitions. The six major factors identified in Guilford's comprehensive factor analysis of human interest—mechanical, scientific, social welfare, clerical, business, and aesthetic—approximate the present types. To the best of my knowledge, Guilford's factor analysis is the most explicit forerunner of the present typology.

The following descriptions of the six types, drawn from work by Holland (1973), also provide definitions of the six General Occupational Themes. (Additional interpretive information and sample items for each General Occupational Theme are reported in the *User's Guide*.)

REALISTIC: Persons of this type are robust, rugged, practical, and physically strong; have good motor coordination and skills; usually perceive themselves as mechanically inclined; are direct, stable, natural, and persistent; prefer concrete to abstract problems; avoid social settings that require verbal and interpersonal skills; and like to build things with tools. Realistic types prefer such occupations as mechanic, engineer, electrician, fish and wildlife specialist, crane operator, and tool designer.

INVESTIGATIVE: This category includes those with a strong scientific orientation; they usually are task-oriented, introspective, and asocial; prefer to think problems through rather than act them out; have a great need to understand the physical world; enjoy ambiguous tasks; prefer to work independently; have unconventional values and attitudes; are confident of their scholarly and intellectual abilities; describe themselves as analytical, curious, independent, and reserved; and especially dislike repetitive activities. Vocational preferences include astronomer, biologist, chemist, technical writer, zoologist, and psychologist.

ARTISTIC: Persons of the artistic type prefer free, unstructured situations with maximum opportunity for self-expression; resemble investigative types in being introspective and asocial but differ in having a greater need for individual expression; are creative, especially in artistic and musical media; avoid problems that are highly structured; prefer dealing with problems through self-expression in artistic media; perform well on standard measures of creativity, and value aesthetic qualities; see themselves as expressive, original, intuitive, creative, nonconforming, introspective, and independent. Vocational preferences include artist, author, composer, writer, musician, stage director, and symphony conductor.

SOCIAL: Persons of this type are sociable, responsible, humanistic; like to work in groups, and enjoy being at the center of the group; have good verbal and interpersonal skills; avoid highly ordered activities; prefer to solve problems through feelings and interpersonal manipulation of others; enjoy activities that involve informing, training, developing, curing, or enlightening others; perceive themselves as understanding, responsible, idealistic, and helpful. Vocational preferences include social worker, special education teacher, high school teacher, guidance counselor, school administrator, recreation leader, and speech therapist.

ENTERPRISING: Persons of this type have verbal skills suited to selling, dominating, and leading; are strong leaders; have a strong drive to attain organizational goals or economic aims; tend to avoid work situations requiring long periods of intellectual effort; differ from conventional types in having a greater preference for social tasks and an even greater concern for power, status, and leadership; see themselves as aggressive, popular, self-confident, cheerful, and sociable; generally have a high energy level; and show an aversion to scientific activities. Vocational preferences include business executive, political campaign manager, real estate salesperson, buyer, and retail merchandiser.

CONVENTIONAL: Conventional people prefer well-ordered environments and like systematic verbal and numerical activities; are effective at well-structured tasks, but avoid ambiguous situations and problems involving interpersonal relationships; describe themselves as conscientious, efficient, obedient, calm, orderly, and practical; identify with power; and value material possessions and status. Vocational preferences include accountant, credit manager, business education teacher, bookkeeper, clerical worker, and quality control expert.

Holland's classification system is an extension of the trait and factor theory that dominated occupational theory from the 1920's to the 1950's. That approach, at its worst and simplest, implied that the main goal of vocational counseling is to match people and jobs—in other words, to see that round pegs find their way into round holes.

Holland's theory, which considers such broad concepts as the individual's total life style and the global occupational environment, is a more sophisticated version of this earlier approach. Although the concept of matching the individual to a setting is still salient, Holland addresses other concerns, especially developmental issues. He describes the effects of different environments on various types: for example, he points out that investigative types usually do well in school because they have attitudes and values compatible with those of their teachers and thus find the atmosphere supportive; in contrast, realistic types tend to do poorly because the match between their dominant characteristics and the dominant characteristics of academic environments is poor.

Constructing the Scales

A detailed account of the construction of the SVIB General Occupational Theme scales for men is given in Campbell and Holland (1972); a similar project for women was reported by Hansen and Johansson (1972). Essentially, what was done in both projects was to select 20 SVIB items to represent each type, on the basis of the descriptions given by Holland (1966). A variety of statistical evidence was used in the selection of specific items: item intercorrelations, popularity of the items among occupations of designated Holland types, and item-scale correlations.

Item selection. The same procedure was followed in constructing the General Occupational Themes for the 1974 SCII. In most instances, the SVIB and SCII Theme scales are nearly identical, although a few new items had to be substituted for those dropped in developing the combined-sex SCII booklet. The 1985 SCII General Occupational Themes have the same item content as the 1974 scales, but they have been renormed on the new 1985 General Reference Sample.

The items making up each SCII General Occupational Theme scale are all "reasonable," in the sense that they correspond either obviously or intuitively to the description of that occupational-personality type. The same items are used for both men and women, and the items

TABLE 4.1
Intercorrelations Between the General Occupational Themes
(Correlations above the diagonal based on 300 women; those below the diagonal based on 300 men)

Scale	REAL-ISTIC	INVESTI-GATIVE	ARTIS-TIC	SOCIAL	ENTER-PRISING	CONVEN-TIONAL
REALISTIC	—	.62	.25	.25	.19	.32
INVESTIGATIVE	.59	—	.40	.25	.10	.25
ARTISTIC	.15	.38	—	.19	.13	-.11
SOCIAL	.33	.33	.26	—	.37	.41
ENTERPRISING	.37	.15	.10	.42	—	.47
CONVENTIONAL	.41	.41	.08	.37	.51	—

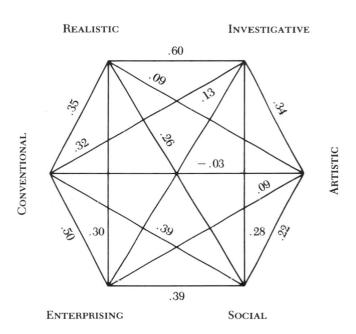

Fig. 4.1. Intercorrelations between the General Occupational Themes, arranged in hexagonal order (correlations based on 300 females and 300 males).

are weighted +1, 0, and −1, respectively, for the "Like," "Indifferent," and "Dislike" responses. This pattern of item weights was used because the "Likes" of each of these patterns are more precisely defined by Holland's theory than are the "Dislikes." In addition, as experience with the Basic Interest Scales has shown (Campbell, Borgen, Eastes, Johansson, and Peterson, 1968), "Likes" tend to cluster statistically, whereas "Dislikes" do not.

Theme intercorrelations. Scale intercorrelations for the General Occupational Themes are presented in Table 4.1. On the strength of such correlations, Holland suggested that his types be arranged in a hexagon, as shown in Fig. 4.1. Although the sides of the hexagon may not be as regular as Holland's theory suggests, the patterns of intercorrelations support the overall structure; especially for men, the strongest correlations occur between adjacent scales, the weakest usually between scales directly opposite each other. Probably because women were excluded from many occupations until recent years, the hexagon arrangement is not as obvious for them at this time as it is for men. But as women move into occupations previously restricted to men, and vice versa, the world-of-work map will undoubtedly be rearranged, and a clearer configuration should emerge.

Norming the Scales

The raw-score-to-standard-score conversion of the General Occupational Themes is based on a distribution of 600 people, called the General Reference Sample (half males, half females), constructed to represent the interests of People-in-General. They represent women and men from professional, vocational/technical, and nonprofessional occupations in all six of the General Occupational Theme types. The mean age for the sample is 38.2 years, and the educational level of the subjects ranges from those without a high school diploma to those with Ph.D. degrees. Their raw-score means and standard deviations on the six scales are used in a standardization

formula that converts all scores into distributions with standard-score means of 50 and standard deviations of 10. By this formula

$$\text{standard score} = \left(\frac{X - Mc}{SDc}\right)10 + 50$$

where X is an individual's raw score, and Mc and SDc are the General Reference Sample raw-score mean and raw-score standard deviation. Thus, a respondent's scores on the General Occupational Themes can be compared quickly on common numerical measures; a standard score of 60, for example, falls one standard deviation (50 plus 10) above the combined mean, no matter which of the Themes is being scored.

Because men and women have different distributions on these scales, interpretation usually should be pursued separately for the two sexes. Consequently, the interpretive comment printed on the profile for each of the General Occupational Themes is based on the distribution for the respondent's sex (either Women-in-General or Men-in-General). For each Theme, the computer prints one of the comments in the lefthand column

TABLE 4.2

Means, Standard Deviations, and Standard-Score Interpretive Boundaries of the General Occupational Theme Scales for the Women- and Men-in-General Samples (Each *N*=300)

(Numbers in parentheses are percentiles)

Scale	Sex	Mean	S.D.	Very low (0–6)	Low (7–15)	Mod. low (16–30)	Average (31–69)	Mod. high (70–84)	High (85–93)	Very high (94–100)
REALISTIC	f	46.5	9.1	29–32	33–37	38–41	42–51	52–55	56–59	60–72
	m	53.5	9.6	29–37	38–42	43–48	49–58	59–63	64–67	68–72
INVESTIGATIVE	f	48.9	10.3	22–33	34–37	38–42	43–55	56–59	60–62	63–69
	m	51.1	9.6	22–35	36–40	41–46	47–56	57–61	62–64	65–69
ARTISTIC	f	52.6	9.2	24–37	38–41	42–48	49–58	59–62	63–64	65–66
	m	47.4	10.1	24–31	32–35	36–41	42–53	54–58	59–62	63–66
SOCIAL	f	50.1	10.2	21–33	34–39	40–43	44–56	57–61	62–66	67–74
	m	49.9	9.8	21–33	34–39	40–44	45–54	55–60	61–64	65–74
ENTERPRISING	f	49.2	9.4	27–35	36–38	39–43	44–54	55–59	60–64	65–77
	m	50.8	10.5	27–33	34–38	39–44	45–55	56–61	62–66	67–77
CONVENTIONAL	f	49.6	10.4	23–33	34–37	38–43	44–56	57–60	61–67	68–79
	m	50.4	9.5	23–36	37–39	40–44	45–54	55–60	61–64	65–79

TABLE 4.3

Test-Retest Reliability Statistics for the General Occupational Themes

Theme	Two-week statistics (*N*=106 women, 74 men)					Thirty-day statistics (*N*=35 women, 67 men)					Three-year statistics (*N*=65 women, 75 men)				
	Test retest correlation[a]	Test		Retest		Test retest correlation[b]	Test		Retest		Test retest correlation[c]	Test		Retest	
		Mean	S.D.	Mean	S.D.		Mean	S.D.	Mean	S.D.		Mean	S.D.	Mean	S.D.
REALISTIC	.91	47	9.7	49	10.7	.87	50	8.7	51	9.2	.82	51	9.8	51	10.1
INVESTIGATIVE	.90	48	9.8	49	11.1	.84	52	8.6	52	8.9	.78	53	8.6	52	9.3
ARTISTIC	.93	48	10.2	49	11.0	.91	51	10.2	53	10.4	.87	50	10.2	51	10.7
SOCIAL	.89	50	10.9	50	11.8	.86	51	9.4	51	10.2	.82	49	10.4	48	10.0
ENTERPRISING	.85	45	9.1	47	10.7	.85	50	10.0	52	11.0	.80	48	10.0	48	10.2
CONVENTIONAL	.91	47	10.9	48	11.7	.84	48	9.8	49	10.1	.79	49	9.9	49	10.9

[a]Median correlation = .91   [b]Median correlation = .86   [c]Median correlation = .81

below; the comment selected corresponds to the particular percentile band in the righthand column that includes, for the in-general sample of the appropriate sex, the respondent's score on that scale.

Comment printed	Percentile of in general sample
Very high	94th and above
High	85th to 93rd
Moderately high	70th to 84th
Average	31st to 69th
Moderately low	16th to 30th
Low	7th to 15th
Very low	6th and below

Again, an individual's score may be compared to the combined male and female distribution by using the printed standard scores, or to the distribution of scores for the respondent's sex by using the interpretive comments and bars.

Table 4.2 lists the standard-score means and standard deviations of the Women- and Men-in-General samples (p. 49) and the ranges used to define each interpretive category. The lower and upper bounds for each scale are the minimum and maximum possible scores; these are the scores that will be earned by anyone answering all items "Dislike" or "Like," respectively.

The distributions of the Men- and Women-in-General samples are illustrated on the profile form by two bars for each scale. The shaded bar represents the men's distribution, the open bar the women's. For each of the two distributions for every scale, the vertical line in the middle indicates the mean; the thick portion of the bar represents the middle 50 percent of the sample (from the 25th to the 75th percentiles); and the thin-line extensions represent the middle 80 percent (from the 10th to the 90th percentiles).

Reliability

Three samples have been tested and then retested over various time intervals to determine the stability of the SCII scales. Test-retest statistics for the three samples on the General Occupational Themes are presented in Table 4.3; analogous statistics for the Basic Interest and Occupational Scales are reported in Tables 5.5 and 6.2 and 6.3, respectively.

The two-week sample was collected by Mary Whitton of North Carolina State University. She tested and retested 180 people—106 females and 74 males—who were mostly high school seniors or college students who had volunteered for this project. Their average age was 18.7 years. The test-retest interval ranged from 11 to 22 days, with a mean of 14 days. As shown in Table 4.3, the median test-retest correlation over this short time period was .91, indicating substantial stability.

The thirty-day sample, which included 35 women and 67 men, came from three sources: an Army Reserve unit; students at the University of Minnesota; and women in a career development course. It was a diverse sample, mainly in the 25 to 40 age range. The median test-retest correlation in this sample was .86, somewhat lower than that for the two-week sample, but still comfortably high.

The three-year test-retest sample, collected by the

TABLE 4.4
Correlations Between SCII General Occupational Themes and Vocational Preference Inventory (VPI) Scales
(Based on 97 subjects)

VPI scales	SCII General Occupational Themes					
	REAL- ISTIC	INVESTI- GATIVE	ARTIS- TIC	SOCIAL	ENTER- PRISING	CONVEN- TIONAL
REALISTIC	.73	.40	−.05	.20	.39	.44
INVESTIGATIVE	.38	.77	.09	.02	.06	.27
ARTISTIC	−.13	.09	.78	.15	−.08	−.20
SOCIAL	.15	.03	.09	.72	.20	.21
ENTERPRISING	.38	.14	−.15	.28	.79	.63
CONVENTIONAL	.32	.20	−.37	.16	.41	.76

Center for Interest Measurement Research at the University of Minnesota, included 65 women and 75 men; all were employed full-time, both when tested and when retested, in occupations ranging from semi-skilled to professional—again, a diverse sample. The median test-retest correlation over the three-year period was .81, a figure high enough to indicate that the Theme scores generally are stable, but low enough to indicate that some shifting around did occur.

In all three of the test-retest samples, the means were roughly 50, indicating that they were indeed general samples. The means also were quite stable between testing and retesting, never changing more than 2 points, usually less; again, these scales are quite reliable.

Internal-consistency reliabilities of the six General Occupational Themes also were computed (Larkin, pers. comm., 1984). Coefficient alphas, derived using a sample of 1,445 males, ranged from .90 to .95 with a median of .92; for 1,410 females, the range was .90 to .93 with a median of .91. These data indicate the high degree of internal consistency of the Themes.

Validity

Several studies have added to the construct validity of the General Occupational Themes. Table 4.4 reports data collected at the University of Minnesota's Center for Interest Measurement Research. Ninety-seven subjects completed both the Vocational Preference Inventory (VPI) and the Strong Blank. Correlations between the same-named General Occupational Themes and VPI Scales are high (median = .765), indicating that the two inventories are measuring similar interest traits.

Another study used the Edwards Personal Preference Schedule (EPPS), an instrument based on Murray's need theory, to identify personality characteristics associated with the General Occupational Themes (Utz & Korben, 1976). Although few of the product-moment correlation coefficients between the EPPS and SVIB-SCII scales were even moderately high (only three out of 182 over .30), several were significant in the expected direction on the basis of definitions of the General Occupational Themes. For example, the Realistic Theme correlated negatively with Affiliation; the Investigative Theme correlated positively with Achievement; the Artistic Theme correlated negatively with Order and positively with

TABLE 4.5
Occupations Scoring High and Low on Each General Occupational Theme

REALISTIC	INVESTIGATIVE	ARTISTIC	SOCIAL	ENTERPRISING	CONVENTIONAL
		High Scores			
Agribusiness managers	Biologists	Advertising executives	Auto sales dealers	Agribusiness managers	Accountants
Carpenters	Chemists	Art teachers	Guidance counselors	Auto sales dealers	Auto sales dealers
Electricians	Engineers	Artists	Home economics teachers	Business education teachers	Bankers
Engineers	Geologists	Broadcasters	Mental health workers	Buyers	Bookkeepers
Farmers	Mathematicians	English teachers	Ministers	Chamber of Commerce executives	Business education teachers
Foresters	Medical technologists	Interior decorators	Physical education teachers	Funeral directors	Credit managers
Highway patrol officers	Physicians	Medical illustrators	Recreation leaders	Life insurance agents	Executive housekeepers
Horticultural workers	Physicists	Ministers	School administrators	Purchasing agents	Food service managers
Industrial arts teachers	Psychologists	Musicians	Social science teachers	Realtors	IRS agents
Military enlisted personnel	Research and development managers	Photographers	Social workers	Restaurant managers	Mathematics teachers
Military officers	Science teachers	Public relations directors	Special education teachers	Retail clerks	Military enlisted personnel
Vocational agricultural teachers	Sociologists	Reporters	YMCA/YWCA directors	Store managers	Secretaries
		Low Scores			
Advertising executives	Bankers	Accountants	Architects	Artists	Art teachers
Artists	Beauticians	Agribusiness managers	Artists	Biologists	Artists
Bankers	Business education teachers	Bus drivers	Cartographers	Chemists	Broadcasters
Broadcasters	Buyers	Credit managers	Computer programmers	College professors	Flight attendants
Buyers	Chamber of Commerce executives	Farmers	Engineers	Foresters	Medical illustrators
English teachers	Farmers	Foresters	Farmers	Geographers	Ministers
Florists	Florists	Military enlisted personnel	Geologists	Geologists	Musicians
Interior decorators	Food service managers	Military officers	Investments managers	Mathematicians	Occupational therapists
Mental health workers	Funeral directors	Pest controllers	Mathematicians	Medical illustrators	Photographers
Reporters	Realtors	Physical education teachers	Medical illustrators	Physicians	Psychologists
Secretaries	Retail clerks	Veterinarians	Physicists	Physicists	Reporters
Travel agents	Secretaries	Vocational agricultural teachers	Veterinarians	Sociologists	Speech pathologists

Change; Social negatively with Autonomy and positively with Nurturance and Dominance; Enterprising positively with Dominance; and Conventional negatively with Autonomy and positively with Endurance.

A third study, conducted by Varca and Shaffer (1982), used adolescent and adult participants to show that the General Occupational Themes are useful for identifying the avocational activities in which an individual will participate. They found that people picked avocational and leisure activities that were congruent with their General Occupational Theme types and that, like vocational interests, avocational interests were stable over time.

Interpreting the Scores

The six General Occupational Theme scores provide a global view of the respondent's occupational orientation.

High scores suggest the general range of activities the person will enjoy, the type of occupational environment she/he will find most comfortable, the problems she/he will be most willing to tackle, and the kinds of people who will be most appealing as co-workers. The scores offer a useful, immediate overview of an individual's interests.

To understand each type or combination of types better, the counselor should study the descriptions given above and the occupations scoring high and low on each scale (see Table 4.5 and Appendix B). Most people do not score high on just one Theme; some have several high scores, some have few, and some have none; many have two high scores, usually on adjacent Themes. More extensive information on the use and interpretation of the General Occupational Themes is given in Chapter 10 and in the *User's Guide* (Chapters 4, 6, 7, 9, 11, and 15).

Assigning occupations to code types. One of the most important contributions of the General Occupational Themes is the structure accorded the profile by assigning the Basic Interest Scales and Occupational Scales to code types based on the Themes. Table 6.4 (in Chapter 6) demonstrates how this was done. Essentially, each Occupational Scale was assigned to a code type corresponding to the highest Theme scores of the people in that occupation. With scales then arranged on the profile in the R-I-A-S-E-C order, the interpretation of the scores and patterns of scores is greatly enhanced; similarities and dissimilarities between occupations become more obvious, and the clustering of occupations along lines of common interests becomes more apparent. (The inter-pretive value of the code types is discussed at length in the *User's Guide*, Chapter 9.)

The code types for several hundred occupations are given in Appendix B; students often find it useful to identify occupations with codes similar to their own.

Consistency among scales. Normally, there is considerable consistency among an individual's scores on the General Occupational Themes, the Basic Interest Scales (see Chapter 5), and the Occupational Scales (see Chapter 6). One of the counselor's main tasks is to help the respondent perceive that pattern in his/her scores or, if the consistency is in fact low, to help the person understand what causes the inconsistency. More is said on this subject in Chapter 5 and in the *User's Guide*.

CHAPTER FIVE

The Basic Interest Scales

The Basic Interest Scales were constructed by gathering together clusters of statistically related items. This technique generates homogeneous scales, that is, scales with items highly consistent in content. For example, the ART Basic Interest Scale includes, among others, the following items: *Artist*, *Cartoonist*, and *Interior Decorator*. These items and others, all similar, were clustered together because most people tend to react to them in one of two ways, by responding either "Like" to all (or nearly all) of them or "Indifferent" or "Dislike" to all (or nearly all) of them.

The strength of this tendency to respond in a similar way to two items can be measured by assigning weights of $+1$, 0, and -1, respectively, to the three possible responses for each item and then calculating the product-moment correlations between the two items. Among 500 women in a general sample, the correlation between *Artist* and *Cartoonist* was .47, between *Artist* and *Interior decorator* .52, and between *Cartoonist* and *Interior decorator* .27; the analogous figures among 500 men were .49, .45, and .37. As discussed in Chapter 3, item intercorrelations of this size indicate a substantial relationship between the items.

A scale formed by using clusters of statistically related items has three important characteristics: first, it represents, by virtue of its internal consistency, an important focus around which people can group their own interests; second, because the items are all drawn from one area, the content of the scale is easy to understand; and third, the concentration of related items in a single scale provides a more reliable measure than the same number of unrelated items would.

Purpose and Origin of the Basic Interest Scales

The main purpose in developing the Basic Interest Scales was to improve the understanding of the Occupational Scales. The latter, which historically preceded the former, are constructed by gathering together into a scale all items that discriminate between an occupational Criterion Sample and a General Reference Sample, no matter what the item content. The resulting scale, though powerful statistically, may be difficult to interpret because the items are quite varied. The PSYCHOLOGIST Occupational Scale, for example, incorporates a wide range of items, including subgroups that reflect interests in science, social service, and the arts,

weighted positively, and other subgroups encompassing religion, business, and military activities, weighted negatively. A person can score high (or low) on this scale in countless ways, and only those counselors with extensive clinical experience can search out the factors underlying a particular profile.

Kenneth Clark, in his work with the Minnesota Vocational Interest Inventory (Clark, 1961), proposed the use of two types of scales to overcome this problem: empirically developed Occupational Scales, such as those that always had been part of the SVIB, and statistically developed homogeneous scales. Clark's rationale was that the combination of these two types of scales would provide more information than would either type used separately. For example, if a person scored high on an Occupational Scale, such as the PSYCHOLOGIST scale, her/his scores on the homogeneous scales could be scanned to see precisely what combination of interests was present—science, social service, art, or whatever. The homogeneous scales could be used to describe the general patterns reflected in the scores of empirical scales. For this reason, the profile for the Minnesota Vocational Interest Inventory contained both types of scales; at the time it was published, it was the only inventory to do so (Clark & Campbell, 1965). Shortly thereafter, the SVIB profile also was expanded to include both types of scales (Campbell, 1969).

Clark, in his award-winning book *Vocational Interests of Non-Professional Men* (1961), discussed at length the differences between the two types of scales: empirical scales are heterogeneous in content and constitute an "open" system to which new occupations can continually be added as they are tested. Homogeneous scales, by contrast, each focus on only one area of item content and constitute a "closed" system, since the number of scales in the system will never be increased unless the inventory itself is expanded.

The two types of scales serve different purposes, and to understand their complementary nature one must understand the differences in their development and in their operating characteristics.

Constructing the Scales

To some extent, the Basic Interest Scales formed themselves; for the most part, the clusters of correlated items making up the scales fell out of the item-intercorrelation matrix. A few arbitrary decisions were made in borderline cases, especially in those instances where an item correlated highly with some items in a cluster but not with others. And in a few instances an item was not used because it did not "feel" right for a given scale. For example, the item *Sculptor* correlated moderately with the science items but was not added to that scale because it seemed out of place. Such decisions were rare; the bulk of the scale-construction decisions were based on hard data.

The details of the construction of the Basic Interest Scales are given in the *Handbook for the SVIB*. Briefly, the procedure was as follows:

First, item-intercorrelation matrices containing correlation coefficients between all possible pairs of items were generated for both female and male samples.

Second, frequency distributions of these correlations were made for each sex. The two distributions, presented in the *Handbook*, were virtually identical, with means of about .03 and standard deviations of about .12. Because most of the correlations were less than .30, that figure was considered "high," and pairs of items with correlations of .30 or greater were considered closely related.

Third, scales were constructed by gathering together those items with intercorrelations of .30 or higher. In many cases, the selection criterion had to be dropped to .20, especially in those instances where, for example, item A correlated .30 with B and .30 with C, but B correlated only .20 with C.

The item-intercorrelation matrices for all of the earlier (1969) SVIB Basic Interest Scales are presented in the *Handbook*; scanning them affords a good impression of the level of correlation one can expect when working with individual items.

The 1969 Basic Interest Scales were constructed separately for the women's and men's booklets. In constructing the 1974 scales, the female and male SVIB scale sets were merged into a single set, in most cases by combining the parallel women's and men's scales. If a scale appeared on only one form of the SVIB, it was nonetheless retained in most cases (e.g., DOMESTIC ACTIVITIES appeared only on the women's form of the SVIB). Dropping or rewording of items in the booklet also led to minor changes in a few of the scales. (Scale-by-scale changes are given in the 1974 *Manual for the SVIB-SCII*.)

This work resulted in the construction of 23 Basic Interest Scales ranging in length from five to 24 items, with a median length of 11 items. The 1985 SCII Basic Interest Scales have the same item content as the 1974 scales, but the 1985 scales have been renormed on the 1985 General Reference Sample.

Norming the Scales

The Basic Interest Scales have been renormed against the 1985 General Reference Sample, a sample of 300 women and 300 men described in Chapter 4. For each scale, the mean and standard deviation of this sample

were set equal to 50 and 10, respectively, and all future scores are converted to this distribution for ready comparison.

As is the case with the General Occupational Themes, the Basic Interest Scale standard-score column on the profile is followed by a column of interpretive comments. These comments are based on the distribution for the respondent's own sex, and the comments for the Basic Interest Scales correspond to the percentile bands used for the General Occupational Themes (p. 30). Table 5.1 lists the standard-score means and standard deviations of the Women- and Men-in-General samples and the ranges used to define each interpretive category. The extremes of the lower and upper bands for each scale are the minimum and maximum possible scores; these are the scores that will be earned by anyone answering all items "Dislike" or "Like," respectively—and they are thus the same for both sexes, on all scales.

The distributions of the Men- and Women-in-General samples are illustrated on the profile by two bars for each scale. The shaded bar represents the men's distribution, the open bar the women's. For each distribution for each scale, the vertical line in the middle indicates the mean; the thick portion of the bar represents the middle 50 percent of the sample (from the 25th to the 75th percentiles); and the thin-line extensions represent the middle 80 percent (from the 10th to the 90th percentiles). With the use of standard scores, bars, and interpretive comments, an individual's score may be compared with either the male or female distribution or the combined male and female distribution.

Relationships to the General Occupational Themes

The SCII Basic Interest Scales are clustered on the profile into the six General Occupational Theme categories, as indicated in the lefthand column of Table 5.1. This clustering was based on the scale intercorrelations given in Tables 5.2 and 5.3. In most cases, the Basic Interest Scales in the same category correlate at least moderately with each other, and in some cases correlate so highly that the decision to create two scales instead of one was all but arbitrary. For example, the MERCHANDISING and BUSINESS MANAGEMENT scales, both of which fit easily into Holland's ENTERPRISING category, might well have been combined; they were kept separate, even though their intercorrelation is high, because they have different item content. Other pairs—SCIENCE and MEDICAL SCIENCE, MUSIC and ART, TEACHING and SOCIAL SERVICE—are similarly related. One must opt either for parsimony and a small number of scales, or for purity of item content and a larger number. The two types of scales—the General Occupational Themes and the Basic Interest Scales—provide the best of both approaches; and their high correlations suggest that the two types rest on the same underlying structure. Only one Basic Interest Scale, OFFICE PRACTICES, fits into Holland's CONVENTIONAL category, which has a smaller bandwidth than the others.

TABLE 5.1
Means, Standard Deviations, and Standard-Score Interpretive Boundaries of the Basic Interest Scales for the Women- and Men-in-General Samples
(Each N = 300; numbers in parentheses are percentiles)

General Theme[a]	Scale	Sex	Mean	S.D.	Very low (0–6)	Low (7–15)	Mod. low (16–30)	Average (30–69)	Mod. high (70–84)	High (85–93)	Very high (94–100)
R	AGRICULTURE	f	47.9	9.9	31–33	34–36	37–42	43–51	52–58	59–61	62–68
		m	52.1	9.7	31–36	37–39	40–45	46–58	59–61	62–64	65–68
R	NATURE	f	50.7	10.1	21–34	35–38	39–44	45–57	58–61	62–63	64–66
		m	49.3	9.9	21–32	33–38	39–42	43–55	56–61	62–63	64–66
R	ADVENTURE	f	47.3	9.5	30–33	34–37	38–41	42–52	53–58	59–62	63–71
		m	52.7	9.7	30–37	38–41	42–46	47–58	59–64	65–66	67–71
R	MILITARY ACTIVITIES	f	46.9	8.1	40–41	42–43	44–45	46–47	48–56	57–62	63–73
		m	53.1	10.8	40–41	42–43	44–45	46–59	60–66	67–71	72–73
R	MECHANICAL ACTIVITIES	f	46.7	9.1	32–34	35–36	37–40	41–50	51–56	57–64	65–70
		m	53.3	9.7	32–36	37–41	42–47	48–59	60–63	64–66	67–70
I	SCIENCE	f	48.6	10.0	31–33	34–36	37–41	42–55	56–59	60–64	65–69
		m	51.4	9.8	31–35	36–39	40–44	45–58	59–62	63–64	65–69
I	MATHEMATICS	f	48.7	9.9	32–33	34–35	36–43	44–45	56–59	60–62	63–67
		m	51.3	10.0	32–33	34–39	40–45	46–57	58–62	63–64	65–67
I	MEDICAL SCIENCE	f	49.1	10.1	30–31	32–35	36–44	45–56	57–60	61–63	64–66
		m	50.9	9.8	30–33	34–40	41–44	45–56	57–60	61–63	64–66
I	MEDICAL SERVICE	f	50.2	10.6	34–35	36–38	39–42	43–54	55–61	62–68	69–76
		m	49.8	9.4	34–35	36–40	41–42	43–54	55–58	59–65	66–76
A	MUSIC/ DRAMATICS	f	53.1	9.0	26–38	39–43	44–47	48–58	59–63	64–65	66–70
		m	46.9	9.9	26–30	31–35	36–39	40–52	53–57	58–61	62–70
A	ART	f	53.5	9.0	27–36	37–43	44–49	50–59	60–61	62–64	65–67
		m	46.5	9.8	27–30	31–35	36–40	41–51	52–57	58–61	62–67
A	WRITING	f	52.5	9.0	27–35	36–42	43–48	49–58	59–60	61–63	64–66
		m	47.5	10.3	27–30	31–34	35–41	42–53	54–59	60–62	63–66
S	TEACHING	f	50.0	10.4	26–32	33–37	38–44	45–55	56–60	61–65	66–68
		m	50.0	9.6	26–34	35–37	38–44	45–55	56–60	61–62	63–68
S	SOCIAL SERVICE	f	51.7	10.2	26–36	37–40	41–44	45–57	58–63	64–67	68–72
		m	48.3	9.5	26–34	35–38	39–42	43–53	54–59	60–63	64–72
S	ATHLETICS	f	46.9	9.3	29–33	34–37	38–39	40–52	53–57	58–61	62–70
		m	53.1	9.8	29–35	36–42	43–47	48–59	60–62	63–66	67–70
S	DOMESTIC ACTIVITIES	f	54.1	9.1	29–39	40–43	44–48	49–59	60–63	64–65	66–73
		m	45.9	9.1	29–32	33–34	35–41	42–50	51–54	55–59	60–73
S	RELIGIOUS ACTIVITIES	f	50.4	10.1	33–34	35–38	39–42	43–56	57–61	62–65	66–68
		m	49.6	9.9	33–34	35–38	39–42	43–54	55–61	62–65	66–68
E	PUBLIC SPEAKING	f	49.4	9.8	29–34	35–38	39–42	43–55	56–59	60–65	66–70
		m	50.6	10.1	29–34	35–38	39–44	45–55	56–61	62–65	66–70
E	LAW/ POLITICS	f	48.9	10.0	30–34	35–37	38–42	43–53	54–60	61–64	65–69
		m	51.1	8.6	30–35	36–39	40–45	46–56	57–61	62–64	65–69
E	MERCHANDISING	f	50.6	9.9	28–34	35–38	39–45	46–56	57–61	62–64	65–70
		m	49.4	10.1	28–33	34–37	38–43	44–55	56–59	60–63	64–70
E	SALES	f	48.7	9.4	36–37	38–39	40–42	43–52	53–58	59–65	66–82
		m	51.3	10.4	36–37	38–39	40–44	45–56	57–61	62–69	70–82
E	BUSINESS MANAGEMENT	f	48.9	9.9	26–33	34–37	38–42	43–55	56–59	60–63	64–70
		m	51.1	10.0	26–34	35–39	40–45	46–56	57–61	62–66	67–70
C	OFFICE PRACTICES	f	51.3	11.1	36–37	38–40	41–42	43–54	55–62	63–72	73–81
		m	48.7	8.6	36–37	38–39	40–42	43–52	53–58	59–63	64–81

[a]R = REALISTIC; I = INVESTIGATIVE; A = ARTISTIC; S = SOCIAL; E = ENTERPRISING; C = CONVENTIONAL.

TABLE 5.2
Intercorrelations Between the Basic Interest Scales for Women and Men
(Correlations above the diagonal based on 300 women; those below, on 300 men. Decimal points have been omitted.)

Basic Interest Scale	AGR	NAT	ADV	MIL	MEC	SCI	MAT	MSC	MSE	MUS	ART	WRI	TEA	SOC	ATH	DOM	REL	PUB	LAW	MER	SAL	BUS	OFF
AGRICULTURE	—	70	16	17	41	28	05	27	24	01	12	−06	08	06	42	21	21	−12	−10	−02	04	−08	03
NATURE	65	—	12	02	46	51	18	48	34	22	40	14	24	13	33	31	24	−12	−08	03	−12	−11	−01
ADVENTURE	35	15	—	33	32	28	12	30	16	27	15	28	−02	04	35	−10	−05	32	35	16	14	16	−19
MILITARY ACTIVITIES	15	08	35	—	25	12	04	18	22	−01	−10	02	09	20	26	01	22	21	23	17	22	34	17
MECHANICAL ACTIVITIES	38	51	29	15	—	68	55	42	29	10	18	16	18	06	33	15	04	04	18	07	−01	16	07
SCIENCE	21	49	17	14	68	—	64	66	39	14	18	18	22	03	20	07	06	−01	15	−08	−19	−04	−02
MATHEMATICS	10	18	15	06	51	61	—	30	15	03	03	08	15	01	20	10	06	06	20	07	−04	16	20
MEDICAL SCIENCE	26	49	32	26	46	64	30	—	68	23	26	22	25	24	25	17	23	07	17	09	02	06	02
MEDICAL SERVICE	16	37	24	26	40	48	19	71	—	06	09	00	28	44	34	38	44	01	00	08	12	09	33
MUSIC/DRAMATICS	−04	22	04	04	09	14	−04	16	21	—	71	63	29	24	06	06	12	31	20	21	04	09	−14
ART	03	40	−05	−06	21	21	−03	15	14	75	—	60	23	13	−05	11	08	18	11	25	−03	03	−19
WRITING	−11	16	06	01	02	19	04	14	09	63	61	—	34	20	−02	01	04	45	39	23	−01	19	−12
TEACHING	−01	19	05	06	09	22	07	27	28	32	26	43	—	50	21	34	41	19	12	10	−04	16	23
SOCIAL SERVICE	02	19	05	14	10	09	−04	24	39	37	26	33	51	—	37	47	54	36	30	33	25	38	41
ATHLETICS	32	14	51	26	21	11	20	26	20	−11	−17	−04	12	23	—	22	22	14	20	19	17	22	26
DOMESTIC ACTIVITIES	10	40	−08	01	28	17	04	23	43	40	44	26	35	43	04	—	42	−01	−10	22	18	18	46
RELIGIOUS ACTIVITIES	14	23	02	23	16	16	04	26	39	20	10	04	27	52	19	28	—	22	06	15	22	21	41
PUBLIC SPEAKING	03	01	32	30	03	−00	05	22	15	32	16	41	35	48	26	16	32	—	79	44	33	54	02
LAW/POLITICS	03	03	34	31	08	10	16	25	14	26	14	38	34	49	31	16	23	84	—	41	29	52	−01
MERCHANDISING	02	07	19	15	17	−09	07	16	15	19	19	19	00	33	25	32	20	50	49	—	69	78	30
SALES	14	00	25	20	14	−11	12	12	16	−04	−05	−10	−18	20	29	12	16	34	34	75	—	65	39
BUSINESS MANAGEMENT	02	02	24	28	13	−04	15	18	14	08	01	18	14	42	32	25	24	63	65	78	62	—	43
OFFICE PRACTICES	−06	11	−09	09	18	13	26	13	41	10	07	09	18	30	03	44	21	13	14	40	27	41	—

Reliability

The median test-retest correlations for the Basic Interest Scales, over two-week, thirty-day, and three-year periods, are .91, .88, and .82, respectively, as reported in Table 5.4. Correlations of this magnitude indicate substantial short-term stability. Analogous statistics for the General Occupational Themes and Occupational Scales are reported in Table 4.3 and Tables 6.2 and 6.3, respectively.

Test-retest reliability of the earlier SVIB Basic Interest Scales was thoroughly studied. Generally the correlations range from the .50's, for 16-year-olds retested 36 years later, to the .90's, for samples tested and retested over a few weeks. The correlations vary mainly with the age of the person at the time of the first testing and the length of the retest interval, with the first factor being more important. A study of the interests of high school and college students (Hansen and Stocco, 1980) once again demonstrated the effect of age on test-retest reliabilities. Although Basic Interest Scale median three-year test-retest correlations were lower for high school students ($r = .56$) and college students ($r = .68$) than for adults ($r = .82$), the correlations were nonetheless sufficiently high to warrant the use of the Basic Interest Scales with young adults. But especially with high school students, some score changes are likely over a three-year period.

Internal-consistency reliabilities for the Basic Interest Scales also were computed (Larkin, pers. comm., 1984). Coefficient alphas, derived using a sample of 1,445 males, range from .77 to .96 with a median of .90; for 1,410 females, the range is .77 to .95 with a median of .90. These data indicate the high degree of internal consistency of the Basic Interest Scales.

Validity

There is no single index of validity for the Basic Interest Scales; instead, a variety of information has been drawn together to show that scores on these scales are reasonable and are related to the respondent's behavior.

Content validity. The emphasis in constructing these scales was to pull together related items; hence, each scale is focused on one content area, and the items reflect this focus. For example, the SCIENCE scale contains items like *Astronomer, Biologist, Chemist,* and *Working in a research laboratory.* Obviously, these items have content validity; responses to them provide direct information about the person's feelings toward scientific activities. The same is true of the other scales.

Concurrent validity. *Concurrent* validity is the power of a psychological measure to discriminate between two groups whose behavior at the same point in time differs; *predictive* validity is the power to discriminate between two groups who will behave differently sometime in the future.

The concurrent validity of the Basic Interest Scales can be checked by comparing the scores of people who are currently in different occupations; if the scales are working as they should, such people should score high on scales relevant to their own occupations; artists should

TABLE 5.3
Correlations Between the General Occupational Themes and the Basic Interest Scales for Women and Men
(Female correlations based on 300 women; male, on 300 men. Decimal points have been omitted.)

Basic Interest Scale	REALISTIC F	REALISTIC M	INVESTIGATIVE F	INVESTIGATIVE M	ARTISTIC F	ARTISTIC M	SOCIAL F	SOCIAL M	ENTERPRISING F	ENTERPRISING M	CONVENTIONAL F	CONVENTIONAL M
AGRICULTURE	62	60	23	21	07	−03	15	18	02	14	02	04
NATURE	59	62	51	50	32	32	24	32	−02	11	04	18
ADVENTURE	41	47	36	27	30	05	11	20	23	31	−04	11
MILITARY ACTIVITIES	34	30	13	16	−02	−01	26	28	27	22	23	17
MECHANICAL ACTIVITIES	91	91	64	62	22	16	18	22	10	25	34	42
SCIENCE	63	60	91	90	22	23	13	19	−03	02	25	35
MATHEMATICS	45	44	64	63	08	00	12	08	06	18	54	55
MEDICAL SCIENCE	48	52	74	70	29	19	34	40	15	25	15	26
MEDICAL SERVICE	35	42	40	46	06	14	54	51	18	24	30	36
MUSIC/DRAMATICS	13	09	28	27	85	87	24	30	17	11	−06	08
ART	21	18	33	30	87	90	13	20	12	10	−11	06
WRITING	16	02	36	36	81	81	21	28	15	11	−02	12
TEACHING	19	09	30	36	27	36	70	66	10	00	24	18
SOCIAL SERVICE	12	15	13	22	19	33	84	82	36	36	35	31
ATHLETICS	44	34	23	17	06	−08	44	42	24	34	29	24
DOMESTIC ACTIVITIES	19	29	08	20	03	39	49	46	20	28	38	38
RELIGIOUS ACTIVITIES	12	23	11	18	06	10	70	67	23	26	32	23
PUBLIC SPEAKING	08	14	16	21	34	29	39	54	48	52	17	28
LAW/POLITICS	20	20	31	31	27	27	28	51	46	53	24	36
MERCHANDISING	13	25	08	06	23	19	31	34	86	88	42	51
SALES	06	26	−09	−02	−04	−09	25	25	84	88	39	36
BUSINESS MANAGEMENT	20	25	09	12	08	07	42	49	81	79	59	58
OFFICE PRACTICES	09	17	−04	14	−23	04	43	31	38	37	80	79

TABLE 5.4
Test-Retest Reliability Statistics for the Basic Interest Scales

Scale	Two-week statistics (N=106 women, 74 men) Test retest correlation[a]	Test Mean	Test S.D.	Retest Mean	Retest S.D.	Thirty-day statistics (N=35 women, 67 men) Test retest correlation[b]	Test Mean	Test S.D.	Retest Mean	Retest S.D.	Three-year statistics (N=65 women, 75 men) Test retest correlation[c]	Test Mean	Test S.D.	Retest Mean	Retest S.D.
AGRICULTURE	.87	50	9.8	52	9.5	.84	50	9.3	49	8.9	.81	51	9.2	51	9.4
NATURE	.92	49	10.0	49	10.2	.87	48	9.0	48	9.4	.81	51	9.4	51	9.0
ADVENTURE	.90	52	10.6	54	11.1	.89	53	9.9	54	9.7	.81	49	10.1	49	9.7
MILITARY ACTIVITIES	.83	47	8.4	48	9.1	.90	50	10.3	51	11.1	.82	49	9.4	50	9.0
MECHANICAL ACTIVITIES	.92	48	9.6	49	10.4	.90	50	9.1	51	9.4	.87	51	10.2	51	10.3
SCIENCE	.91	49	9.3	50	10.2	.85	51	9.2	51	9.4	.84	53	9.1	53	9.6
MATHEMATICS	.91	48	9.6	48	10.2	.89	49	11.0	49	10.7	.92	52	11.4	52	11.6
MEDICAL SCIENCE	.86	48	10.0	49	10.4	.82	50	9.0	51	9.2	.74	50	8.3	50	9.2
MEDICAL SERVICE	.82	51	9.9	52	10.5	.86	49	10.2	49	10.6	.75	49	9.2	48	9.7
MUSIC/DRAMATICS	.91	49	11.1	50	11.3	.93	50	10.8	51	11.2	.84	50	10.6	50	11.1
ART	.91	49	10.0	50	10.6	.91	50	10.7	52	10.8	.87	50	10.4	50	11.0
WRITING	.93	46	10.6	47	11.0	.87	51	9.7	52	9.8	.83	51	9.3	51	10.0
TEACHING	.89	48	10.6	50	11.5	.83	51	9.2	51	9.5	.78	51	9.6	50	9.9
SOCIAL SERVICE	.90	53	10.9	53	11.7	.79	53	9.3	53	9.8	.80	50	10.6	48	10.0
ATHLETICS	.92	53	9.4	54	10.1	.89	52	9.7	53	9.7	.91	50	10.4	49	10.4
DOMESTIC ACTIVITIES	.93	49	12.5	50	12.7	.86	48	10.8	48	11.4	.82	48	11.4	49	11.0
RELIGIOUS ACTIVITIES	.92	50	9.9	50	10.2	.91	48	9.2	48	9.1	.86	50	9.8	50	9.8
PUBLIC SPEAKING	.88	45	9.3	46	10.3	.89	51	9.6	52	9.8	.83	49	10.7	48	11.0
LAW/POLITICS	.91	47	9.5	48	10.4	.89	52	9.6	53	10.2	.82	49	10.3	49	10.4
MERCHANDISING	.87	44	9.4	45	10.6	.89	50	10.6	51	10.9	.76	48	9.7	47	10.0
SALES	.83	47	8.1	48	9.0	.85	50	9.7	52	10.2	.82	48	10.4	48	10.5
BUSINESS MANAGEMENT	.87	43	10.2	44	11.2	.83	50	9.6	51	10.0	.81	47	9.6	48	10.3
OFFICE PRACTICES	.92	49	10.7	50	11.0	.84	47	8.0	49	9.4	.84	49	10.4	50	10.7

[a]Median correlation = .91   [b]Median correlation = .88   [c]Median correlation = .82

score high on the ART scale, scientists high on the SCI-ENCE scale, teachers high on the TEACHING scale; further, people in unrelated occupations should score at only average levels or lower on scales *not* related to their occupations.

A substantial body of such data has been collected for the Strong during the last 12 years. In addition, data are available for the earlier SVIB Basic Interest Scales; and because the SCII scales are based directly on these earlier scales, these data also are relevant. The data include scores for over 500 occupational samples ranging in size from seven to over 1,000 people, with a median sample size of about 250. These samples, stored in the Center for Interest Measurement Research at the University of Minnesota, include a majority of the adults ever tested for research purposes with the Strong Blank.

Each of these samples has been scored on the Basic Interest Scales. Generally, the occupations' scores on each scale are spread over two to two-and-one-half standard deviations, or a range of 20 to 25 points, demonstrating that the scales spread the occupations apart in a reasonable fashion. Table 5.5 lists the highest- and lowest-scoring samples on each scale. The patterns of high- and low-scoring occupations demonstrate that scores on these scales are substantially related to the occupations that people pursue. Accordingly, counselors should study these lists of occupations carefully, for they are useful in helping students think about their high and low scores.

Predictive validity.   The predictive validity of the Basic Interest Scales—that is, their ability to discriminate between two groups who will at some future time behave differently—is not as good as their concurrent validity, since a long-range discrimination is harder to make than a concurrent one. Nevertheless, there is considerable agreement between the scores earned by students and their eventual occupations. Because the nature of the scales does not permit detailed predictions, there is no way of tallying "hits" or "misses"; all one can say is that students with high scores on, for example, the SCIENCE scale tend to end up in occupations of a generally scientific character. Studies documenting that conclusion are summarized in the *Handbook*.

Some of the scales are less predictive than others. Scores on the ADVENTURE scale, in particular, decrease with age and do not seem particularly related to eventual occupation. People who are in "adventuresome" occupations, such as astronauts, police officers, and military officers, have high scores, but so do many young people who will not be entering such occupations.

A study by Douce (1978) investigated that relationship between scores on the ADVENTURE scale and various aspects of career development of women. She found that scores on ADVENTURE were related to both current and future status. High-adventure women reported extroverted interests; they were more autonomous and independent, more willing to take physical and social risks; they expected to marry later than the low-adventure

women did; and they had higher salaries and held more full-time positions.

Douce also found that ADVENTURE scores were not significantly related to the sex-role traditionalism of occupations actually entered; nor were they related to educational aspirations or to parental variables such as education level, number of years mothers worked outside the home, or the sex-role traditionalism of parents' occupations.

In general, the less a student's pattern resembles the typical teenage pattern, the more predictive it is. Any student with high scores on such scales as SCIENCE, ART, or BUSINESS MANAGEMENT, which are fairly uncommon high scores among young people, is likely to be more predictable in career selection than are students with high scores on the more "adolescent" scales.

Also, the more consistent the pattern is across the entire profile, the more predictive. Johnson and Johansson (1972) have shown that consistency between scores on the Basic Interest Scales and the Occupational Scales leads to greater predictive accuracy. A student with a high score on one of the sales-area Occupational Scales—such as REALTOR or LIFE INSURANCE AGENT—and a high score on the SALES Basic Interest Scale is more likely to enter sales work than is a student with an equally high score on these same Occupational Scales but a low or moderate score on the SALES Basic Interest Scale. Students with the latter pattern of scores are more likely to enter a people-oriented but non-sales occupation, such as public relations.

Inconsistencies with the Occupational Scales

From his research on the relationships between the Basic Interest Scales and the Occupational Scales, Johnson (1972) reported that approximately 50 percent of SVIB profiles exhibit one or more apparent inconsistencies between the Basic Interest and Occupational Scales. Because these profiles occur often, counselors must understand the implications of the inconsistencies and how to explain them to the respondents.

The inconsistencies appear as highly contrasted scores on pairs of scales that are obviously related, such as ART and FINE ARTIST, MATHEMATICS and MATHEMATICIAN, MILITARY ACTIVITIES and ARMY OFFICER. Such situations provide excellent examples of the effects of the different strategies used to construct the Basic Interest and Occupational Scales; properly interpreted, they can give the student (and the counselor) considerable insight into what the scores mean for each type of scale. That is, the inconsistency can be turned to positive advantage.

An example: Mathematics/Mathematician.   The Basic Interest Scales reflect the respondent's answers to items directly concerned with certain well-defined areas of activity; the score on the MATHEMATICS Basic Scale, for example, is based on responses to only nine items, all heavily mathematical in nature. The "Like" responses for

TABLE 5.5
Occupations Scoring High and Low on Each Basic Interest Scale

ADVENTURE	BUSINESS MANAGEMENT	MECHANICAL ACTIVITIES	MILITARY ACTIVITIES	PUBLIC SPEAKING	SOCIAL SERVICE
			High Scores		
Advertising executives	Bankers	Auto sales dealers	Auto sales dealers	Broadcasters	Guidance counselors
Astronauts	Business education teachers	Carpenters	Bankers	Chamber of Commerce executives	Home economics teachers
Auto sales dealers	Chamber of Commerce executives	Cartographers	Bus drivers	Elected public officials	Mental health workers
Bus drivers	Credit managers	Electricians	Elected public officials	Lawyers	Ministers
Carpenters	Food service managers	Emergency medical technicians	Emergency medical technicians	Life insurance agents	Nurses, LPN
Electricians	Life insurance agents	Engineers	Executive housekeepers	Ministers	Occupational therapists
Emergency medical technicians	Nursing home administrators	Medical technicians	Food service managers	Personnel directors	Recreation leaders
Military officers	Personnel directors	Medical technologists	Life insurance agents	Public administrators	Social science teachers
Physical education teachers	Purchasing agents	Military enlisted personnel	Military enlisted personnel	Public relations directors	Social workers
Police officers	Restaurant managers	Research and development managers	Military officers	School administrators	Special education teachers
Realtors	School administrators	Science teachers	Police officers	Social science teachers	Speech pathologists
Restaurant managers	Store managers	Vocational agricultural teachers	Physical education teachers	YMCA/YWCA directors	YMCA/YWCA directors
			Low Scores		
Business education teachers	Artists	Bankers	Architects	Chemists	Artists
Dietitians	Biologists	Broadcasters	Artists	Computer programmers	Cartographers
Elementary teachers	Carpenters	Buyers	Marketing executives	Farmers	Chemists
English teachers	Chemists	English teachers	Mathematicians	Mathematicians	Engineers
Farmers	College professors	Foreign language teachers	Medical illustrators	Medical illustrators	Farmers
Food service managers	Electricians	Funeral directors	Ministers	Medical technicians	Foresters
Foreign language teachers	Foresters	Mental health workers	Musicians	Medical technologists	Geologists
Home economics teachers	Geologists	Nursing home administrators	Physicists	Radiologic technologists	Horticultural workers
Mathematicians	Mathematicians	Public relations directors	Psychologists	Respiratory therapists	Investments managers
Medical technicians	Medical illustrators	Reporters	Social workers	Physical therapists	Mathematicians
Nurses, LPN	Physicists	Secretaries	Sociologists	Physicists	Physicists
Social workers	Veterinarians	Travel agents	Speech pathologists	Veterinarians	Systems analysts

AGRICULTURE	DOMESTIC ACTIVITIES	MEDICAL SCIENCE	MUSIC/DRAMATICS	RELIGIOUS ACTIVITIES	TEACHING
			High Scores		
Agribusiness managers	Beauticians	Athletic trainers	Actors/Actresses	Christian education directors	Art teachers
Athletic trainers	Chefs	Biologists	Art teachers	Executive housekeepers	Business education teachers
Carpenters	Dental assistants	Dentists	Artists	Farmers	Elementary teachers
Farmers	Dental hygienists	Medical technicians	Broadcasters	Food service managers	English teachers
Foresters	Dietitians	Nurses, LPN	Chefs	Funeral directors	Foreign language teachers
Geologists	Elementary teachers	Nurses, RN	English teachers	Guidance counselors	Guidance counselors
Horticultural workers	Executive housekeepers	Pharmacists	Flight attendants	Home economics teachers	Home economics teachers
Physical education teachers	Food service managers	Physical therapists	Ministers	Mental health workers	Mathematics teachers
Physical therapists	Home economics teachers	Physicians	Music teachers	Ministers	Physical education teachers
Science teachers	Nurses, LPN	Respiratory therapists	Musicians	Nurses, LPN	School administrators
Veterinarians	Occupational therapists	Science teachers	Nightclub entertainers	Special education teachers	Social science teachers
Vocational agricultural teachers	Special education teachers	Veterinarians	Public relations directors	YMCA/YWCA directors	Special education teachers

(Continued)

TABLE 5.5 (continued)

AGRICULTURE	DOMESTIC ACTIVITIES	MEDICAL SCIENCE	MUSIC/DRAMATICS	RELIGIOUS ACTIVITIES	TEACHING
			Low Scores		
Artists	Accountants	Bankers	Accountants	Architects	Agribusiness
Bankers	Agribusiness	Business education	Agribusiness	Artists	managers
Credit managers	managers	teachers	managers	Carpenters	Beauticians
English teachers	Bankers	Buyers	Credit managers	Electricians	Carpenters
Foreign language	Elected public	Chamber of	Electricians	Geographers	Farmers
teachers	officials	Commerce	Emergency medical	Geologists	Florists
Guidance	Farmers	executives	technicians	Investments	Funeral directors
counselors	Investments	Credit managers	Farmers	managers	Interior decorators
Librarians	managers	English teachers	Foresters	Marketing	Investments
Marketing	IRS agents	Florists	Military enlisted	executives	managers
executives	Life insurance	Interior decorators	personnel	Medical illustrators	Opticians
Mathematicians	agents	Public relations	Military officers	Physicists	Purchasing agents
Psychologists	Marketing	directors	Pharmacists	Psychologists	Realtors
Public relations	executives	Realtors	Veterinarians	Research and	Restaurant
directors	Physicists	Retail clerks	Vocational	development	managers
Speech pathologists	Research and	Secretaries	agricultural	managers	
	development		teachers		
	managers				
	Systems analysts				

ART	LAW/POLITICS	MEDICAL SERVICE	NATURE	SALES	WRITING
			High Scores		
Actors/Actresses	Bankers	Athletic trainers	Biologists	Agribusiness	Advertising
Advertising	Chamber of	Chiropractors	Carpenters	managers	executives
executives	Commerce	Dental assistants	Farmers	Auto sales dealers	Artists
Architects	executives	Dental hygienists	Foresters	Beauticians	Broadcasters
Art teachers	Elected public	Emergency medical	Geologists	Buyers	English teachers
Artists	officials	technicians	Horticultural	Chamber of	Lawyers
Chefs	Lawyers	Medical technicians	workers	Commerce	Librarians
Interior decorators	Life insurance	Nurses, LPN	Medical illustrators	executives	Ministers
Medical illustrators	agents	Nurses, RN	Occupational	Funeral directors	Psychologists
Musicians	Personnel directors	Nursing home	therapists	Life insurance	Public relations
Occupational	Public	administrators	Physical therapists	agents	directors
therapists	administrators	Physical therapists	Physicists	Opticians	Reporters
Photographers	Public relations	Radiologic	Veterinarians	Realtors	Social science
Public relations	directors	technologists	Vocational	Restaurant	teachers
directors	School	Respiratory	agricultural	managers	Sociologists
	administrators	therapists	teachers	Retail clerks	
	Social science			Store managers	
	teachers				
	Social workers				
	Sociologists				
			Low Scores		
Accountants	Art teachers	Accountants	Accountants	Artists	Agribusiness
Agribusiness	Artists	Advertising	Bankers	Biologists	managers
managers	Athletic trainers	executives	Broadcasters	Chemists	Athletic trainers
Athletic trainers	Beauticians	Architects	Chamber of	College professors	Bus drivers
Emergency medical	Bus drivers	Art teachers	Commerce	Foresters	Electricians
technicians	Horticultural	Artists	executives	Geologists	Emergency medical
Farmers	workers	Bankers	Credit managers	Mathematicians	technicians
Foresters	Medical illustrators	Broadcasters	Elected public	Medical illustrators	Farmers
Military enlisted	Medical technicians	Chamber of	officials	Physicians	Funeral directors
personnel	Musicians	Commerce	Investments	Physicists	Mathematics
Military officers	Nurses, LPN	executives	managers	Psychologists	teachers
Pest controllers	Respiratory	Interior decorators	Life insurance	Sociologists	Medical technicians
Police officers	therapists	Investments	agents		Military enlisted
Veterinarians	Vocational	managers	Marketing		personnel
Vocational	agricultural	Marketing	executives		Radiologic
agricultural	teachers	executives	Public relations		technologists
teachers		Public relations	directors		Vocational
		directors	Restaurant		agricultural
			managers		teachers
			Travel agents		

(Continued)

TABLE 5.5 (*continued*)

ATHLETICS	MATHEMATICS	MERCHANDISING	OFFICE PRACTICES	SCIENCE
High Scores				
Athletic trainers	Accountants	Auto sales dealers	Bankers	Biologists
Auto sales dealers	Biologists	Business education	Business education	Chemists
Credit managers	Chemists	teachers	teachers	Computer
IRS agents	Computer	Buyers	Chamber of	programmers
Life insurance	programmers	Florists	Commerce	Engineers
agents	Engineers	Funeral directors	executives	Geologists
Military enlisted	Geologists	Life insurance	Credit managers	Mathematicians
personnel	Mathematicians	agents	Dental assistants	Medical technicians
Physical education	Mathematics	Purchasing agents	Executive	Medical
teachers	teachers	Realtors	housekeepers	technologists
Physical therapists	Medical technicians	Restaurant	Food service	Physicians
Police officers	Physicists	managers	managers	Physicists
Recreation leaders	Research and	Retail clerks	IRS agents	Research and
School	development	Store managers	Military enlisted	development
administrators	managers	Travel agents	personnel	managers
YMCA/YWCA	Systems analysts		Nursing home	Science teachers
directors			administrators	
			Retail clerks	
			Secretaries	
Low Scores				
Architects	Artists	Artists	Advertising	Bankers
Art teachers	Art teachers	Biologists	executives	Beauticians
Artists	Beauticians	Carpenters	Architects	Business education
College professors	Broadcasters	Chemists	Art teachers	teachers
Foreign language	English teachers	College professors	Artists	Buyers
teachers	Flight attendants	Foresters	Broadcasters	Chamber of
Interior decorators	Interior decorators	Geographers	Geologists	Commerce
Librarians	Mental health	Geologists	Marketing	executives
Mathematicians	workers	Medical illustrators	executives	English teachers
Musicians	Public relations	Physicians	Medical illustrators	Florists
Physicists	directors	Physicists	Musicians	Interior decorators
Psychologists	Reporters	Sociologists	Photographers	Public relations
Sociologists	Retail clerks		Physicians	directors
	Social workers		Psychologists	Realtors
				Retail clerks
				Secretaries

these items are all weighted positively, the "Dislikes" negatively; thus, the only way an individual can score high on the MATHEMATICS Scale is by indicating "Like" to most of the specifically mathematical items, and the only way to score low is by indicating "Dislike" to most of these items.

In contrast, the Occupational Scales are much more heterogeneous in content. The male MATHEMATICIAN Occupational Scale includes 70 items covering a wide range of subjects and activities. Each item was included because mathematicians responded differently to it than Men-in-General did. (The female MATHEMATICIAN scale was analogously constructed.) The heterogeneity of item content of the Occupational Scales is illustrated in the following sample of items from the MATHEMATICIAN Occupational Scale:

Items weighted positively

Astronomer	*Geometry*
Author of technical books	*Physics*
Designer, electronic	*Doing research work*
equipment	*Teaching adults*
Scientific research worker	
Statistician	

Items weighted negatively

Advertising executive	*Penmanship*
Athletic director	*Public speaking*
Employment manager	*Boxing*
Flight attendant	*Drilling in a military company*
Interior decorator	*Meeting and directing people*
Manager, Chamber of	*Leading a scout troop*
Commerce	*Formal dress affairs*
Public relations director	*Planning a large party*
Realtor	

Again, these items were included in the MATHEMATICIAN Scale because (and only because) of the large difference in response frequencies between mathematicians and Men-in-General; there was no attempt to screen them intuitively for any special type of content.

Both the number and the diversity of the items emphasize the many ways male mathematicians differ from other men in their interests. Mathematicians are particularly interesting because their scale has more items weighted negatively than do most scales; they are, in a sense, "Dislikers." Consequently, one way of scoring high on the MATHEMATICIAN Scale, or "looking like a mathematician," is to answer "Dislike" to all the negatively weighted items in the above list, and thus to share the aversions of mathematicians—a different way of expressing commonality of interests than is generally the case. This is a valuable illustration of the psychometric differences between the Basic Interest and Occupational Scales, for one cannot score high on a Basic Interest Scale by reporting a particular pattern of aversions.

An analogous explanation holds for other pairs of scales where apparent inconsistencies can occur—ART and FINE ARTIST, SOCIAL SERVICE and SOCIAL WORKER, MILITARY ACTIVITIES and ARMY OFFICER. The explanation is always the same: the Basic Interest Scales are homogeneous, and high scores can be earned only by indicating preferences for those activities; the Occupational Scales are heterogeneous, and high scores can be earned in many different ways, including reporting the same pattern of dislikes that people in the indicated occupation do.

If there is a conflict between related scales of the two types, the Basic Interest Scale score usually will be high and the related Occupational Scale score low, seldom the reverse.

Interpreting the inconsistencies. Conflicting scores on the profile provide an opportunity to discuss the all-encompassing nature of occupations; they emphasize vividly that interest in one particular activity is not sufficient for a person to enjoy the occupational environment surrounding that activity. An intense interest in mathematics is only one element in the interests of professional mathematicians; artists are unique in ways other than their interest in artistic activities; people in social-service settings stand apart on factors other than "service-to-humanity" concerns.

Patterns of scores that appear to be inconsistencies are an asset to the system, because they literally force the counselor and the client to understand the meaning of the scales. Integrating the two types of scales in the discussion of the profile leads to the realization that they are reflecting interest in two different, but related, ways—a realization that in turn leads to more accurate interpretation. For more information on interpreting profile score inconsistencies, see the *User's Guide* (Chapter 11).

Changes with Age

Most of the SCII Basic Interest Scales are quite similar to the older SVIB scales; consequently, research findings based on earlier SVIB scales can be generalized to the SCII scales. The following discussion does that, using the results from several samples tested two, three, or even four times over periods of two weeks to 36 years.

Stability over time. The most important finding is that mean scores on these scales usually are quite stable, even over long time spans, seldom shifting more than 2 or 3 points except in certain situations discussed below. Of course, these are averages; some individuals show much greater changes. In working with individual scores on these scales, the counselor must be aware of the possibility of such changes; still, on the average, stability, not change, is the norm.

Scores increasing over time. The level of scores on most of the Basic Interest Scales tends to increase slightly from age 15 into adulthood. Teenagers tend to mark "Like" to a smaller number of items than adults do; why this is so is not clear. Probably because students have not been exposed yet to a wide range of occupational activities, they tend to say "Indifferent" more often. As their experience expands, so does the number of their likes. One could suppose that an increasing self-confidence and sense of personal identity also are involved.

The general increase in number of likes is most apparent in areas where students accumulate the greatest experience. The most obvious example is the TEACHING scale, which shows the largest gain across many different samples; the gains are most evident in those samples continuing further in school, especially those continuing on to advanced professional degrees. Other scales showing substantial gains among samples continuing in school are the ART, MUSIC/DRAMATICS, and WRITING scales, those generally reflecting a liberal-arts orientation.

Another scale that shows a mild increase in mean score into the adult years is the NATURE scale, which contains items such as *Gardening, Raising flowers and vegetables*, and other outdoor activities. Many people in all occupations show an increased interest in such activities as they grow older.

Scores decreasing with age. The only scale showing a consistent, sizable decrease with age is the ADVENTURE scale. On the average, people score about 10 points lower—a full standard deviation—on this scale as adults than they did as teenagers. This decrease, along with increasing scores on the NATURE scale, reflects the general mellowing of people's interests with age, particularly a decreasing interest in physically risky activities. Related scales showing smaller decreases are the ATHLETICS and MILITARY ACTIVITIES scales—again, scales covering physically demanding and adventuresome activities.

These changes reflect the aging process; one of its components is an increased reluctance to participate in rough, boisterous, physically dangerous pursuits.

Change across time in specific samples. Occasionally, some interesting changes appear in particular samples, changes that evidently occur only within those samples. The best documented example concerns medical school students. Several samples were tested on entrance to medical school and retested at exit four years later. The results, which were quite consistent over several schools, showed a sizable decrease on the SOCIAL SERVICE, MEDICAL SERVICE, SCIENCE, and RELIGIOUS ACTIVITIES scales and a modest increase on the ADVENTURE scale. The increase on ADVENTURE is quite significant, for these medical students are the only samples ever tested that showed an increase with age on this scale; usually this scale shows a substantial drop.

One explanation might be that these students, who were first tested upon entering medical school, were trying either consciously or unconsciously to appear as intense, dedicated young scientists, and as humanists with strong social-service drives. Consequently, they scored high on these scales, perhaps—to some extent—

artificially high. They also may have repressed some of their youthful energy and recklessness, thus scoring artificially low on the ADVENTURE scale. Four years later, as graduating seniors, they perhaps were more realistic about their interests in both science and social service—which were still quite high but no longer so overwhelming. The increase on the ADVENTURE scale, unique to these samples, reflects the same reaction in the contrasting direction; generally, medical school students were more open, daring, and less conscientious as seniors than as freshmen.

Almost certainly, these trends do *not* represent simple regression toward the mean, which has not shown up in any other samples tested and retested with these scales. Most likely, these decreases in mean scores were reflecting some human process.

More information on these students and their scores can be found in the *Handbook*; they provide a model of how the Basic Interest Scales can be used to study changes within a population.

Interpreting the Scores

The Basic Interest Scales are easily interpreted, since their item content is straightforward: the items on the ART scale are concerned exclusively with artistic activities; the items on the MECHANICAL ACTIVITIES scale, with mechanical activities; those on the SALES scale, with sales. High scores can be achieved only by answering "Like" to the items on a scale, low scores only by answering "Dislike." Additional interpretive information and samples of item content are given for each Basic Interest Scale in Chapter 10 and in Chapter 5 of the *User's Guide*.

Profile plotting. The plotting arrangement on the profile is designed to make the scores easy to interpret, in a normative sense. Plotted asterisks in the extreme ranges indicate the most noteworthy Basic Interest scores on each profile. For each scale, the distributions of scores for the Women-in-General and Men-in-General samples are indicated by the horizontal bars, as discussed above, under "Norming the Scales."

High and low scores. Experienced workers usually average 58 or above on the Basic Interest Scale that most closely corresponds to their particular occupation: artists, photographers, and interior decorators average 58 or above on the ART scale; ministers, 58 or above on the RELIGIOUS ACTIVITIES scale; and lawyers, elected public officials, and public administrators, 58 or above on the LAW/POLITICS scale. Thus, scores that high and above can be considered high.

Conversely, scores of 42 and below can be considered low. Scores at this level indicate that the respondent reported substantially more dislikes than average for the activities represented by the scale.

Relationships to the LP, IP, and DP percentages. The level of scores on the Basic Interest Scales is influenced by the percentages of "Like," "Indifferent," and "Dislike" responses given. Because the items on these scales are weighted +1 for the "Like" response and −1 for "Dislike," people who give many more "Like" than "Dislike" responses usually will have higher scores on these scales. Those who give an unusually high number of "Like" responses—60 to 70 percent or higher—will have several scores in the High or Very High ranges. But although these high scores indicate a positive response to a large number of activities in each of the designated areas, they probably are not as important indicators of strong interests as are scores of the same level that are the *only* high scores among the Basic Interest Scales.

This artifact means that allowances should be made in profile interpretation when a person has responded with a high percentage of "Likes" or "Dislikes." In such cases, the *ranking* of scores must be considered, as well as the absolute *level* of scores. The three or four highest—and the three or four lowest—scores are worth noting, no matter the level, since these are the areas where the individual has most consistently responded "Like" or "Dislike."

Sensitivity to overall level of "Like" and "Dislike" responses is a minor disadvantage of the SCII item format, but only minor, since not many individuals give extreme numbers of either "Like" or "Dislike" responses. The problem could be eliminated entirely, of course, by the use of a forced-choice item format that requires the respondent to give a fixed number of likes and dislikes. However, forced-choice formats have serious drawbacks: they irritate respondents; the decisiveness they force upon the respondent is artificial; these formats therefore tend to produce scales with lower reliabilities; and they have no demonstrated advantage in validity.

Further, people do differ dramatically both in the numbers of activities they like and in how they go about taking pencil-and-paper tests, and this in itself is useful information. We must learn to use it, not ignore it. For more information on the interpretation of elevated, flat, and depressed profiles, refer to the *User's Guide* (Chapter 15) and to Chapter 9 in this manual.

Underlying themes. The Basic Interest Scales were developed to help users in the difficult task of interpreting the profile scores. The pre-1969 versions of the profile had no Basic Interest Scales, only Occupational Scales, and interpretation proceeded by inferring the underlying themes of the respondent's interest from the pattern of scores on the Occupational Scales. Because those scales are complex in content, interpretation was difficult, especially for inexperienced counselors. And even experienced counselors often could not be sure which factors had led to the observed patterns of scores.

The Basic Interest Scales are particularly useful in providing a direct reflection of the clustering in the person's responses. Used in conjunction with the Occupational Scales, they provide information about major themes in the individual's interests, which can then be mapped into the occupational world via scores on the Occupational Scales.

But again, the rationale for selecting items for the Basic Interest Scales is fundamentally different from that used in making up the Occupational Scales: the former use only "direct" items (*Artist*, for example, for the ART scale); the latter use both "direct" and "indirect" items (including, for example the minister's aversion to *Poker*). The discussion above, "Inconsistencies with the Occupational Scales," shows how this distinction can be turned to advantage in interpreting the profile.

An example: social-service interests. The Basic Interest Scales can be used to sharpen profile interpretation beyond the Occupational Scales. For example, one presumably established finding in interest measurement is that as people grow older, their level of social-service interests increases. This "truth" was first established in Strong's longitudinal study of Stanford students over 18 years; his data showed that their scores increased on the Social Service cluster of Occupational Scales. This finding appealed particularly to social service types such as psychologists, possibly because it implied, "As people grew older and wiser, they came around more to an appreciation of what we [social service types] do." Perhaps for this reason, this finding was commented on frequently in counseling sessions and in training programs for new counselors.

That comforting thought was shaken, however, by the development of the Basic Interest Scales, including the SOCIAL SERVICE scale, which contains items such as *Social worker*, *Sociology*, *Work in a YMCA/YWCA*, and *Contributing to charities*. When this scale was used to score the SVIB test-retest samples, not one of them showed any noteworthy increase of scores on this scale with age. Because that was an unexpected finding, the figures were studied carefully. The changes that did occur in these samples, which are reported in detail in Chapter 5 of the *Handbook*, were increases on the TEACHING, MEDICAL SERVICE, ART, MUSIC/DRAMATICS, and WRITING scales. Because these areas are popular among people in social-service occupations, items from them appear on their Occupational Scales; consequently, when interests

in these areas increase, the Occupational Scale scores are raised. Although these areas do have a social-service flavor to them, especially the TEACHING and MEDICAL SERVICE scales, the dominant theme here is *not* social service *but rather a more generalized cultural interest*. By using the specific Basic Interest Scales to help explain the changes observed in the more global Occupational Scales, we can better understand the change that occurred. The two scale types, then, are complementary; they are more effective used jointly than either is used separately.

Using the Scales in Assessing Leisure Interests

The Basic Interest Scales may be used to help a client explore not only vocational interests but also avocational interests, and counselors should encourage their clients to consider both work and leisure interests as they examine their SCII results.

Cairo (1979), in a study designed to determine the validity of the Basic Interest Scales, found that the scales identify leisure interests as well as they identify occupational interests. Although the scales used to measure leisure activities were, in most cases, different from the scales used to measure occupations, 79 percent of the subjects had Basic Interest Scale scores that were congruent with occupational or avocational activities; and about half of the subjects who had congruent measured interests and occupations also had congruent measured interests and leisure activities.

Cairo's findings suggest that the Basic Interest Scales may be used to explore the entire interest pattern of an individual rather than vocational interests alone. Additional suggestions for using the SCII to explore nonoccupational interests are given in the *User's Guide* (Chapter 7).

CHAPTER SIX

The Occupational Scales

The Occupational Scales have been the bulwark of the Strong Inventory since its inception in 1927. Strong constructed them by comparing the item responses of an Occupational Criterion Sample with those of a General Reference Sample, identifying items yielding large response differences between the two samples, and then drawing these items together into a scale. The scale was normed on the occupational sample, and raw scores were converted to standard scores on the basis of the occupational sample's distribution.

Essentially the same methods are used today. Strong's original techniques have been refined, and the important ingredients in scale construction are more systematized, but the empirical brilliance of the approach can be traced to E. K. Strong, Jr.

The 1985 Revision

Between 1927 and 1969, the SVIB was revised infrequently—the male form only twice (1938 and 1966) and the female form only twice (1946 and 1969). Thus, the 1974 SCII (revised in 1981 and again in 1985) has emerged from the most active period of research in the inventory's history. One of the major goals of the 1985 revision was to extend the Occupational Scale offerings beyond a predominantly professional orientation to one that includes more vocational/technical and nonprofessional Occupational Scales. A second objective was to add scales representing new professional occupations. A third was to update the 1981 Occupational Scales that had been developed with Criterion Samples collected prior to 1972. The fourth was to match all extant male-normed Occupational Scales with the corresponding female-normed scales, and vice versa. The fifth objective was to collect at least representative samples of those nonprofessional occupations for whom it was impossible to collect Criterion Samples, from which to develop mean profiles (reported in Appendix D). The sixth was to enlarge the smallest 1981 Criterion Samples. The final goal was to develop new Women-in-General and Men-in-General samples to use both in constructing the Occupational Scales and in renorming the General Occupational Themes and Basic Interest Scales.

Adding vocational-technical and nonprofessional occupations. Over the years the Strong has developed a reputation of being oriented exclusively toward exploration of career opportunities in occupations requiring a college education. This, however, has not been the intent of the authors; rather, as educational requirements for entry into occupations have become more stringent over the decades the Strong has appeared to become more professional. For example, E. K. Strong, Jr.'s original police officer Criterion Sample had an average educational level of 10.0 years, whereas the male Criterion Sample for the SCII has a mean educational level of 14.7 years and the female Criterion Sample a mean of 14.8 years. The current revision effort offered an opportunity to expand the profile to include once again a large number of scales oriented toward vocational-technical or nonprofessional occupations. Thus, 32 percent of the 1985 Occupational Scales were developed from Criterion Samples whose mean educational level is less than 16 years or whose requirements for entry into the occupation do not include a college degree. About half of these scales (e.g., FARMER, POLICE OFFICER, BEAUTICIAN, EXECUTIVE HOUSEKEEPER) were represented on earlier forms of the Strong; the 17 new occupations, all of which are represented on the profile by both female- and male-normed scales (34 scales) are as follows:

Code		
f	m	Scale
C	R	AIR FORCE ENLISTED PERSONNEL
CRS	CR	ARMY ENLISTED PERSONNEL
R	R	BUS DRIVER
RI	R	CARPENTER
AR	EA	CHEF
RI	R	ELECTRICIAN
RS	R	EMERGENCY MEDICAL TECHNICIAN
E	E	FLORIST
CS	CE	FOOD SERVICE MANAGER
ECS	E	FUNERAL DIRECTOR
R	R	HORTICULTURAL WORKER
CRS	RC	MARINE CORPS ENLISTED PERSONNEL
IC	IR	MEDICAL TECHNICIAN
RC	RC	NAVY ENLISTED PERSONNEL
EC	ER	OPTICIAN
IR	IRS	RESPIRATORY THERAPIST
EC	E	TRAVEL AGENT

The first step in identifying nonprofessional occupations that might be added to the 1985 profile was to consult information predicting the employment outlook for such occupations. All of the vocational-technical jobs added have at least an average or an above-average outlook for the future. Once the list of occupations with good employment outlooks was developed, the second step was to consult census data for each occupation to determine if enough women and men were employed in that occupation to permit the collection of a Criterion Sample that would be sufficiently large to construct a reliable and valid Occupational Scale.

The third step was to attempt to predict which occupations would represent the six General Occupational Themes and to select at least one new occupation from each theme. The effort was reasonably successful. For example, bus drivers, carpenters, electricians, emergency medical technicians, and horticultural workers represent the Realistic type; medical technicians and respiratory therapists represent the Investigative type; chefs, the Artistic type; florists, funeral directors, opticians, and travel agents, the Enterprising type; and food service managers, the Conventional type. None of the new nonprofessional Occupational Scales represents the Social type, but the female and male Licensed Practical Nurse scales, which already were on the profile, are coded "S."

The fourth step was to obtain the cooperation of unions or other organizations in acquiring mailing lists, and the fifth step, finally, was the actual sample collection. Generally, the response rate for the nonprofessional groups was lower than is typical for professional occupations—about 21 percent, compared to 36 percent. The nonprofessional subjects were more often rejected, too, either because they did not meet such sample criteria as minimum age or minimum length of experience, or because they did not like their work. The same criteria (described in detail on p. 51) as those established for the professional occupations were imposed on the nonprofessional subjects, and the same sample-collection methods (described on pp. 51–52) were used.

These new vocational/technical Occupational Scales should make the Strong more useful with people who have a wide range of educational and occupational goals—whether professional or nonprofessional in nature—and should improve the utility of the profile when it is used in conjunction with Appendixes A and B to generalize to occupations not represented on the profile—occupations that have a wide range of educational levels.

Adding professional occupations. Six new professional occupations (12 scales) have been added to the profile. Here, too, predictions of future employment growth and opportunity were considered in selecting these occupations. For example, faster-than-average growth is predicted for athletic trainers, broadcasters, medical illustrators, and research and development managers. Scales for mathematics teachers and science teachers, which are among the disciplines within education that still are in demand, were developed to replace the more general MATH-SCIENCE TEACHER scale. All of these have been added to the profile; all are represented by scales for both sexes.

Updating Criterion Samples. Any scale developed before 1972 used samples collected on the T399 and TW398 forms. This meant that the item-response data for these scales were incomplete, since samples collected on T399 responded to only 254 of the 325 items, and those collected on TW398 responded to only 249 items. Although the scales developed with these reduced item pools were reliable—testimony to the excellence of the empirical technique of scale development—scales drawing upon response data to all of the items tend to be longer and therefore even more stable.

Occupations do not change much, across time, in their item-endorsement frequency. Nonetheless, Criterion Samples should be updated periodically to reflect such fluctuations as occasionally occur. For that reason, all scales based on Criterion Samples collected prior to 1972 have been revised.

All of the new scales are based on occupational groups tested with the T325 booklet. Whereas in 1974, when the SCII was introduced, all but 15 of the 124 Occupational Scales were based on Criterion Samples tested on the old single-sex inventories, for the 1985 edition all 207 of the Occupational Scales are based on samples tested on the merged-form T325. (Data on all Criterion Samples are given in Appendix A.)

Matching female- and male-normed Occupational Scales. The 1985 SVIB-SCII profile carries 207 Occupational Scales representing 106 occupations. All but five of the 207 scales are in matched pairs: for each of 101 occupations there is a scale based on a female-normed Criterion Sample and a scale based on a male-normed sample; this almost triples the analogous number of matched pairs (37 occupations) on the first merged-sex form of the Strong published in 1974.

Every new occupation added to the profile in this revision is represented by matched-sex scales as reported above, and every effort was made to obtain Criterion Samples for the development of matched-sex scales for the eight occupations represented on the 1981 Strong by only one sex or the other. Generally the effort was successful, especially for women. Two of the new scales on the profile are female-normed scales developed to match existing male-normed scales: INVESTMENTS MANAGER (formerly called INVESTMENT FUND MANAGER) and VOCATIONAL AGRICULTURE TEACHER.

The SKILLED CRAFTS scale, which appeared on the 1974 and 1981 profiles and was constructed with only a male Criterion Sample, is replaced on the 1985 profile by female- and male-normed CARPENTER and ELECTRICIAN scales.

On occasion, the obstacles to collecting a sample large enough for valid scale construction could not be overcome. For example, the American Dental Assistants Association was very willing to assist our attempts to sample male dental assistants, and offered the names and addresses of the *two* men who belonged to the ADAA. Thinking that the military might provide a source, we undertook a pilot study of a dozen male dental assistants stationed around the country. Universally, they reported that they disliked being dental assistants, had not chosen to be trained in dental assisting, but rather had been assigned arbitrarily to that specialty by the military, and would not pursue careers as dental assistants once they left the service.

Four occupations are represented now only by female-normed scales, compared to 20 on the 1974 profile; one is represented only by a male-normed scale, compared to 30 in 1974. These five scales have proved useful for occupational exploration in the past, and they have been retained on the profile to augment the many other occupations representing the world of work. The Occupational Scales normed only for women are DENTAL ASSISTANT, DENTAL HYGIENIST, HOME ECONOMICS TEACHER, and SECRETARY. The scale normed only for men is AGRIBUSINESS MANAGER.

Mean profiles for male dental hygienists, male secretaries, and female agribusiness managers are presented in Appendix C to help guide interpretation for the unrepresented sex. Unfortunately, even the effort to obtain small samples of male dental assistants and male home economics teachers was unsuccessful, and therefore no mean profiles are available for those occupations.

Developing mean profiles for vocational-technical occupations. In a few cases, vocational-technical and nonprofessional occupations with good employment outlooks did not have a sufficient representation of one sex or the other in the field to allow the collection of a sample large enough for valid scale construction. To increase the usefulness of the SCII with non-college-bound clients, samples were collected for these occupations and their mean SCII profiles calculated; their profiles are reported in Appendix D. The samples, smaller than those needed for scale construction but large enough to provide reliable mean profiles, were collected using the same method (described on p. 51) that is used to collect Criterion Samples. The occupations also were assigned General Occupational Theme codes, using the method detailed on p. 58; the occupations and their codes are as follows:

Code	Female samples	Code	Male samples
CE	Baker	RE	Baker
RI	Cartographer	RI	Cartographer
C	Office manager	EC	Office manager
R	Painter	R	Painter
CE	Pest controller	ER	Pest controller
EC	Retail clerk	ECS	Retail clerk

Adding subjects to existing small samples. One task in every revision is to increase the size of the smaller extant Criterion Samples, in particular those samples that included substantially less than 200 subjects. Although valid scales can be constructed with samples as small as 50 subjects by using rigorous item-selection standards (see p. 52 for a thorough discussion), the reliability of the item content generally is greater if the occupation is represented by 200 to 300 subjects. Sixteen of the 1981 Criterion Samples (female and male) were enlarged for the 1985 revision:

Sample	Sex	1981 N	1985 N
Artist, commercial	f	123	222
Artist, commercial	m	199	206
Beautician	f	103	181
Beautician	m	186	195
Credit manager	f	192	193
Credit manager	m	199	203
Forester	f	165	174
Geographer	f	187	195
Nurse, LPN	m	100	128
Optometrist	f	190	191
Public administrator	f	195	202
Purchasing agent	f	158	247
Restaurant manager	f	92	152
Restaurant manager	m	159	193
Store manager	f	166	176
Store manager	m	200	238

Constructing New Women- and Men-in-General Samples

A key feature of the Strong scoring system is the General Reference Sample, which is for all practical purposes *two* samples: Women-in-General (WIG) and Men-in-General (MIG). These samples are used to determine the popularity of each item across the general population—usually termed base-rate popularity—for comparison with the popularity of that item within a specific occupational sample. Those items that provoke one response from the occupational sample and another from the Reference Sample are the items used in that occupation's Occupational Scale.

The Reference Sample is necessary because the base-rate popularity varies considerably from item to item; to ignore this variance would be to add considerable error to the scales. For example, if the scoring system weighted items with respect only to their popularity within the various occupations, the most popular items would appear in most of the scales, and their discriminating power would be reduced or even nullified. Conversely, the relatively unpopular items would appear in so few scales as to be almost useless. Thus, using a Reference Sample to control for item popularity results in a scoring system that reacts more to differences between occupations than to similarities among them.

The composition of the Reference Samples (Women- and Men-in-General) is critical to the development of valid, useful scales. Conceptually, each Reference Sample should be centered at the intersection of all the dimensions within the domain of interests. Operationally, the goal is to select a sample that falls collectively at the mean of all the item-response distributions, such as those shown in Chapter 3 (Figs. 3.1, 3.2, and 3.3). To find such a sample for the earlier SVIB Women-in-General and Men-in-General samples, roughly 20 people were drawn from each of 50 occupations for each sex; thus each sample contained 1,000 people, one sample consisting of men who responded to the men's booklet, the other of women who responded to the women's booklet. (The precise composition of the two samples is described in the *Handbook for the SVIB*.)

The 1974 Women- and Men-in-General samples. When the two booklets were merged into the T325 booklet in 1974, the two samples, though large and well selected, could no longer be used, because neither of them had responded to all of the items in the combined booklet. But they clearly were the model to be emulated. Thus, in the development of the 1974 Reference Samples, the goal was to match the composition and characteristics of the old Women-in-General and Men-in-General samples—to generate new samples that had item-response percentages identical to those of the old samples on those items that were common to the old (SVIB) and new (T325) booklets. The rationale was that if new samples could be matched with the old ones on the 250 common items, then the responses of the new samples to the 75 new items could be assumed to represent roughly the response percentages that the old, carefully selected samples would have given, had they responded to the new items. To achieve this matching, several hundred men and women were tested with the new inventory, however they could be found—in occupational groups, university classes, neighborhood clubs, among friends, friends of friends, and schoolteachers, in the local Jaycees, in Army Reserve units, and so forth. This diverse pool was fed into a computer that was programmed to select a sample randomly and compare it with the old In-General samples on the items to which both groups had responded (for the MIG, 254 items; for the WIG, 249 items); and to continue doing this until new samples matching the old had been found. Then, the assumption was made—in the absence of a more reasonable approach—that the percentage response of these new samples to the Form T325 items was roughly what that of the former In-General samples would have been. The new samples offered the considerable advantage that item popularities for all items, based on the responses of samples almost identical to the previous Women-in-General and Men-in-General samples, were available for both sexes. The new samples, 300 males and 300 females, were designated the 1974 WIG and MIG samples. When combined, they were the 1974 General Reference Sample.

The 1985 Women- and Men-in-General samples. The major deficiency of the 1974 General Reference Sample was that the matching technique employed to select subjects perpetuated the item response rates of Women- and Men-in-General of the 1960's. To eliminate the possibility that societal changes in interests (and consequently in response rates) had occurred during the 1970's and early 1980's, a new General Reference Sample was constructed for use in the 1985 revision.

The 1985 General Reference Sample was drawn from a pool of 1,588 subjects (794 women and 794 men). This initial pool was developed by collecting subjects from occupations represented on the 1981 Strong profile, as well as from those occupations anticipated to be included for the first time on the 1985 profile. The pool included both professional and vocational-technical or nonprofes-

sional subjects (loosely categorized by the mean educational level of their occupational group). For the first time, the female and male subjects in the pools were matched by occupational title. For example, if the female sample contained two secretaries, so did the male sample; if the male sample contained five electricians, so did the female. Ninety-three occupations were represented in the initial pool of 1,588 subjects.

From the original pool of 794 women, 150 professional and 150 nonprofessional women were selected (for a total of 300 Women-in-General) using a random numbers table. Then, the 300 Men-in-General were identified simply by randomly selecting male subjects from the same occupations as those already represented in the Women-in-General sample. The women and men included in the General Reference Sample represent all six of the General Occupational Theme areas of interest. The average age for the sample, 38 years, matches closely the average age of the Criterion Samples used for Occupational Scale construction.

Comparison of the 1974 and 1985 General Reference samples. Comparisons of the item-response rates for the 1974 and 1985 Women-in-General and the 1974 and 1985 Men-in-General show how stable interests are over substantial periods of time, even at the item level. The 1974 samples, which as explained earlier were intentionally matched to the interests of women and men in the 1960's, exhibited very few response rates that were significantly different from those of the 1985 sample: for the Women-in-General, only 18 items significantly differentiated the 1974 and 1985 samples, and for the Men-in-General, only five.

The interests of the 1974 and 1985 Women-in-General and Men-in-General also were compared on the General Occupational Themes to determine if significant shifts in interest had occurred. For the male sample, the largest difference was on the Artistic Theme, with the 1985 Men-in-General scoring 1.2 points higher than the 1974 Men-in-General. The 1985 Women-in-General scored 2.7 points lower on the Social Theme and 1.8 points higher on the Enterprising Theme, suggesting a shift among women in the areas of work involving contact with people: from a concentration of social-service activities with a humanitarian orientation to a more business-oriented focus. This modest trend also appears on the Introversion-Extroversion scale, where there is a slight shift toward extroversion among the 1985 Women-in-General (48 compared to 50). (The Men-in-General scored 50 on the IE scale in both 1974 and 1985.) The shift in women's interests probably reflects a better balance of enterprising women in the new sample than were included in the past. Compared to the 1974 samples, the stability of interests of these samples is especially noteworthy, given the very divergent methods used by Campbell in 1974 and Hansen in 1985 in developing the samples, as well as the societal changes that have occurred, especially for women, in the work force during the last 15 years.

Even though the interests of the 1974 and 1985 samples are very similar, the 1985 General Reference Sample represents a huge step forward in the effort to comparatively study the interests of women and men. For the first time, the Strong Blank now has Women- and Men-in-General samples matched on occupational title. Because of the importance of these Reference Samples to the development of the Occupational Scales, as well as their importance in the standardization of the General Occupational Themes and Basic Interest Scales, the development of matched Women- and Men-in-General Samples is critical to the inventory at this stage in the history of interest measurement.

Characteristics of the Occupational Samples

The first step in the construction of an Occupational Scale is testing a sample from that occupation; and because the characteristics of the sample greatly influence the characteristics of the resulting scale, the sample should be selected with care. Through years of research with the SVIB, the following sample characteristics have emerged as important.

Job satisfaction. Because the inventory is so often used in career planning, the eventual scale should reflect the interests of *satisfied* workers. The most practical way to ascertain job satisfaction for the purposes of scale construction is to use the item *How do you like your work?* (I couldn't be more satisfied; I like it; I am indifferent to it; I dislike it), and then eliminate from the sample any respondent choosing either of the last two options.

Success. Whenever possible, some measure of success or achievement should be used to screen the sample; the measure might be sales-production figures, or ratings by superiors, or an index of formal achievement such as earning an advanced degree or being licensed or certified. Occasionally, qualifications specific to the occupation also are imposed. For example, subjects selected for the female farmer sample were women who spent at least 50 percent of their work time engaged in outdoor activities; this criterion was imposed to ensure that the women resembled male farmers on this dimension of interests.

The purpose of imposing a criterion of success is not to restrict the sample to outstanding people, but to exclude the bottom 10 to 15 percent of the working population— the inadequate practitioners—from the sample.

Age. Where possible samples are restricted to people between the ages of 25 and 60. These limits exclude the very young members of the occupation, whose interests may not have stabilized, and the older members, who entered the occupation several decades earlier.

A study by Hansen (1978) examined the possible effects of age differences on measured occupational interests. She studied three age groups (26-35; 36-45; 46-55) for each of six occupational samples that represented a mixture of occupations that are traditional or nontraditional for one sex or the other. Her findings indicated that people of different ages who are in the same occupation do not have different interests. Nor was any evidence found to suggest a female/male role reversal in the home: younger men are not beginning to say "Like"

to more domestic activities than older men do, and there were no large differences between age groups on the Academic Comfort scale. Thus, the current practice of combining people from across a wide age range into one occupational Criterion Group is both suitable and valid.

Experience. Almost all of the SCII samples are restricted to workers who have been on the job at least three years. Experience is a crude but effective index of many pertinent qualities, and screening for it helps purify the final sample. After three years, workers know enough about their occupation to answer validly the question whether they like their jobs. Thus, persistence in an occupation for three years represents, at the minimum, a modest level of both achievement and satisfaction.

"Performing in the typical manner." The samples also are screened to reject people who are not performing the occupation in the typical way. A physician who is now a writer would not be included with the physician sample; a lawyer who is now an actor would likewise be rejected. Although this circumstance usually affects less than 1 or 2 percent of an occupational base, some address lists carry numerous "nontypical" individuals.

An unintended criterion. Since most of the data collection is done by mail, a criterion that inevitably imposes itself is willingness to cooperate with the research project. Self-selection—the automatic implication of cooperation—raises the question of sample bias, which is worth discussing at length.

Bias in the Occupational Samples

Random influences. When questionnaires are collected by mail, as is usually the case, a few members of the intended sample can be expected not to respond because of some current, usually transient, disruption in their lives. Years of interest-measurement research, requiring large-scale sample collection, indicate that this particular influence is harmless. The reasons people fail to respond are legion, and most of them are completely irrelevant to the research. On any address list, for example, a few people will be deceased, and their failure to respond scarcely constitutes harmful bias. Others do not respond because they are in the hospital, or their spouse is, or they are in the middle of an exhausting divorce, or they have just won a trip to the Caribbean, or their house was flooded, or their dog chewed up the test booklet— all of these are circumstances reported in past SVIB research projects, and all are apparently random events unrelated to any sample bias. Another 2 or 3 percent will not respond because they are opposed to psychological tests, questionnaires, surveys, opinion polls, and other "nefarious devices of manipulative social scientists." For these and similar reasons about 15 percent of most samples will be inaccessible for research; thus a return of no more than about 85 percent is the most one can expect.

Self-selection. That some recipients fail to respond may actually be an advantage. A few do not answer simply because they think they do not belong in the Criterion Sample: if the covering letter states that we are attempting to develop a job-interest profile of physical therapists, and one of the recipients is trying to leave this field for another, she/he may conclude, correctly, that we would not want her/his response. Another source of probable positive bias is general identification with the occupation: although there are no hard data on this point, the people most committed to their occupation tend to cooperate more earnestly with research studying the occupation than do those who feel more indifferent about it; to whatever extent this bias exists, it is desirable.

The initial SVIB samples, collected by E. K. Strong in the 1920's, 1930's, and 1940's, capitalized on these sources of respondent bias. Though he never reported, or perhaps even calculated, his percent returns, informal comments by Strong suggest that the effective rate of return in his research was about 25 percent. In a letter to a student who had asked about using the SVIB with an occupational sample, Strong commented that about four inventories had to be mailed out to get one usable one in return. That estimate agrees with more recent research: there is no evidence in Strong's research files to suggest that he ever used follow-up letters, and our experience at Minnesota has been that a one-time mailing, with no special care, will result in about a 25- to 30-percent return. Because Strong's samples have proved useful, one can conclude that the sampling bias was not too debilitating. Indeed, some self-selection may be an advantage.

From a well-executed mailing, one can expect about a 30- to 35-percent return, assuming an up-to-date address list, a good covering letter, and one follow-up postcard. To push the return rate higher requires an inordinate amount of time, energy, and money, with no guarantee that the quality of the final sample will be improved— and the uneasy suspicion that the quality could in fact be lowered (the survey mavericks could be occupational mavericks as well).

Practical constraints. In inventory research, samples are drawn from the real world, and the investigator has to work within practical constraints; that is, the samples cannot always be collected in precisely the preferred way. Simply to reach 300 bona fide actors, let alone persuade them to fill in a psychological test, would be a fair achievement, since there is no place to go to find a mailing list for that occupation. Theater programs or advertisements in *Variety* offer some possibilities, but thorny problems arise in ascertaining age, experience, and job satisfaction, not to mention the sample's willingness to cooperate. The same problems occur with many other occupations. Consequently, one takes one's data where one finds them, and the sampling methods used cannot always be described precisely. In any case, sampling issues often have been overemphasized; the crucial issue is not the sampling method, but the characteristics of the final sample.

Reporting of return rates. One criticism leveled at earlier editions of the SVIB *Manual* is that the percent of returned forms for each occupational sample was not reported. There are two reasons for the omissions. First,

in some cases the figure is not available. For example, if biologists are tested by handing out test booklets to everyone in sight at a national biological convention, what is the percent return? Second, the return rate is a meaningless number. If 1,000 forms are sent to entertainers featured in nightclub advertisements and only 100 are returned, and if, concurrently, 500 forms are sent to military officers through official channels and 450 are returned, does a comparison between the 10-percent and 90-percent returns say anything useful about the people who do or do not respond? Not likely. These results say more about the collection mechanism than about the people involved.

Quality of address lists. As noted above, many extraneous factors influence the percent usable response in an occupational sampling. The most important of these is the quality of the address list. If one is working with a professional organization with a well-established membership—an organization with annual dues, perhaps a professional journal, and an annual convention— then the quality of addresses will be high, and one can count on about a 40-percent return. But if the national organization is loose, the return will be much lower. (One address list included names that were 20 years out of date; some quiet investigation revealed that this organization benefited in lobbying with its state legislature by showing as large a membership as possible, and for this reason no one ever was removed from the roster.)

Quality of the final sample. Percent return, then, has practically nothing to do with the quality of the final sample. A low rate of return does not necessarily project a poor sample, nor does a 100-percent response guarantee a useful sample. The payoff lies in the *characteristics* of the sample, no matter how the people were surveyed; and in close attention to the issues of job satisfaction, experience, and "performing the occupation in the typical manner."

Some factors that do *not* relate to sample quality are race, geographic location, method tested (whether by mail or in person), and again, percentage return. Neither randomness, nor representativeness, nor selection precision is necessarily the best predictor of whether the sample will meet the criteria of experience, success, and satisfaction. In the end, the quality of the sample used for the construction of a scale is reflected in the validity data—the scale works, or it does not.

The particular characteristics of each SCII Occupational Sample, or Criterion Group, are reported in Appendix A.

Constructing the Scales

Step 1. Once an Occupational Criterion Sample has been tested, the first step in item analysis is to compare the sample's item responses with those of the appropriate-sex Reference Sample. This is done by computing the percent of both samples answering "Like," "Indifferent," and "Dislike" to each of the 325 items, and then calculating the differences. For example, the result of comparing the Criterion Sample for female physicists to

Women-in-General on the item *Repairing electrical wiring* is:

Sample	Item-response percentages			
	Like	Indifferent	Dislike	Total
f Physicist	49	36	15	100
Women-in-General	16	26	58	100
Difference	+33	+10	−43	

Step 2. The next step is to identify those items that differentiate the Criterion and the General Reference Samples at a significant level. The goal is to have about 60 to 70 items with a 16-percent or larger difference in the "Like" or "Dislike" response rate between the Criterion Sample and the Reference Sample. Scales of this length will have good test-retest reliability, and items with a minimum difference of 16 percent will provide a valid scale, capable of discriminating between people in different occupations and resistant to cross-validation shrinkage.

Step 3. The next step is to assign scoring weights to these differences. For the 1985 SCII Occupational Scales, item selection and weighting proceeded as follows:

1. For each item in the inventory, the Criterion Sample's response percentage for each of the three alternatives ("Like," "Indifferent," "Dislike") was calculated. The analogous percentages for the Reference Sample, either female or male as appropriate, also were calculated, and then subtracted from the Criterion Sample's percentages. The resulting differences were used to identify the discriminating items.

2. Typically, 60 to 70 items showing a minimum difference of 16 percent between the Criterion and Reference Samples were found. If more were available, the minimum cutoff was raised to 17 percent, or 18, or 19, until the number of items had dropped to roughly 65. In no case was the minimum lowered below 16 percent. The minimum cutoff ("Min. percent diff.") and number of items used, for each scale, are shown in Table 6.1 (below).

3. After the discriminating items were identified, the "Like" or "Dislike" response choice that showed the larger difference was weighted +1 or −1 depending on the direction of the difference; for example, the "Like" response for the item *College professor* received a +1 weight on the female PHYSICIST scale:

Sample	Item-response percentages		
	Like	Indifferent	Dislike
f Physicist	86	10	4
Women-in-General	47	29	24
Difference	+39	−19	−20
Item weights	[+1]	[ ]	[ ]

4. The opposite response choice (in this case, "Dislike") automatically was weighted in the opposite direction, even if the percent difference of that particular response was not above the minimum cutoff (that is, no matter how small the empirical difference). This technique, which assumes each item to be a miniature di-

mension, increases the reliability of the scale about .03–.04 correlational points and does not affect validity (percent overlap) either way. Thus for the item *College Professor* on the female PHYSICIST scale, the weighting became:

Sample	Item-response percentages		
	Like	Indifferent	Dislike
f Physicist	86	10	4
Women-in-General	47	29	24
Difference	+39	−19	−20
Item weights	[+1]	[ ]	[−1]

5. Once the "Like" and "Dislike" choices for an item had been weighted, the "Indifferent" response choice also was weighted, but only if the difference between the samples on that response was sufficiently large. For those scales with a minimum item-selection cutoff between 16 and 20 percent, the "Indifferent" difference had to be 10 percent or higher to be weighted. When the minimum "Like" or "Dislike" difference cutoff was raised to 21 percent or higher, as in the case of the female PHYSICIST scale (29 percent), the "Indifferent" difference had to be 13 percent or higher to be weighted. If the difference was positive, the "Indifferent" response was weighted +1; if negative, −1. Thus, the final weighting scheme for the item *College professor* on the female PHYSICIST scale was:

Sample	Item-response percentages		
	Like	Indifferent	Dislike
f Physicist	86	10	4
Women-in-General	47	29	24
Difference	+39	−19	−20
Item weights	[+1]	[−1]	[−1]

If a woman answers "Like" to the item *College professor*, she is responding like a female physicist, and her score on the female PHYSICIST scale will increase (+1). Conversely, if she says "Dislike" or "Indifferent," her score on this scale will decrease (−1).

Of course, the items also identify interests that the Criterion Samples *dislike*. For example, the item *Beauty and haircare consultant* is an aversion of female physicists; therefore, on the female PHYSICIST scale the item was weighted:

Sample	Item-response percentages		
	Like	Indifferent	Dislike
f Physicist	2	16	82
Women-in-General	24	28	48
Difference	−22	−12	+34
Item weights	[−1]	[0]	[+1]

In this case, a person responding "Dislike" to the item is responding the same way that female physicists do, and the score on the f PHYSICIST scale will *increase* (+1). Conversely, a "Like" response would result in a lower score (−1) on the f PHYSICIST scale. In other words, a high score on an Occupational Scale is the result of a person's having both interests and aversions that match those of the Occupational Criterion Sample.

For this item, the "Indifferent" response is weighted 0

because the item did not reach a satisfactory level of difference in response rate between the Criterion Sample and the Reference Sample (13 percent) to be weighted.

Reliability versus validity in item weighting. Ever since unit weights were adopted, the system of selecting and weighting items has varied in its details, because empirical scale construction always involves a trade-off between item validity and scale reliability: emphasizing the former, which is directly related to scale validity, produces short scales: emphasizing the latter, which is based on test-retest correlations, produces long scales. The relative importance attached to the two factors has changed from time to time, depending on the bias of the test reviser. Thus, if scale validity is stressed, only those items showing large differences between the Criterion and Reference Samples are weighted; if scale reliability is stressed, then as many "good" items as possible are weighted, even those of moderate or low validity, because longer scales are more stable over time than shorter scales are. Unfortunately, there is no automatic procedure by which to resolve this trade-off. Many statistics can be adduced to demonstrate the presence of the dilemma, but its resolution even in this, the most empirical of tests, must be to some extent arbitrary.

In the past, more consideration was given to scale reliability than to scale validity; stability in the scores was deemed more important than accuracy. In the development of the SCII, the strategy has shifted slightly toward giving each of these factors roughly equal weight. If more than 60 to 70 items are available at the 16-percent difference level, the cutoff is raised to 17 or 18 or 19 percent, until the number of items selected for the scale drops to roughly 60. For example, the minimum item-response difference selected for the female PHYSICIST scale was 29 percent; 60 items differentiate the interests of female physicists and Women-in-General at this level.

Variable and unit weights. The technique used to assign scoring weights has changed through the years. For earlier versions of the scales, E. K. Strong used variable weights based on the ratio of the Criterion- and Reference-Sample response percentages. Essentially, he calculated the ratio for each difference by dividing the response percentage of the Criterion Sample by that of the Reference Sample. When the ratio was large, a large scoring weight was assigned to that response; smaller ratios were assigned smaller weights. (This is only an approximation of the technique; for a more precise description, see Strong, 1943.) One problem with this technique is that it treated a comparison between 2 and 4 percent in the same manner as a comparison between 20 and 40 percent, because it was based on the *ratio* of the response percentages rather than the *magnitude* of the difference.

For his first scales, developed in 1927, Strong used scoring weights as great as ±30: the largest ratios were assigned scoring weights of +30 or −30; the smallest ones, a weight of 0. Such a large range of weights made scoring very difficult, and because he could find no benefit in a large weight range, Strong dropped his weights to ±15 in 1930, then to ±4 in 1938. Finally, in 1966, Campbell completed the trend by establishing unit scoring weights of +1, 0, or −1. Although the concept of variable weights—varying according to the size of the differences in response percentages—is intuitively appealing, empirical comparisons between variable weights and unit weights show the latter to be just as effective and sometimes better (as, for example, in cross-validation studies with new samples). Consequently, the SCII system continues to be based completely on unit weights.

Scale characteristics. The number of items weighted and the minimum response-percentage difference used, for each 1985 scale, are shown in Table 6.1, along with the percent overlap between the Criterion and Reference Samples on that scale (the calculation of percent overlap is explained below under "Concurrent Validity"). The most important column is the one showing percent overlap, since these figures indicate concurrent validity, that is, how well the scales separate the Criterion and Reference Samples. The 1985 Occupational Scales are, on the average, the same length as the 1981 scales; the 1985 percent overlap between the scores of the Criterion and Reference Samples is also about the same as before.

Table 6.1 also lists the means and standard deviations for the MIG and WIG samples used to build the 1985 Occupational Scales. If the scales are separating the Occupational Samples from the Reference Samples as they should, the MIG and WIG samples should score as low on the various 1985 SCII scales as.they did on the 1981 or 1974 scales. Comparisons of the mean scores in Table 6.1 to the 1974 and 1981 data (Campbell, 1974; Campbell and Hansen, 1981) indicate that many of the standard scores for the MIG and WIG actually are lower on the 1985 SCII scales than they were on the earlier scales. To the extent they *are* lower, the 1985 scales are more powerful.

Table 6.1 also reports the differences between the MIG and WIG samples on all of the 1985 Occupational Scales (thus the MIG and WIG samples are both scored on opposite-sex scales as well as same-sex scales). These differences demonstrate the normative problem in working with male and female samples; frequently women scored much higher on the male-normed scales than the men did, and vice versa. For this reason, scales based on appropriate-sex samples are more useful for any given individual. Chapter 7 examines this issue more thoroughly.

Norming the Scales

Once the items were selected, the scales were normed by scoring the original Occupational Criterion Samples on the scales and using their raw-score means and standard deviations in the standard score-conversion formula, yielding for the Criterion Sample a mean of 50 and a standard deviation of 10. All future individual scores are converted to this distribution for easy comparison.

TABLE 6.1
Scale Characteristics, Concurrent Validities (Percent Overlap), and Minimum and Maximum Possible Scores,
for the 1985 Occupational Scales

Scale	Sex	Number of items	Min. percent diff.	Tilton percent overlap	WIG mean	WIG S.D.	MIG mean	MIG S.D.	WIG–MIG diff.	Minimum possible score	Maximum possible score
ACCOUNTANT	f	61	18	31	27.8	11.8	35.8	11.1	−8.0	−14	85
ACCOUNTANT	m	54	16	33	21.7	11.6	28.3	12.1	−6.6	−18	81
ADVERTISING EXECUTIVE	f	43	16	50	35.1	11.9	30.1	11.0	+5.0	−4	75
ADVERTISING EXECUTIVE	m	56	21	40	40.0	12.4	31.0	12.7	+9.0	−9	71
AGRIBUSINESS MANAGER	m	63	23	28	20.5	10.7	26.8	11.4	−6.3	−7	76
AIR FORCE ENLISTED PERSONNEL	f	62	18	33	28.0	12.6	32.3	10.8	−4.3	−8	89
AIR FORCE ENLISTED PERSONNEL	m	60	18	37	22.2	10.4	30.4	11.8	−8.2	−10	86
AIR FORCE OFFICER	f	46	16	35	30.8	10.6	42.4	10.8	−11.6	−2	86
AIR FORCE OFFICER	m	52	16	43	18.2	11.2	32.3	12.4	−14.1	−16	78
ARCHITECT	f	66	23	29	23.6	14.9	33.0	12.5	−9.4	−25	80
ARCHITECT	m	61	19	30	29.3	13.1	26.2	12.8	+3.1	−22	77
ARMY ENLISTED PERSONNEL	f	53	18	35	29.4	12.1	35.4	11.8	−6.0	1	82
ARMY ENLISTED PERSONNEL	m	55	17	32	22.2	11.5	28.1	12.1	−5.9	−12	92
ARMY OFFICER	f	49	16	37	31,4	10.8	43.0	11.3	−11.6	0	78
ARMY OFFICER	m	50	16	41	21.3	10.7	32.2	11.8	−10.9	−9	78
ART TEACHER	f	60	18	18	12.6	17.7	4.1	17.2	+8.5	−53	80
ART TEACHER	m	65	24	18	29.9	13.8	17.8	14.2	+12.1	−27	75
ARTIST, COMMERCIAL	f	64	21	29	20.1	18.0	15.4	15.5	+4.7	−45	76
ARTIST, COMMERCIAL	m	61	25	26	33.4	12.6	25.0	12.3	+8.4	−9	72
ARTIST, FINE	f	66	25	32	26.1	13.8	24.7	12.4	+1.4	−17	68
ARTIST, FINE	m	71	29	21	28.4	13.2	21.0	13.2	+7.4	−12	69
ATHLETIC TRAINER	f	64	24	19	16.8	15.1	25.3	14.2	−8.5	−28	78
ATHLETIC TRAINER	m	65	19	22	18.1	12.4	22.2	12.5	−4.1	−29	82
BANKER	f	45	18	44	33.2	11.9	34.6	10.5	−1.4	1	75
BANKER	m	48	19	39	28.1	12.3	31.1	12.2	−3.0	−10	77
BEAUTICIAN	f	55	19	41	31.9	11.9	30.1	10.3	+1.8	−1	81
BEAUTICIAN	m	54	18	34	42.9	9.5	31.8	9.2	+11.1	5	74
BIOLOGIST	f	66	26	22	18.1	15.9	26.0	14.6	−7.9	−24	73
BIOLOGIST	m	64	22	30	27.5	12.8	26.2	13.0	+1.3	−12	70
BROADCASTER	f	61	16	46	34.0	11.5	30.4	11.4	+3.6	−6	75
BROADCASTER	m	69	18	41	39.6	11.6	32.4	11.4	+7.2	−3	74
BUS DRIVER	f	44	22	36	31.7	9.8	38.9	10.0	−7.2	5	80
BUS DRIVER	m	51	17	49	32.5	7.5	36.9	8.9	−4.4	10	79
BUSINESS EDUCATION TEACHER	f	62	22	17	18.2	13.2	19.2	10.4	−1.0	−19	74
BUSINESS EDUCATION TEACHER	m	59	21	21	27.0	12.1	24.5	10.4	+2.5	−7	73
BUYER	f	53	18	30	23.1	15.7	21.5	14.4	+1.6	−25	83
BUYER	m	50	16	36	34.1	14.1	28.0	13.8	+6.1	−13	81
CARPENTER	f	60	25	21	21.1	13.0	31.8	13.1	−10.7	−11	74
CARPENTER	m	58	19	28	16.8	12.4	24.4	13.9	−7.6	−17	87
CHAMBER OF COMMERCE EXECUTIVE	f	67	17	42	32.0	12.5	30.7	10.6	+1.3	−5	80
CHAMBER OF COMMERCE EXECUTIVE	m	58	20	34	26.2	13.7	26.1	14.8	+0.1	−13	72
CHEF	f	42	16	35	27.7	13.7	22.2	12.6	+5.5	−31	84
CHEF	m	36	16	24	33.2	12.2	23.4	12.7	+9.8	−24	87
CHEMIST	f	67	25	23	20.0	15.0	29.7	13.9	−9.7	−17	73
CHEMIST	m	61	22	25	17.9	14.5	21.1	15.1	−3.2	−25	73
CHIROPRACTOR	f	35	16	42	31.2	13.2	33.8	12.7	−2.6	−10	79
CHIROPRACTOR	m	29	16	33	28.1	13.3	27.6	13.2	+0.5	−22	80
COLLEGE PROFESSOR	f	57	18	42	33.0	11.0	36.5	10.4	−3.5	−1	72
COLLEGE PROFESSOR	m	54	17	46	36.2	10.4	34.5	11.0	+1.7	−5	74
COMPUTER PROGRAMMER	f	64	19	39	32.4	10.6	37.9	10.5	−5.5	4	74
COMPUTER PROGRAMMER	m	59	17	44	27.4	11.6	32.7	12.4	−5.3	−4	76
CREDIT MANAGER	f	59	18	40	30.7	12.9	33.4	10.5	−2.7	−4	79
CREDIT MANAGER	m	58	17	42	25.7	12.4	31.8	12.8	−6.1	−9	79
DENTAL ASSISTANT	f	58	19	39	30.8	12.5	30.6	9.9	+0.2	−1	79
DENTAL HYGIENIST	f	61	16	40	31.2	12.5	31.1	11.2	+0.1	−13	84
DENTIST	f	59	18	38	29.2	13.7	37.1	13.5	−7.9	−8	78
DENTIST	m	45	17	34	24.4	14.7	27.0	13.9	−2.6	−24	79

(*Continued*)

TABLE 6.1 (*continued*)

Scale	Sex	Number of items	Min. percent diff.	Tilton percent overlap	WIG mean	WIG S.D.	MIG mean	MIG S.D.	WIG–MIG diff.	Minimum possible score	Maximum possible score
DIETITIAN	f	28	16	44	33.1	12.1	35.9	11.0	−2.8	−6	77
DIETITIAN	m	39	16	41	41.2	10.0	33.4	10.2	+7.8	4	76
ELECTED PUBLIC OFFICIAL	f	45	16	39	29.6	13.8	30.0	14.5	−0.4	−9	70
ELECTED PUBLIC OFFICIAL	m	55	19	36	31.3	11.7	29.8	12.2	+1.5	−7	72
ELECTRICIAN	f	58	25	25	22.9	13.6	33.9	13.6	−11.0	−10	73
ELECTRICIAN	m	60	20	32	17.6	11.3	26.6	13.4	−9.0	−16	79
ELEMENTARY TEACHER	f	64	16	41	31.4	12.5	26.6	9.6	+4.8	−10	82
ELEMENTARY TEACHER	m	34	16	35	30.3	14.9	28.0	13.5	+2.3	−20	82
EMERGENCY MEDICAL TECHNICIAN	f	65	18	28	25.1	13.0	32.0	11.9	−6.9	−15	84
EMERGENCY MEDICAL TECHNICIAN	m	57	19	34	20.9	11.1	29.0	12.2	−8.1	−13	79
ENGINEER	f	53	23	34	27.2	13.7	37.4	13.3	−10.2	−3	72
ENGINEER	m	66	19	37	19.8	13.8	28.5	13.8	−8.7	−11	74
ENGLISH TEACHER	f	57	18	30	24.2	14.8	14.9	15.7	+9.3	−31	75
ENGLISH TEACHER	m	62	22	30	36.1	12.8	24.9	14.4	+11.2	−14	72
EXECUTIVE HOUSEKEEPER	f	60	19	44	33.4	11.6	35.5	9.7	−2.1	8	76
EXECUTIVE HOUSEKEEPER	m	61	25	51	33.6	9.5	36.4	10.5	−2.8	9	78
FARMER	f	66	21	36	31.5	10.3	33.9	8.2	−2.4	5	78
FARMER	m	61	25	35	24.5	9.1	30.8	10.4	−6.3	3	70
FLIGHT ATTENDANT	f	51	17	41	32.1	11.7	28.2	9.8	+3.9	−9	77
FLIGHT ATTENDANT	m	56	18	42	42.7	9.4	33.7	10.0	+9.0	6	69
FLORIST	f	57	16	44	33.4	11.5	30.3	10.9	+3.1	−6	81
FLORIST	m	48	16	37	35.7	11.3	30.9	11.2	+4.8	−4	80
FOOD SERVICE MANAGER	f	53	20	47	34.8	11.1	34.6	8.1	+0.2	9	75
FOOD SERVICE MANAGER	m	35	16	41	36.8	10.5	33.1	10.5	+3.7	2	76
FOREIGN LANGUAGE TEACHER	f	48	16	25	23.2	13.4	15.6	13.5	+7.6	−33	82
FOREIGN LANGUAGE TEACHER	m	51	20	34	38.8	10.9	28.6	12.3	+10.2	−9	74
FORESTER	f	64	24	27	23.3	14.2	31.6	12.5	−8.3	−18	76
FORESTER	m	50	20	33	22.0	12.0	28.1	12.4	−6.1	−15	75
FUNERAL DIRECTOR	f	59	16	53	36.7	11.3	34.4	9.7	+2.3	6	75
FUNERAL DIRECTOR	m	62	16	45	30.3	11.2	33.6	11.8	−3.3	−9	83
GEOGRAPHER	f	55	19	43	32.2	12.3	42.9	10.0	−10.7	−7	78
GEOGRAPHER	m	62	19	29	25.1	13.8	25.0	13.5	+0.1	−30	83
GEOLOGIST	f	70	25	25	21.4	14.8	31.3	12.9	−9.9	−20	75
GEOLOGIST	m	67	23	31	25.3	12.4	27.3	12.2	−2.0	−13	70
GUIDANCE COUNSELOR	f	62	16	44	32.3	12.7	28.7	11.7	+3.6	−9	73
GUIDANCE COUNSELOR	m	54	18	35	37.2	11.4	29.7	11.5	+7.5	−2	73
HOME ECONOMICS TEACHER	f	64	21	28	24.9	13.4	19.1	9.6	+5.8	−18	78
HORTICULTURAL WORKER	f	55	17	40	31.8	11.6	34.5	11.4	−2.7	−3	77
HORTICULTURAL WORKER	m	57	16	36	30.0	12.2	29.2	12.8	+0.8	−15	83
INTERIOR DECORATOR	f	61	19	28	23.2	14.6	15.9	12.5	+7.3	−34	80
INTERIOR DECORATOR	m	62	26	26	38.8	10.9	27.2	10.4	+11.6	−4	69
INVESTMENTS MANAGER	f	43	20	38	29.5	13.3	37.4	10.8	−7.9	−15	72
INVESTMENTS MANAGER	m	51	17	35	26.6	12.5	30.0	11.2	−3.4	−20	78
IRS AGENT	f	49	16	51	34.4	13.9	40.2	13.4	−5.8	−2	76
IRS AGENT	m	47	16	45	28.6	10.0	34.5	10.3	−5.9	−5	81
LAWYER	f	67	16	39	28.4	15.3	33.8	11.9	−5.4	−25	81
LAWYER	m	52	16	41	32.3	12.9	31.4	12.7	+0.9	−20	78
LIBRARIAN	f	36	16	42	29.4	15.4	26.8	15.5	+2.6	−26	83
LIBRARIAN	m	66	19	41	42.2	10.4	31.1	12.7	+11.3	−7	76
LIFE INSURANCE AGENT	f	61	18	33	28.8	11.9	30.6	12.6	−1.8	−5	72
LIFE INSURANCE AGENT	m	60	22	25	19.6	12.6	22.3	14.2	−2.7	−20	73
MARINE CORPS ENLISTED PERSONNEL	f	62	18	32	28.1	11.8	35.8	11.4	−7.7	−4	84
MARINE CORPS ENLISTED PERSONNEL	m	49	19	33	18.9	11.4	27.6	13.2	−8.7	−15	81
MARKETING EXECUTIVE	f	48	18	38	28.9	14.2	34.3	11.4	−5.4	−19	78
MARKETING EXECUTIVE	m	52	16	45	33.1	12.5	34.1	11.2	−1.0	−8	74
MATHEMATICIAN	f	64	26	18	16.7	15.0	27.3	13.7	−10.6	−24	74
MATHEMATICIAN	m	70	26	20	18.6	12.6	19.5	13.9	−0.9	−22	71
MATHEMATICS TEACHER	f	63	18	27	25.5	12.3	31.7	12.3	−6.2	−9	78
MATHEMATICS TEACHER	m	67	17	28	22.4	10.3	27.8	10.7	−5.4	−13	76

(*Continued*)

TABLE 6.1 (*continued*)

Scale	Sex	Number of items	Min. percent diff.	Tilton percent overlap	WIG mean	WIG S.D.	MIG mean	MIG S.D.	WIG–MIG diff.	Minimum possible score	Maximum possible score
MEDICAL ILLUSTRATOR	f	55	25	22	18.3	15.9	18.3	15.0	0.0	−35	72
MEDICAL ILLUSTRATOR	m	56	27	15	22.5	15.6	12.4	16.3	−10.1	−35	72
MEDICAL TECHNICIAN	f	51	21	34	28.6	12.4	31.5	11.8	−2.9	−7	80
MEDICAL TECHNICIAN	m	45	17	36	23.7	14.7	27.3	14.7	−3.6	−17	80
MEDICAL TECHNOLOGIST	f	65	19	34	27.1	13.9	33.5	13.6	−6.4	−9	78
MEDICAL TECHNOLOGIST	m	61	17	43	25.9	13.7	30.7	14.2	−4.8	−7	72
MINISTER	f	58	21	23	20.2	15.0	15.4	14.9	+4.8	−28	73
MINISTER	m	54	22	35	35.1	12.1	29.1	12.5	+6.0	−3	68
MUSICIAN	f	64	17	41	32.0	12.0	26.0	12.9	+6.0	−15	75
MUSICIAN	m	51	21	36	38.5	11.1	30.0	11.9	+8.5	−3	73
NAVY ENLISTED PERSONNEL	f	61	17	35	30.9	10.5	39.5	10.3	−8.6	−1	84
NAVY ENLISTED PERSONNEL	m	52	20	38	22.0	10.5	30.6	12.2	−8.6	−10	83
NAVY OFFICER	f	41	16	42	33.9	10.1	43.5	10.5	−9.6	7	75
NAVY OFFICER	m	63	16	45	22.4	11.5	32.9	12.5	−10.5	−11	76
NURSE, LPN	f	65	20	31	26.2	13.5	25.2	10.9	+1.0	−10	81
NURSE, LPN	m	61	18	32	34.8	11.4	30.2	10.0	+4.6	0	79
NURSE, RN	f	30	16	48	33.0	13.8	31.9	12.1	+1.1	−5	72
NURSE, RN	m	42	16	39	29.7	13.2	30.1	13.0	−0.4	−7	79
NURSING HOME ADMINISTRATOR	f	55	16	45	33.7	11.7	32.8	10.2	+0.9	−2	77
NURSING HOME ADMINISTRATOR	m	45	16	51	37.8	11.3	35.8	11.5	+2.0	3	75
OCCUPATIONAL THERAPIST	f	54	18	39	29.4	13.8	30.8	12.2	−1.4	−18	78
OCCUPATIONAL THERAPIST	m	60	19	31	33.3	12.4	27.4	12.3	+5.9	−14	78
OPTICIAN	f	42	16	49	34.3	12.8	36.3	11.2	−2.0	−2	82
OPTICIAN	m	36	16	47	30.4	10.3	34.0	11.9	−3.6	−5	82
OPTOMETRIST	f	51	16	53	35.8	12.4	41.7	12.1	−5.9	3	77
OPTOMETRIST	m	28	16	53	30.9	14.3	35.0	13.6	−4.1	−8	74
PERSONNEL DIRECTOR	f	37	16	49	33.7	13.4	34.7	14.1	−1.0	−6	71
PERSONNEL DIRECTOR	m	58	16	45	29.7	12.8	32.1	13.7	−2.4	−10	73
PHARMACIST	f	53	17	40	31.5	12.1	36.1	11.7	−4.6	−7	80
PHARMACIST	m	40	16	38	27.2	11.1	30.8	12.0	−3.6	−12	78
PHOTOGRAPHER	f	47	16	45	33.1	12.4	32.0	11.3	+1.1	−12	75
PHOTOGRAPHER	m	58	17	38	34.8	12.4	31.2	11.4	+3.6	−16	78
PHYSICAL EDUCATION TEACHER	f	63	21	19	19.9	13.2	29.5	12.3	−9.6	−23	83
PHYSICAL EDUCATION TEACHER	m	56	17	19	11.4	14.9	17.1	15.1	−5.7	−40	83
PHYSICAL THERAPIST	f	57	18	38	28.0	14.9	30.9	12.9	−2.9	−22	79
PHYSICAL THERAPIST	m	54	16	33	23.1	14.5	27.1	13.7	−4.0	−24	77
PHYSICIAN	f	60	21	33	25.1	15.3	30.5	13.6	−5.4	−25	74
PHYSICIAN	m	60	20	32	27.6	13.4	27.0	13.1	+0.6	−13	73
PHYSICIST	f	60	29	13	9.6	16.6	19.7	15.6	−10.1	−30	73
PHYSICIST	m	63	26	18	10.6	15.8	14.7	16.2	−4.1	−31	71
POLICE OFFICER	f	42	16	34	29.6	11.2	38.7	12.8	−9.1	−5	76
POLICE OFFICER	m	45	16	35	19.1	10.5	28.5	13.2	−9.4	−16	77
PSYCHOLOGIST	f	56	21	31	25.8	14.0	29.0	12.1	−3.2	−29	74
PSYCHOLOGIST	m	62	23	30	29.4	13.9	25.5	13.6	+3.9	−20	73
PUBLIC ADMINISTRATOR	f	45	18	38	27.4	16.0	32.0	12.9	−4.6	−21	75
PUBLIC ADMINISTRATOR	m	56	17	45	35.7	13.5	32.2	13.6	+3.5	−4	72
PUBLIC RELATIONS DIRECTOR	f	60	19	37	27.1	15.8	24.1	14.8	+3.0	−21	75
PUBLIC RELATIONS DIRECTOR	m	61	21	30	31.2	14.3	24.0	15.1	+7.2	−22	73
PURCHASING AGENT	f	37	16	53	35.8	12.7	41.0	13.2	−5.2	5	74
PURCHASING AGENT	m	44	16	49	28.6	11.0	34.3	12.5	−5.7	−3	77
RADIOLOGIC TECHNOLOGIST	f	52	17	40	30.3	13.3	32.1	11.7	−1.8	−8	82
RADIOLOGIC TECHNOLOGIST	m	50	16	42	27.3	13.1	30.8	13.8	−3.5	−12	84
REALTOR	f	63	18	33	26,2	14,2	26,8	14.2	−0.6	−16	75
REALTOR	m	46	16	45	30.5	11.1	33.1	12.3	−2.6	−1	73
RECREATION LEADER	f	43	17	49	35.3	11.2	36.9	10.8	−1.6	0	71
RECREATION LEADER	m	49	16	46	33.9	10.4	34.2	11.4	−0.3	−7	74
REPORTER	f	57	16	39	28.1	15.3	24.5	14.5	+3.6	−26	77
REPORTER	m	62	19	28	32.6	12.2	24.6	13.6	+8.0	−24	77
RESEARCH & DEVELOPMENT MANAGER	f	61	19	31	25.1	14.5	35.4	13.5	−10.3	−18	79

TABLE 6.1 (continued)

Scale	Sex	Number of items	Min. percent diff.	Tilton percent overlap	WIG mean	WIG S.D.	MIG mean	MIG S.D.	WIG–MIG diff.	Minimum possible score	Maximum possible score
RESEARCH & DEVELOPMENT MANAGER	m	63	18	30	16.1	14.0	25.6	13.6	−9.5	−22	76
RESPIRATORY THERAPIST	f	55	16	42	30.8	13.8	35.2	13.3	−4.4	−13	84
RESPIRATORY THERAPIST	m	64	16	43	29.3	15.1	30.3	15.2	−1.0	−24	80
RESTAURANT MANAGER	f	37	16	52	34.4	14.4	36.2	15.0	−1.8	−6	78
RESTAURANT MANAGER	m	41	18	42	32.5	12.2	31.1	13.4	+1.1	−6	79
SCHOOL ADMINISTRATOR	f	53	16	48	34.0	12.8	33.6	13.3	+0.4	−5	67
SCHOOL ADMINISTRATOR	m	51	19	44	31.8	11.1	33.2	11.8	−1.4	2	70
SCIENCE TEACHER	f	62	18	29	23.0	15.3	27.3	15.1	−4.3	−19	78
SCIENCE TEACHER	m	61	18	33	25.0	13.0	27.1	13.3	−2.1	−14	75
SECRETARY	f	54	18	41	31.8	12.2	30.4	9.2	+1.4	0	77
SOCIAL SCIENCE TEACHER	f	42	16	39	31.2	11.8	30.6	12.6	+0.6	−8	72
SOCIAL SCIENCE TEACHER	m	55	16	42	35.6	11.1	32.5	11.9	+3.1	−5	79
SOCIAL WORKER	f	44	16	34	28.3	12.7	24.7	13.0	+3.6	−23	75
SOCIAL WORKER	m	61	17	33	34.0	13.8	26.3	14.5	+7.7	−21	79
SOCIOLOGIST	f	62	22	23	21.0	14.4	26.2	12.4	−5.2	−31	76
SOCIOLOGIST	m	70	21	28	29.3	12.3	24.9	13.3	+4.4	−24	77
SPECIAL EDUCATION TEACHER	f	45	16	48	32.9	14.2	29.3	11.3	+3.6	−8	75
SPECIAL EDUCATION TEACHER	m	40	16	37	33.4	15.6	27.8	14.9	+5.6	−15	78
SPEECH PATHOLOGIST	f	45	16	41	30.9	13.0	25.0	13.1	+5.9	−23	74
SPEECH PATHOLOGIST	m	54	16	38	35.0	13.2	29.0	13.7	+6.0	−24	80
STORE MANAGER	f	35	16	46	33.7	11.9	31.4	11.5	+2.3	+1	70
STORE MANAGER	m	40	17	43	33.1	11.5	32.3	12.2	−0.8	+1	73
SYSTEMS ANALYST	f	64	18	44	32.7	12.2	39.7	11.1	−7.0	−1	76
SYSTEMS ANALYST	m	56	16	43	24.6	12.8	32.2	12.7	−7.6	−12	79
TRAVEL AGENT	f	39	16	42	31.1	13.2	32.2	12.7	−1.1	−15	79
TRAVEL AGENT	m	44	16	50	41.4	11.1	36.0	10.7	+5.4	1	78
VETERINARIAN	f	66	21	28	23.9	14.1	29.6	13.0	−5.7	−16	79
VETERINARIAN	m	67	18	29	20.5	12.5	25.5	13.1	−5.0	−21	81
VOCATIONAL AGRICULTURE TEACHER	f	60	17	27	26.2	11.6	31.8	11.5	−5.6	−15	82
VOCATIONAL AGRICULTURE TEACHER	m	64	21	28	18.7	11.0	26.1	12.0	−7.4	−17	77
YWCA DIRECTOR	f	42	16	51	35.0	13.0	36.5	12.7	−1.5	−5	72
YMCA DIRECTOR	m	51	19	39	30.7	12.6	30.3	12.8	+0.4	−4	70

Ordering the Occupational Scales on the Profile

The Occupational Scales are ordered on the profile in the six categories represented by the General Occupation Themes classification system (see Chapter 4); the code letters next to each Occupational Scale on the profile indicate the one, two, or three General Occupational Themes most closely associated statistically with that scale.

Earlier groupings. Earlier forms of the Strong profile organized scales into occupational groups developed from the statistical relationships between the scales. Generally, scales were grouped together if they correlated .65 or above with each other, or if the Criterion Samples had standard-score means of 40 or higher on each other's scales. These groupings were not entirely satisfactory for a variety of reasons: some scales had only small correlations with other scales and could not be grouped with any others; some scales seemed to belong, statistically, to more than one group; some pairs of scales were asymmetrical (for example, veterinarians belonged with farmers, but farmers did not belong with veterinar-

ians); and some groupings just did not seem reasonable (for example, the clustering of artists with the biological scientists). The most serious problem was the lack of a unifying theory to guide the grouping or to use in understanding the groups once they were formed.

Despite the attendant problems, the profile groupings were useful in interpreting the profiles—they provided more focus than did no groupings at all. Instead of the sterile statement, "You have the interests of a physician," the groupings provided a broader interpretation, "You have interests similar to those of physicians and other biological scientists, such as _____." Although this approach was decidedly superior to listing the scales alphabetically, it was not completely satisfactory, because the particular characteristics of each group were not well described.

New groupings. Because the SVIB profile groupings and Holland's occupational types were similar, his occupational-classification system offered some potential for improvement. And because Holland drew many of his ideas about occupational types from research on the

Strong, the substantial overlap between the two systems comes as no surprise.

The major advantage of Holland's categories is that he paid closer attention to the theoretical concerns of classification systems than had Strong. He constructed categories that were both exhaustive and mutually exclusive; and most important, he developed a rationale for his classification and described it at length (Holland, 1966, 1973). As discussed in Chapter 4, his descriptions of the six types were used to establish the General Occupational Theme scales, and the six Themes were used as the basis for organizing the Occupational Scales on the 1974, 1981, and 1985 profiles.

Several kinds of information were used to derive the codes for the 1985 Occupational Scales. The most important were the mean scores of the Criterion Samples on the six General Occupational Themes normed on each sample's appropriate-sex Reference Sample; next were the correlations between the Themes and the Occupational Scales; next, the mean scores of the Criterion Samples on the combined-sex-normed Themes; then, the mean scores of the Criterion Samples on the Basic Interest Scales; and last, the overall rank order of the scores of all of the Criterion Samples on all of the Occupational Scales.

Table 6.2 lists, for each occupational sample, the same-sex and combined-sex General Occupational Theme means and the correlations between the Themes and the 1985 Occupational Scales. Correlation coefficients for the Occupational Scales were based on the 1985 General Reference Sample, which is composed of 300 women and 300 men. Code types, as listed in Table 6.2, were then assigned to the Occupational Scales. Usually, only means of 53 or higher were considered in the coding, but a few samples had no means that high. Conversely, only two occupational groups—female mathematics teachers and male executive housekeepers—had more than three means of 53 or higher. In both cases, the correlation coefficients were examined along with the mean Theme and Basic Interest Scale scores to choose the most appropriate code for the occupation.

The hexagonal arrangement. After the codes had been assigned, the Occupational Scales were ordered on the profile to conform to the R-I-A-S-E-C hexagon order. Most of the Occupational Scales fell into code types that ordered themselves reasonably around the perimeter of the hexagon. Only nine of the 207 Occupational Scales— f Emergency Medical Technician (RS), m Pharmacist (IE), f and m Marketing Executive (EI), f and m Physical Education Teacher (SR), m Athletic Trainer (SR), f Occupational Therapist (SRI), and f Recreation Leader (SRE) — were assigned to unexpected categories represented by the diagonals of the hexagon (that is, IE or EI, AC or CA, and SR or RS). A few occupations, notably m and f Investments Manager, m and f Public Administrator, f Beautician, and f Dietitian, had no high mean scores, which probably means that these occupations are not psychologically homogeneous. The remainder of the occupations, the vast majority, clustered neatly into the designated code types.

Interpretive value of code types. Profile interpretation is greatly facilitated by the code types and their use in ordering the scales on the profile. Clusters of identical code types, such as the SR cluster containing Athletic Trainer, Occupational Therapist, Physical Education Teacher, and Recreation Leader, help draw attention to the similarities between occupations. Comparisons between similar code types, such as EC and CE—the former including Chamber of Commerce Executive, Store Manager, Purchasing Agent, Restaurant Manager, and Travel Agent, the latter including IRS Agent, Credit Manager, and Business Education Teacher— draw attention to the nuances often separating closely related occupations. Respondents should therefore be encouraged to compare their highest one, two, or three General Occupational Theme scores (depending on the point spread of the scores) with the various possible combinations of the codes for these Themes.

The interpretive value of the codes is discussed at length in the *User's Guide*.

Occupations not listed on the profile. The occupations listed in Table 6.2 are only those that were used to develop empirical scales; consequently their number is restricted. Many other occupational samples have been collected over the years, but for a variety of reasons they were not used to construct Occupational Scales, usually because they were too small but occasionally for other reasons, such as a close intuitive and statistical relationship with some other occupation already on the profile. Although these samples have not proved to be appropriate for scale construction, they can nonetheless provide useful data. Their mean scores are especially useful, since samples used for the calculation of mean scores need not be as stringently selected as those used to establish item-scoring weights. All of these samples were scored on the General Occupational Themes and assigned a code type. They are listed, along with the occupations accorded Occupational Scales on the profile, in Appendix B, ordered according to the R-I-A-S-E-C classification system. Counselors and their clients should refer to this appendix for further information on the classification of occupations.

Reliability

Test-retest statistics for the 1985 Occupational Scales are reported in Tables 6.3 and 6.4 for three samples tested and retested over two-week, thirty-day, and three-year periods. These are the same samples used to study the reliability of the General Occupational Themes (Table 4.3) and the Basic Interest Scales (Table 5.4); the samples are described on p. 31.

The median correlations over these three periods were .92, .89, and .87, respectively, almost identical to the comparable statistics for the 1981 Occupational Scales, which were .91, .89, and .87, respectively.

The magnitude of the test-retest correlations and the stability of the means over the three testing periods demonstrate that the SCII scales are quite stable over short time periods. Over longer time periods, the stability will be somewhat less but still high.

TABLE 6.2

Data Used to Classify Occupational Scales:
General Occupational Theme Scale Means and Correlations for Each Occupational Scale Criterion Sample

Occupational Scale	Sex	Code	Separate-sex-normed GOT mean for each Occupational Sample[a]						Combined-sex-normed GOT mean for each Occupational Sample[b]						Correlations between GOT Scales and Occupational Scales (decimal points omitted)[c]					
			R	I	A	S	E	C	R	I	A	S	E	C	R	I	A	S	E	C
ACCOUNTANT	f	C	50	51	45	46	48	58	47	50	48	46	48	57	25	09	−53	−24	14	47
ACCOUNTANT	m	C	49	50	46	48	50	56	53	51	43	48	51	56	09	−02	−41	−13	27	46
ADVERTISING EXECUTIVE	f	A	47	48	54	47	50	47	44	47	56	47	49	46	−42	−31	53	−16	06	−38
ADVERTISING EXECUTIVE	m	A	46	47	57	47	48	44	49	48	55	47	49	45	−46	−19	66	−13	−20	−52
AGRIBUSINESS MANAGER	m	ECR	56	45	41	50	58	56	59	46	38	50	60	56	24	−26	−75	−04	33	34
AIR FORCE ENLISTED PERSONNEL	f	C	52	48	45	51	50	56	48	46	48	52	49	56	26	−05	−51	21	18	51
AIR FORCE ENLISTED PERSONNEL	m	R	55	49	48	48	48	52	58	46	42	50	49	52	61	20	−50	00	02	29
AIR FORCE OFFICER	f	R	56	52	48	48	49	52	52	51	50	48	48	52	70	42	−15	06	23	40
AIR FORCE OFFICER	m	R	55	51	46	49	50	52	58	52	43	49	51	53	72	43	−32	09	26	33
ARCHITECT	f	RIA	57	55	54	42	44	47	53	54	56	42	44	46	59	55	17	−30	−20	−06
ARCHITECT	m	ARI	53	52	57	44	43	46	56	53	54	44	44	46	07	19	44	−39	−51	−46
ARMY ENLISTED PERSONNEL	f	CRS	54	50	48	54	52	57	50	49	51	54	51	57	52	26	−15	52	48	66
ARMY ENLISTED PERSONNEL	m	CR	53	46	46	51	50	54	57	48	43	51	51	55	48	04	−47	24	28	50
ARMY OFFICER	f	RC	57	51	49	51	51	53	53	50	52	51	50	53	74	49	−03	41	40	42
ARMY OFFICER	m	RC	55	52	46	51	51	54	59	53	44	51	51	54	66	43	−31	26	30	41
ART TEACHER	f	A	52	50	57	52	48	46	48	48	59	52	48	45	11	19	69	21	−14	−18
ART TEACHER	m	A	47	47	61	50	45	42	51	48	58	49	45	42	−35	−14	63	01	−33	−49
ARTIST, COMMERCIAL	f	A	51	51	57	44	45	42	48	50	59	44	45	41	00	16	62	−32	−34	−54
ARTIST, COMMERCIAL	m	A	47	47	60	43	42	40	51	48	57	43	43	41	−41	−21	46	−36	−50	−66
ARTIST, FINE	f	A	49	50	56	41	42	39	45	49	58	41	42	38	−23	−10	21	−57	−63	−76
ARTIST, FINE	m	A	47	49	60	40	39	36	50	50	58	40	40	37	−37	−17	32	−46	−68	−70
ATHLETIC TRAINER	f	RIS	58	54	45	54	46	49	54	53	48	55	46	49	75	56	−04	31	04	18
ATHLETIC TRAINER	m	SR	52	51	45	54	45	48	55	52	42	54	46	49	28	15	−42	24	−16	08
BANKER	f	C	46	45	48	49	52	58	43	44	48	49	52	58	−39	−63	−59	−08	19	28
BANKER	m	C	49	48	48	49	52	54	52	46	46	49	53	55	−20	−28	−10	−05	38	15
BEAUTICIAN	f	E	49	45	47	49	51	50	45	44	50	49	50	50	−17	−51	−50	−15	−09	−01
BEAUTICIAN	m	AE	46	46	55	48	52	48	50	48	52	48	53	48	−28	−23	55	09	22	−08
BIOLOGIST	f	IR	56	61	51	46	40	46	52	60	53	46	40	46	50	67	04	−10	−43	−02
BIOLOGIST	m	I	50	58	52	46	40	45	54	59	49	46	41	46	07	39	10	−21	−74	−32
BROADCASTER	f	A	46	47	54	49	51	46	43	46	56	50	50	46	−39	−23	51	10	19	−22
BROADCASTER	m	A	44	46	55	46	47	44	48	47	52	46	48	45	−66	−47	39	−23	−19	−51
BUS DRIVER	f	R	56	47	44	50	48	52	52	46	47	50	48	51	45	−09	−57	−04	05	18
BUS DRIVER	m	R	54	45	46	50	50	50	57	46	43	50	51	51	26	−28	−68	−17	−04	04
BUSINESS EDUCATION TEACHER	f	CES	48	45	44	55	55	65	45	44	47	55	54	65	−01	−21	−32	46	41	67
BUSINESS EDUCATION TEACHER	m	CES	48	45	46	56	56	64	52	46	44	56	58	64	−04	−16	−00	53	55	68
BUYER	f	EC	46	45	47	49	60	53	43	44	50	49	58	53	−31	−55	−19	−06	54	16
BUYER	m	E	47	46	49	49	57	51	50	47	46	49	58	51	−37	−51	00	−03	55	10
CARPENTER	f	RI	64	53	52	49	44	46	59	52	54	49	44	46	82	52	00	−02	−13	06
CARPENTER	m	R	57	49	51	48	48	49	60	50	48	48	48	49	76	38	−09	−03	−02	16
CHAMBER OF COMMERCE EXECUTIVE	f	EC	46	45	47	50	55	56	43	44	50	50	54	56	−25	−46	−23	25	56	48
CHAMBER OF COMMERCE EXECUTIVE	m	E	47	45	50	51	56	52	51	47	47	51	57	52	−10	−16	15	28	58	20
CHEF	f	AR	53	49	50	49	51	48	49	47	53	49	50	48	26	18	35	03	−07	−08

TABLE 6.2 (continued)

Occupational Scale	Sex	Code	Separate-sex-normed GOT mean for each Occupational Sample[a]						Combined-sex-normed GOT mean for each Occupational Sample[b]						Correlations between GOT Scales and Occupational Scales (decimal points omitted)[c]					
			R	I	A	S	E	C	R	I	A	S	E	C	R	I	A	S	E	C
CHEF	m	EA	51	49	50	50	52	50	54	50	48	50	52	50	−09	−17	30	20	32	05
CHEMIST	f	IR	56	62	50	46	42	50	52	62	52	46	42	50	62	73	00	−06	−25	15
CHEMIST	m	IR	52	61	51	45	42	49	55	62	49	45	51	49	37	64	07	−17	−51	00
CHIROPRACTOR	f	IR	53	53	50	51	50	50	49	52	52	51	49	50	54	62	05	46	18	27
CHIROPRACTOR	m	I	51	53	51	50	48	48	54	54	48	50	48	48	25	47	15	11	−14	−21
COLLEGE PROFESSOR	f	I	51	57	52	49	42	48	54	56	54	49	42	47	17	46	01	−21	−66	−22
COLLEGE PROFESSOR	m	I	48	55	52	48	43	47	52	56	50	48	43	48	00	44	24	−12	−64	−26
COMPUTER PROGRAMMER	f	IRC	55	56	48	45	45	53	51	55	51	45	45	53	63	64	−09	−11	−15	31
COMPUTER PROGRAMMER	m	IRC	54	54	48	46	46	53	57	55	46	46	46	53	53	54	−10	−18	−26	21
CREDIT MANAGER	f	CES	48	47	45	52	55	61	45	46	48	52	54	61	05	−17	−41	33	49	71
CREDIT MANAGER	m	CES	52	49	46	53	55	58	56	50	43	52	56	58	35	05	−25	33	68	71
DENTAL ASSISTANT	f	CS	49	49	47	53	49	53	46	48	50	53	48	52	23	05	−26	38	11	42
DENTAL HYGIENIST	f	SCI	50	51	49	52	50	52	46	50	52	53	50	51	40	31	−09	32	15	32
DENTIST	f	IR	55	57	50	48	45	49	51	56	53	48	45	48	69	74	01	01	−10	16
DENTIST	m	IR	54	55	50	48	47	48	57	56	47	48	47	48	53	62	06	04	−12	02
DIETITIAN	f	ISR	50	52	47	52	49	51	47	51	50	52	48	50	50	56	−15	40	12	31
DIETITIAN	m	CSE	49	50	50	53	52	53	53	52	47	53	52	54	06	18	29	59	27	40
ELECTED PUBLIC OFFICIAL	f	ES	50	51	51	53	54	51	47	50	54	53	53	51	11	23	36	46	51	25
ELECTED PUBLIC OFFICIAL	m	E	48	47	50	52	53	49	51	48	47	52	54	49	−20	−11	31	23	39	00
ELECTRICIAN	f	RI	62	55	52	48	45	47	58	54	54	48	45	47	87	66	07	06	05	22
ELECTRICIAN	m	R	57	50	46	47	47	50	60	51	43	47	48	50	64	26	−41	−13	−06	15
ELEMENTARY TEACHER	f	S	48	47	50	54	49	52	45	46	52	54	49	52	−07	−17	03	45	04	34
ELEMENTARY TEACHER	m	S	52	50	49	55	49	51	55	51	47	55	50	52	33	29	15	53	−09	23
EMERGENCY MEDICAL TECHNICIAN	f	RS	53	51	45	53	47	52	49	50	48	53	46	51	46	28	−40	29	04	28
EMERGENCY MEDICAL TECHNICIAN	m	R	55	51	44	51	47	50	58	52	41	51	48	51	45	21	−60	08	−05	17
ENGINEER	f	RI	60	58	47	45	45	51	56	57	50	45	45	50	79	73	00	00	03	28
ENGINEER	m	RI	56	56	47	46	45	50	60	57	44	46	46	51	68	62	−16	−13	−15	22
ENGLISH TEACHER	f	AS	46	48	56	55	50	49	43	47	58	55	49	48	−28	02	68	37	09	−01
ENGLISH TEACHER	m	AS	44	48	59	54	46	48	48	50	56	54	47	48	−25	13	80	31	−06	−10
EXECUTIVE HOUSEKEEPER	f	CSE	52	49	48	55	54	57	48	48	50	55	53	57	36	13	−18	61	46	68
EXECUTIVE HOUSEKEEPER	m	CSE	54	49	47	54	53	54	57	50	45	54	54	54	43	21	−05	60	65	60
FARMER	f	RC	53	45	43	51	50	55	50	44	46	51	49	54	15	−24	−63	15	08	36
FARMER	m	R	56	45	40	45	49	50	60	47	37	45	50	51	16	−26	−84	−35	−13	−04
FLIGHT ATTENDANT	f	AE	50	49	54	51	52	46	46	48	56	51	51	45	12	−05	38	37	40	04
FLIGHT ATTENDANT	m	A	48	49	56	51	51	47	51	50	54	51	52	47	−08	09	74	30	33	06
FLORIST	f	E	48	45	49	48	54	50	45	44	51	48	53	50	−32	−70	−33	−25	04	−15
FLORIST	m	E	47	45	50	47	54	50	51	46	47	47	55	50	−36	−70	−21	−21	25	−06
FOOD SERVICE MANAGER	f	CS	50	46	44	53	52	56	46	45	47	53	51	56	02	−21	−53	32	16	48
FOOD SERVICE MANAGER	m	CES	51	48	48	51	54	56	54	49	45	51	55	56	15	04	02	51	58	68
FOREIGN LANGUAGE TEACHER	f	SA	47	48	53	54	48	50	44	47	55	54	48	49	−18	07	48	51	−01	16
FOREIGN LANGUAGE TEACHER	m	AS	45	48	55	53	46	49	49	49	53	53	47	49	−25	14	69	35	−17	−08
FORESTER	f	RI	58	54	48	47	43	49	54	53	51	47	42	49	71	60	01	−02	−28	02
FORESTER	m	R	56	51	45	47	46	50	59	52	42	47	46	50	53	28	−29	−15	−34	−03

(Continued)

TABLE 6.2 (continued)

Occupational Scale	Sex	Code	Separate-sex-normed GOT mean for each Occupational Sample[a]						Combined-sex-normed GOT mean for each Occupational Sample[b]						Correlations between GOT Scales and Occupational Scales (decimal points omitted)[c]					
			R	I	A	S	E	C	R	I	A	S	E	C	R	I	A	S	E	C
Funeral Director	f	ECS	48	48	48	53	56	56	44	47	51	53	55	56	13	04	01	59	67	69
Funeral Director	m	E	50	47	45	51	55	51	54	48	42	51	56	51	02	-34	-64	18	47	22
Geographer	f	IR	54	55	49	46	46	50	50	54	51	46	45	49	51	59	-09	-21	-26	06
Geographer	m	I	48	53	50	45	43	48	51	54	48	45	44	48	-01	31	22	-30	-61	-27
Geologist	f	IR	57	59	50	43	41	46	53	58	52	43	41	46	59	64	-01	-21	-36	-03
Geologist	m	IR	52	57	50	43	40	44	56	58	47	43	41	45	11	29	-08	-49	-74	-39
Guidance Counselor	f	S	48	50	50	58	51	52	44	49	52	59	50	52	-05	10	27	81	38	34
Guidance Counselor	m	S	48	50	51	60	50	52	51	51	48	60	50	52	-22	00	35	70	15	17
Home Economics Teacher	f	SCE	51	48	46	57	53	53	48	46	49	57	52	53	01	-10	-03	56	28	44
Horticultural Worker	f	R	55	51	48	50	51	51	51	51	45	50	52	50	47	23	-18	-13	-22	02
Horticultural Worker	m	R	55	50	48	48	51	49	58	51	45	48	52	50	38	08	-05	-20	-26	-10
Interior Decorator	f	AE	48	47	54	45	54	45	45	46	56	45	53	45	-29	-30	42	-30	18	-25
Interior Decorator	m	A	44	43	57	43	51	44	48	45	55	43	52	45	-64	-53	39	-19	-10	-39
Investments Manager	f	EIC	51	52	49	44	51	50	47	51	52	44	50	50	12	20	-09	-48	-08	-12
Investments Manager	m	ECI	47	50	48	46	48	52	50	51	46	46	49	52	-25	-13	-16	-52	-15	-09
IRS Agent	f	CE	51	52	49	52	53	58	47	51	52	52	52	58	54	53	06	45	56	79
IRS Agent	m	CE	50	50	47	52	52	57	54	51	44	52	53	57	42	24	-23	37	48	67
Lawyer	f	A	49	52	52	47	48	47	46	51	55	47	47	46	-06	12	27	-30	-05	-31
Lawyer	m	A	49	50	52	49	47	46	52	51	50	49	48	47	-08	16	52	09	-01	-22
Librarian	f	A	51	51	53	48	47	51	47	50	56	48	46	51	05	38	63	04	-18	03
Librarian	m	A	45	50	57	48	44	49	49	51	54	47	44	50	-40	04	64	-11	-38	-24
Life Insurance Agent	f	ES	48	50	50	53	64	52	45	49	53	53	62	52	08	05	10	42	78	38
Life Insurance Agent	m	ES	49	48	47	55	62	50	52	50	44	55	64	51	12	01	06	39	76	33
Marine Corps Enlisted Personnel	f	CRS	55	48	47	53	50	57	51	47	50	53	49	57	54	23	-26	37	34	62
Marine Corps Enlisted Personnel	m	RC	55	48	45	52	50	53	59	49	42	52	51	53	71	29	-28	28	28	43
Marketing Executive	f	EI	49	52	51	46	52	51	45	51	53	46	51	50	00	07	-03	-51	06	-05
Marketing Executive	m	EI	48	51	50	47	52	50	51	52	48	47	52	51	-31	-24	-06	-54	-08	-33
Mathematician	f	I	52	59	48	46	40	51	48	59	51	46	40	51	39	55	-12	-21	-45	01
Mathematician	m	I	48	58	51	43	39	49	51	59	48	43	39	49	04	32	-05	-36	-75	-20
Mathematics Teacher	f	CIR	54	56	45	53	48	60	50	55	48	53	48	60	57	60	-24	28	11	65
Mathematics Teacher	m	CIR	53	54	46	52	46	54	56	55	44	52	46	54	43	39	-37	-04	-30	23
Medical Illustrator	f	AI	51	54	54	43	42	43	48	53	56	43	42	43	20	38	35	-36	-49	-44
Medical Illustrator	m	AI	51	54	59	46	41	42	54	55	57	46	42	42	04	28	66	-07	-40	-38
Medical Technician	f	IC	51	52	45	48	47	52	47	51	48	49	46	52	30	22	-40	-02	-22	15
Medical Technician	m	IR	53	55	47	49	49	51	56	56	44	49	50	51	54	59	-13	13	-05	19
Medical Technologist	f	IRC	54	57	47	49	46	54	50	56	50	49	45	54	65	73	-06	04	-11	30
Medical Technologist	m	IR	55	57	49	51	46	52	58	58	46	50	47	52	74	79	10	17	-03	29
Minister	f	SA	51	52	55	60	45	45	47	51	57	61	44	45	03	28	52	69	04	05
Minister	m	SA	50	51	55	60	48	50	53	52	53	50	49	50	03	30	62	73	22	18
Musician	f	A	48	51	57	48	45	46	45	50	59	48	44	45	-22	05	55	-21	-62	-48
Musician	m	A	46	50	58	45	44	42	50	51	56	45	44	43	-31	-03	59	-31	-51	-52
Navy Enlisted Personnel	f	RC	56	48	47	52	50	55	52	47	50	52	49	55	68	31	-27	30	29	53
Navy Enlisted Personnel	m	RC	56	48	44	49	49	53	59	49	42	49	49	53	58	09	-52	-05	00	26

TABLE 6.2 (continued)

Occupational Scale	Sex	Code	Separate-sex-normed GOT mean for each Occupational Sample[a]						Combined-sex-normed GOT mean for each Occupational Sample[b]						Correlations between GOT Scales and Occupational Scales (decimal points omitted)[c]					
			R	I	A	S	E	C	R	I	A	S	E	C	R	I	A	S	E	C
NAVY OFFICER	f	RI	57	52	50	48	49	51	53	51	53	49	49	51	85	55	02	26	31	38
NAVY OFFICER	m	RIC	57	52	47	50	50	53	60	54	44	50	51	53	82	57	-11	23	30	43
NURSE, LPN	f	SC	48	48	45	53	48	52	45	46	48	53	47	51	07	-05	-35	30	-08	26
NURSE, LPN	m	SC	48	50	50	55	49	52	51	52	47	55	49	53	07	18	09	63	15	39
NURSE, RN	f	SI	51	53	50	55	48	48	47	52	53	55	48	47	31	55	28	73	11	17
NURSE, RN	m	ISR	52	53	50	53	48	49	56	54	47	53	48	49	42	55	11	53	10	25
NURSING HOME ADMINISTRATOR	f	CSE	47	49	46	53	53	56	44	48	49	53	52	56	06	01	-16	63	53	66
NURSING HOME ADMINISTRATOR	m	ESC	51	49	48	55	54	54	54	50	45	54	56	54	11	06	11	68	70	55
OCCUPATIONAL THERAPIST	f	SRI	54	52	51	54	46	46	54	51	54	54	45	45	55	48	22	52	-08	06
OCCUPATIONAL THERAPIST	m	SAR	53	51	54	55	46	44	50	52	51	55	46	44	16	31	52	45	-19	-19
OPTICIAN	f	EC	50	49	47	49	54	53	47	48	49	49	52	53	22	-06	-33	15	48	49
OPTICIAN	m	ER	53	50	48	48	54	50	57	51	45	48	55	51	38	02	-33	-15	32	18
OPTOMETRIST	f	IR	52	56	48	49	48	51	48	55	50	48	47	51	69	79	01	14	03	33
OPTOMETRIST	m	IR	51	55	49	48	47	49	55	56	46	48	48	50	55	77	06	-03	-13	10
PERSONNEL DIRECTOR	f	E	49	49	49	51	54	52	45	48	52	52	53	52	10	09	15	46	69	44
PERSONNEL DIRECTOR	m	ES	51	50	49	55	53	51	54	51	46	54	54	52	13	12	12	52	64	40
PHARMACIST	f	IC	50	55	47	49	48	52	47	54	50	49	47	51	43	52	-27	-07	-21	13
PHARMACIST	m	IE	50	54	46	50	52	51	54	54	44	49	52	51	45	51	-26	20	21	25
PHOTOGRAPHER	f	A	52	50	55	46	47	45	48	49	57	46	46	44	00	08	59	-29	-30	-56
PHOTOGRAPHER	m	A	51	49	55	46	47	44	55	50	52	46	48	45	-04	05	55	-34	-30	-59
PHYSICAL EDUCATION TEACHER	f	SR	56	50	44	57	48	52	52	49	47	57	47	52	55	18	-38	37	05	21
PHYSICAL EDUCATION TEACHER	m	SR	53	49	46	58	48	50	56	50	44	58	49	50	35	14	-23	56	06	19
PHYSICAL THERAPIST	f	IRS	53	54	49	53	45	47	49	53	52	53	44	46	48	51	01	22	-29	-05
PHYSICAL THERAPIST	m	IRS	54	54	49	54	47	48	57	55	46	53	47	48	52	58	04	36	-17	03
PHYSICIAN	f	I	52	58	51	50	42	47	49	57	54	50	41	46	38	68	07	-05	-48	-12
PHYSICIAN	m	IA	50	58	54	47	42	47	53	58	51	47	42	47	16	51	12	-17	-65	-24
PHYSICIST	f	IR	54	62	50	44	39	48	50	61	52	44	39	47	53	67	-01	-13	-36	09
PHYSICIST	m	IR	53	61	52	43	39	46	56	62	49	43	39	47	31	54	-01	-27	-59	-10
POLICE OFFICER	f	R	53	50	48	52	50	50	49	49	51	52	49	49	55	25	-20	28	29	21
POLICE OFFICER	m	R	54	49	46	51	49	48	57	50	44	51	50	49	43	10	-41	20	15	11
PSYCHOLOGIST	f	IA	49	57	53	50	44	46	45	56	56	50	43	46	20	60	28	-11	-37	-19
PSYCHOLOGIST	m	IA	46	56	55	47	43	45	50	57	52	47	43	45	-16	25	37	-29	-58	-48
PUBLIC ADMINISTRATOR	f	A	50	51	52	48	50	51	47	50	54	48	49	51	02	15	20	-13	13	-01
PUBLIC ADMINISTRATOR	m	AS	49	52	54	52	48	52	52	53	52	52	49	52	01	28	61	35	28	12
PUBLIC RELATIONS DIRECTOR	f	A	46	48	55	48	51	46	52	53	57	48	50	46	-24	-10	51	07	22	-16
PUBLIC RELATIONS DIRECTOR	m	A	45	46	56	49	49	46	48	47	57	49	50	46	-48	-32	45	05	10	-29
PURCHASING AGENT	f	EC	52	49	49	50	57	55	49	48	51	50	56	55	40	17	01	38	89	61
PURCHASING AGENT	m	EC	52	49	47	50	55	54	56	50	45	50	56	54	27	09	-14	29	75	54
RADIOLOGIC TECHNICIAN	f	RI	52	52	47	52	48	50	49	51	50	52	48	50	33	25	-29	17	-17	16
RADIOLOGIC TECHNICIAN	m	RI	53	53	48	50	48	50	56	54	45	50	49	50	55	48	-20	16	-05	25
REALTOR	f	E	47	46	48	51	62	52	44	45	51	51	61	52	-06	-18	04	39	77	34
REALTOR	m	E	50	49	49	50	59	51	53	50	46	50	60	52	14	-04	-01	30	85	39
RECREATION LEADER	f	SRE	53	51	52	57	51	49	50	50	55	57	50	49	45	39	33	72	48	35

(Continued)

TABLE 6.2 (continued)

Occupational Scale	Sex	Code	Separate-sex-normed GOT mean for each Occupational Sample[a]						Combined-sex-normed GOT mean for each Occupational Sample[b]						Correlations between GOT Scales and Occupational Scales (decimal points omitted)[c]					
			R	I	A	S	E	C	R	I	A	S	E	C	R	I	A	S	E	C
Recreation Leader	m	SE	51	48	49	55	50	50	54	49	46	55	51	50	17	12	23	61	43	22
Reporter	f	A	48	50	55	49	47	45	45	49	57	49	46	44	-09	18	70	08	-04	-30
Reporter	m	A	46	48	56	47	44	45	49	49	54	47	44	46	-42	-09	56	-16	-45	-46
Research & Development Manager	f	IR	54	59	48	45	47	51	50	58	51	45	46	50	61	73	-05	-15	-09	18
Research & Development Manager	m	IR	55	58	47	46	47	51	58	59	45	46	47	51	55	65	-07	-18	-17	10
Respiratory Therapist	f	IR	53	53	49	52	46	49	49	52	52	52	46	48	56	55	-06	18	-18	16
Respiratory Therapist	m	IRS	52	55	51	53	46	50	56	56	49	53	47	50	57	73	26	32	-11	17
Restaurant Manager	f	EC	50	48	48	50	57	54	46	46	51	51	56	54	17	-02	02	38	88	60
Restaurant Manager	m	E	49	45	46	48	55	51	52	47	44	48	56	51	-27	-59	-33	-12	46	07
School Administrator	f	SEC	50	52	50	57	53	53	47	51	53	58	52	53	13	25	36	67	52	37
School Administrator	m	SCE	52	52	49	59	54	55	55	53	46	58	55	56	28	29	21	76	59	54
Science Teacher	f	IRS	53	59	48	53	46	51	50	58	50	54	45	51	61	83	13	35	-04	30
Science Teacher	m	IR	54	58	47	52	45	49	57	58	45	52	46	50	53	70	08	18	-26	11
Secretary	f	C	47	45	47	51	52	57	44	43	50	51	51	57	-24	-52	-41	16	28	48
Social Science Teacher	f	S	48	49	51	55	49	51	45	48	53	55	48	51	11	32	41	59	36	38
Social Science Teacher	m	S	48	47	50	56	49	50	52	49	48	56	50	50	-08	05	40	71	31	21
Social Worker	f	SA	48	50	53	55	49	46	45	49	55	55	48	46	-12	09	41	65	08	-04
Social Worker	m	SA	48	50	53	57	47	47	51	51	51	57	47	47	-17	10	55	56	12	-04
Sociologist	f	IA	50	58	53	48	43	47	46	57	55	48	43	47	24	59	21	-06	-37	-05
Sociologist	m	IA	46	55	55	49	42	48	50	56	52	49	43	48	-05	45	54	02	-39	-14
Special Education Teacher	f	S	49	49	51	57	50	51	45	48	53	57	49	51	13	18	20	83	24	44
Special Education Teacher	m	S	52	50	52	58	50	49	55	51	49	57	50	49	22	31	38	80	16	30
Speech Pathologist	f	SIA	45	52	51	55	48	46	42	50	54	55	48	45	-21	12	47	64	03	-06
Speech Pathologist	m	SAI	48	53	53	54	46	46	51	54	51	54	47	47	-06	31	54	61	-05	-09
Store Manager	f	EC	48	47	50	51	58	52	44	46	52	51	57	52	-05	-26	08	27	79	37
Store Manager	m	EC	49	46	48	50	59	53	52	48	45	50	60	53	01	-20	00	26	81	38
Systems Analyst	f	IRC	55	57	49	46	47	53	51	56	52	46	47	53	67	72	01	-12	-08	32
Systems Analyst	m	IRC	53	55	48	46	48	54	56	56	46	46	48	54	60	68	-03	-09	00	40
Travel Agent	f	EC	47	47	50	48	56	53	44	46	52	48	54	52	-09	-25	-03	14	73	37
Travel Agent	m	E	46	45	49	47	52	51	50	46	46	47	53	52	-61	-67	-09	-05	30	00
Veterinarian	f	IR	55	56	48	45	43	46	51	55	50	45	43	46	55	59	01	-10	-34	-07
Veterinarian	m	RI	54	54	45	48	46	47	57	54	42	48	47	48	42	33	-33	-12	-33	-13
Vocational Agriculture Teacher	f	R	56	50	45	52	49	49	52	49	48	52	48	49	52	20	-40	14	-12	11
Vocational Agriculture Teacher	m	RCS	57	50	43	53	52	53	60	51	40	53	53	53	66	28	-41	28	09	31
YWCA Director	f	SE	51	50	50	59	52	52	47	49	53	59	51	52	30	27	18	85	52	45
YMCA Director	m	SE	50	49	49	62	53	51	53	50	47	62	54	51	12	11	21	81	50	35

[a]Female Criterion Samples were scored on GOT normed on the Women-in-General; male Criterion Samples on GOT normed on the Men-in-General.
[b]Female and male Criterion Samples were scored on the GOT normed on the General Reference Sample (300 women and 300 men).
[c]Correlations are based on the General Reference Sample (300 women and 300 men).

TABLE 6.3
Two-Week and Thirty-Day Test-Retest Correlations for Scores on the 1985 Occupational Scales

Scale	Sex	Test-retest correlation[a]	Test Mean	Test S.D.	Retest Mean	Retest S.D.	Test-retest correlation[b]	Test Mean	Test S.D.	Retest Mean	Retest S.D.
		Two-week statistics (N = 106 women, 74 men)					Thirty-day statistics (N = 35 women, 67 men)				
ACCOUNTANT	f	.93	28.7	12.5	28.9	12.0	.92	30.1	14.3	30.2	12.9
ACCOUNTANT	m	.92	21.9	12.9	22.1	12.0	.91	25.4	13.9	25.1	13.0
ADVERTISING EXECUTIVE	f	.89	31.2	10.4	31.5	10.7	.88	34.9	11.3	36.2	11.4
ADVERTISING EXECUTIVE	m	.93	35.6	12.4	35.0	12.2	.92	37.6	13.4	38.2	13.3
AGRIBUSINESS MANAGER	m	.94	25.3	10.9	25.5	11.2	.90	22.5	10.6	21.7	9.9
AIR FORCE ENLISTED PERSONNEL	f	.92	36.6	11.2	37.5	11.1	.91	28.3	11.4	28.6	11.7
AIR FORCE ENLISTED PERSONNEL	m	.93	32.7	11.3	32.9	11.1	.92	26.0	12.2	26.1	12.0
AIR FORCE OFFICER	f	.89	33.1	10.8	34.6	10.8	.89	36.7	12.6	37.8	12.9
AIR FORCE OFFICER	m	.94	23.6	13.8	24.5	13.8	.93	27.8	14.5	28.0	14.2
ARCHITECT	f	.95	25.5	14.8	26.2	15.2	.88	29.6	12.1	30.4	12.2
ARCHITECT	m	.90	29.1	12.8	28.5	13.3	.86	28.5	11.5	29.0	11.5
ARMY ENLISTED PERSONNEL	f	.87	36.6	11.2	39.0	12.0	.84	33.1	10.7	35.0	11.7
ARMY ENLISTED PERSONNEL	m	.91	30.9	11.9	32.3	11.9	.90	24.3	11.7	25.3	11.7
ARMY OFFICER	f	.88	35.4	10.8	37.2	11.6	.89	39.5	11.7	40.8	12.3
ARMY OFFICER	m	.92	24.4	11.9	25.0	12.1	.92	28.3	14.0	29.0	13.6
ART TEACHER	f	.92	10.1	18.8	11.5	19.1	.89	9.4	19.6	11.3	20.0
ART TEACHER	m	.94	27.9	14.2	27.7	14.3	.92	25.6	15.7	26.1	15.3
ARTIST, COMMERCIAL	f	.93	19.4	17.1	19.6	17.1	.90	20.2	14.8	20.5	14.7
ARTIST, COMMERCIAL	m	.90	31.8	12.4	30.9	12.9	.87	29.6	12.2	30.0	12.7
ARTIST, FINE	f	.92	27.7	13.7	26.7	14.4	.83	26.7	11.1	26.2	12.3
ARTIST, FINE	m	.91	30.0	13.6	28.7	14.5	.86	25.4	12.5	24.8	13.4
ATHLETIC TRAINER	f	.90	26.4	12.7	28.3	13.4	.86	22.2	14.4	22.8	14.2
ATHLETIC TRAINER	m	.89	28.7	10.8	29.0	10.8	.89	20.0	12.9	19.2	12.9
BANKER	f	.92	33.2	11.5	32.7	11.6	.90	31.8	10.8	31.4	10.4
BANKER	m	.89	22.8	10.7	23.2	11.2	.90	29.9	13.1	30.2	13.3
BEAUTICIAN	f	.93	38.1	10.9	38.1	11.4	.88	28.3	9.9	27.6	10.1
BEAUTICIAN	m	.94	38.3	11.4	38.9	11.2	.94	37.4	12.2	38.1	11.9
BIOLOGIST	f	.94	22.0	15.0	22.3	15.3	.90	21.9	14.0	21.4	14.0
BIOLOGIST	m	.90	30.1	11.7	29.3	12.6	.90	26.4	12.7	25.5	12.7
BROADCASTER	f	.93	32.4	11.1	33.4	11.5	.93	34.5	12.1	35.9	12.0
BROADCASTER	m	.91	36.8	10.4	36.0	10.5	.91	37.6	11.5	37.8	11.6
BUS DRIVER	f	.90	40.1	10.5	40.7	10.1	.90	34.3	10.0	34.8	10.1
BUS DRIVER	m	.92	39.8	9.1	39.7	9.5	.85	34.1	8.2	33.7	8.2
BUSINESS EDUCATION TEACHER	f	.93	18.0	13.2	18.6	13.2	.89	17.0	10.0	17.4	10.7
BUSINESS EDUCATION TEACHER	m	.93	22.8	12.5	23.8	13.0	.87	24.4	9.6	25.3	10.6
BUYER	f	.92	20.5	13.4	20.7	14.5	.88	20.9	14.4	22.0	14.9
BUYER	m	.92	29.9	12.8	29.8	12.9	.89	31.6	13.5	32.5	14.1
CARPENTER	f	.94	28.6	13.4	30.2	13.9	.86	27.4	12.3	28.6	12.6
CARPENTER	m	.92	27.6	12.8	28.8	13.3	.90	21.9	13.5	23.1	13.5
CHAMBER OF COMMERCE EXECUTIVE	f	.93	29.4	12.3	29.8	12.2	.89	30.3	9.9	30.7	10.3
CHAMBER OF COMMERCE EXECUTIVE	m	.91	17.9	12.4	18.3	13.0	.91	27.3	13.5	27.9	13.9
CHEF	f	.91	28.2	14.8	29.8	14.3	.84	21.9	13.7	22.7	14.2
CHEF	m	.86	26.5	14.7	27.6	14.4	.87	25.7	13.9	26.3	14.1
CHEMIST	f	.95	23.8	14.4	24.9	14.9	.92	25.2	14.2	25.6	13.7
CHEMIST	m	.92	21.2	14.0	21.4	14.6	.89	19.9	14.5	19.5	13.7
CHIROPRACTOR	f	.84	31.0	11.3	32.4	11.9	.84	29.8	11.2	30.3	11.7
CHIROPRACTOR	m	.87	30.7	14.3	31.6	14.3	.84	27.9	12.4	28.1	12.8
COLLEGE PROFESSOR	f	.91	35.1	9.9	34.7	10.3	.90	35.4	10.3	34.3	10.7
COLLEGE PROFESSOR	m	.90	36.6	9.8	36.4	10.7	.86	36.1	10.1	35.7	10.6
COMPUTER PROGRAMMER	f	.94	36.4	10.0	36.9	10.0	.92	35.8	11.1	36.1	10.6
COMPUTER PROGRAMMER	m	.93	33.8	11.4	34.0	11.4	.92	31.1	11.5	30.8	11.9
CREDIT MANAGER	f	.92	29.1	11.9	29.9	12.1	.86	29.1	10.5	29.7	11.1
CREDIT MANAGER	m	.92	25.9	12.7	27.7	13.3	.88	29.2	12.7	30.0	12.6
DENTAL ASSISTANT	f	.92	36.5	10.9	37.7	10.7	.90	28.6	10.9	28.8	11.4
DENTAL HYGIENIST	f	.89	36.8	10.9	38.1	11.0	.90	29.9	12.2	30.2	12.7
DENTIST	f	.92	34.2	13.2	35.7	13.8	.91	32.7	13.5	33.5	12.8

(*Continued*)

TABLE 6.3 (continued)

| Scale | Sex | Two-week statistics (N = 106 women, 74 men) | | | | | Thirty-day statistics (N = 35 women, 67 men) | | | | |
| | | Test-retest correlation[a] | Test | | Retest | | Test-retest correlation[b] | Test | | Retest | |
			Mean	S.D.	Mean	S.D.		Mean	S.D.	Mean	S.D.
DENTIST	m	.91	28.4	14.4	29.1	14.3	.86	25.1	13.6	25.1	12.6
DIETITIAN	f	.87	33.6	10.5	33.8	10.8	.79	32.9	10.6	33.3	10.5
DIETITIAN	m	.90	35.1	12.0	36.0	12.5	.85	35.0	10.7	36.1	11.4
ELECTED PUBLIC OFFICIAL	f	.91	22.9	12.9	23.6	14.3	.89	34.1	13.1	34.6	13.7
ELECTED PUBLIC OFFICIAL	m	.92	26.5	10.3	26.7	10.8	.92	33.6	12.0	33.9	12.3
ELECTRICIAN	f	.93	29.2	13.6	30.9	14.3	.90	30.0	12.7	31.9	12.7
ELECTRICIAN	m	.94	28.7	13.0	29.4	12.8	.91	22.4	13.0	22.9	12.8
ELEMENTARY TEACHER	f	.94	33.9	12.3	34.7	12.6	.92	27.8	11.3	28.2	12.3
ELEMENTARY TEACHER	m	.88	35.9	12.5	36.8	13.2	.84	30.6	13.6	29.9	14.0
EMERGENCY MEDICAL TECHNICIAN	f	.89	33.9	10.7	35.0	10.5	.89	27.5	12.2	27.3	12.7
EMERGENCY MEDICAL TECHNICIAN	m	.93	29.9	12.5	29.6	12.0	.92	24.6	12.1	23.7	12.3
ENGINEER	f	.95	29.9	14.0	31.3	14.6	.91	32.6	14.1	33.6	13.7
ENGINEER	m	.95	23.7	13.1	24.8	13.9	.93	23.5	13.6	24.0	13.2
ENGLISH TEACHER	f	.94	15.6	15.8	17.4	16.7	.89	20.9	15.5	22.1	15.9
ENGLISH TEACHER	m	.95	28.3	14.0	29.1	14.6	.93	31.4	14.5	32.2	14.0
EXECUTIVE HOUSEKEEPER	f	.89	34.2	10.2	35.6	10.6	.88	31.8	9.8	32.9	10.1
EXECUTIVE HOUSEKEEPER	m	.87	32.0	9.7	32.6	10.5	.83	35.1	9.0	36.4	10.5
FARMER	f	.93	36.2	8.5	36.2	8.6	.92	30.6	8.1	30.0	8.1
FARMER	m	.93	31.5	10.4	30.9	11.4	.90	26.5	9.8	25.0	9.8
FLIGHT ATTENDANT	f	.90	35.0	11.8	36.5	11.9	.84	32.3	11.7	33.9	11.6
FLIGHT ATTENDANT	m	.93	39.0	11.6	39.8	12.1	.90	40.0	10.7	41.4	11.6
FLORIST	f	.91	34.8	10.9	34.3	11.5	.89	29.0	10.2	29.1	9.9
FLORIST	m	.88	33.3	10.8	32.8	11.8	.85	31.2	10.7	31.2	10.5
FOOD SERVICE MANAGER	f	.94	37.9	9.7	37.8	9.7	.91	31.8	8.3	31.6	8.4
FOOD SERVICE MANAGER	m	.90	30.9	12.1	31.9	12.1	.85	32.5	10.2	33.5	11.3
FOREIGN LANGUAGE TEACHER	f	.91	18.7	14.6	19.5	15.5	.87	21.1	14.5	21.0	15.0
FOREIGN LANGUAGE TEACHER	m	.93	33.2	11.8	33.2	12.2	.91	34.5	12.0	34.8	12.1
FORESTER	f	.94	30.4	13.0	31.0	13.5	.90	27.0	12.6	27.0	12.3
FORESTER	m	.90	27.6	12.8	27.3	12.6	.89	23.3	11.1	22.5	10.6
FUNERAL DIRECTOR	f	.91	33.7	11.2	34.9	11.9	.87	33.1	9.2	34.7	10.5
FUNERAL DIRECTOR	m	.93	34.1	10.8	33.6	11.0	.88	31.2	10.3	30.6	10.1
GEOGRAPHER	f	.94	35.0	12.0	35.9	12.2	.93	38.2	12.0	38.2	11.9
GEOGRAPHER	m	.86	25.1	12.1	24.6	12.0	.86	27.2	12.5	26.7	13.0
GEOLOGIST	f	.95	26.9	14.9	28.1	14.8	.91	26.7	13.8	26.7	13.6
GEOLOGIST	m	.90	30.5	12.2	30.0	13.0	.90	26.2	11.7	25.3	12.4
GUIDANCE COUNSELOR	f	.93	29.3	13.2	29.6	14.0	.86	32.0	10.6	32.1	11.5
GUIDANCE COUNSELOR	m	.92	35.0	12.8	34.8	13.1	.85	35.9	11.2	35.7	11.8
HOME ECONOMICS TEACHER	f	.95	23.8	13.8	24.5	14.1	.92	21.1	12.1	20.9	12.8
HORTICULTURAL WORKER	f	.91	37.2	10.4	37.4	10.1	.88	31.2	10.6	30.5	10.1
HORTICULTURAL WORKER	m	.88	33.6	11.3	33.8	11.4	.88	27.0	11.1	26.8	11.4
INTERIOR DECORATOR	f	.90	16.1	12.0	16.2	12.7	.88	19.9	13.7	21.9	13.8
INTERIOR DECORATOR	m	.94	33.5	11.1	32.3	11.3	.92	32.9	11.6	33.1	11.7
IRS AGENT	f	.90	31.9	13.1	33.6	14.5	.83	38.3	12.9	39.8	13.9
IRS AGENT	m	.90	32.1	10.9	32.7	11.2	.86	33.0	10.6	33.8	10.8
INVESTMENTS MANAGER	f	.92	28.4	11.8	27.5	11.9	.88	34.6	13.0	33.6	13.5
INVESTMENTS MANAGER	m	.86	24.2	11.0	23.3	10.8	.85	28.3	12.8	27.8	13.0
LAWYER	f	.94	27.0	13.0	26.8	12.8	.94	35.2	14.3	35.6	15.0
LAWYER	m	.90	28.3	11.6	28.6	11.4	.92	35.7	13.8	36.0	13.7
LIBRARIAN	f	.88	22.7	13.4	23.1	13.5	.83	30.0	13.7	31.8	12.9
LIBRARIAN	m	.94	35.1	11.1	34.4	11.2	.92	37.0	12.2	37.5	11.9
LIFE INSURANCE AGENT	f	.90	23.4	10.9	24.8	12.1	.90	31.3	11.6	32.2	12.2
LIFE INSURANCE AGENT	m	.91	16.8	12.4	17.7	13.7	.88	23.2	12.9	24.4	13.2
MARINE CORPS ENLISTED PERSONNEL	f	.87	35.4	10.3	37.4	10.5	.87	31.4	11.2	32.4	11.7
MARINE CORPS ENLISTED PERSONNEL	m	.91	28.2	11.4	29.4	11.7	.90	23.7	12.5	24.8	12.7
MARKETING EXECUTIVE	f	.91	25.6	11.4	25.3	11.3	.86	33.5	12.3	33.7	12.5
MARKETING EXECUTIVE	m	.82	29.7	9.5	28.5	9.8	.82	34.9	12.1	34.1	12.6
MATHEMATICIAN	f	.94	22.0	15.0	22.4	14.9	.92	22.3	15.1	21.8	14.2

(Continued)

TABLE 6.3 (continued)

| Scale | Sex | Two-week statistics (N = 106 women, 74 men) | | | | | Thirty-day statistics (N = 35 women, 67 men) | | | | |
| | | Test-retest correlation[a] | Test | | Retest | | Test-retest correlation[b] | Test | | Retest | |
			Mean	S.D.	Mean	S.D.		Mean	S.D.	Mean	S.D.
MATHEMATICIAN	m	.88	23.2	12.4	22.1	12.7	.89	18.9	12.6	17.5	12.7
MATHEMATICS TEACHER	f	.93	29.6	12.0	30.5	12.4	.90	27.4	12.8	27.7	13.0
MATHEMATICS TEACHER	m	.91	29.0	10.3	29.2	9.8	.91	24.4	11.9	24.1	11.4
MEDICAL ILLUSTRATOR	f	.92	20.5	15.6	20.7	15.7	.87	17.6	13.8	18.0	14.0
MEDICAL ILLUSTRATOR	m	.93	21.0	16.4	21.5	16.6	.92	16.9	17.4	18.6	16.6
MEDICAL TECHNICIAN	f	.92	35.5	10.7	35.8	10.9	.91	27.0	11.6	26.7	11.0
MEDICAL TECHNICIAN	m	.91	27.8	13.1	28.7	14.0	.87	22.9	13.7	23.1	13.2
MEDICAL TECHNOLOGIST	f	.93	31.9	12.4	32.6	12.8	.92	29.0	13.9	30.0	13.0
MEDICAL TECHNOLOGIST	m	.93	29.3	12.0	30.6	13.2	.89	27.4	13.1	28.6	12.8
MINISTER	f	.94	19.4	14.4	19.6	15.2	.89	20.3	14.4	20.7	14.4
MINISTER	m	.94	30.3	12.8	31.0	14.2	.89	33.2	11.5	33.9	12.1
MUSICIAN	f	.94	34.6	12.5	34.6	12.9	.92	30.0	13.3	30.1	13.2
MUSICIAN	m	.93	38.6	11.6	38.0	11.9	.93	36.2	12.6	36.2	12.4
NAVY ENLISTED PERSONNEL	f	.89	38.6	9.9	40.3	9.8	.88	35.4	10.4	36.6	11.1
NAVY ENLISTED PERSONNEL	m	.93	30.4	12.0	30.6	12.1	.91	25.4	12.7	25.3	12.3
NAVY OFFICER	f	.88	35.0	10.7	36.8	11.0	.87	39.4	11.0	41.1	11.7
NAVY OFFICER	m	.91	25.2	12.3	26.6	13.0	.90	29.4	13.5	30.5	13.5
NURSE, LPN	f	.93	32.1	11.4	32.6	11.1	.92	22.1	11.0	21.6	11.3
NURSE, LPN	m	.90	36.6	10.5	37.2	10.8	.89	31.5	10.1	31.8	10.9
NURSE, RN	f	.89	34.1	12.6	34.9	13.3	.83	33.9	12.8	34.2	12.9
NURSE, RN	m	.89	32.3	11.4	33.4	12.2	.88	30.7	12.6	31.7	13.0
NURSING HOME ADMINISTRATOR	f	.91	30.2	11.3	31.0	11.6	.86	30.9	8.8	31.5	9.7
NURSING HOME ADMINISTRATOR	m	.90	33.2	11.9	33.9	12.6	.84	36.9	9.8	37.8	11.0
OCCUPATIONAL THERAPIST	f	.88	34.1	11.1	34.7	11.7	.89	31.8	14.0	31.5	13.6
OCCUPATIONAL THERAPIST	m	.92	33.7	11.7	33.4	12.2	.89	32.5	14.4	32.7	13.8
OPTICIAN	f	.86	36.7	10.7	38.0	10.9	.85	33.1	11.2	33.8	11.9
OPTICIAN	m	.86	35.8	10.5	36.2	10.3	.84	32.0	10.7	32.6	10.1
OPTOMETRIST	f	.92	40.3	11.4	41.3	11.9	.90	39.3	12.0	40.1	11.8
OPTOMETRIST	m	.91	33.2	13.9	34.3	14.3	.86	32.9	12.9	33.3	12.4
PERSONNEL DIRECTOR	f	.89	25.3	13.0	26.5	14.0	.87	36.0	12.8	37.3	13.9
PERSONNEL DIRECTOR	m	.93	25.1	12.9	26.0	13.9	.87	34.0	12.0	35.5	13.2
PHARMACIST	f	.92	38.5	11.6	38.9	11.7	.90	32.8	12.0	32.4	11.4
PHARMACIST	m	.90	29.7	11.3	29.4	11.7	.79	28.3	11.3	28.7	10.4
PHOTOGRAPHER	f	.94	33.1	12.7	33.8	12.8	.91	35.3	11.7	36.2	11.3
PHOTOGRAPHER	m	.92	34.8	12.3	34.4	12.6	.91	35.6	12.0	35.8	11.1
PHYSICAL EDUCATION TEACHER	f	.90	30.7	11.2	32.1	10.9	.88	25.0	13.0	23.8	13.2
PHYSICAL EDUCATION TEACHER	m	.88	20.6	14.1	21.7	14.6	.88	14.8	15.4	14.2	16.0
PHYSICAL THERAPIST	f	.90	36.2	12.0	36.1	11.7	.91	28.8	14.2	28.7	13.5
PHYSICAL THERAPIST	m	.89	30.9	13.0	31.6	13.0	.89	26.3	14.2	26.0	13.8
PHYSICIAN	f	.93	28.2	15.0	28.3	15.6	.91	27.7	14.1	27.0	13.9
PHYSICIAN	m	.91	29.7	13.5	29.4	14.2	.87	27.3	13.3	26.4	13.2
PHYSICIST	f	.94	15.2	16.4	16.1	16.5	.90	15.3	16.8	15.4	15.9
PHYSICIST	m	.92	15.4	15.3	15.2	16.1	.88	12.4	15.3	12.0	15.4
POLICE OFFICER	f	.88	37.8	11.0	39.6	11.4	.90	36.1	12.6	37.3	13.1
POLICE OFFICER	m	.90	29.2	12.4	29.8	12.3	.92	25.6	14.1	26.2	14.7
PSYCHOLOGIST	f	.91	25.4	12.8	24.7	12.8	.86	30.8	11.4	30.0	11.2
PSYCHOLOGIST	m	.88	28.2	12.6	27.5	12.9	.85	30.2	13.0	30.0	13.3
PUBLIC ADMINISTRATOR	f	.91	23.3	13.4	22.0	12.9	.91	32.6	14.3	32.7	15.6
PUBLIC ADMINISTRATOR	m	.92	28.6	12.8	29.2	14.0	.87	36.9	12.9	38.6	13.1
PUBLIC RELATIONS DIRECTOR	f	.93	17.9	13.6	18.5	14.2	.92	27.8	15.4	29.4	15.5
PUBLIC RELATIONS DIRECTOR	m	.94	23.9	13.5	23.5	13.5	.94	29.8	15.9	30.1	15.5
PURCHASING AGENT	f	.89	30.7	12.3	32.6	14.3	.88	38.9	12.8	40.7	14.0
PURCHASING AGENT	m	.90	25.4	11.3	25.9	12.3	.88	32.8	12.7	33.4	12.8
RADIOLOGIC TECHNOLOGIST	f	.89	38.2	10.3	38.9	10.2	.89	29.8	12.3	29.5	12.2
RADIOLOGIC TECHNOLOGIST	m	.90	33.1	12.3	33.7	12.7	.90	28.0	14.0	28.6	13.9
REALTOR	f	.90	19.9	12.7	21.1	13.8	.90	27.3	13.5	28.3	13.8
REALTOR	m	.90	26.7	9.9	27.9	11.3	.89	33.2	11.4	34.3	11.9

(Continued)

TABLE 6.3 *(continued)*

Scale	Sex	Two-week statistics (N = 106 women, 74 men)					Thirty-day statistics (N = 35 women, 67 men)				
		Test-retest correlation[a]	Test Mean	S.D.	Retest Mean	S.D.	Test-retest correlation[b]	Test Mean	S.D.	Retest Mean	S.D.
RECREATION LEADER	f	.92	37.3	11.9	38.4	13.0	.81	39.0	10.5	39.9	11.4
RECREATION LEADER	m	.91	33.4	12.4	33.9	12.9	.84	36.6	11.1	36.9	11.1
REPORTER	f	.94	23.9	15.1	24.7	14.8	.91	29.9	14.9	31.6	15.4
REPORTER	m	.93	31.7	12.4	31.3	12.5	.92	30.5	13.5	31.0	13.9
RESEARCH & DEVELOPMENT MANAGER	f	.94	26.4	14.3	27.6	14.5	.90	30.1	15.0	30.6	14.4
RESEARCH & DEVELOPMENT MANAGER	m	.94	19.1	14.4	19.6	15.0	.89	23.1	14.5	23.2	14.1
RESPIRATORY THERAPIST	f	.89	39.0	11.0	40.1	10.9	.89	31.8	13.4	32.4	12.8
RESPIRATORY THERAPIST	m	.90	35.6	12.7	36.2	13.8	.87	30.5	14.0	31.8	13.7
RESTAURANT MANAGER	f	.86	26.4	14.3	28.4	15.4	.87	33.6	14.2	35.3	15.7
RESTAURANT MANAGER	m	.87	30.0	10.8	29.3	11.4	.83	30.6	10.8	30.1	11.0
SCHOOL ADMINISTRATOR	f	.92	27.0	12.6	28.2	14.5	.84	35.3	11.7	36.4	12.8
SCHOOL ADMINISTRATOR	m	.92	29.6	11.7	31.0	13.4	.82	34.6	10.3	35.2	11.6
SCIENCE TEACHER	f	.92	26.6	13.9	28.2	15.3	.87	24.4	14.3	25.1	14.5
SCIENCE TEACHER	m	.92	29.6	11.5	30.7	12.3	.87	25.8	12.4	26.0	12.6
SECRETARY	f	.93	31.6	11.5	32.0	11.4	.88	27.9	9.2	28.3	9.5
SOCIAL SCIENCE TEACHER	f	.91	26.3	12.4	27.4	13.5	.86	32.8	11.2	33.6	11.8
SOCIAL SCIENCE TEACHER	m	.92	34.6	11.7	35.5	12.5	.87	37.0	11.2	36.8	11.7
SOCIAL WORKER	f	.90	29.6	12.2	29.3	13.1	.86	33.4	12.8	32.7	13.1
SOCIAL WORKER	m	.92	30.3	14.7	30.2	15.6	.89	34.9	15.4	35.2	15.5
SOCIOLOGIST	f	.92	19.8	13.0	20.2	12.9	.91	26.2	13.1	26.2	12.8
SOCIOLOGIST	m	.91	27.3	11.9	27.2	11.9	.89	30.3	12.2	30.5	12.0
SPECIAL EDUCATION TEACHER	f	.93	35.5	13.7	36.9	14.9	.86	31.9	12.1	32.5	12.9
SPECIAL EDUCATION TEACHER	m	.90	34.6	15.0	35.7	16.6	.83	34.2	14.7	34.1	15.6
SPEECH PATHOLOGIST	f	.90	28.8	13.5	29.1	14.5	.85	30.9	13.2	31.1	13.5
SPEECH PATHOLOGIST	m	.90	34.8	12.9	34.9	14.0	.86	35.6	13.2	35.9	13.3
STORE MANAGER	f	.90	29.0	10.9	29.9	11.6	.89	33.6	11.8	34.5	12.4
STORE MANAGER	m	.90	29.0	11.0	29.8	11.7	.88	34.0	11.7	34.9	12.6
SYSTEMS ANALYST	f	.93	35.2	11.4	35.9	11.8	.91	37.1	11.9	37.3	11.5
SYSTEMS ANALYST	m	.93	25.9	12.4	26.6	12.8	.91	29.7	12.9	30.0	12.5
TRAVEL AGENT	f	.85	24.9	10.9	26.6	11.9	.86	31.1	12.2	32.1	13.1
TRAVEL AGENT	m	.92	36.7	10.1	35.8	10.6	.89	37.7	9.8	37.3	10.1
VETERINARIAN	f	.93	31.4	13.6	32.0	13.5	.91	26.5	12.6	26.0	12.1
VETERINARIAN	m	.90	28.8	13.2	28.4	13.2	.89	21.7	12.1	20.0	11.6
VOCATIONAL AGRICULTURE TEACHER	f	.91	32.5	10.4	32.9	10.4	.86	26.7	10.5	26.0	10.3
VOCATIONAL AGRICULTURE TEACHER	m	.93	24.3	10.6	25.0	10.9	.85	20.7	9.9	20.4	9.8
YWCA DIRECTOR	f	.92	35.9	14.1	37.3	15.2	.80	39.5	11.5	40.1	12.2
YMCA DIRECTOR	m	.93	29.8	13.6	30.5	14.9	.86	33.2	11.8	33.3	11.9

[a]Median correlation = .92   [b]Median correlation = .89

Concurrent Validity

Concurrent validity is the power of a scale to discriminate between people concurrently in different occupations. Two types of validity information are relevant: first, the contrast between the Criterion (occupational) Samples and the Reference (MIG or WIG) Samples; second, the mean scores of occupations on each other's scales.

Percent overlap. The contrast between the Criterion and Reference Samples usually is expressed in terms of *percent overlap*, a statistic suggested by Tilton (1937). This statistic, which ranges from zero to 100 percent, gives the percentage of scores in one distribution (Criterion Sample) that are matched by scores in another distribution (Reference Sample). If the scale discriminates perfectly between the two samples, so that their distributions are entirely separated, the overlap is zero percent; if the scale does not discriminate at all and the

two distributions are identical, the overlap is 100 percent. Fig. 6.1 (p. 76) illustrates the distribution of scores for Women-in-General and female physicists on the f PHYSICIST scale; the overlap is 13 percent, which translates roughly into three standard deviations of separation between the samples.

Although the percent overlap can be calculated by actually counting the overlapping scores and converting the resulting figure to a percentage, Tilton provides a table that permits the calculation of this statistic by using the means and standard deviations of the two samples in the formula

$$Q = \frac{M_1 - M_2}{(SD_1 + SD_2)/2}$$

where M_1 and M_2 are the two mean scores and SD_1 and SD_2 are the two standard deviations. The index Q is used to enter Tilton's overlap table (Table 6.5) to determine

TABLE 6.4
Three-Year Test-Retest Correlations for Scores on the 1985 Occupational Scales

Scale	Sex	Test-retest correlation (median = .87)	Test		Retest	
			Mean	S.D.	Mean	S.D.
ACCOUNTANT	f	.89	32.7	14.2	33.5	14.6
ACCOUNTANT	m	.89	26.3	14.4	26.5	14.5
ADVERTISING EXECUTIVE	f	.90	32.2	11.5	32.5	12.2
ADVERTISING EXECUTIVE	m	.90	35.8	13.6	35.8	14.2
AGRIBUSINESS MANAGER	m	.90	22.9	11.5	22.6	11.9
AIR FORCE ENLISTED PERSONNEL	f	.87	30.2	12.0	29.2	12.8
AIR FORCE ENLISTED PERSONNEL	m	.91	28.0	12.9	27.3	13.7
AIR FORCE OFFICER	f	.87	37.1	13.0	37.8	12.7
AIR FORCE OFFICER	m	.92	27.2	15.7	27.2	16.0
ARCHITECT	f	.93	32.5	16.6	32.6	16.1
ARCHITECT	m	.87	30.8	14.0	31.0	13.5
ARMY ENLISTED PERSONNEL	f	.79	32.3	11.5	31.1	12.1
ARMY ENLISTED PERSONNEL	m	.82	25.2	11.6	24.5	11.8
ARMY OFFICER	f	.84	37.8	12.0	37.6	12.0
ARMY OFFICER	m	.87	27.0	13.4	27.0	13.6
ART TEACHER	f	.88	12.0	19.4	11.2	19.1
ART TEACHER	m	.91	26.2	16.9	25.6	17.2
ARTIST, COMMERCIAL	f	.91	20.2	17.7	19.9	18.5
ARTIST, COMMERCIAL	m	.87	31.0	13.4	31.3	13.7
ARTIST, FINE	f	.84	28.8	13.5	28.8	14.1
ARTIST, FINE	m	.86	27.9	14.7	28.0	14.8
ATHLETIC TRAINER	f	.88	23.6	12.0	22.8	14.7
ATHLETIC TRAINER	m	.86	22.1	11.8	20.4	12.6
BANKER	f	.85	31.7	11.4	32.4	11.0
BANKER	m	.86	27.7	12.9	28.6	13.9
BEAUTICIAN	f	.84	30.6	10.9	30.1	10.9
BEAUTICIAN	m	.93	35.3	11.7	35.5	12.2
BIOLOGIST	f	.93	28.3	17.4	28.4	17.3
BIOLOGIST	m	.90	31.7	13.8	31.8	13.7
BROADCASTER	f	.89	30.9	11.9	30.8	12.4
BROADCASTER	m	.88	35.7	11.8	35.6	12.5
BUS DRIVER	f	.87	35.6	10.3	35.3	10.8
BUS DRIVER	m	.85	34.3	8.6	34.4	9.1
BUSINESS EDUCATION TEACHER	f	.86	18.3	12.2	18.2	12.8
BUSINESS EDUCATION TEACHER	m	.84	24.9	11.2	24.8	11.5
BUYER	f	.84	17.9	14.4	18.7	14.2
BUYER	m	.89	26.5	14.0	26.7	14.1
CARPENTER	f	.88	29.6	15.4	29.5	15.1
CARPENTER	m	.90	22.8	14.6	22.3	15.1
CHAMBER OF COMMERCE EXECUTIVE	f	.88	28.2	11.9	28.8	12.2
CHAMBER OF COMMERCE EXECUTIVE	m	.88	22.1	13.8	23.5	14.8
CHEF	f	.79	26.5	13.6	25.9	12.7
CHEF	m	.75	26.1	13.9	25.4	14.2
CHEMIST	f	.93	30.6	17.7	30.6	17.3
CHEMIST	m	.93	26.3	18.3	26.4	18.0
CHIROPRACTOR	f	.77	33.4	10.7	32.7	11.9
CHIROPRACTOR	m	.75	29.3	13.1	28.2	12.9
COLLEGE PROFESSOR	f	.91	39.9	12.0	39.9	11.8
COLLEGE PROFESSOR	m	.87	39.6	12.3	39.6	11.6
COMPUTER PROGRAMMER	f	.93	39.4	12.8	39.3	13.3
COMPUTER PROGRAMMER	m	.93	35.1	14.1	34.6	14.7
CREDIT MANAGER	f	.85	30.3	12.4	31.2	12.6
CREDIT MANAGER	m	.85	27.5	14.0	27.3	14.3
DENTAL ASSISTANT	f	.90	30.6	11.4	29.6	12.2
DENTAL HYGIENIST	f	.86	30.8	10.8	30.1	11.6
DENTIST	f	.90	36.5	14.9	36.3	15.1
DENTIST	m	.84	29.0	13.5	28.3	14.5
DIETITIAN	f	.86	35.7	10.5	35.5	11.5

(Continued)

TABLE 6.4 (*continued*)

Scale	Sex	Test-retest correlation (median = 87)	Test		Retest	
			Mean	S.D.	Mean	S.D.
Dietitian	m	.81	36.4	11.9	36.9	11.8
Elected Public Official	f	.87	29.2	13.9	29.4	14.8
Elected Public Official	m	.90	29.8	12.4	29.8	13.4
Electrician	f	.90	31.5	15.1	30.9	15.2
Electrician	m	.92	24.3	14.6	23.3	14.8
Elementary Teacher	f	.90	30.3	13.2	29.6	12.6
Elementary Teacher	m	.82	33.0	14.4	30.8	14.2
Emergency Medical Technician	f	.87	29.7	11.7	28.4	12.8
Emergency Medical Technician	m	.90	24.9	12.0	24.2	12.9
Engineer	f	.92	35.7	16.1	36.0	16.1
Engineer	m	.94	28.7	16.3	29.2	16.8
English Teacher	f	.87	20.8	17.5	20.4	17.2
English Teacher	m	.89	31.6	16.0	31.5	15.7
Executive Housekeeper	f	.84	33.4	10.6	33.5	10.8
Executive Housekeeper	m	.74	33.6	9.1	33.4	8.8
Farmer	f	.91	33.5	9.5	33.7	9.8
Farmer	m	.87	28.7	10.1	28.3	10.6
Flight Attendant	f	.84	29.6	11.2	28.5	11.2
Flight Attendant	m	.85	37.1	10.6	37.0	11.4
Florist	f	.84	30.0	11.4	30.4	11.0
Florist	m	.82	31.0	11.5	31.6	10.6
Food Service Manager	f	.91	33.8	9.4	33.9	9.8
Food Service Manager	m	.73	32.1	10.9	32.3	10.9
Foreign Language Teacher	f	.84	21.8	16.3	21.2	15.2
Foreign Language Teacher	m	.90	36.1	14.2	35.5	13.3
Forester	f	.90	31.5	14.1	31.2	14.3
Forester	m	.87	29.3	12.7	28.9	13.5
Funeral Director	f	.82	32.9	10.4	33.2	11.1
Funeral Director	m	.88	28.9	11.6	28.8	11.8
Geographer	f	.90	41.3	14.3	41.3	13.6
Geographer	m	.87	30.3	15.2	30.7	14.5
Geologist	f	.93	31.5	16.7	31.2	16.9
Geologist	m	.89	31.3	13.9	30.8	14.0
Guidance Counselor	f	.86	30.9	13.0	30.0	12.8
Guidance Counselor	m	.87	33.7	13.0	32.7	12.3
Home Economics Teacher	f	.87	22.4	13.2	22.2	13.0
Horticultural Worker	f	.89	35.5	11.4	34.9	11.8
Horticultural Worker	m	.86	32.2	12.3	32.3	12.2
Interior Decorator	f	.86	17.9	13.9	19.4	14.7
Interior Decorator	m	.91	31.7	13.2	32.0	13.4
IRS Agent	f	.78	37.6	13.1	37.5	14.6
IRS Agent	m	.87	31.6	11.7	31.4	12.3
Investments Manager	f	.89	34.2	14.6	34.7	14.3
Investments Manager	m	.83	30.0	12.9	30.5	13.2
Lawyer	f	.91	33.1	13.7	33.1	14.5
Lawyer	m	.87	33.5	12.9	33.3	13.3
Librarian	f	.82	32.9	15.3	34.0	14.9
Librarian	m	.92	38.8	13.7	39.3	13.4
Life Insurance Agent	f	.87	27.6	12.9	27.6	13.4
Life Insurance Agent	m	.87	18.3	13.9	17.9	14.7
Marine Corps Enlisted Personnel	f	.85	32.2	12.0	31.8	12.6
Marine Corps Enlisted Personnel	m	.86	23.7	12.7	22.3	13.1
Marketing Executive	f	.88	31.5	13.6	32.3	13.7
Marketing Executive	m	.81	33.4	11.2	34.1	11.9
Mathematician	f	.95	28.8	18.1	28.5	17.5
Mathematician	m	.92	25.0	16.2	25.2	16.0
Mathematics Teacher	f	.90	31.8	13.2	31.2	14.4
Mathematics Teacher	m	.92	29.4	12.5	28.8	12.9
Medical Illustrator	f	.87	21.5	15.8	21.2	15.7

TABLE 6.4 (*continued*)

Scale	Sex	Test-retest correlation (median = .87)	Test		Retest	
			Mean	S.D.	Mean	S.D.
MEDICAL ILLUSTRATOR	m	.89	20.1	17.2	20.2	17.2
MEDICAL TECHNICIAN	f	.90	31.8	11.6	31.4	12.7
MEDICAL TECHNICIAN	m	.86	27.6	13.6	26.8	15.4
MEDICAL TECHNOLOGIST	f	.91	34.0	14.8	33.7	15.6
MEDICAL TECHNOLOGIST	m	.88	31.8	13.9	31.2	14.9
MINISTER	f	.86	20.3	15.5	19.5	14.8
MINISTER	m	.86	33.2	12.6	32.5	12.3
MUSICIAN	f	.89	32.7	13.7	32.9	14.0
MUSICIAN	m	.90	37.3	13.5	36.9	13.7
NAVY ENLISTED PERSONNEL	f	.86	35.4	11.1	34.8	11.6
NAVY ENLISTED PERSONNEL	m	.90	27.8	13.3	27.7	13.9
NAVY OFFICER	f	.84	39.4	11.1	39.7	11.0
NAVY OFFICER	m	.90	29.5	13.8	29.3	14.2
NURSE, LPN	f	.92	26.2	12.1	26.1	12.6
NURSE, LPN	m	.84	32.2	10.9	31.8	10.9
NURSE, RN	f	.82	33.8	12.0	31.9	12.4
NURSE, RN	m	.80	31.1	10.7	29.9	11.7
NURSING HOME ADMINISTRATOR	f	.84	30.8	10.7	31.1	11.5
NURSING HOME ADMINISTRATOR	m	.81	33.2	11.4	32.9	11.8
OCCUPATIONAL THERAPIST	f	.84	33.2	12.9	31.9	12.8
OCCUPATIONAL THERAPIST	m	.85	33.0	13.4	32.0	13.6
OPTICIAN	f	.83	33.7	12.2	34.0	12.1
OPTICIAN	m	.82	31.3	11.3	31.7	11.5
OPTOMETRIST	f	.88	41.9	12.3	41.5	13.2
OPTOMETRIST	m	.87	36.6	13.9	36.3	14.9
PERSONNEL DIRECTOR	f	.84	30.6	13.6	31.1	14.6
PERSONNEL DIRECTOR	m	.85	28.5	13.6	28.8	14.0
PHARMACIST	f	.92	36.7	12.3	36.1	13.4
PHARMACIST	m	.84	30.1	11.0	29.2	12.3
PHOTOGRAPHER	f	.86	34.9	13.0	35.0	13.5
PHOTOGRAPHER	m	.86	34.4	12.7	34.0	13.0
PHYSICAL EDUCATION TEACHER	f	.89	27.4	13.3	25.7	13.9
PHYSICAL EDUCATION TEACHER	m	.83	16.0	14.0	13.9	14.9
PHYSICAL THERAPIST	f	.91	33.7	13.2	32.5	14.0
PHYSICAL THERAPIST	m	.88	27.8	13.3	26.1	13.7
PHYSICIAN	f	.91	32.2	15.8	31.7	15.8
PHYSICIAN	m	.90	32.0	15.0	31.7	14.7
PHYSICIST	f	.94	21.9	20.8	22.2	20.2
PHYSICIST	m	.93	19.5	20.1	19.3	19.6
POLICE OFFICER	f	.89	34.0	13.1	32.8	12.7
POLICE OFFICER	m	.90	23.8	13.6	22.4	13.3
PSYCHOLOGIST	f	.89	32.8	14.2	32.0	13.9
PSYCHOLOGIST	m	.87	32.2	15.2	31.8	15.3
PUBLIC ADMINISTRATOR	f	.87	29.6	14.1	30.4	14.4
PUBLIC ADMINISTRATOR	m	.86	33.7	12.6	33.9	13.3
PUBLIC RELATIONS DIRECTOR	f	.90	24.0	14.5	25.3	15.3
PUBLIC RELATIONS DIRECTOR	m	.91	25.7	15.7	26.5	16.1
PURCHASING AGENT	f	.81	35.4	12.6	35.5	13.7
PURCHASING AGENT	m	.84	30.2	12.4	30.1	13.2
RADIOLOGIC TECHNOLOGIST	f	.90	32.8	11.8	31.5	12.1
RADIOLOGIC TECHNOLOGIST	m	.88	30.4	12.6	30.0	13.6
REALTOR	f	.89	23.1	14.8	23.4	15.4
REALTOR	m	.90	28.5	12.4	28.7	12.8
RECREATION LEADER	f	.81	36.0	10.5	35.2	10.7
RECREATION LEADER	m	.85	32.7	11.6	32.3	11.6
REPORTER	f	.85	28.5	14.8	28.5	14.7
REPORTER	m	.84	31.3	13.9	31.2	13.7
RESEARCH & DEVELOPMENT MANAGER	f	.92	34.3	17.6	34.8	17.5
RESEARCH & DEVELOPMENT MANAGER	m	.93	25.8	17.9	26.2	17.6

(*Continued*)

TABLE 6.4 (*continued*)

Scale	Sex	Test-retest correlation (median = .87)	Test Mean	Test S.D.	Retest Mean	Retest S.D.
RESPIRATORY THERAPIST	f	.90	35.8	12.8	34.7	13.7
RESPIRATORY THERAPIST	m	.84	33.5	14.1	31.8	15.1
RESTAURANT MANAGER	f	.81	30.2	14.9	31.4	15.3
RESTAURANT MANAGER	m	.81	27.3	12.3	27.1	12.4
SCHOOL ADMINISTRATOR	f	.82	32.5	12.3	32.0	12.8
SCHOOL ADMINISTRATOR	m	.80	32.1	11.0	31.3	11.5
SCIENCE TEACHER	f	.86	29.7	14.2	28.7	15.2
SCIENCE TEACHER	m	.88	30.9	13.3	30.0	13.4
SECRETARY	f	.88	28.7	11.7	29.0	11.5
SOCIAL SCIENCE TEACHER	f	.82	32.2	11.5	31.7	12.2
SOCIAL SCIENCE TEACHER	m	.86	34.1	12.1	33.5	12.0
SOCIAL WORKER	f	.83	29.8	13.8	28.2	13.8
SOCIAL WORKER	m	.88	30.9	15.9	30.0	15.5
SOCIOLOGIST	f	.90	28.6	15.7	29.1	14.9
SOCIOLOGIST	m	.89	31.5	14.4	31.7	13.2
SPECIAL EDUCATION TEACHER	f	.86	32.8	13.9	31.2	13.2
SPECIAL EDUCATION TEACHER	m	.80	33.8	15.9	31.7	15.0
SPEECH PATHOLOGIST	f	.87	30.2	15.0	28.9	14.5
SPEECH PATHOLOGIST	m	.83	34.4	14.8	32.9	14.2
STORE MANAGER	f	.83	29.7	12.0	29.8	11.4
STORE MANAGER	m	.85	29.4	11.8	29.8	11.9
SYSTEMS ANALYST	f	.93	40.5	14.4	40.3	14.4
SYSTEMS ANALYST	m	.92	33.2	15.5	33.8	16.3
TRAVEL AGENT	f	.84	27.6	12.7	28.4	13.9
TRAVEL AGENT	m	.86	35.4	11.4	35.9	11.6
VETERINARIAN	f	.90	31.8	14.3	31.0	14.6
VETERINARIAN	m	.86	27.1	12.8	26.0	13.8
VOCATIONAL AGRICULTURE TEACHER	f	.88	31.1	10.8	30.2	11.8
VOCATIONAL AGRICULTURE TEACHER	m	.88	24.3	11.9	23.8	12.9
YWCA DIRECTOR	f	.82	35.1	12.4	33.3	12.8
YMCA DIRECTOR	m	.85	29.1	12.6	28.5	12.8

the percent overlap of the two distributions. The use of this formula assumes that the two distributions are normally distributed, although we have found from experience that the formula is quite robust even with skewed distributions.

The Q index is essentially a measure of the number of standard-deviation units separating the two distributions; as such, it reflects the magnitude of the difference. Table 6.5 shows the amount of separation, in terms of standard-deviation units, that is associated with various levels of percent overlap. For example, a Q index of 2.00, associated with a percent overlap of about 32, represents a separation of two standard deviations between the distributions, an enormous separation by the usual standards of psychological research. For some perspective with other measures, it is worth noting that two standard deviations correspond roughly to differences of 30 IQ points, or 6 inches in height, or 1.8 grade points (on a four-point scale), or the difference between the 16th and 86th percentiles.

Percent overlaps for the SCII Occupational Scales are given in Table 6.1 (above). The median overlap for both the women's and the men's scales is 36 percent. This degree of overlap is associated with a Q index of 1.83, which means that the scales are separating the Criterion Samples from the Reference Samples by slightly less

than two standard deviations, on the average. The best scale in this respect is the female PHYSICIST scale, which has an overlap of only 13 percent (Q index = 3.03) between the Criterion Sample and the WIG; the best male scale is MEDICAL ILLUSTRATOR, which has an overlap of only 15 percent (Q index = 2.88) between the Criterion Sample and the MIG. The poorest scales are the male and female OPTOMETRIST, female FUNERAL DIRECTOR, and female PURCHASING AGENT scales, all with overlaps of 53 percent (Q index = 1.26) between the Criterion Sample and the WIG or MIG sample, indicating that the Criterion Samples representing these occupations are less homogeneous than the other samples and are therefore harder to separate from the Reference Sample.

This wide range of percent overlap indicates that the scales vary considerably in their validities. Scales with the highest validities (the lowest overlaps) are usually those for occupations that are tightly defined and quite distinct from most other occupations, as is the case with medical illustrators, physicists, chemists, and interior decorators. Scales with low validities (high overlaps) are usually those for occupations that are not as well defined.

Mean scores of occupations on each other's scales. Another important type of concurrent-validity information is the mean scores of the occupational samples on

TABLE 6.5
Tilton Percent–Overlap Table
(See text for derivation of Q index)

Q	Percent overlap	Q	Percent overlap	Q	Percent overlap	Q	Percent overlap
0.00	100	0.63	75	1.35	50	2.30	25
0.02	99	0.66	74	1.38	49	2.35	24
0.05	98	0.69	73	1.41	48	2.40	23
0.08	97	0.72	72	1.44	47	2.45	22
0.10	96	0.74	71	1.48	46	2.51	21
0.12	95	0.77	70	1.51	45	2.56	20
0.15	94	0.80	69	1.54	44	2.62	19
0.18	93	0.82	68	1.58	43	2.68	18
0.20	92	0.85	67	1.61	42	2.74	17
0.23	91	0.88	66	1.65	41	2.81	16
0.25	90	0.91	65	1.68	40	2.88	15
0.28	89	0.94	64	1.72	39	2.95	14
0.30	88	0.96	63	1.76	38	3.03	13
0.33	87	0.99	62	1.79	37	3.11	12
0.35	86	1.02	61	1.83	36	3.20	11
0.38	85	1.05	60	1.87	35	3.29	10
0.40	84	1.08	59	1.91	34	3.39	9
0.43	83	1.11	58	1.95	33	3.50	8
0.46	82	1.14	57	1.99	32	3.62	7
0.48	81	1.17	56	2.03	31	3.76	6
0.51	80	1.20	55	2.07	30	3.92	5
0.53	79	1.23	54	2.12	29	4.11	4
0.56	78	1.26	53	2.16	28	4.34	3
0.58	77	1.29	52	2.21	27	4.65	2
0.61	76	1.32	51	2.25	26	5.15	1

Source: J. W. Tilton, "The Measurement of Overlapping," *Journal of Educational Psychology*, 28: 656–60.

each other's scales. Because these data are so voluminous, they are not included in this *Manual*; a table of mean scores for 207 occupational samples on 207 scales would have to include 42,849 numbers.

The mean scores for the SCII scales follow the same pattern as the earlier SVIB means, which are reported in the *Handbook for the SVIB*. Mean scores for the various occupations on a given Occupational Scale tend to be normally distributed around the General Reference Sample mean, and range roughly across 30 to 40 scale points, that is, three to four standard deviations.

Predictive Validity

The predictive validity of an Occupational Scale is the scale's power to distinguish between people who will eventually enter different occupations—to distinguish, for example, between students who will become bankers and those who will become artists or farmers. This is an important attribute, because the inventory is generally used to help make long-term decisions; thus it is important that there be data to support the long-range predictive power of these scales.

Strong's studies of validity. The SVIB has a long history of research on predictive validity, beginning with E. K. Strong's attempts in the 1930's. He believed intensely in the value of empirical data, and very early he began collecting longitudinal data to use in studying the practical usefulness of his inventory. During the year following initial publication of the inventory (1927),

Strong administered it to the senior class of Stanford University; five years later he asked these students, in a survey (see Table 6.6), which occupations they had entered, to determine if the inventory had accurately predicted their career choices. The results were published in the *Journal of Educational Psychology* in 1935 under the title, "Predictive Value of the Vocational Interest Test" (Strong, 1935). In this report (p. 334), Strong grappled (as every investigator has since) with the issue of what constitutes predictive validity:

Determination of the validity of a vocational test is fraught with many difficulties. What should be the criterion? At first thought "final vocational choice" appears to be the only ultimate criterion in guidance. But. . . . one cannot assume that every man [or woman] eventually enters the occupation for which he [or she] is best fitted. If this were true there would be no great need for vocational tests. . . . Because final occupational choice cannot be accepted as a perfect criterion, it necessarily follows that a vocational test which correlates perfectly with final occupational choice is as faulty as the present system of finding one's livelihood.

This fact is of crucial importance in understanding why the SVIB, or the SCII, or any other interest inventory, cannot, by the nature of the problem, approach perfect predictive validity.

Strong concluded, however, that a substantial relationship should exist between scores on his test and eventual occupational choice, and he argued that the following four propositions, if true, would constitute persuasive evidence of high validity:

1. People continuing in occupation X should obtain higher interest scores on the scale for X than they do on scales for any other occupations.

2. Interest scores *on scale X* should be higher for people continuing in occupation X than for people in occupation Y.

3. Interest scores *on scale X* should be higher for people continuing in occupation X than for people who change from X to occupation Y.

4. People changing from occupation Y to occupation X should have scored higher on the X scale *prior to the change* than they scored on the Y scale.

Strong used the results of his five-year follow-up of Stanford seniors to evaluate the inventory on these four propositions and concluded, as summarized in the 1938 *Manual* for the Strong: "The first three propositions are true with respect to averages but, of course, there were some individual exceptions. . . . The fourth proposition is approximately true."

Several years later Strong studied the predictive validity of the test for these students and several hundred of their peers (combined *N*: 524) over a longer time period and reported the results in his book *Vocational Interests 18 Years After College* (Strong, 1955). In general, his results supported the propositions he had advanced 20 years earlier.

Validity studies since Strong. Following Strong's lead, a number of other investigators have conducted studies of the validity of the inventory over long time periods (see Table 6.6). The usual paradigm is to test a group of students, put the data away, let several years pass, locate the students, ascertain their current occupations (and their perseverance, satisfaction, and success in those occupations), then study the degree of correspondence between their earlier scores and their current occupations. The basic finding of these studies is that there is a substantial relationship between high scores on the Occupational Scales and eventual occupation entered. Depending on how the hit rate is calculated, between one-half and two-thirds of all college students enter occupations that are predictable from their earlier scores.

The level of accuracy is influenced, as one might suppose, by various external factors. McArthur (1954), for example, showed that Harvard students from homes of high socioeconomic status (and private schools) are less predictable than are other Harvard students (those from public schools): the former are more likely to enter occupations dictated by the family fortunes, such as banking or trusteeships, than they are to follow their own interests—sometimes, according to McArthur's observations, to the considerable detriment of their occupational satisfaction. Campbell (1966a) showed that predictability is higher for students who have well-defined interest patterns, an outcome that also appeared in Strong's 18-year follow-up of Stanford students. Brandt and Hood (1968), using the files of the Counseling Service at the University of Iowa, demonstrated that students with severe emotional problems are less predictable than normal students. Harmon (1969) has provided evidence showing that, for women making a career commitment outside of the home, measured interests are as predictive of career choices as they are for men. Swanson and Hansen (1985) found that academic comfort is a moderator variable of the predictive validity of the Strong for college-major choices; those students with high scores (≥56) on the ACADEMIC COMFORT scale were twice as likely to choose majors predicted by their Strong profile as were those students with low (≤35) scores on the ACADEMIC COMFORT scale. They also found (Hansen & Swanson, 1983) that the predictive validity of the Strong for choosing a college major increases if the students are satisfied with their college experience and is greater for those students whose interests were most stable during the 3 1/2-year test-retest interval.

In general, these studies support Strong's original proposition that measured interests are predictive of occupational choice; and, they extend his original work by documenting situations in which the predictive validity is higher or lower than average.

One of the last predictive-validity studies on the SVIB—before its conversion to the merged-sex form—was conducted using subjects who had been students at the University of Missouri. Dolliver, Irvin, and Bigley (1972) searched the files of the Testing and Counseling Service for SVIB's completed at least nine years earlier and found 1,000 men who had been tested, on the average, 12 years earlier. They managed to collect follow-up data from 130 of them who were in occupations for which the SVIB had a corresponding Occupational

Scale. (They actually received data from 220 men; 90 were in occupations with no SVIB scale.) Using classification methods developed by McArthur (1954), they classified these men into three categories according to the predictive level of their earlier scores.

Their results are reported in Table 6.6, which also includes the results from several of the predictive-validity studies just discussed. The data in the first row of Table 6.6 were taken from Strong's 18-year follow-up of Stanford students: Excellent Hits were those with standard scores of 45 or above on the scale for the occupation they ultimately entered; Moderate Hits were standard scores of 40-44; and Poor Hits were scores of 39 or below. As mentioned above, McArthur (1954) split his sample of Harvard students into students from private and public high schools. Brandt and Hood (1968) studied two groups, normal and deviant (so classified on the basis of their MMPI profiles).

Scanning the table gives a general picture of the level of predictive accuracy one can expect: the Excellent and Moderate Hit rate centers around 65 percent, from McArthur's high of 61 percent for predicting job entry to Dolliver et al.'s low of 54 percent. The results, though ranging over 20 percentage points, are *relatively* consistent, especially given the variability in age of the subjects when tested, purpose of testing, particular techniques of investigators, percent of earlier sample reassessed, and variability of classification techniques. All things considered, the hit rate looks to be about 65 percent.

In an extension of this work, Dolliver and Kunce (1973) identified another source of error in validity studies that depend on following up individuals over time—that is, the characteristics of people who choose not to cooperate with the researcher. They asked the question, "Who drops out of an SVIB follow-up study?" then answered it using data from the original testing of these dropouts. "We found [that] those in intellectual occupations and those with the most accurate SVIB results show greater likelihood of dropping out. . . . Those for whom the [earlier] SVIB was most accurate did not make themselves available for further study." Their data thus suggest that the level of predictive accuracy reported by follow-up studies is a conservative estimate of true validity.

Validity studies based on the SVIB-SCII. Most predictive-validity studies for the Strong are based on initial and follow-up testing with the older forms of the SVIB. However, Spokane (1979) examined the predictive validity of the 1974 SCII for college women and men over a 3 1/2-year span. Excellent and Moderate predictive validity was found for 59 percent of the females and 71 percent of the males. Spokane also found that students who stated interests consistent with their measured interests reported higher levels of job satisfaction.

Occupational entry or expressed occupational choice usually is identified as the criterion for prediction for the Strong. The usefulness of the 1981 Strong in exploring college majors was examined in a study that also considered concurrent validity, differential validity for females and males, and the moderating effect of interest stability

TABLE 6.6
Summary of SVIB and SVIB-SCII Predictive-Validity Studies:
Percentages of Sample Falling in Three Hit Categories

Study[a]	Sex	N	Study span (years)	Hit category (and standard scores)		
				Excellent hits (≥45)	Moderate hits (40–44)	Poor hits (≤39)
Strong (direct scale)	m	524	18	48%	18%	34%
McArthur (total sample)	m	60	14	45	20	35
McArthur (public school)	m	31	14	61	13	26
Brandt and Hood (total)	m	259	7	47	20	33
Brandt and Hood (normals)	m	129	7	56	16	28
Dolliver et al. (total sample)	m	130	12	42	12	46
Spokane (direct scale)	f	120	3½	42	17	41
Spokane (direct scale)	m	236	3½	59	12	29
Hansen and Swanson (total sample)	f	245	3½	44	14	42
Hansen and Swanson (total sample)	m	183	3½	38	26	36
Hansen and Swanson (satisfied)	f & m	130	3½	51	20	29
Hansen and Swanson (unsatisfied)	f & m	298	3½	38	15	47
Hansen and Swanson (stable profiles)	f & m	95	3½	59	7	34
Hansen and Swanson (unstable profiles)	f & m	88	3½	24	16	50
Swanson and Hansen (high AC scores)	f & m	115	3½	50	17	33
Swanson and Hansen (low AC scores)	f & m	64	3½	27	9	64

[a]See text for an explanation of the parenthetical qualifications.

on predictive validity (Hansen & Swanson, 1983). The validity hit rates were similar to those reported in previous studies, indicating that the Strong can be used with confidence for choosing a college major. Also, entry into both *direct* majors (those with a major clearly represented by an Occupational Scale, e.g., psychology, geography, social work), and *indirect* majors (those not clearly represented, e.g., industrial relations, art history, music therapy) were predictive. This finding is especially important, since no interest-inventory profile can provide a scale to measure interests in every occupation or major. Thus, generalizing beyond the profile with the related scales expands the usefulness of the instrument. The results, summarized in Table 6.6, also showed that the Strong is more predictive for students who are satisfied with their majors or who have stable interests during their college careers. Finally, the results suggest that as the number of Occupational Scales developed on female Criterion Samples has increased with each revision (57 scales in 1974, 76 in 1981, 105 in 1985), the predictive validity of the Strong for women has improved slightly. Thus, predictive-validity hit rates for the merged-sex form of the Strong compare favorably with the older SVIB hit rates, which averaged around 65 percent.

Predictive accuracy among Black students. Racial differences in interests have not been a problem with interest inventories, for no appreciable differences have been identified. An important study of predictive accuracy for Blacks tested with the earlier SVIB Occupational Scales was reported by Borgen and Harper (1973). They compared predictive accuracy for White and Black students who had been winners of the National Achievement and National Merit Scholarships and concluded

that "membership in career groups was predicted at least as well for these able Blacks as it was for the Whites." Nor is that finding restricted to high academic achievers: in a study of vocational high school students, Barnette and McCall (1964) reported no differences between Blacks and Whites.

Predictive validity and the Basic Interest Scales. Another study related to the predictive validity of the Occupational Scales was published by Johnson and Johansson (1972). They reanalyzed data from earlier studies of male students who had had high scores on either the LIFE INSURANCE AGENT or PHYSICIST scales. Ten years later, about 75 percent of these students were in occupations related to their earlier profiles. But what was more revealing was that whether a student with a high score on an Occupational Scale went directly into that occupation or into a related occupation was influenced considerably by his score on the appropriate Basic Interest Scale. For example, a student with a high score on the LIFE INSURANCE AGENT scale and a high score on the SALES Basic Interest Scale was likely to become a salesman; another student, with the same score on the LIFE INSURANCE AGENT scale but a low score on the SALES scale (which meant that his common interests with salesmen were in areas other than sales), was more likely to enter a related occupation, such as advertising.

The principal result of their study was to show that the more consistency there is between scores on the Occupational Scales and scores on the Basic Interest Scales, the more specific (and more confident) the counselor can be in predicting outcomes from the profile. Chapter 5 of the *Manual* and Chapter 11 of the *User's Guide* discuss the issue of consistency (or inconsistency) further.

Unpredictable Scales

One anomaly in working with empirical scales is that they do not always behave predictably. If several scales are constructed under precisely the same rules for item selection, weighting, and norming, then the scales should operate in similar fashion—yet often they do not. Their validities, as measured by percent overlap between samples, sometimes vary markedly; their reliabilities also vary, though they usually are more consistent, given equal scale length, than are the validities. When this variation between scales constructed by similar items is combined with the variations created by differing numbers of items per scale and differing levels of item validity, the result is a broad range in characteristics across the total set of scales.

The most noticeable variation from one Occupational Scale to another is in the population mean—that is, the average score earned on an Occupational Scale by people not in that occupation. In every form of the inventory, there have been scales with high population means. On the 1938 men's form, for example, it was the FARMER scale—over 50 percent of high school senior boys scored at or above the mean of farmers. Other scales with high population mean scores were the REAL ESTATE SALESMAN scale, which had the greatest overlap with Men-in-General of any scale on the profile, and MUSICIAN-PERFORMER, a scale on which the majority of liberal arts students scored high. On the 1946 women's form, it was the ELEMENTARY TEACHER and SECRETARY scales; high scores for young women were common on these scales. On the 1966 men's form, the PHYSICAL THERAPIST and COMPUTER PROGRAMMER scales showed many more high scores than the other scales, and on the 1969 women's form, the same was true for the ARMY OFFICER and NAVY OFFICER scales. Much of what is known as "shrewd, clinical interpretive skill" comes from knowing about and having a reasonable explanation for these high population means.

Though good counselors learn to overcome, and even profit by, these aberrations, we should not forget that that is exactly what they are—aberrations. We do not intend that the scales behave differently; they just do, and we have to learn to deal with their idiosyncrasies. Why scales with apparently similar items have different scale characteristics is something that remains unexplained.

Additional information on the interpretation of the Occupational Scales is given in Chapter 10 and in many chapters of the *User's Guide*.

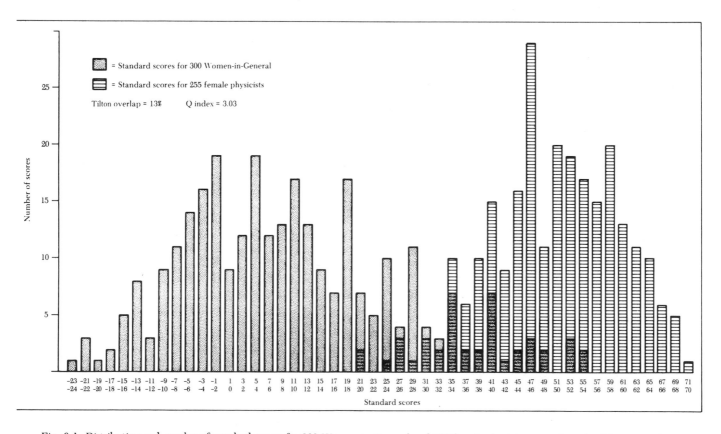

Fig. 6.1. Distribution and overlap of standard scores for 300 Women-in-General and 255 female physicists scored on the f PHYSICIST scale.

CHAPTER SEVEN

Research on Women's and Men's Measured Interests

The SVIB-SCII is designed for use by both women and men. Historically, beginning with the men's form published in 1927 and the women's in 1933, the interests of the two sexes were analyzed separately. Two reasons may be cited for Strong's decision to make that enduring distinction: first, the item responses of women and men were different in the 1930's; second, the employment patterns of women and men differed markedly, not only in the large number of women in the housewife-mother role but also in the radically different distribution of the sexes in most occupations. Given these two factors, the provision of a single inventory seemed inappropriate.

For nearly four decades, dissatisfaction with this system was minimal, though Strong himself was always eager for people to undertake research on the women's form. For its part, the counseling profession never really settled upon a philosophy for handling the two forms: some counselors, for example, used the men's form with career-oriented women. Moreover, the dual system was cumbersome: for example, a researcher testing a group of 20 women and 20 men was forced to choose among giving everybody one form, eliminating one sex from the sample, or using two different forms with two small subsamples.

More profound concerns began to merge in the 1960's. As attention focused on the inequalities of the sex roles, and as pressures increased on institutions and programs that were continuing to separate the sexes artificially, the necessity and wisdom of two separate systems was questioned more often, and more vigorously.

One of the main goals in developing the 1974 SCII and in constructing the 1985 SCII was to eliminate completely any differential treatment of the sexes. Pursuing this goal has proved difficult, since women and men continue to respond differently to the individual inventory items.

Differences Between Women and Men

Women and men, *on the average*, report somewhat different interests; no one who works closely with the results from interest inventories can avoid coming to that conclusion. That fact must be handled carefully, however, when working with any single individual, for she/he easily can fall outside of the averages; the existence of average differences is no justification for limiting the options of either sex, because the overlap is so large that the ranges are almost identical.

The problem confronting those responsible for interest inventories is how to work with the differences that do occur—so that the unique qualities of every individual of either sex can be addressed by the scoring system—without using the group differences to restrict the choices of any one person.

The nature of the difference. Women and men differ substantially in their responses to many inventory items. Specifically, the response differences between the Women- and Men-in-General samples are 16 percent or larger on 109 of the 325 items. Because the importance attached to any particular response is a direct function of the frequency of that response among various samples—the criterion samples, the Reference Samples, and the Special Scale normative samples—these differences between women and men become a major factor in determining how the data for any single individual are to be analyzed.

For example, the item *Interior decorator* is marked "Like" by a substantial majority of women (64 percent of the Women-in-General sample) though by only a minority of men (29 percent of the Men-in-General sample). Consequently, when a woman gives this response, she is not telling us anything very useful; she is responding in a way typical of most women, and we have made only minimal progress toward understanding her occupational interests. But when a man responds "Like," he has chosen an unusual response, one suggesting that he, unlike most men, has interests in common with men in such occupations as interior decoration, art, and architecture. Because of these patterns, the sex of the respondent must be considered when the answer sheet is scored.

Teenage sex differences. Differences between the sexes in vocational interests appear early; in fact, they overwhelm all other considerations in the vocational musings of grade school children. Data illustrating this point are listed in Table 7.1, which reports the most popular occupations in terms of percent "Like" responses to particular items, for the girls and boys in a typical eighth-grade class tested with the Strong. Obviously, sex role was the most important ingredient in their responses. Only one occupational item, *Cartoonist*, ap-

TABLE 7.1
Popular Occupations Among Female (N = 81) and
Male (N = 76) Eighth-Graders

Occupation item	Percentage "Like"		
	Girls	Boys	Difference
Occupations marked "Like" by more than half of the boys			
Auto racer	24%	65%	41
Jet pilot	22	57	35
Cartoonist	61	57	−4
Professional athlete	45	53	8
Inventor	17	51	34
Occupations marked "Like" by more than half of the girls			
Children's clothes designer	76%	14%	62
Interior decorator	68	21	47
Fashion model	66	11	55
Costume designer	64	13	51
Flight attendant	64	20	44
Actor/Actress	63	33	30
Home economics teacher	61	12	49
Cartoonist	61	57	4
Elementary school teacher	61	26	35
Nurse's aide/Orderly	59	10	49
Manager, child care center	58	11	47
Dressmaker/Tailor	57	15	42
Photographer	56	34	22
Manager, women's style shop	55	10	45
Waiter/Waitress	55	16	39
Artist	54	35	19
Typist	53	9	44

TABLE 7.2
Item-Response Comparisons to the Item *Operating Machinery*
for Twelve Pairs of Male-Female Samples

Sample	Response	N and response percentage		Difference
		Males	Females	
Eighth-graders (1972)	N	81	76	
	Like	33%	14%	19%
	Indifferent	32	28	4
	Dislike	35	58	−23
Ninth-graders (1972)	N	91	108	
	Like	62%	14%	48%
	Indifferent	25	32	−7
	Dislike	13	54	−41
Twelfth-graders (1976)	N	31	39	
	Like	52%	13%	39%
	Indifferent	19	.38	−19
	Dislike	29	49	−20
National Merit Scholarship winners (1973)	N	75	37	
	Like	24%	14%	10%
	Indifferent	40	45	−5
	Dislike	36	41	−5
University freshmen (1974)	N	261	354	
	Like	33%	15%	18%
	Indifferent	34	36	−2
	Dislike	33	49	−16
Introductory psychology students (1984)	N	61	67	
	Like	44%	18%	26%
	Indifferent	33	43	−10
	Dislike	23	39	−16
University seniors (1978)	N	261	354	
	Like	34%	17%	17%
	Indifferent	38	38	0
	Dislike	28	45	−17
Husbands and wives (1972)	N	42	42	
	Like	52%	14%	38%
	Indifferent	24	36	−12
	Dislike	24	50	−26
Men- and Women-In-General (1938, 1946)	N	500	500	
	Like	54%	27%	27%
	Indifferent	26	34	−8
	Dislike	20	39	−19
Men- and Women-In-General (1969)	N	1,000	1,000	
	Like	42%	26%	16
	Indifferent	34	32	2
	Dislike	24	42	−18
Men- and Women-In-General (1974)	N	300	300	
	Like	47%	23%	24%
	Indifferent	34	36	−2
	Dislike	19	41	−22
Men- and Women-In-General (1985)	N	300	300	
	Like	45%	22%	23%
	Indifferent	35	39	−4
	Dislike	20	39	−19

peared on both lists; every other occupation among the popular items has a strong sex-role identification.

Adult sex differences. Differences between the sexes diminish with age but never become trivial. An example of an item showing differences over all ages is given in Table 7.2, which lists the response data for several samples to the item *Operating machinery*. These are samples of convenience, and are used only for illustrative purposes; several comparisons, are between small samples and must be viewed with caution. (As explained in more detail in Chapter 3, item-response comparisons are more valid and more stable when the samples contain at least 200 individuals.)

The first sample is an eighth-grade class from a typical suburban school. The second is a ninth-grade class from a slightly more rural setting; the third is a suburban twelfth-grade class; the fourth consists of 112 National Merit Scholarship finalists in Kansas. The fifth, sixth, and seventh samples are groups collected at the University of Minnesota; the eighth is 42 pairs of wives and husbands. The ninth is Strong's original Women- and Men-in-General samples collected during the 1930's and 1940's. The tenth is the SVIB Women- and Men-in-General samples tested during the 1960's. The eleventh is the 1974 SCII Women- and Men-in-General samples (the General Reference Sample), tested in the 1970's, and the twelfth is the 1985 Women- and Men-in-General samples.

The response percentages listed in Table 7.2 show that the male-female difference on this item, reported in the last column for each sample, was relatively constant over all samples. Although the percentages vary from sample to sample, generally about half of the males, compared with a fifth of the females, answered "Like." The smallest difference, that between the small samples of National Merit Scholarship winners, is attributable to the low response among the males.

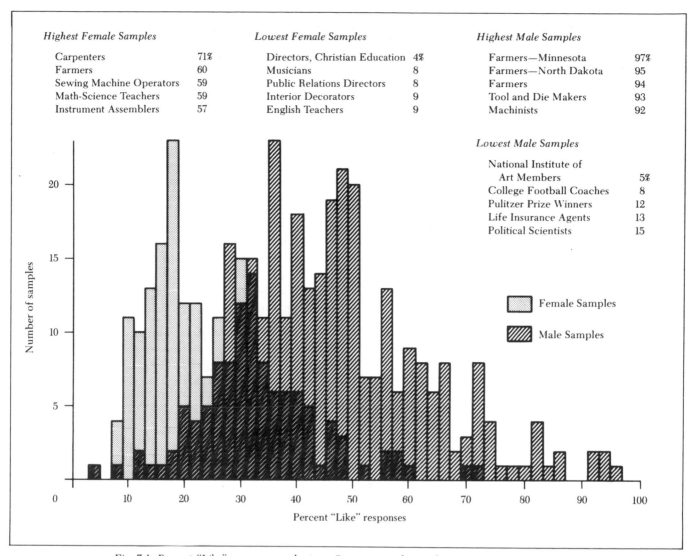

Highest Female Samples

Carpenters	71%
Farmers	60
Sewing Machine Operators	59
Math-Science Teachers	59
Instrument Assemblers	57

Lowest Female Samples

Directors, Christian Education	4%
Musicians	8
Public Relations Directors	8
Interior Decorators	9
English Teachers	9

Highest Male Samples

Farmers—Minnesota	97%
Farmers—North Dakota	95
Farmers	94
Tool and Die Makers	93
Machinists	92

Lowest Male Samples

National Institute of Art Members	5%
College Football Coaches	8
Pulitzer Prize Winners	12
Life Insurance Agents	13
Political Scientists	15

Fig. 7.1. Percent "Like" responses to the item *Operating machinery* for 523 occupational samples.

The strong and consistent male-female difference in mechanical interests is shown graphically in Fig. 7.1, which plots the distribution of "Like" percentages to the item *Operating machinery* for over 500 occupational samples. Female samples are distinguished graphically from male samples. The distributions overlap considerably, but the separation between the sexes is obvious. The samples with the highest and lowest percentages for each sex, listed at the top of the table, are interesting.

This figure, incidentally, is another illustration of the varied popularity of items over many occupations (see Chapter 3). The range of percent "Like" responses was from 4 percent (Christian education directors) to 97 percent (farmers).

Sex differences within the same occupation. Although female-male differences are obvious when general female groups are compared with general male groups, one might suppose that such differences do not

appear when women and men in the same occupation are compared. Table 7.3 demonstrates that the differences persist. These data consider women and men in the same occupation, contrasting their responses to those items showing large differences between Women- and Men-in-General. Twelve pairs of samples, all of them Criterion Samples used in this revision of the SCII, were selected, with each of the six General Occupational Theme types represented by two pairs of samples. The samples were large and well selected: each individual had had at least two years of experience; all reported that they liked their work; and whenever appropriate, all had the necessary degree or certification in their field.

These samples can be used to determine whether the contrasts in interests between women and men disappear when samples from the same occupation are compared. There are three possibilities:

1. Women and men in the same occupation have the same interests.

TABLE 7.3

SCII Items Showing Large Differences Between Men and Women in the Same Occupations

(Percentage difference between the two sexes in "Like" response to designated item)

Item	MIG vs. WIG	Farmers	Police officers	Physical therapists	Physicists	Musicians	Photographers	Elementary education teachers	Social workers	Chamber of Commerce executives	Buyers	Accountants	Credit managers	Average of 12 samples
Items favored by women														
Decorating a room with flowers	54%	56%	65%	62%	39%	57%	53%	60%	56%	37%	56%	49%	56%	54%
Sewing	43	55	33	51	38	47	33	45	38	52	42	47	46	44
Costume designer	38	36	43	34	25	43	36	43	32	38	45	37	46	38
Looking at things in a clothing store	36	48	33	24	30	35	34	47	28	29	11	33	35	32
Family pages in newspapers	36	52	35	39	24	38	28	47	30	45	42	35	39	39
Interior decorator	35	47	48	42	25	38	26	46	40	42	45	45	45	41
Preparing dinner for guests	34	56	32	43	32	23	29	34	34	37	28	33	43	35
Trying new cooking recipes	34	60	34	36	32	24	28	38	41	41	30	39	36	37
Children's clothes designer	32	35	34	42	24	36	32	55	33	36	35	30	34	36
Home economics	32	60	33	27	8	26	20	39	22	42	40	25	37	32
Items favored by men														
Enjoy tinkering with small hand tools	31%	25%	29%	22%	26%	29%	21%	41%	26%	33%	28%	21%	41%	28%
Sports pages in the newspaper	30	29	39	46	25	26	18	38	37	34	37	46	41	34
Popular mechanics magazines	28	42	38	38	37	27	36	41	34	30	21	21	40	34
Manufacturer	24	30	18	31	23	10	23	24	18	52	11	25	34	25
Operating machinery	23	35	28	31	12	22	17	32	20	17	20	16	24	23
Mechanical engineer	22	40	26	21	8	15	19	28	16	14	16	15	25	20
Boxing	22	18	38	23	10	23	16	23	18	20	21	20	16	21
Repairing electrical wiring	21	39	27	23	6	26	20	33	25	18	23	20	26	23
Military officers	19	11	28	18	14	8	15	15	15	35	6	18	21	17
Building a radio or stereo	19	16	20	14	21	34	23	29	14	21	18	8	22	20

2. They have different interests, but the differences are specific to each occupation.

3. They have different interests, and the differences are constant across all occupations.

To study this point, the 10 SCII items that Men-in-General prefer more often than Women-in-General (19 percent or greater difference) and the 10 items that Women-in-General prefer more often than Men-in-General (32 percent or greater difference) are listed in Table 7.3. The percentages in the table indicate the contrast between the male and female occupational samples in their percentage "Like" responses to these items. For example, the first number in the first row shows the MIG-WIG comparison on the item *Decorating a room with flowers*, a 54-percent difference (74 percent of the women versus 20 percent of the men responded "Like"). The numbers in the succeeding columns report the analogous figures for male and female farmers, male and female police officers, and so forth. The last number shows the average difference for this item across the 12 samples. The figures in the first and last columns are in most cases quite similar, differing by only 2 or 3 percentage points.

These data indicate that the differences in interests

between women and men are relatively constant across all occupations in all of the General Occupational Theme areas; no occupation is free of them, nor does any occupation studied have any novel pattern of differences that does not appear in other occupations.

The data in Table 7.3, then, clearly show that sex cannot (or should not) be ignored in norming interest inventories. No matter how samples are selected, women and men respond differently to some items. To ignore this fact would introduce unnecessary error variance. Somehow, the method of analysis must accommodate these differences without penalizing either sex.

Sex differences over time. Differences between the sexes in vocational interests may be diminishing, in response to the growing awareness that many aspects of traditional sex roles are arbitrary. That possibility can be studied empirically, using data from the archives at the Center for Interest Measurement Research. Male and female samples from eight occupations tested during the 1930's are available for comparison with similar samples from the 1960's and with samples from the 1970's or 1980's; Table 7.4 reports the results.

Four items showing male-female response differences

TABLE 7.4
Male-Female Response Differences on Selected SCII Items:
1930's versus 1960's versus 1970's or 1980's Samples
(Percent of each sample responding "Like")

Occupation	Samples	Decorating a room with flowers			Regular hours for work			Repairing electrical wiring			Expressing judgments publicly		
		Male	Female	Difference	Male	Female	Difference	Male	Female	Difference	Male	Female	Difference
Artists	1930's	42%	87%	−45	39%	63%	−24	29%	17%	+12	30%	32%	+6
	1960's	31	80	−49	29	48	−19	24	11	+13	60	40	+20
	1970's	34	73	−39	15	25	−10	23	15	+8	51	45	+6
Lawyers	1930's	21	79	−58	57	59	−2	31	23	+8	55	49	+6
	1960's	9	63	−54	30	40	−10	32	8	+24	66	49	+17
	1970's	15	62	−47	27	29	−2	31	16	+15	60	62	−2
Life insurance agents	1930's	34	85	−51	49	56	−7	35	15	+20	41	32	+9
	1960's	14	76	−62	14	26	−12	31	8	+23	56	38	+18
	1970's	12	71	−59	14	17	−3	33	9	+24	50	44	+6
Physicians	1930's	26	80	−54	60	67	−7	51	40	+11	26	28	−2
	1960's	13	71	−58	40	50	−10	53	28	+25	58	27	+31
	1980's	19	72	−53	40	53	−13	40	25	+15	41	35	+6
Psychologists	1930's	15	80	−65	37	60	−23	50	33	+17	34	26	+8
	1960's	13	72	−59	27	32	−5	38	17	+21	60	49	+11
	1980's	14	62	−48	25	24	+1	37	20	+17	51	41	+10
Reporters	1930's	30	83	−53	47	72	−25	22	12	+10	56	38	+18
	1960's	12	78	−66	24	36	−12	25	9	+16	68	49	+19
	1970's	16	69	−53	36	38	−2	18	12	+6	62	51	+11
Social science teachers	1930's	19	90	−71	72	83	−11	36	14	+22	38	31	+7
	1960's	7	69	−62	42	68	−26	26	7	+19	66	40	+26
	1980's	17	70	−53	56	67	−11	28	9	+17	55	50	+5
YMCA-YWCA staff	1930's	31	92	−61	55	60	−5	50	23	+27	37	21	+16
	1960's	10	70	−60	36	33	+3	40	20	+20	35	38	−3
	1970's	14	70	−56	29	42	−13	34	17	+17	47	38	+9

were used, two chosen more often by men (*Repairing electrical wiring* and *Expressing judgments publicly, regardless of what others say*) and two chosen more often by women (*Decorating a room with flowers* and *Regular hours for work*). For each item, the percentage of each male and female sample responding "Like" is listed in the table, as well as the difference between the two. These four items were not selected in an attempt to exaggerate differences; they were chosen because they are typical of male-female high-contrast items. Of the 32 comparisons (four items over eight occupations), 21 show larger differences in the 1960's than in the 1930's. In general, the gap between men and women on these items in the 1960's was at least as great as and perhaps greater than it was in the 1930's. Data for the 1970's and 1980's samples indicate differences comparable to those in the 1930's, suggesting a slight trend toward reduced male-female differences since the 1960's. But certainly, the differences have not disappeared; until they do, the major research effort should be directed toward developing a system that accommodates the contrasts.

Item changes over time. Although the main purpose of preparing Table 7.4 was to study male-female differences over time, the arrangement of the data also permits analysis of the change in popularity for each of the four items. Each had a different pattern. The first, *Decorating a room with flowers*, showed a mild decrease in popularity over time, roughly 10 percentage points among men and 15 among women. The second, *Regular hours for work*, showed a marked decrease in popularity in both sexes, with differences between the 1930's and 1970's or 1980's samples amounting to an average of 22 percent for men and 30 percent for women, a considerable shift. The third, *Repairing electrical wiring*, showed little change for either sex. The fourth, *Expressing judgments publicly, regardless of what others say*, showed an increase in popularity, especially among the female samples.

Such changes in item responses over time, which are reported in greater detail in the *Handbook for the SVIB*, demonstrate why psychological tests must be renormed periodically.

Options in Constructing the SCII Occupational Scales

In recent years, several experimental methods of Occupational Scale construction were studied in an attempt to develop the best possible procedure for measuring the interests of women and men (Hansen, 1976). All of the methods begin with one of two approaches. One approach assumes that occupationally relevant sex differences exist, and that the best technique is separate-sex scale construction that provides a female and a male scale for each occupation. The other approach assumes that the sex differences in interests documented in previous sections of this chapter are irrelevant to interest measurement, and that the preferred technique is the development of combined-sex scales that differentiate people in the same occupation from People-in-General.

Separate-sex approach, two methods. Method 1 is the empirical-scale-construction technique used with the Strong for the past 60 years; the method involves contrasting criterion subjects, all of the same sex and same occupation, with an in-general sample of the same sex. Method 2, a modification of the separate-sex construction technique, was developed to eliminate items that differentiate women from men. This method is based on work by Johansson and Harmon (1972) that distinguished between valid and nonvalid sex-differentiating items: items that differentiated Women-in-General from Men-in-General were defined as nonvalid discriminators; but items differentiating women from men in the same occupation were defined as valid discriminators. They suggested, as has Rayman (1976), that when nonvalid sex-differentiating items are eliminated, women and men should score similarly on the resulting scales, and also that scales developed on that basis should be more valid and reliable than those developed using Method 1.

Combined-sex approach, two methods. Method 3 is an extension of Method 1 that uses the entire SCII item pool (325 items) to build the best possible scale, using combined-sex criterion and contrast samples. Method 4 also develops a combined-sex scale, but like Method 2, eliminates nonvalid sex-differentiating items from the available SCII item pool.

Studies examining the four experimental methods. All four of the experimental methods were explored in a study by Hansen (1976), who used Criterion Samples of female and male sociologists; Methods 1, 3, and 4 were studied by Webber and Harmon (1978), who used Criterion Samples of female and male veterinarians and life insurance agents.

Both studies found, for all of the methods, that results vary depending on the sex and occupation of the Criterion Sample. To summarize: Hansen found that the method that produced the most valid scale for female sociologists was Method 1 (separate sexes, sex-differentiating items retained) or Method 4 (combined sexes, sex-differentiating items eliminated); and that the most valid scale for male sociologists was Method 1. Webber and Harmon found that the most valid scales for both female veterinarians and female life insurance agents were developed using Method 3 (combined sexes, sex-differentiating items retained); and that the most valid scales for both male veterinarians and male life insurance agents were developed using Method 1.

Hansen also examined the item overlap of the separate-sex female and male Occupational Scales developed with Method 1 (separate sexes, sex-differentiating items

retained) and Method 2 (separate sexes, sex-differentiating items eliminated). She found that, for the sociologists, only 27 percent of the items on the female and male scales (Method 1) were identical. Eliminating the sex-differentiating items (Method 2) increased the item overlap for the separate-sex scales, but still only 41 percent of the items were shared. The non-overlapping items, according to Johansson and Harmon (1972), reflect real occupational differences between women and men in sociology.

The 1981 *Manual* presented additional data on combined-sex scale construction derived from the application of the four experimental methods to other occupations, including radiologic technologists, physicists, librarians, social workers, personnel directors, and credit managers. *For every occupation the best scale for at least one of the two sexes was the scale developed using Method 1, the method currently used for Occupational Scale construction.*

For example, Method 1 produced the most valid scale for male radiologic technologists, female physicists, male librarians, male social workers, female and male personnel directors, and female credit managers. In most of the instances where Method 1 was the most successful for one sex, Method 3 was the most successful for the opposite sex. Thus, Method 3 worked best (produced the most valid scales) for female radiologic technologists, male physicists, female librarians, female social workers, and male credit managers. In no instance was either Method 2 or Method 4, both of which eliminate sex-differentiating items, the technique that produced the most valid scale.

Table 7.5 presents data derived from the application of three of the four experimental methods to six occupations: two of the occupations used in 1981 (a replication for physicists and social workers) and four additional occupations. Method 2 (separate sexes, sex-differentiating items eliminated) was not used to develop experimental scales because it had not proved useful in previous studies and because it does nothing to further the effort to produce combined-sex Occupational Scales. The occupations, selected to represent each of the six Holland types, are presented in the table in RIASEC order. In all instances the samples are large, well-selected groups composed of people who said that they like their work, were at least 25 years old, and had been in the occupations for at least three years. All of the occupations have been open to both women and men for a sufficient number of years to ensure the measurement of truly representative interests.

Tilton percentage-overlap validities for the experimental scales are summarized in Table 7.5 (see Chapter 6 for a thorough discussion of the Tilton overlap statistic). The Criterion Samples used in calculating the overlap percentages were, for the female scales, the female Criterion Samples and Women-in-General; for the male scales, the male Criterion Samples and Men-in-General; and, for the combined scales, the combined-sex Criterion Samples and the General Reference Sample.

TABLE 7.5
Tilton Percent-Overlap Statistics for the Experimental Scales

Experimental method	Method number	Sex of scale	Occupational Scale (sex indicated in column 3)											
			ENGINEER		PHYSICIST		REPORTER		SOCIAL WORKER		REALTOR		ACCOUNTANT	
			Q	%OV	Q	%OV	Q	%OV	Q	%OV	Q	%OV	Q	%OV
Separate sexes, sex-differentiating items retained	1	f	1.92	34	3.04	13	1.73	39	1.91	34	1.97	33	2.04	31
Separate sexes, sex-differentiating items retained	1	m	1.81	37	2.69	18	2.15	28	1.93	33	1.52	45	1.96	33
Combined sexes, sex-differentiating items retained	3	—	−1.69	40	−2.79	16	−1.87	35	−1.80	37	−1.64	41	−1.89	35
Combined sexes, sex-differentiating items eliminated	4	—	−1.64	41	−2.63	19	−1.84	36	−1.72	39	−1.61	42	−1.92	34

As was found in 1981, *for every occupation the best scale for at least one of the two sexes was the scale developed using Method 1, the method currently used for Occupational Scale construction.* In fact, for three of the six occupations—engineers, social workers, and accountants—Method 1 (separate sexes, sex-differentiating items retained) was the most valid for both females and males. Method 1 also was most valid for female physicists, female realtors, and male reporters. For these three occupations, Method 3 (combined sexes, sex-differentiating items retained) was most valid for the sample of the other sex. The results confirm those in the 1981 study, which indicated that Method 4 (combined sexes, sex-differentiating items eliminated) in no instance produces the most valid scales.

The optimum strategy. As these data demonstrate, developing a strategy for the construction of empirical Occupational Scales is a complicated issue. What works best (is most valid) for one occupation may be the least valid for another. But if users are to accept and understand the results on the Occupational Scales, the same method of scale construction must be used for both sexes and all occupations. To mix the modes of scale construction would lead to unimaginable confusion. Thus, because combined-sex construction is not the most *valid* approach for most occupations, and because combined-sex scales are often less *reliable* than separate-sex scales, single-sex construction continues to be the strategy used to develop the SCII Occupational Scales. Moreover, Method 1 (separate sexes, sex-differentiating items retained), or even Method 3 (combined sexes, sex-differentiating items retained), is superior to Method 4 (combined sexes, sex-differentiating items eliminated) because Method 1 (and 3) takes advantage of *all* the differences in interests between people in an occupation and people not in the occupation, whereas Method 4 (and in earlier studies Method 2) ignores those differences that are sex-related.

Intuitively, scale constructors would expect these results, but of course only the results of careful studies can validate the intuition.

Using Opposite-Sex Scales

The results of constructing separate-sex scales can be studied by inspecting occupations for which scales for both sexes are available. These scales are listed in Table 7.6, along with the results from the General Reference Samples of 300 women and 300 men. The critical issue is whether the two scales for each occupation (for example, female and male ELEMENTARY TEACHER) perform equally well with either sex, or whether the scales perform better when used with the appropriate sex. (The third possibility, that the scales perform *better* when used for the *opposite* sex was not considered; but as the data demonstrate, that is not the case.) The data most useful in answering the question are the mean differences listed in Table 7.6 (along with the WIG and MIG mean scores on the Occupational Scales). If the scales perform equally well with both sexes, those differences should be roughly zero. They are not; they are mostly negative, showing that each sex usually scores lower on its own scale than on the scale for the other sex. *Assuming that low scores are good*—because low scores indicate good separation between the General Reference Sample and the occupational samples—the differences show that the appropriate-sex scale usually is superior. Empirical scales developed on female samples work better for women; those developed on male samples work better for men.

This conclusion does not always hold, since the item-by-item sex differences influence each scale differently. Although the influence in not consistent, the tendency is for women to score higher than men on those pairs of scales dominated by items representing traditionally "female" activities and for men to score higher than women on those pairs dominated by items representing traditionally "male" activities. "Female" and "male," here,

TABLE 7.6
Women- and Men-in-General Mean Scores on, and Correlations Between,
the 101 Pairs of Women's and Men's Occupational Scales

Scale	Women-in-General				Men-in-General			
	Correlation between m & f scales	Mean score on female scale	Mean score on male scale	Mean difference	Correlation between m & f scales	Mean score on male scale	Mean score on female scale	Mean difference
ACCOUNTANT	.83	28	22	+6	.82	28	36	−8
ADVERTISING EXECUTIVE	.85	35	40	−5	.86	31	30	+1
AIR FORCE ENLISTED PERSONNEL	.74	28	22	+6	.73	30	32	−2
AIR FORCE OFFICER	.83	31	18	+13	.81	32	42	−10
ARCHITECT	.74	24	29	−5	.73	26	33	−7
ARMY ENLISTED PERSONNEL	.81	29	22	+7	.74	28	35	−7
ARMY OFFICER	.84	31	21	+10	.87	32	43	−11
ART TEACHER	.82	13	30	−17	.80	18	4	+14
ARTIST, COMMERCIAL	.84	20	33	−13	.84	25	15	+10
ARTIST, FINE	.94	26	28	−2	.94	21	25	−4
ATHLETIC TRAINER	.73	17	18	−1	.73	22	25	−3
BANKER	.47	33	28	+5	.58	31	35	−4
BEAUTICIAN	.26	32	43	−11	.08	30	32	−2
BIOLOGIST	.87	18	28	−10	.86	26	26	0
BROADCASTER	.83	34	40	−6	.79	32	30	+2
BUS DRIVER	.79	32	32	0	.84	37	39	−2
BUSINESS EDUCATION TEACHER	.92	18	27	−9	.89	24	19	+5
BUYER	.93	23	34	−11	.92	28	22	+6
CARPENTER	.85	21	17	+4	.86	24	32	−8
CHAMBER OF COMMERCE EXECUTIVE	.60	32	26	+6	.69	26	31	−5
CHEF	.48	28	33	−5	.51	23	22	+1
CHEMIST	.92	20	18	+2	.92	21	30	−9
CHIROPRACTOR	.66	31	28	+3	.68	28	34	−6
COLLEGE PROFESSOR	.86	33	36	−3	.89	34	36	−2
COMPUTER PROGRAMMER	.95	32	27	+5	.95	33	38	−5
CREDIT MANAGER	.80	31	26	+5	.80	32	33	−1
DENTIST	.86	29	24	+5	.88	27	37	−10
DIETITIAN	.57	33	41	−8	.47	33	36	−3
ELECTED PUBLIC OFFICIAL	.86	30	31	−1	.86	30	30	0
ELECTRICIAN	.67	23	18	+5	.72	27	34	−7
ELEMENTARY TEACHER	.70	31	30	+1	.67	28	27	+1
EMERGENCY MEDICAL TECHNICIAN	.85	25	21	+4	.85	29	32	−3
ENGINEER	.90	27	20	+7	.92	28	37	−9
ENGLISH TEACHER	.90	24	36	−12	.92	25	15	+10
EXECUTIVE HOUSEKEEPER	.70	33	34	−1	.73	36	36	0
FARMER	.67	32	24	+8	.70	31	34	−3
FLIGHT ATTENDANT	.72	32	43	−11	.71	34	28	+6
FLORIST	.85	33	36	−3	.84	31	30	+1
FOOD SERVICE MANAGER	.61	35	37	−2	.45	33	35	−2
FOREIGN LANGUAGE TEACHER	.79	23	39	−16	.86	29	16	+13
FORESTER	.82	23	22	+1	.82	28	32	−4
FUNERAL DIRECTOR	.60	37	30	+7	.49	34	34	0
GEOGRAPHER	.77	32	25	+7	.63	25	43	−18
GEOLOGIST	.82	21	25	−4	.80	27	31	−4
GUIDANCE COUNSELOR	.92	32	37	−5	.91	30	29	+1
HORTICULTURAL WORKER	.89	32	30	+2	.91	29	34	−5
INTERIOR DECORATOR	.82	23	39	−16	.75	27	16	+11
INVESTMENTS MANAGER	.81	30	27	+3	.79	30	37	−7
IRS AGENT	.77	34	29	+5	.76	34	40	−6
LAWYER	.82	28	32	−4	.79	31	34	−3
LIBRARIAN	.75	29	42	−13	.83	31	27	+4
LIFE INSURANCE AGENT	.94	29	20	+9	.94	22	31	−9
MARINE CORPS ENLISTED PERSONNEL	.81	28	19	+9	.82	28	36	−8
MARKETING EXECUTIVE	.86	29	33	−4	.82	34	34	0
MATHEMATICIAN	.87	17	19	−2	.88	20	27	−7
MATHEMATICS TEACHER	.81	26	22	+4	.77	28	32	−4

(Continued)

TABLE 7.6 (*continued*)

Scale	Women-in-General				Men-in-General			
	Correlation between m & f scales	Mean score on female scale	Mean score on male scale	Mean difference	Correlation between m & f scales	Mean score on male scale	Mean score on female scale	Mean difference
MEDICAL ILLUSTRATOR	.84	18	22	−4	.85	12	18	−6
MEDICAL TECHNICIAN	.80	29	24	+5	.83	27	32	−5
MEDICAL TECHNOLOGIST	.94	27	26	+1	.94	31	34	−3
MINISTER	.93	20	35	−15	.94	29	15	+14
MUSICIAN	.90	32	38	−6	.93	30	26	+4
NAVY ENLISTED PERSONNEL	.72	31	22	+9	.73	31	40	−9
NAVY OFFICER	.86	34	22	+12	.88	33	44	−11
NURSE, LPN	.81	26	35	−9	.71	30	25	+5
NURSE, RN	.82	33	30	+3	.81	30	32	−2
NURSING HOME ADMINISTRATOR	.82	34	38	−4	.84	36	33	+3
OCCUPATIONAL THERAPIST	.78	29	33	−4	.78	27	31	−4
OPTICIAN	.70	34	30	+4	.70	34	36	−2
OPTOMETRIST	.88	36	31	+5	.87	35	42	−7
PERSONNEL DIRECTOR	.94	34	30	+4	.94	32	35	−3
PHARMACIST	.73	32	27	+5	.71	31	36	−5
PHOTOGRAPHER	.92	33	35	−2	.90	31	32	−1
PHYSICAL EDUCATION TEACHER	.87	20	11	+9	.84	17	30	−13
PHYSICAL THERAPIST	.90	28	23	+5	.89	27	31	−4
PHYSICIAN	.93	25	28	−3	.92	27	30	−3
PHYSICIST	.92	10	11	−1	.92	15	20	−5
POLICE OFFICER	.87	30	19	+11	.92	28	39	−11
PSYCHOLOGIST	.85	26	29	−3	.83	26	29	−3
PUBLIC ADMINISTRATOR	.75	27	36	−9	.75	32	32	0
PUBLIC RELATIONS DIRECTOR	.92	27	31	−4	.93	24	24	0
PURCHASING AGENT	.86	36	29	+7	.88	34	41	−7
RADIOLOGIC TECHNOLOGIST	.85	30	27	+3	.84	31	32	−1
REALTOR	.90	26	30	−4	.92	33	27	+6
RECREATION LEADER	.85	35	34	+1	.87	34	37	−3
REPORTER	.82	28	33	−5	.81	25	24	+1
RESEARCH & DEVELOPMENT MANAGER	.94	25	16	+9	.92	26	35	−9
RESPIRATORY THERAPIST	.88	31	29	+2	.89	30	35	−5
RESTAURANT MANAGER	.57	34	32	+2	.59	31	36	−5
SCHOOL ADMINISTRATOR	.89	34	32	+2	.90	33	34	−1
SCIENCE TEACHER	.93	23	25	−2	.92	27	27	0
SOCIAL SCIENCE TEACHER	.80	31	36	−5	.88	32	31	+1
SOCIAL WORKER	.88	28	34	−6	.90	26	25	+1
SOCIOLOGIST	.86	21	29	−8	.86	25	26	−1
SPECIAL EDUCATION TEACHER	.86	33	33	0	.87	28	29	−1
SPEECH PATHOLOGIST	.90	31	35	−4	.91	29	25	+4
STORE MANAGER	.94	34	33	+1	.93	32	31	+1
SYSTEMS ANALYST	.91	33	25	+8	.92	32	40	−8
TRAVEL AGENT	.77	31	41	−10	.73	36	32	+4
VETERINARIAN	.87	24	20	+4	.84	26	30	−4
VOCATIONAL AGRICULTURE TEACHER	.89	26	19	+7	.89	26	32	−6
YMCA/YWCA DIRECTOR	.91	35	31	+4	.92	30	36	−6

refer to items showing large differences in popularity between Women- and Men-in-General. Consequently, on scales such as ARMY OFFICER and CARPENTER, men ("Men-in-General sample," in the table) have higher means than women, on both men's *and* women's scales; whereas on scales such as MUSICIAN and ART TEACHER, women ("Women-in-General sample") have higher means than men, again on both men's and women's scales.

This relationship leads to complexity in the interpre-

tation of Occupational Scales developed for women and men who are in occupations stereotypically associated with the opposite sex—for example, the scales for male ART TEACHER and female ARMY OFFICER. Because these scales are dominated by items favored by the opposite sex, opposite-sex samples tend to score higher than appropriate-sex samples. The net effect at the individual level is that many people score higher on some of the Occupational Scales for the other sex than they do on the same Occupational Scales for their own sex.

The soundest conclusion to be drawn from the data in Table 7.6 is that, where possible, Occupational Scales should be developed in pairs, one for women, one for men, and this has been the primary goal for the 1985 SVIB-SCII.

Profiling the Results

To provide a system that recognizes sex differences yet does not penalize either sex, separate scales have been maintained for the two sexes in the 1985 revision of the SCII. Scales for both women and men have been developed for 101 of the 106 occupations represented on the profile, and everyone is scored on all scales.

There were two possible approaches to profiling the Occupational Scales: (1) score each person only on scales developed for her or his own sex or (2) score each person on all scales, regardless of the individual's sex. The data in Tables 6.1 and 7.6 indicate from a purely technical standpoint the best way to profile the results would be to report only the female-scale scores for women and only the male-scale scores for men. When scales such as INTERIOR DECORATOR show a 17-point difference between women's and men's scales in the female sample and an 11-point difference in the male sample, the two scales cannot be considered interchangeable. However, since one of the chief goals in the development of this edition of the Strong was to encourage both women and men to consider occupations heretofore dominated by the other sex, the resolution to this dilemma on the SCII has been to score everyone on every scale. Although this approach does increase the problems of interpretation, it also offers the individual a maximum of information, and encourages each person at least to ponder the similarity, or lack of it, between her/his interests and those of women and men in a wide range of occupations.

Substantial problems were encountered in furnishing the respondent with scores on both same-sex and opposite-sex scales in ways that would minimize misinterpretation, and accommodations have been made on the profile to help make interpretation more accurate. First, interpretive comments on the General Occupational Themes and Basic Interest Scales, based on the respondent's sex and on the distributions for that sex, are printed out on the profile. Second, the norms for each sex on each of the General Occupational Themes and Basic Interest Scales are printed on the profile. Third,

the Occupational Scale scores are presented on the profile in both numerical and graphic manner. The intent is to make all of the scores available, while at the same time providing the appropriate normative information for each sex.

Sex Differences and Scoring Policy

The data in this chapter document clearly that:

1. Women and men, on the average, respond differently to about one-third of the inventory items.

2. The size of the differences is considerable.

3. The differences do not disappear when only women and men who have made the same occupational choice are compared.

4. The differences have not lessened appreciably since 1930.

5. Attempts to develop combined-sex scales appear to be premature, and the validity of such scales varies from occupation to occupation.

6. Empirical scales constructed on the basis of same-sex criterion and reference samples work better (are more valid) than scales based on opposite-sex samples.

The emphasis in this chapter has been on female-male response differences. A statement of policy is therefore appropriate at this point: these differences should in no way be used to discriminate against or repress any individual of either sex. Women with mechanical interests, no matter how common or rare they are, should have the same range of options open to them as do men with such interests; analogously, men with domestic or artistic interests should not find their way barred by either formal or informal barriers. People should be permitted and encouraged to follow their own inclinations; no societal need requires that individuals be limited to arbitrary occupational sex roles.

Yet the data in this chapter also demonstrate that the route to *equal* treatment is not necessarily through *identical* treatment, for identical treatment of groups that are dissimilar will not have identical impact. Thus, separate scales and separate norms are necessary, but we must be certain that they are used as a means of expanding options, not of limiting them. Chapter 10 of the *User's Guide* explains two basic approaches that aid in the interpretation of scores on opposite-sex scales, and presents several case studies that illustrate the use of opposite-sex Occupational Scales.

CHAPTER EIGHT

The Special Scales

The two Special Scales are extreme examples of the empirical approach that dominated the early history of the Strong. Each Special Scale is composed of items selected strictly according to a statistical criterion, just as the items in the Occupational Scales are selected.

The Academic Comfort Scale

This scale was initially labeled ACADEMIC ACHIEVEMENT, but when experience indicated that this was not quite the scale's flavor, the name was changed to ACADEMIC ORIENTATION. And when further experience indicated that the scale was most closely associated with degree of comfort in being in an academic setting, the name was changed again in 1981 to ACADEMIC COMFORT (AC).

Constructing the AC scale. The predecessors of the ACADEMIC COMFORT scale originally were constructed by comparing the item responses of good and poor students at the University of Minnesota's College of Liberal Arts; because women and men were scored on separate inventories at that time, the result was separate female and male scales. The single scale for the 1974 SCII, which remains in use on the 1985 SCII, was constructed by using items that were common to the previous SVIB women's and men's ACADEMIC ACHIEVEMENT scales and had survived the screening for the merged booklet. Because all of the items on the scale are included in all three booklets, every sample in the Strong archives that responded to any of these booklets can be scored on this scale. The items that are weighted positively cover a wide range of academic topics, with emphasis on the arts and sciences. Items weighted negatively are fewer in number, with no particular common theme, except for minor clusters of sales and blue-collar items.

Norming the AC scale. The earlier forms of the scale were normed by scoring samples of liberal arts college graduates and setting their mean equal to 50. On scales developed in that fashion, samples of Ph.D.'s usually scored around 60.

For the 1974 ACADEMIC ORIENTATION scale, samples of Ph.D.'s were used as the normative groups, since several good samples were available; the same normative groups were used for the 1985 ACADEMIC COMFORT scale. For the men, the 1974 criterion sample of college professors ($N = 421$) was used; for the women, the 1974 criterion samples of psychologists ($N = 275$) and mathematicians

($N = 119$) were used. The raw-score means and standard deviations of these three samples were averaged (although, because they were within 2 points of each other, the effect of averaging was slight), and the results were used in a raw-score-to-standard-score conversion formula that placed these samples at a standard-score mean of 60 and a standard deviation of 10. The item selection and scale-norming process was successful; both female and male occupational samples scored at virtually the same level on the AC scale as they had on the earlier ACADEMIC ACHIEVEMENT scale, and those 1985 criterion samples collected for the SCII revision that represent groups of Ph.D.'s continue to have scores around 60 (see Table 8.2).

One potential complication in developing the combined-sex AC scale was that the earlier scale norms might have been quite different for women and men. Because the sexes had never been combined on this scale, there was no way of knowing if one sex had "greater" academic interest than the other. If they did, then women and men from the same occupation would score differently on this scale. As the data in Table 8.1 demonstrate, women and men in 29 of the 101 pairs of matched-sex occupational samples differed by one-half standard deviation or more; in 72 pairs, they differed less. But almost all of the female samples showed more academic interest than the male samples did.

No particular characteristic distinguishes the occupations with large (± 5) female-male differences from those occupations showing only minor differences. Perhaps this is simply a manifestation of a common observation: that women are usually more comfortable in classroom settings than men. In any event, the sizable differences appeared in about 30 percent of the occupations.

Data on the 1985 Women-in-General and Men-in-General samples show that the 300 women scored higher than the 300 men did, with means of 47 and 44 respectively, indicating that the general sample of women was more academically oriented than the analogous sample of men. The two standard deviations were 14.7 and 14.9, respectively, much larger than the 10.0 of the scale-standardization sample—which is good, because diversity in the reference sample is desirable. The nonprofessional women and nonprofessional men in the General Reference Sample scored 43 and 39, respectively, on the

TABLE 8.1
Mean Scores of Female versus Male Occupational Samples on the ACADEMIC COMFORT Scale

Occupational sample	Female mean	Male mean	Difference	Occupational sample	Female mean	Male mean	Difference
Accountants	46	42	+4	Marine Corps enlisted personnel	42	39	+3
Advertising executives	44	42	+2	Marketing executives	48	44	+4
Air Force enlisted personnel	40	39	+1	Mathematicians	63	60	+3
Air Force officers	48	43	+5	Mathematics teachers	54	50	+4
Architects	53	47	+6	Medical illustrators	51	52	−1
Army enlisted personnel	44	37	+7	Medical technicians	47	47	0
Army officers	47	45	+2	Medical technologists	56	53	+3
Art teachers	48	46	+2	Ministers	56	52	+4
Artists, commercial	46	42	+4	Musicians	52	47	+5
Artists, fine	49	48	+1	Navy enlisted personnel	42	39	+3
Athletic trainers	49	44	+5	Navy officers	48	46	+2
Bankers	39	42	−3	Nurses, licensed practical	43	46	−3
Beauticians	36	38	−2	Nurses, registered	52	49	+3
Biologists	65	61	+4	Nursing home administrators	44	40	+4
Broadcasters	43	41	+2	Occupational therapists	49	46	+3
Bus drivers	38	34	+4	Opticians	40	39	+1
Business education teachers	41	39	+2	Optometrists	53	48	+5
Buyers	36	35	+1	Personnel directors	44	41	+3
Carpenters	49	39	+10	Pharmacists	53	47	+6
Chamber of Commerce executives	39	37	+2	Photographers	45	42	+3
Chefs	43	41	+2	Physical education teachers	45	43	+2
Chemists	65	62	+3	Physical therapists	52	48	+4
Chiropractors	50	48	+2	Physicians	61	59	+2
College professors	60	56	+4	Physicists	64	61	+3
Computer programmers	53	48	+5	Police officers	44	39	+5
Credit managers	42	39	+3	Psychologists	59	55	+4
Dentists	54	48	+6	Public administrators	50	50	0
Dietitians	50	47	+3	Public relations directors	46	44	+2
Elected public officials	49	42	+7	Purchasing agents	42	41	+1
Electricians	50	38	+12	Radiologic technologists	47	45	+2
Elementary teachers	44	44	0	Realtors	39	39	0
Emergency medical technicians	46	42	+4	Recreation leaders	47	41	+6
Engineers	54	51	+3	Reporters	49	48	+1
English teachers	53	54	−1	Research and development managers	58	53	+5
Executive housekeepers	43	40	+3	Respiratory therapists	50	52	−2
Farmers	38	33	+5	Restaurant managers	42	34	+8
Flight attendants	42	43	−1	School administrators	51	46	+5
Florists	37	36	+1	Science teachers	61	54	+7
Food service managers	40	40	0	Social science teachers	50	44	+6
Foreign language teachers	52	52	0	Social workers	50	47	+3
Foresters	53	45	+8	Sociologists	60	56	+4
Funeral directors	43	35	+8	Special education teachers	46	45	+1
Geographers	55	54	+1	Speech pathologists	50	50	0
Geologists	59	56	+3	Store managers	41	36	+5
Guidance counselors	50	47	+3	Systems analysts	54	49	+5
Horticultural workers	45	41	+4	Travel agents	41	38	+3
Interior decorators	39	36	+3	Veterinarians	54	46	+8
Investments managers	48	45	+3	Vocational agriculture teachers	46	42	+4
IRS agents	49	42	+7	YWCA/YMCA directors	46	41	+5
Lawyers	52	47	+5	Nonprofessional women/men	43	39	+4
Librarians	52	53	−1	Professional women/men	50	48	+2
Life insurance agents	45	38	+7	Women/Men-In-General	47	44	+3

AC scale, and professional women and professional men scored 50 and 48.

AC scale validity. Table 8.2 lists mean AC scores for 254 occupational samples; these data constitute the validity foundation for this scale. The rank-ordering of the scale means is reassuringly sensible. Occupations requiring a high level of academic training—biologists, chemists, physicists, psychologists, mathematicians, college professors, physicians—scored the highest, all in the high 50's or low to middle 60's. At the bottom of the distribution, with means more than three standard deviations lower, were occupational samples with much lower requisite educational levels—farmers, instrument assemblers, agribusiness managers, funeral directors, and sewing machine operators. When occupations such as these can be spread apart by 3-1/2 standard deviations, the scale clearly is related to educational level. Of course, this scale is not a measure of ability, but only of interests, although interests are probably as important as ability if a student is to persist to the end of graduate training.

Correlations of AC scores with grades usually range between .10 and .30. Correlations of this magnitude, indicating that the level of the score is only slightly related to grades, have been found at the University of Massachusetts, the United States Military Academy, Pennsylvania State University, and the University of California (Berkeley), as well as the University of Minnesota.

Yet, mean scores for students entering these institutions vary widely, in meaningful ways. Students entering Minnesota junior colleges have average scores of about 30–35. Freshmen at Pennsylvania State University and the University of Massachusetts have average scores of about 40–45. Freshmen entering the University of Minnesota College of Liberal Arts average about 46. Students entering the University of California (Berkeley) and Dartmouth College average about 45–50, and entering freshmen at Harvard University average 55–60. These are large differences, and, again, the rank order is eminently reasonable, suggesting that the student's score has some relationship to the institution entered.

AC scale reliability. Test-retest statistics for the AC scale over 14-day, 30-day, and 3-year intervals are presented in Table 8.3, along with similar data on the INTROVERSION-EXTROVERSION scale, which is discussed in the next section of this chapter. (The samples used to calculate these statistics are described on p. 31.) As the data in Table 8.3 indicate, the AC scale is stable over both short and long time periods, with test-retest correlations of .91 to .85 and test-retest means within a point of each other.

Interpreting the AC scale. Scores on the AC scale should be interpreted as the name implies: as an indication of the degree to which the respondent is comfortable in academic settings. High scores will be found among people who are well educated or who intend to become well educated; low scores will be found among those who are uncomfortable in academic settings and who find intellectual exercises boring. Most people with advanced degrees will score high on this scale; high school dropouts will score low. Those who drop out of college also will score low, though not as low as high school dropouts.

College and university students who have high scores on this scale normally will be doing well in school and usually will report satisfaction with their educational experience, though they may be dissatisfied with particular teachers or courses. In contrast, students with low scores frequently will be doing poorly and usually will be thinking about dropping out of school and looking for outside activities. Their dissatisfaction is generally diffuse, likely to be directed toward the entire educational experience.

Most graduate students score at least 50 on the AC scale, with the majority scoring between 55 and 60. Students seeking advanced degrees who score low (40 and below, for example) usually report that they view their education as a means to an end, as a necessary hurdle to be cleared on the way to the career they are seeking; they are seldom enchanted with the academic nature of their study. When queried about their similarity or dissimilarity with other students in their program, they report themselves to be less concerned with the academic and more concerned with the practical nature of their education than are their classmates. These generalizations vary from program to program—typically, even the most academically oriented business school student scores lower than the average student in the philosophy department, which is to be expected in light of the item content of the scale. Still, the overall trends are consistent.

A recent study (Swanson & Hansen, 1985) examining the construct of academic comfort as measured by the AC scale has shown that:

1. Samples composed of people completing B.A. and M.A. degrees are no longer differentiated on the AC scale as they once were (Campbell, 1971). The convergence of these two groups probably reflects the increased number of occupations that require the accumulation of graduate degree credits to retain licensure, to maintain status, or to move upward in an occupation.

2. The correlation between mean AC scale scores and mean years of education for the Strong occupational criterion samples is high, .79 for women and .73 for men.

3. In a liberal arts sample, even students scoring in the lowest quartile (mid-30's and lower) on the AC scale had a passing cumulative GPA (mean = 2.6 on a 4.0 scale). These data emphasize that low scores on the AC scale do not indicate an inability to successfully complete college-level work.

4. The AC scale is related to educational expectations of college freshmen; those who viewed college as preparation for further education (e.g., graduate or professional school) scored about 52; those who indicated that they were in college to have a good time scored about 38; and those who indicated their reason as career training, general education, or personal growth scored about 46.

Chapter 12 of the *User's Guide* contains more infor-

TABLE 8.2
Mean Scores on the ACADEMIC COMFORT Scale for 254 Occupational Samples

Scale mean	Occupational samples	Scale mean	Occupational samples
65	Biologists f, Chemists f		Mental health workers m, Radiologic technologists m, Special education teachers m
64	Physicists f	44	Advertising executives f, Army enlisted personnel f, Elementary teachers f, Nursing home administrators f, Personnel directors f, Police officers f; Athletic trainers m, Elementary teachers m, Marketing executives m, Men-in-General m, Public relations directors m, Social science teachers m
63	Mathematicians f		
62	Chemists m		
61	Science teachers f, Physicians f; Biologists m, Physicists m		
60	College professors f, Sociologists f, Mathematicians m		
59	Geologists f, Psychologists f; Physicians m	43	Army noncommissioned officers f, Broadcasters f, Chefs f, Dental assistants f, Executive housekeepers f, Funeral directors f, Nightclub entertainers f, Nonprofessionals-in-general f, Pest controllers f; Air Force officers m, Flight attendants m, Physical education teachers m, Revenue agents m, Revenue officers m, Tax auditors m
58	Language interpreters f, Research and development managers f		
57			
56	Medical technologists f, Ministers f; College professors m, Geologists m, Sociologists m		
55	Geographers f; Psychologists m	42	Credit managers f, Flight attendants f, Home economics teachers f, Marine Corps enlisted personnel f, Navy enlisted personnel f, Nurses, LPN f, Purchasing agents f, Restaurant managers f, Stockbrokers f; Accountants m, Advertising executives m, Artists, commercial m, Bankers m, Elected public officials m, Emergency medical technicians m, IRS agents m, Photographers m, Vocational agriculture teachers m
54	Dentists f, Engineers f, Mathematics teachers f, Systems analysts f, Veterinarians f; English teachers m, Geographers m, Science teachers m		
53	Architects f, Computer programmers f, English teachers f, Foresters f, Marine Corps officers f, Optometrists f, Pharmacists f; Librarians m, Medical technologists m, Research and development managers m		
52	Foreign language teachers f, Lawyers f, Librarians f, Musicians f, Nurses, RN f, Physical therapists f; Foreign language teachers m, Medical illustrators m, Respiratory therapists m	41	Business education teachers f, Navy Noncommissioned officers f, Store managers f, Travel agents f; Broadcasters m, Chefs m, Horticultural workers m, Industrial arts teachers m, Personnel directors m, Purchasing agents m, Recreation leaders m, YMCA directors m
51	Medical illustrators f, School administrators f; Engineers m, Food scientists m, Ministers m, Priests m		
50	Cartographers f, Chiropractors f, Dietitians f, Electricians f, Guidance counselors f, Nurses, public health f, Professionals-in-general f, Public administrators f, Respiratory therapists f, Social science teachers f, Social workers f, Speech pathologists f; Mathematics teachers m, Public administrators m, Speech pathologists m	40	Air Force enlisted personnel f, Food service managers f, Opticians f; Executive housekeepers m, Food service managers m, Highway Patrol officers m, Nursing home administrators m, Stockbrokers m, Union leaders m
		39	Agribusiness managers f, Bankers f, Chamber of Commerce executives f, Interior decorators f, Realtors f; Air Force enlisted personnel m, Auto sales dealers m, Business education teachers m, Carpenters m, Credit managers m, Marine Corps enlisted personnel m, Navy enlisted personnel m, Nonprofessionals-in-general m, Opticians m, Police officers m, Realtors m
49	Artists, fine f, Athletic trainers f, Carpenters f, Elected public officials f, IRS agents f, Occupational therapists f, Reporters f; Nurses, RN m, Systems analysts m		
48	Air Force officers f, Art teachers f, Christian education directors f, Investments managers f, Marketing executives f, Navy officers f, Revenue agents f, Revenue officers f, Tax auditors f; Artists, fine m, Cartographers m, Chiropractors m, Computer programmers m, Dentists m, Optometrists m, Physical therapists m, Professionals-in-general m, Reporters m		
		38	Bus drivers f, Farmers f, Secretaries f, Telephone operators f; Beauticians m, Life insurance agents m, Retail clerks m
		37	Florists f; Army enlisted personnel m, Chamber of Commerce executives m, Electricians m, Pest controllers m, Sales managers m, Travel agents m
47	Army officers f, Medical technicians f, Nurses, occupational health f, Radiological technologists f, Recreation leaders f, Women-in-General f; Architects m, Dietitians m, Guidance counselors m, Lawyers m, Marine Corps officers m, Medical technicians m, Musicians m, Pharmacists m, Social workers m	36	Beauticians f, Buyers f; Florists m, Interior decorators m, Nursery managers m, Store managers m
		35	Instrument assemblers f; Buyers m, Funeral directors m
46	Accountants f, Artists, commercial f, Dental hygienist f, Emergency medical technicians f, Mental health workers f, Public relations directors f, Special education teachers f, Vocational agriculture teachers f, YWCA directors f; Art teachers m, Navy officers m, Nurses, LPN m, Occupational therapists m, School administrators m, Veterinarians m	34	Bus drivers m, Restaurant managers m
		33	Retail clerks f, Sewing machine operators f; Dairy processing managers m, Farmers m
		32	
		31	Agribusiness managers m, Grain elevator managers m
		30	
		29	
45	Horticultural workers f, Life insurance agents f, Photographers f, Physical education teachers f; Army officers m, Foresters m, Investments managers m,	28	Farm implement managers m, Farm supply managers m

TABLE 8.3

Test-Retest Statistics over 14-Day, 30-Day, and 3-Year
Intervals for the ACADEMIC COMFORT and
INTROVERSION-EXTROVERSION Scales

Scale	Test-retest correlation	Test Mean	Test S.D.	Retest Mean	Retest S.D.
14-day interval ($N = 180$)					
ACADEMIC COMFORT	.91	39	15.4	40	16.6
INTROVERSION-EXTROVERSION	.91	53	12.3	52	13.8
30-day interval ($N = 102$)					
ACADEMIC COMFORT	.86	46	13.5	46	13.5
INTROVERSION-EXTROVERSION	.90	39	12.0	38	12.0
3-year interval ($N = 140$)					
ACADEMIC COMFORT	.85	49	13.7	49	14.3
INTROVERSION-EXTROVERSION	.82	51	11.5	52	12.0

TABLE 8.4

Normative Samples for the INTROVERSION-EXTROVERSION Scale

Normative sample	N	Earlier scale Mean	1974 scale (raw scores) Mean	S.D.
Male samples				
Investments managers	237	44	10.5	13.1
Purchasing agents	164	44	8.6	14.5
Vocational agriculture teachers	395	44	7.8	13.7
Female samples				
Business education teachers	300	50	6.5	13.7
Home economics teachers	373	50	5.8	13.1
Registered nurses	263	50	7.9	13.2

mation on the AC scale, as well as case studies that illustrate its use with clients.

The Introversion-Extroversion Scale

The INTROVERSION-EXTROVERSION (IE) scale is another special scale retained from the earlier form of the Strong because it proved useful in understanding a person's pattern of interests. Psychologists have long realized the importance of the introversion-extroversion dimension, one that continually reasserts itself in research studies. Scores on the IE scale reflect a person's interest in working with things or ideas, or in working with people.

The IE scale appears on the SCII profile for two reasons: first, the scale is clinically helpful, since the score gives a quick index of a person's attitude toward working with others; second, the validity statistics, as reported below, demonstrate that the IE scale successfully discriminates between people-oriented occupations and non-people-oriented occupations.

Constructing the IE scale. The original scales were constructed by comparing the SVIB item responses of MMPI-defined extroverts with those of MMPI-defined introverts among the student body of the University of Minnesota; separate scales were developed for the male and female booklets. Details are reported in the *Handbook for the SVIB*.

The single IE scale for the 1974 SCII (which is the same scale now on the 1985 profile) was constructed by using the items that had survived the screening for the merged booklet. Again, as with the ACADEMIC COMFORT scale, only those items common to both the former female (Form TW398) and male (Form T399) booklets were used, so that all of the occupational criterion groups could be scored on the new scale.

Norming the IE scale. The 1974 IE scale was normed by using information generated by the earlier SVIB scales, and the same samples were used to norm the 1985 IE scale. A wide range of both female and male occupational samples had been scored on the SVIB scales (their means are presented in the *Handbook*). As usual, the IE means formed a reasonably normal curve, but the male samples were distributed around a standard score of 44

on the men's scales and the women's samples were distributed around a standard score of 50 on the women's scale. Because the scales for women and men were separate, no direct comparison was possible, and one could not say whether the 6-point difference in means reflected a "true" sex difference on the introversion-extroversion dimension or whether the two scales were not equivalent. As discussed below, data from the SCII INTROVERSION-EXTROVERSION scale suggest that the latter explanation is the more reasonable.

The intent in norming the IE scale was to locate a standard score of 50 in the middle of the curve, halfway between the extroversion and introversion extremes. To ensure this, three samples of each sex with mean scores on the earlier scales falling at the peak of a bell-shaped distribution were selected as the norming samples. Three samples of each sex, rather than one, were used to protect the norming from any potential disruption created by the unknown idiosyncrasies of a single sample. The samples selected, their means on the older scales, and their raw-score statistic on the new scale are listed in Table 8.4. The raw-score means and standard deviations of these six samples on the new scale were averaged, and these data were then used in the usual raw-score-to-standard-score conversion formula. The net effect was to convert the scores into a distribution with a population mean of about 50, the most extroverted occupations averaging about 40, and the most introverted about 60.

Female samples scored on the earlier women's IE scale (TW398) and on the SCII IE scale compare very well; most of the samples had mean scores on the new scale within 2 or 3 points of their mean scores on the earlier scale. For the male samples scored on the earlier men's (T399) scale and on the SCII scale, however, the differences were larger and more consistent: most of the male samples scored 4 to 6 points higher on the SCII scale than they did on the older scale (see the 1974 *Manual*). These results answer a question posed earlier in this chapter: the data on the new scale indicate that the differences on the older scales between the male and female distribution means were due to lack of equivalence in the norms, not to some difference between the sexes on the introversion-extroversion dimension. On

TABLE 8.5
Mean Scores of Female versus Male Occupational Samples on the INTROVERSION-EXTROVERSION Scale

Occupational sample	Female mean	Male mean	Differ-ence	Occupational sample	Female mean	Male mean	Differ-ence
Accountants	53	50	+3	Marine corps enlisted personnel	50	51	−1
Advertising executives	47	46	+1	Marketing executives	47	47	0
Air Force enlisted personnel	52	54	−2	Mathematicians	57	60	−3
Air Force officers	50	51	−1	Mathematics teachers	53	55	−2
Architects	55	54	+1	Medical illustrators	56	54	+2
Army enlisted personnel	48	52	−4	Medical technicians	56	53	+3
Army officers	47	49	−2	Medical technologists	56	54	+2
Art teachers	49	50	−1	Ministers	42	43	−1
Artists, commercial	52	54	−2	Musicians	52	53	−1
Artists, fine	55	57	−2	Navy enlisted personnel	50	54	−4
Athletic trainers	51	51	0	Navy officers	50	50	0
Bankers	48	45	+3	Nurses, licensed practical	54	50	+4
Beauticians	52	50	+2	Nurses, registered	47	51	−4
Biologists	57	56	+1	Nursing home administrators	45	45	0
Broadcasters	42	45	−3	Occupational therapists	50	49	+1
Bus drivers	54	54	0	Opticians	50	53	−3
Business education teachers	50	49	+1	Optometrists	53	53	0
Buyers	48	48	0	Personnel directors	44	44	0
Carpenters	52	54	−2	Pharmacists	54	53	+1
Chamber of Commerce executives	46	41	+5	Photographers	50	51	−1
Chefs	50	50	0	Physical education teachers	51	49	+2
Chemists	56	56	0	Physical therapists	52	51	+1
Chiropractors	49	50	−1	Physicians	53	54	−1
College professors	52	52	0	Physicists	58	59	−1
Computer programmers	58	58	0	Police officers	45	48	−3
Credit managers	48	48	0	Psychologists	47	49	−2
Dentists	54	55	−1	Public administrators	45	43	+2
Dietitians	50	48	+2	Public relations directors	43	43	0
Elected public officials	40	41	−1	Purchasing agents	46	46	0
Electricians	53	56	−3	Radiologic technologists	52	53	−1
Elementary teachers	52	51	+1	Realtors	42	45	−3
Emergency medical technicians	50	52	−2	Recreation leaders	42	44	−2
Engineers	54	56	−2	Reporters	46	48	−2
English teachers	43	44	−1	Research and development managers	52	53	−1
Executive housekeepers	47	48	−1	Respiratory therapists	52	51	+1
Farmers	54	60	−6	Restaurant managers	46	48	−2
Flight attendants	46	44	+2	School administrators	41	43	−2
Florists	52	53	−1	Science teachers	53	54	−1
Food service managers	51	49	+2	Social science teachers	44	46	−2
Foreign language teachers	49	50	−1	Social workers	45	44	+1
Foresters	54	56	−2	Sociologists	47	48	−1
Funeral directors	46	48	−2	Special education teachers	48	47	+1
Geographers	52	53	−1	Speech pathologists	45	46	−1
Geologists	56	58	−2	Store managers	46	47	−1
Guidance counselors	42	44	−2	Systems analysts	53	53	0
Horticultural workers	54	55	−1	Travel agents	47	49	−2
Interior decorators	50	52	−2	Veterinarians	58	57	+1
Investments managers	50	51	−1	Vocational agriculture teachers	51	52	−1
IRS agents	46	49	−3	YWCA/YMCA directors	43	42	+1
Lawyers	45	45	0	Nonprofessional women/men	49	50	−1
Librarians	50	52	−2	Professional women/men	48	49	−1
Life insurance agents	40	41	−1	Women/Men-In-General	48	50	−2

TABLE 8.6
Mean Scores on the Introversion-Extroversion Scale for 254 Occupational Samples

Scale mean	Occupational samples
60	Farmers m, Mathematicians m
59	Sewing machine operators f; Physicists m
58	Computer programmers f, Physicists f, Veterinarians f; Computer programmers m, Geologists m
57	Biologists f, Mathematicians f; Artists, fine m, Veterinarians m
56	Chemists f, Geologists f, Instrument assemblers f, Medical illustrators f, Medical technicians f, Medical technologists f; Biologists m, Cartographers m, Chemists m, Electricians m, Engineers m, Foresters m
55	Architects f, Artists, fine f, Cartographers f; Dentists m, Grain elevator managers m, Horticultural workers m, Mathematics teachers m, Nursery managers m
54	Bus drivers f, Dentists f, Engineers f, Farmers f, Foresters f, Horticultural workers f, Navy Noncommissioned officers f, Nurses, LPN f, Pharmacists f, Telephone operators f; Air Force enlisted personnel m, Architects m, Artists, commercial m, Bus drivers m, Carpenters m, Dairy processing managers m, Industrial arts teachers m, Medical illustrators m, Medical technologists m, Navy enlisted personnel m, Physicians m, Science teachers m
53	Accountants f, Agribusiness managers f, Electricians f, Mathematics teachers f, Optometrists f, Physicians f, Science teachers f, Systems analysts f; Agribusiness managers m, Florists m, Geographers m, Medical technicians m, Musicians m, Opticians m, Optometrists m, Pharmacists m, Radiologic technologists m, Research and development managers m, Systems analysts m
52	Air Force enlisted personnel f, Artists, commercial f, Beauticians f, Carpenters f, College professors f, Dental assistants f, Elementary teachers f, Florists f, Geographers f, Language interpreters f, Musicians f, Physical therapists f, Radiologic technologists f, Research and development managers f, Respiratory therapists f; Army enlisted personnel m, College professors m, Emergency medical technicians m, Farm supply managers m, Interior decorators, m, Librarians m, Pest controllers m, Vocational agriculture teachers m
51	Athletic trainers f, Dental hygienists f, Food service managers f, Home economics teachers f, Nurses, public health f, Pest controllers f, Physical education teachers f, Vocational agriculture teachers f; Air Force officers m, Athletic trainers m, Elementary teachers m, Farm implement dealers m, Highway Patrol officers m, Investments managers m, Marine Corps enlisted personnel m, Nurses, RN m, Photographers m, Physical therapists m, Respiratory therapists m
50	Air Force officers f, Army Noncommissioned officers f, Business education teachers f, Chefs f, Dietitians f, Emergency medical technicians f, Interior decorators f, Investments managers f, Librarians f, Marine Corps enlisted personnel f, Navy enlisted personnel f, Navy officers f, Occupational therapists f, Opticians f, Photographers f, Retail clerks f, Secretaries f; Accountants m, Art teachers m, Beauticians m, Chefs m, Chiropractors m, Food scientists m, Foreign language teachers m, Men-in-General m, Navy officers m, Nonprofessionals-in-general m, Nurses, LPN m, Psychologists m, Revenue agents m
49	Art teachers f, Chiropractors f, Foreign language teachers f, Nonprofessionals-in-general f; Army officers m, Business education teachers m, Food service managers m, IRS agents m, Occupational therapists m, Physical education teachers m, Professionals-in-general m, Tax auditors m, Travel agents m
48	Army enlisted personnel f, Bankers f, Buyers f, Credit managers f, Nightclub entertainers f, Professionals-in-general f, Revenue agents f, Special education teachers f, Tax auditors f, Women-in-General f; Buyers m, Credit managers m, Dietitians m, Executive housekeepers m, Funeral directors m, Police officers m, Reporters m, Restaurant managers m, Revenue officers m, Sociologists m, Union leaders m
47	Advertising executives f, Army officers f, Executive housekeepers f, Marketing executives f, Nurses, occupational health f, Nurses, RN f, Psychologists f, Sociologists f, Travel agents f; Marketing executives m, Special education teachers m, Store managers m
46	Chamber of Commerce executives f, Christian education directors f, Flight attendants f, Funeral directors f, IRS agents f, Purchasing agents f, Reporters f, Restaurant managers f, Store managers f; Advertising executives m, Marine Corps officers m, Priests m, Purchasing agents m, Social science teachers m, Speech pathologists m
45	Lawyers f, Nursing home administrators f, Police officers f, Public administrators f, Revenue officers f, Social workers f, Speech pathologists f; Bankers m, Broadcasters m, Lawyers m, Mental health workers m, Nursing home administrators m, Realtors m, Retail clerks m
44	Mental health workers f, Personnel directors f, Social science teachers f; English teachers m, Flight attendants m, Guidance counselors m, Personnel directors m, Recreation leaders m, Social workers m
43	English teachers f, Marine Corps officers f, Public relations directors f, YWCA directors f; Ministers m, Public administrators m, Public relations directors m, School administrators m
42	Broadcasters f, Guidance counselors f, Ministers f, Realtors f, Recreation leaders f, Stockbrokers f; YMCA directors m
41	School administrators f; Chamber of Commerce executives m, Elected public officials m, Life insurance agents m, Sales managers m
40	Elected public officials f, Life insurance agents f
39	Auto sales dealers m
38	Stockbrokers m

the current IE scale, where a direct comparison can be made, the sexes have similar scores.

This point is made even more strikingly by the data presented in Table 8.5, which lists the mean scores for male and female samples from the same occupations. The differences are minimal; all but six of the 101 pairs of means are within three points of each other. Women have a slight—very slight—tendency to score more in the extroverted direction, but the differences between women and men in the same occupations are trivial compared to the much larger differences between occupations.

The scores of the 1985 Women-in-General and Men-in-General samples reflect the occupational-sample tendency of women to score slightly lower than men on the IE scale: the 300 women averaged 48, with a standard deviation of 10.4; the 300 men averaged 50, with a standard deviation of 11.2. The nonprofessional women and the nonprofessional men scored 49 and 50, respectively, and the professional women and professional men scored 48 and 49.

IE scale validity.   Table 8.6 lists mean IE scores for 254 occupational samples. The samples are spread over a range of about two standard deviations. Occupations at the high or introverted end of the distribution—in the upper 50's and low 60's—are those that work with things and ideas, such as farmers, mathematicians, sewing machine operators, physicists, computer programmers, and geologists. Occupations at the low or extroverted end of the distribution—in the low 40's and high 30's—are those that work with people, such as stockbrokers, auto sales dealers, life insurance agents, elected public officials, school administrators, sales managers, and Chamber of Commerce executives.

IE scale reliability.   Test-retest statistics for the IE scale over 14-day, 30-day, and 3-year intervals are presented in Table 8.3, along with similar data for the ACADEMIC COMFORT scale. (The samples used to calculate these statistics are described on p. 31) As the data in Table 8.3 indicate, the IE scale is stable over both short and long time periods, with test-retest correlations of .91 to .82 and test-retest means within a point of each other.

Interpreting the IE scale.   A person's score on the IE scale reflects her/his interest in being alone, as opposed to working closely with people: high scores are earned by introverts, people who would rather work with things or ideas; low scores are earned by people who enjoy working with others, especially in sales and social service occupations.

Students with high scores—60 or over—frequently are shy; often they feel great discomfort in any social setting, and they may even find it hard to talk with a counselor in a private office. Many such students express dissatisfaction with their lack of social ease and want to change. Others are comfortable with that aspect of themselves and seek a career that will allow them to remain in the background of public attention.

Occasionally, adults who appear to be outgoing and socially adept score high, toward the introverted end, on the IE scale; the test appears to have "missed." Interview inquiries in such cases frequently reveal that these people do indeed see themselves as introverts, but for some practical reason they have learned to exhibit extroverted behavior—"to close more sales, to get reelected, to keep the office going." Such people usually report that their extroversion operates in relatively short bursts of a few hours or perhaps a day or two; then, they retreat to regenerate their capacity for that behavior. The extroversion skills seem to form with age; this pattern of introverted score and extroverted skill is seldom seen among students.

Students with low scores—40 or under—usually converse easily, and are often among the leaders of their peer groups because of their eagerness to assume substantial social responsibility. Such students frequently are involved in clubs or organizations and many times take leadership roles. Adults with low scores on the IE scale usually are active in community activities or professional organizations.

Most people are located between the two extremes, and their more moderate IE scores suggest only trends in these directions. Scores of 50 reflect a combination of interests that include activities involving people, ideas, and things. This scale and the ACADEMIC COMFORT scale are particularly useful to the counselor at the outset of the interview. Chapter 13 of the *User's Guide* elaborates on the interpretation of the INTROVERSION-EXTROVERSION scale and provides case studies to illustrate its use.

CHAPTER NINE

The Administrative Indexes

The SVIB-SCII Administrative Indexes are routine clerical checks performed by computer on each answer sheet to make certain that nothing has gone awry during the administration, completion, or processing of the answer sheet. The indexes examine three statistics: total responses, infrequent responses, and the percentage of "Like," "Indifferent," and "Dislike" responses to each part of the inventory booklet. How the three are used in interpreting the profile is discussed comprehensively in Chapter 14 of the *User's Guide*.

The Total Responses Index

The first of these indexes, TOTAL RESPONSES (TR), is the number of item responses read by the computer from the answer sheet. The SCII inventory has 325 items; thus if every item was answered, the number printed on the profile should be 325. Occasionally, the marks on the answer sheet will be too light, and the computer will not pick up all of the responses. Or, the person taking the SCII may overlook a section of items, or neglect to complete the inventory. A few answers may be omitted without appreciably affecting the scoring, but if the TR index drops below about 305, the counselor should check the answer sheet to see what happened.

The Infrequent Response Index

The INFREQUENT RESPONSE (IR) index is based on response choices that are selected infrequently, and is basically used to identify answer sheets that may be marked incorrectly. The item weights are assigned so that any respondent selecting several uncommon choices will receive a low score on the index; if the respondent marks more unusual items than the average person does, the score becomes negative. This inverse-weighting technique was employed to simplify the use of the index by counselors and other users. All that needs to be remembered is that if the index is a negative number, there is likely to be a problem somewhere.

To develop this index, the item-response percentages of the General Reference Sample (GRS) were scanned to locate items that were chosen infrequently. One important criterion in selecting the Strong booklet items was that they be neither extremely popular nor extremely unpopular; thus, not many of the items that survived the item screening were selected infrequently by the total GRS sample. However, when the male and female GRS

samples were separated, several items appeared for which the response rate was 6 percent or less; these items became the INFREQUENT RESPONSE indexes, one index for each sex.

Each item-response choice on the two IR indexes was weighted −1, and the GRS samples, along with several other samples, were scored on the scales. The results for each sample are presented in Table 9.1. Among the women, almost everyone selected seven or fewer of the infrequent-response items. Thus, for women, seven infrequent responses were set as the acceptable number of atypical responses. The analogous figure for men is 8. Almost anyone who chooses more of these responses has given an inordinately large number of infrequent responses. Such cases should be scrutinized carefully to make certain that no problems occurred during test administration or scoring.

In practice, each respondent is given a constant on this index—women 7 points, men 8—and 1 point is subtracted from this constant for each infrequent response selected. The result is printed on the profile as the IR score; the highest possible score for women is 7; for men, it is 8.

The IR can indicate the presence of a problem, but it cannot specify which of many possible circumstances is responsible. In one case successfully flagged by this index, the respondent became confused on the answer sheet, skipped a number, and answered the remainder of the items in the wrong spaces on the answer sheet. In another case, a job applicant who was irritated that she had to take the inventory filled it in randomly. In still another case, an individual tried to fool the system— "just to see what would happen," he said—by marking choices reflecting the exact opposite of his true feelings.

When the index is negative, some confusion probably has occurred, and each case should be checked on its own merits. Occasionally no problem exists; the respondent simply has unique interests. That in itself is useful information.

The LP, IP, and DP Indexes

The LP, IP, and DP indexes show the percent of "Like," "Indifferent," and "Dislike" responses selected in each section of the inventory. These figures reflect something of the respondent's response style in filling in the inventory.

TABLE 9.1
Score Distributions on the Male and Female
INFREQUENT RESPONSE Indexes for Several Samples

Female samples on the female index

Raw score (before constant is added)	1985 General Reference Sample (N = 300)	1974 General Reference Sample (N = 300)	Miscellaneous sample No. 1 (N = 201)	Miscellaneous sample No. 2 (N = 106)
−7	0	0	.5	0
−6	.3	1.0	.5	.9
−5	.7	.3	1.5	2.8
−4	3.7	2.7	1.5	2.8
−3	5.7	7.7	9.0	2.8
−2	10.7	13.7	11.9	16.0
−1	25.3	30.7	32.3	23.6
0	53.7%	44.0%	42.8%	50.9%
Mean	− .84	− .99	−1.03	− .95
S.D.	1.17	1.20	1.26	1.32

Male samples on the male index

−8	0	0	.5	0
−7	0	.3	.5	0
−6	0	.7	.5	0
−5	1.0	1.0	.5	5.4
−4	1.3	3.0	3.0	3.6
−3	4.3	5.7	4.5	5.4
−2	9.0	12.0	14.5	14.3
−1	29.0	27.0	28.5	25.0
0	55.3%	50.3%	47.5%	46.4%
Mean	− .70	− .91	− .96	−1.11
S.D.	1.01	1.25	1.31	1.42

TABLE 9.2
Means and Standard Deviations on the LP, IP, and DP
Indexes for 300 Men, 300 Women,
and Combined Group (300 Men and 300 Women)

		Response-percentage index[a]					
		LP		IP		DP	
Booklet part	Sex	Mean	S.D.	Mean	S.D.	Mean	S.D.
I. Occupations	Men	28	14	32	16	40	19
	Women	30	14	27	14	43	18
	Combined	29	14	30	15	41	19
II. School subjects	Men	41	19	35	17	24	18
	Women	46	18	29	15	25	17
	Combined	43	19	32	16	25	18
III. Activities	Men	38	16	35	15	27	14
	Women	42	14	29	13	29	12
	Combined	40	15	32	14	28	13
IV. Leisure activities	Men	37	16	36	16	27	17
	Women	41	14	29	14	30	15
	Combined	39	15	33	15	28	16
V. Types of people	Men	38	20	43	20	19	15
	Women	44	19	37	19	19	14
	Combined	41	20	40	20	19	14
VI. Preference between two activities	Men	39	10	24	17	36	12
	Women	40	11	23	15	37	10
	Combined	40	11	24	16	37	11
VII. Characteristics	Men	60	17	20	14	20	13
	Women	56	18	19	14	25	14
	Combined	58	17	19	14	22	14
Total	Men	35	12	33	12	32	14
	Women	38	11	28	11	34	12
	Combined	37	12	30	12	33	13

[a]For some parts of the booklet, the three response patterns are labeled differently.

Normal response ranges. Means and standard deviations on the LP, IP, and DP indexes for each section of the SCII booklet are given in Table 9.2 for a sample of 300 men and 300 women. These figures show the normal ranges for each section. Although response percentages vary some from section to section, the mean "Like" response rate to the entire item pool is about 37 percent and the standard deviation is about 12. Scores for most respondents will fall between the mean and ±1-1/2 standard deviations, that is, between 20 and 55 percent. Consequently, a "20-55" boundary is sufficient for most interpretive purposes. Indexes within this range are normal and can be accepted without further thought. If response percentages fall outside these limits, the interpretation of certain portions of the profile may have to be modified, as discussed below.

High LP's. A high percentage of "Like" responses for the entire inventory—for example, 65 percent or higher over several sections—will be reflected in the level of scores on the General Occupational Themes and the Basic Interest Scales; a large number of them will be high. This occurs because these scales assign positive weights only to the "Like" response (in contrast to the Occupational Scales, which also weight the "Dislike" response positively, depending on the direction of the difference between the Criterion and Reference Sam-

ples). Although these scores are accurate—they reflect what the respondent says she/he likes—the interpretation of the profile needs to be modified somewhat. For example, if scores on 15 or 16 Basic Interest Scales are over 60, then the definition of a high score, usually regarded as any score over 58, needs to be altered for this individual. In such cases, only the three to five highest scores should be considered "high." Chapter 15 of the *User's Guide* provides case studies and discussion relevant to elevated profiles.

No single characteristic describes all persons with high LP's, but some combination of the adjectives "enthusiastic," "curious," "diverse," "unfocused," and "energetic" will fit many of them.

High DP's. Conversely, if the "Dislike" response percentage is high over several sections of the booklet, the General Occupational Theme and Basic Interest Scale scores will be low, and the above comments need to be reversed.

Persons with high DP's tend to fall into two categories. One includes those people with an intense occupational focus—they mark almost everything "Dislike" because they are interested in a single area, such as art, or science, or mechanics. The other category includes those

TABLE 9.3
Mean "Like" Response Percentages for 240 Occupational Samples

Mean "Like" percent	Occupational samples	Mean "Like" percent	Occupational samples
47	Marine Corps officers f		ecutives m, Elected public officials m, Food service managers m, Industrial arts teachers m, Medical technologists m, Nurses, RN m, Public relations directors m, Realtors m, Recreation leaders m, Revenue officers m, Social science teachers m
46			
45	Auto sales dealers m		
44			
43	Ministers f, School administrators f		
42	Elected public officials f, Guidance counselors f, Life insurance agents f, Recreation leaders f; Marine Corps officers m, Ministers m	36	Biologists f, Chemists f, Computer programmers f, Emergency medical technicians f, Foresters f, Interior decorators f, Investments managers f, Musicians f, Pest controllers f, Pharmacists f, Retail clerks f, Secretaries f; Advertising executives m, Art teachers m, Bankers m, Beauticians m, Chefs m, Chiropractors m, Credit managers m, Dentists m, Elementary teachers m, Foreign language teachers m, IRS agents m, Marine Corps enlisted personnel m, Marketing executives m, Nurses, LPN m, Opticians m, Physical therapists m, Physicians m, Professionals-in-general m, Psychologists m, Research and development managers m, Respiratory therapists m, Science teachers m, Sociologists m, Speech pathologists m, Store managers m, Vocational agriculture teachers m
41	Executive housekeepers f, Occupational health nurses f, YWCA directors f; School administrators m, Stockbrokers m		
40	Army enlisted personnel f, Army officers f, Art teachers f, Electricians f, English teachers f, Flight attendants f, Funeral directors f, Mathematics teachers f, Navy officers f, Nurses, RN f, Revenue officers f, Science teachers f, Social science teachers f; Guidance counselors m, Mental health workers m, YMCA directors m		
39	Agribusiness managers f, Athletic trainers f, Broadcasters f, Carpenters f, Chiropractors f, Dental hygienists f, Foreign language teachers f, IRS agents f, Mental health workers f, Nursing home administrators f, Personnel directors f, Physical education teachers f, Psychologists f, Professionals-in-general f, Public administrators f, Public health nurses f, Public relations directors f, Purchasing agents f, Realtors f, Sociologists f, Special education teachers f; Executive housekeepers m, Flight attendants m, Life insurance agents m, Public administrators m, Retail clerks m	35	Architects f, Bankers f, Beauticians f, Bus drivers f, Cartographers f, Farmers f, Florists f, Geographers f, Nurses, LPN f, Veterinarians f; Air Force officers m, Army enlisted personnel m, Buyers m, Horticultural workers m, Lawyers m, Medical illustrators m, Medical technicians m, Men-in-General m, Police officers m, Physical education teachers m, Tax auditors m, Union leaders m
38	Advertising executives f, Air Force officers f, Business education teachers f, Chefs f, College professors f, Dietitians f, Elementary teachers f, Home economics teachers f, Marine Corps enlisted personnel f, Marketing executives f, Medical technologists f, Navy enlisted personnel f, Occupational therapists f, Physical therapists f, Physicians f, Police officers f, Radiologic technologists f, Reporters f, Restaurant managers f, Revenue agents f, Social workers f, Speech pathologists f, Stockbrokers f, Store managers f, Tax auditors f, Women-in-General f; Dietitians m, English teachers m, Navy officers m, Nursing home administrators m, Occupational therapists m, Personnel directors m, Purchasing agents m, Social workers m, Special education teachers m	34	Accountants f, Artists, fine f, Geologists f, Mathematicians f, Medical illustrators f, Medical technicians f, Physicists f; Accountants m, Air Force enlisted personnel m, Architects m, Artists, commercial m, Athletic trainers m, Broadcasters m, Bus drivers m, Chemists m, College professors m, Emergency medical technicians m, Engineers m, Funeral directors m, Librarians m, Mathematics teachers m, Musicians m, Nonprofessionals-in-general m, Optometrists m, Pharmacists m, Photographers m, Radiologic technologists m, Restaurant managers m, Revenue agents m, Systems analysts m, Travel agents m
37	Air Force enlisted personnel f, Artists, commercial f, Buyers f, Chamber of Commerce executives f, Credit managers f, Dental assistants f, Dentists f, Engineers f, Food service managers f, Horticultural workers f, Lawyers f, Librarians f, Nonprofessionals-in-general f, Optometrists f, Photographers f, Research and development managers f, Respiratory therapists f, Systems analysts f, Travel agents f, Vocational agriculture teachers f; Army officers m, Business education teachers m, Carpenters m, Chamber of Commerce ex-	33	Opticians f; Agribusiness managers m, Biologists m, Cartographers m, Farm implement managers m, Farm supply managers m, Florists m, Interior decorators m, Navy enlisted personnel m, Pest controllers m, Physicists m, Reporters m, Veterinarians m
		32	Artists, fine m, Computer programmers m, Dairy processing managers m, Electricians m, Foresters m, Grain elevator managers m, Geographers m, Investments managers m
		31	Geologists m, Mathematicians m, Nursery managers m
		30	
		29	
		28	Farmers m

who have few "Likes" in the world and who find virtually everything repugnant. The two types present two very different counseling tasks: the first is no problem, because the person is already committed passionately to a fixed course; the second, however, is a formidable challenge, because the person systematically rejects virtually every choice offered. Chapter 15 of the *User's Guide* presents more information on the interpretation of flat and depressed profiles.

High IP's. Occasionally a respondent will check "Indifferent" to a large majority of items in the booklet. These people usually report considerable vocational confusion or, sometimes, generalized apathy. The inventory cannot be much help in such cases—if a young person has no consistent themes within her or his interests, the inventory cannot manufacture them. Some psychologists have found it helpful to have such a person retake the inventory, stressing that the "Indifferent" response should be avoided. No empirical study has been made of the value of scores under such instructions, but adopting this approach at least helps to break the counseling impasse.

Extreme cases. The LP, IP, and DP percentages can provide other useful information, especially when percentages are either extremely high or extremely low. Profiles with one or more percentages below 20 or over 55 should be studied carefully, for they can provide clues for further exploration by the counselor. For example, an occasional student answers "Dislike" to virtually every occupation in the first section of the booklet, while at the same time giving a fairly normal number of "Likes," "Indifferents," and "Dislikes" to the remaining sections of the booklet; such an unusual response pattern should be noted by the counselor and explored with the student. In other cases, students may answer "Dislike" to most to the school subjects, suggesting another fruitful area of discussion for the counselor and client.

Differences between occupations. The range of LP, IP, and DP scores among occupational samples is substantial. Mean LP scores for 240 occupational samples are reported in Table 9.3. Occupations that require working with a variety of people in "social" or "enterprising" environments—such as auto dealers, military officers, school administrators, recreation leaders, ministers, guidance counselors, elected public officials, and life insurance agents—have high LP scores, averaging around 42 percent. Occupations attracting people who frequently work with things or ideas rather than people and who have intensely focused interests—such as farmers, geologists, agribusiness managers, mathematicians, artists, scientists, and computer programmers—have lower LP scores, around 32 percent. In general, the female occupational samples have slightly higher average "Like" response percentages than the male samples do.

LP intercorrelations. The intercorrelations between the LP indexes for the seven parts of the booklet, as well as the entire item pool (Total), are given in Table 9.4. (The correlations for the IP and DP indexes, not given, are similar in pattern to those for the LP index.) Correlations among the first five parts of the booklet, all of

TABLE 9.4

Intercorrelations of the LIKE PERCENTAGE Indexes for the Seven Parts and Total SCII Booklet

(Figures above the diagonal based on sample of 300 women; those below, on sample of 300 men)

Booklet part	Booklet part							
	I	II	III	IV	V	VI	VII	Total
I. Occupations		.61	.62	.64	.45	.10	.29	.91
II. School subjects	.68		.57	.59	.41	.11	.33	.76
III. Activities	.74	.67		.66	.57	.08	.51	.82
IV. Leisure activities	.64	.57	.74		.52	.13	.37	.81
V. Types of people	.52	.48	.59	.63		.04	.33	.64
VI. Preference between two activities	.04	.04	.03	.07	.08		.09	.21
VII. Characteristics	.18	.23	.38	.30	.31	.07		.48
Total	.92	.80	.88	.82	.70	.14	.36	

which contain only L-I-D items, run about .60, indicating a fair consistency among people in the number of "Like" responses given from section to section in the booklet.

The correlations for Part VI are smaller than are the correlations for Parts I–V. In Part VI, "Preference Between Two Activities," the respondent can choose either the item on the left or the one on the right, or mark in the middle, indicating that the items are equal in attraction. This forced-choice item format controls any tendency for response set, but it also makes statistical analysis more difficult, because the individual's response depends on a combination of attraction or aversion to the two choices offered in an item. If the alternatives in this section were realigned in new item combinations, activities formerly rejected by particular respondents might be selected, and vice versa.

LP, IP, and DP scores for Part VI, "Preference Between Two Activities," are presented on the profile, along with scores for the other six sections, to provide counselor and client with complete information, and to allow determination of the response percentage for the entire profile. But the left and right choices in Part VI do not reflect a systematic arrangement of items, or two poles of a psychological characteristic. For example, responses on the left are not weighted as extrovert items, nor are responses on the right weighted as introvert items, or vice versa. Occasionally, extremely high LP scores on other sections of the inventory will be accompanied by high IP, or "equal," scores on the "Preferences" items. This pattern often reflects the response pattern of an individual who is unwilling to reject anything.

The correlations for "Your Characteristics" also are smaller, averaging about .30. Correlations between the entire item pool and each of the parts reflect the number of items in each section; for example, the largest section of the inventory is Part I: "Occupations," with 131 items; this section has the highest correlation with the full item pool.

The correlations in Table 9.4 indicate a mild tendency for people to adopt the same response strategy over various sections of the booklet, though this tendency is not particularly strong. As demonstrated earlier by Figs. 3.1, 3.2, 3.3, and 7.1, the most important determinant of response is item content. Note in particular that corre-

lations of about .60 do not mean that 36 percent of the variance (.60 x .60) is accounted for by the yea-sayer/nay-sayer phenomenon. For that to be the case, the individual's responses would have to be independent of content, and they clearly are not. What the correlation of .60 indicates is that people do differ in the number of "Likes," "Indifferents," and "Dislikes" they choose, and that they are consistent over a variety of inventory sections.

CHAPTER TEN

Interpreting the Results

This chapter is intended to introduce the counselor to the interpretation of the scores on the SVIB-SCII profile. The *User's Guide*, which is a blend of theoretical possibilities, research findings, and clinical knowledge, provides more detailed interpretive information as well as case studies to illustrate how interpretation proceeds. Additional material on interpretation may be found in the concluding sections of Chapters 4 through 8 and in Chapter 9, as well as in the *User's Guide*. Although the profile may seem complex at first, you will find—after examining a few profiles carefully—that it soon makes sense. Once you have examined an actual case in detail with the help of the *Manual* and the *User's Guide*, and perhaps three or four more cases to cover particular points, you will find the explanation and interpretation of the profile flowing easily, leaving you more time to work with the particular concerns of the individual client.

The interpretive remarks in this chapter assume that the counselor is familiar with the preceding chapters of the *Manual*, and with the remarks on the reverse side of the profile (pp. 14–15).

Pre-Test Orientation

Generally, the SCII should be administered in the larger context of career planning; no one should be asked, out of the blue, to sit down and begin marking an answer sheet. An orientation is required, and the character and extent of the orientation will vary as the situation permits or demands. The remarks made at that point need not be extensive. What is said also may depend on special circumstances: in individual testing, the counselor might perceive an excess of skepticism or apprehension; in another case, a sense of competition (where, for example, students are seeking entrance to medical school) may call for discouragement of "look-good" test-taking strategies. If students are filling in the inventory as part of a college orientation session in a large group, the test administrator will have less opportunity to explain the inventory in detail and answer questions than is the case in the usual counseling setting; at the same time, in large group or classroom settings, more visual aids can be used, and the orientation time available per student can be used more efficiently.

At a minimum, anyone filling in the inventory should be told that it is designed to help people make occupational decisions by identifying patterns in their likes and dislikes, and by showing how these patterns compare with those of people in a wide range of occupations.

Sitting Down with the Profile

In preparation for profile interpretation, the following points should be stressed to the counselee:

First, career planning should not be done randomly. People should take some initiative in planning their careers; in particular they should use the best data available to make their decisions.

Second, this inventory will provide some useful information, but that information should not be followed blindly; other data about abilities, experiences, and motivations also should be considered.

Third, career planning is a lifelong activity, not the work of a single afternoon. The information provided by the inventory should be used in long-range planning, now and in the years to come; it should not be used to make one-time decisions about the immediate future.

In these preliminary discussions, the inventory also should be demystified. The counselor or other test administrator should remind the client that the test is not a magic crystal ball, that it cannot solve problems, that it cannot "tell them what they should be"—it can only provide information.

First Steps in Interpreting the Profile

Ideally, the counselor will have studied the profile at some length before the client arrives for the interview. If this can be managed, the counselor's task will be easier; the interpretation is likely to be more accurate, and the client will be more confident of the entire procedure. Certainly, preparation is warranted until the counselor builds some familiarity with the SCII. In practice, however, preparation is often a luxury, and the counselor must build an impression of the client as the interview proceeds. The counselor should begin with the Administrative Indexes and the Special Scales; they can be important to the validity of the interpretation and the success of the interview.

The Administrative Indexes. The first numbers to look at on the profile are the scores on the Administrative Indexes; these are designed to detect problems in test administration and scoring. *If they indicate problems, the remainder of the profile is suspect.*

The TOTAL RESPONSES index reports how many pencil

marks the computer picked up from the answer sheet. Since the inventory has 325 items, and since each one requires a single response, the number reported for this index should be 325 or close to it. Generally, the SCII scoring routine is not notably affected by a few missing responses. But if more than 20 of the responses are missing, something must be done. If the answer sheet is available, it should be examined; in some cases, making heavier marks and then rescoring (through the computer) solves the problem. More often, the person must be retested—when several responses are omitted, it usually is because the person overlooked a block of questions in the booklet, perhaps an entire column or section.

The next index to examine is the INFREQUENT RESPONSES index. This is a measure of the number of highly unusual responses that the person made to the inventory; it is arranged so that the figure reported will be negative if the person picked an unusually high number of atypical responses. When it is negative, some checking should be done; until a reasonable explanation is found, the profile should be treated skeptically. Usually, some specific explanation emerges: for example, the person inadvertently skipped a number on the answer sheet; or the person failed to take the task seriously and filled in the answer sheet randomly; or the person tried some unusual test-taking strategy.

The remaining Administrative Indexes—the LP, IP, and DP Response Indexes—indicate, for each part of the booklet, how the person distributed her or his responses over the "Like," "Indifferent," and "Dislike" choices. These figures can be clinically useful, though in practice they have been found to be subject to considerable overinterpretation. In large samples, the average response percentages are roughly as follows:

Inventory part	LP	IP	DP
Occupations	30%	30%	40%
School Subjects	45	30	25
Activities	40	30	30
Leisure Activities	40	30	30
Types of People	40	40	20
Preferences	40	20	40
Characteristics	60	20	20
Total	35	30	35

(These figures are only averages to keep in mind during counseling sessions; precise means and standard deviations of these percentages are given in Table 9.2.)

People filling in the inventory's answer sheet deviate some from these averages, but the deviations are rarely troublesome; the SCII scoring techniques are quite robust in the face of substantial individual differences.

The Special Scales. The next step in working with the profile is to look at the Special Scales. These are generally useful in learning something about the client's overall orientation; more specifically, they can tell you something about what is likely to happen in the counseling session.

The client's score on the INTROVERSION-EXTROVERSION (IE) scale is a good predictor of how the interview will go,

since it measures, to some extent, the person's sociability. The scale is normed so that the average person scores about 50, with "introverts" averaging about 60 and "extroverts" about 40.

People with scores in the high range—around 60—are not particularly talkative. They do not volunteer much information, and are not likely to ask many questions; the counselor will have to supply the conversational momentum.

Low scores on the INTROVERSION-EXROVERSION scale—40 or below—indicate a person relatively comfortable in social settings, and the interview probably will flow smoothly; the lower the score, the more this will be true. Anyone with a score of 35 or below will be talkative.

The ACADEMIC COMFORT (AC) scale is a rough index of the degree of comfort that a person feels, or might feel, in an academic environment, especially a high-quality liberal-arts-and-science university environment. Because so much career counseling revolves around the amount and kind of education the person is pursuing or contemplating, this score is frequently useful in understanding how the person views the academic experience.

If the ACADEMIC COMFORT scale is high—50 or above—the person probably will be intellectually curious about the profile and interested in the rationale behind the test and her or his scores. If the scale is low—30 or below—the person will be more practical and just want a quick, straightforward summary of the results, not a discussion of the technical details.

The counselor must stress continually to the client that the ACADEMIC COMFORT scale *is not a measure of abilities*, that it is simply a measure of interest in academic pursuits: some people with high scores will not do well at the university level, though they probably will enjoy it; some low scorers will earn advanced degrees, though they usually will report that the university is not where they would enjoy spending much more time.

In any case, people with high scores—55 or above—should be encouraged to pursue some kind of postgraduate work. Clinical experience suggests that people with high scores who do not continue their education will always wish they had.

Interpreting the Three Main Scale Types

With some practice, it takes only a few moments to glance over the Administrative Indexes and Special Scales and develop an impression of how the person answered the inventory and thus how she or he might react to the interview. Very often what the client volunteers in the discussion of the Administrative Indexes and Special Scales provides useful confirmation or modification of that impression. You can then move on to study other areas of the profile, both to determine the main patterns in the person's interests and to establish the basic code type of the profile—in terms of the six General Occupational Themes.

The General Occupational Themes. The coding process begins with the General Occupational Themes. For each Theme, the computer prints a numerical score and a comment on the profile; of these, the latter is more important, since it interprets how the person scored in relation to others of the same sex.

A useful mnemonic in working with these Themes is RIASEC, which combines the first letters of the six Themes. In that order, the six Themes can be characterized by the following shorthand descriptions:

R – REALISTIC
outdoors, technical, mechanical interests

I – INVESTIGATIVE
scientific, inquiring, analytical interests

A – ARTISTIC
dramatic, musical, self-expressive interests

S – SOCIAL
helping, guiding, group-oriented interests

E – ENTERPRISING
entrepreneurial, persuasive, political interests

C – CONVENTIONAL
methodical, organized, clerical interests

In interpreting the General Occupational Themes, a useful approach is to pinpoint the Themes that have been given the interpretive comments "Very high" or "Very low," by circling the asterisks plotted for them. If there are no "Very highs" or "Very lows," circle the "Highs" and "Lows." If there are none of them either, circle the "Moderately highs" and "Moderately lows." In brief, highlight the extremes. Then, working only with the high scores, write on the profile the one, two, or three letters that capture the strongest Themes, and write them in order of dominance. For example, if the profile has "Very high" after the E-Theme and "High" after the I-Theme, and no other "Very high" or "High" scores, write the letters EI across the Themes portion of the profile. If there are two "Highs," look at the numerical scores to see which is higher and write the letters in the appropriate order. If there is only one "High," write just that letter.

The purpose of this step is to generate a one-, two-, or three-letter code type, using the General Occupational Themes. This code type provides substantial interpretive power, as we shall see below. The idea of circling the "Lows" is to point out to the person some areas of interest that do *not* characterize her or him. Frequently it serves to accent "Highs" by contrast; for example: "Your low score on REALISTIC tends to support your high score on SOCIAL—you really do like people better than machines."

The Basic Interest Scales. The next step in organizing the client's profile pattern is to look at the Basic Interest Scales in the same manner. Again, circle the "Highs" and "Lows." Usually, the "Highs" cluster in one or two of the RIASEC areas; using these concentrations, write across the Basic Interest Scale portion of the profile the appropriate one-, two-, or three-letter code type, using your judgment to decide on rank order. If, for example, the two highest scores are PUBLIC SPEAKING and LAW/POLITICS, and the next two are MATHEMATICS and SCIENCE, the code type would be EI.

While doing this, you can explain to the client the

meaning of the Basic Interest Scales, at least glancing at each one, because these scales are the easiest to interpret. Their meaning is clear, and the character of each is captured well by its name.

The Occupational Scales. The next step in the process of highlighting the patterns in the person's profile is to study the scores on the Occupational Scales, looking again for the high scores—40 and over. Circle the three or four highest scores by locating the asterisks in the "Very similar" or "Similar" columns. If the client has no "Very similar" or "Similar" scores, locate the asterisks in the "Moderately similar" column. Then circle the code types for these occupations; these appear on the profile just to the left of the Occupational Scale titles. Usually, the code types you circle will show some similarity—they will be listed close to each other—and by inspecting all of them you can identify a summary one-, two-, or three-letter code type to write on the profile in the Occupational Scale section.

The Occupational Scales tie the client's pattern of interests into the working world; a high score—which is plotted graphically in the "Moderately similar," "Similar," or "Very similar" column—indicates that the person's interests match those of people happily employed in that occupation. Pointing out the lowest scores also is useful, although it may not serve much of a counseling function because the person usually is well aware that she/he is not interested in those areas.

The counselor and student should work together to try to find a common element among the high scores. Frequently, the student will want to focus on one or two specific Occupational Scales for further discussion. That is perfectly appropriate, and the counselor should be prepared to do that. Concurrently, the counselor should be persistent in pointing out the underlying Themes, indicating how these particular occupations fit into them and, then, in encouraging the client to think about related occupations not on the profile. Appendixes A and B of the *Manual* and the *User's Guide*, which list many occupations and their codes, are useful aids for generalizing to other occupational possibilities.

Searching Out Further Possibilities

The next step in profile interpretation is to help the person understand where people with her or his particular code type tend to settle in the occupational world. This can be done by referring to the profile, paying particular attention to those occupations that have the same Themes represented anywhere within their code types; for example, IR occupations would cluster with IRE, IRS, and IRC occupations, as well as RI occupations. Once the counselee understands the general pattern that is emerging, you can both speculate about other occupations, not given on the profile, that might fall in this segment of the world of work.

The next step in this occupation-seeking stage is to consult Appendixes A and B of this *Manual* (or the *User's Guide*), which list many more occupations and their code types. With the use of these listings, a large group of potential occupations can be constructed for the client to consider.

Since the main purpose of this inventory is to stimulate the counselees to consider occupations that may match their interests, and to help them find other pathways for exploration, these occupation-seeking steps should proceed in ways that maximize the number of opportunities actively considered. In particular, the counselees should be encouraged to consider relevant occupations they may not have considered before because of lack of exposure, or because of some misconception of the nature of an occupation, or preconception that the occupation was not open to them—perhaps on grounds of sex, social class, or ethnic background. Emphatically, clients should be encouraged to consider all relevant occupations.

Although little is known about how a person's patterns of vocational interests are initially formed, it seems likely that the major influence is past experience. If that experience has been limited, the resulting patterns of interests may be constricted. Consequently, every client, no matter what her or his age or specific situation, should be encouraged to engage in wide-ranging vocational exploration, and to gain a broad range of experience.

APPENDIX A

Occupational Criterion Samples, DOT Codes, and Related Job Titles

The samples described below are those used to develop the current SVIB-SCII Occupational Scales. For each, the column headed "Composition" supplies the sample source as well as noteworthy demographic data. The heading "DOT code and description" offers, for each occupation, synopses of the information presented in the *Dictionary of Occupational Titles (DOT)*. The DOT description begins with the three-digit DOT code most appropriate for that sample. These three digits will help your client locate related occupations in the DOT. The first digit indicates within which of the nine very broad categories the occupation fits:

0/1 Professional, technical, and managerial occupations
2 Clerical and sales occupations
3 Service occupations
4 Agricultural, fishery, forestry, and related occupations
5 Processing occupations
6 Machine trades occupations
7 Bench work occupations
8 Structural work occupations
9 Miscellaneous occupations

The second digit indicates a more specific division of work within the nine broad categories, and the third digit locates a particular occupation within that division. The information presented under "Composition" and "DOT code and description" will help you to aid your client in identifying the responsibilities, job tasks, work environments, and skills entailed in each of the occupations represented on the profile.

The last column, "Related occupations," is a list of jobs related to each of the Criterion Samples. As discussed in Chapters 6 and 10 of this *Manual* and in Chapters 9 and 20 of the *User's Guide*, this list, along with the occupations suggested in Appendix B, will help you to broaden your client's career exploration by generalizing beyond the Strong profile to occupations appropriate for her or his consideration.

Sample/ scale	N	Year tested	Mean age	Mean years educ	Mean years exper	Composition	DOT code and description	Related occupations
ACCOUNTANT (f)	294	1977	36.6	16.3	11.3	Members, American Institute of Certified Public Accountants. 75% completed BA degree, 15% MA.	**160.** Designs new systems or modifies existing systems to provide records of assets, liabilities, and financial transactions of establishment. Maintains accounts and records or supervises subordinates in such bookkeeping activities as recording disbursements, expenses, or tax payments or in maintenance of accounting controls over inventories, purchases. Audits contracts, orders, and vouchers and prepares reports that substantiate individual transactions before their settlement. May work independently for a fee, as a member of an accounting firm, or for a corporation.	Auditor Budget accountant City auditor Controller Cost acountant County auditor Internal auditor Property accountant Systems accountant
ACCOUNTANT (m)	317	1977	38.9	16.5	14.6	See women's sample above. 76% completed BA degree, 16% MA.		
ADVERTISING EXECUTIVE (f)	216	1973	39.0	14.9	13.0	Advertising executives listed in *Standard Directory of Advertising Agencies*, with	**164.** Plans or assists in planning advertising programs to promote sale of company's	Advertising manager Advertising pro-

Sample/ scale	N	Year tested	Mean age	Mean years educ	Mean years exper	Composition	DOT code and description	Related occupations
						emphasis on agency executives. 29% completed BA degree, 6% MA. Sample included media directors and buyers, creative directors, art directors, production directors, research directors, account executives, client service directors, and broadcasting directors.	products; consults with company officials, sales department, and advertising agency to develop promotional plans. Prepares advertising brochures and manuals for publication. Reviews and proofreads layout and copy before advertisement or brochure is printed. May	motions manager Advertising sales manager Creative director Display manager Manager, ad agency
ADVERTISING EXECUTIVE (m)	217	1982	38.4	16.2	12.9	See women's sample above. 5% completed AA degree, 66% BA, 17% MA, 12% other. 23% were account executives, 17% art directors, 12% creative directors, 19% other. Major activities included administrative functions (29%), client contact (16%), consultation with artists (10%), a combination of activities (30%), and other (16%). 31% held the title of President or Vice President.	write copy, do layout work, prepare sales kits, set up displays, or write sales outlines for use by sales staff, or direct other workers performing these duties.	Media director Radio advertising director
AGRIBUSINESS MANAGER (m)	297	1972	43.4	N/A	16.0	Grain elevator managers (22%), implement dealers (21%), farm supply managers (21%), dairy processing plant managers (20%), nursery managers (16%).	**180.** Nursery manager: grows plants for sale to trade or retail customers; determines type and quantity to be grown. Selects and purchases seeds, nutrients, and disease-control chemicals. **529.** Dairy processing manager: supervises and coordinates production of dairy products; directs workers in receiving and testing milk and in operations such as pasteurizing and storing dairy products. **529.** Grain elevator manager: supervises and coordinates unloading, loading, storing, cleaning, and blending of grain for milling and shipment. **624.** Implement dealer and farm service supply manager: sells and repairs implements used on farms, such as cultivators, harvesting machines, plows, tractors, and weeders.	Cooperative manager Dairy processing manager Elevator manager Farm implement dealer Farm supply manager Grain buyer Nursery manager
AIR FORCE ENLISTED PERSONNEL (f)	193	1984	29.4	13.3	8.4	Roster of enlistees provided by the Defense Manpower Data Center, Department of Defense. 66% had high school diploma, 15% a degree or certificate from a vocational-technical institution, 12% completed AA degree, 6% BA.	**378.** Provides technical support for the operation of military aircraft. Repairs and maintains aircraft. Aids in the transportation of military passengers, mail, and freight. May aid pilot in navigation of aircraft, may prepare weapons, equipment, and	Aircraft mechanic Airline radio operator Communications system operator Counterintelligence agent

Sample/ scale	N	Year tested	Mean age	Mean years educ	Mean years exper	Composition	DOT code and description	Related occupations
AIR FORCE ENLISTED PERSONNEL (m)	209	1984	33.2	13.2	13.6	See women's sample above. 57% had high school diploma, 16% a degree or certificate from a vocational-technical institution, 21% completed AA degree, 3% BA, 2% MA.	artillery. May participate in drills and operations concerned with protecting the nation from enemies. May be trained in any number of jobs paralleling civilian occupations.	Defense fire control systems operator Electronic intelligence operations specialist Parachute rigger Radiotelephone operator Reconnaissance crew member Recruit instructor Sound technician Survival specialist Target aircraft technician
AIR FORCE OFFICER (f)	234	1979	32.3	17.0	8.7	Roster of commissioned officers provided by Defense Manpower Data Center, Department of Defense. 52% completed BA degree, 47% MA. Rank: lieutenant (4%), captain (77%), major (11%), lt. colonel (8%), colonel (1%).	196. Pilots jets to transport passengers, mail, freight; may pilot combat aircraft or new, experimental aircraft to determine airworthiness. Navigates aircraft, locating position and course using navigation instruments and charts. May take any of a variety of administrative assignments.	Air traffic controller Communications officer Fighter pilot Intelligence officer Navigator Transportation officer Weapons control officer
AIR FORCE OFFICER (m)	292	1979	37.5	16.0	14.3	See women's sample above. 35% completed BA degree, 60% MA. Rank: lieutenant (2%), captain (39%), major (25%), lt. colonel (21%), colonel (13%), higher (1%).		
ARCHITECT (f)	215	1979	40.3	18.1	14.9	Roster from 44 state registration boards, obtained with assistance of National Council of Architectural Registration Boards. 71% completed BA degree, 22% MA. Areas of specialty included housing (26%), institutional (21%), commercial (15%), and a combination (24%).	001. Plans and designs private residences, office buildings, theaters, public buildings, factories, and other structures, and organizes services necessary for construction. Consults with client to determine size and space requirements, and provides information regarding cost, design, materials, equipment, and estimated building time. Plans layout of project; integrates structural, mechanical, and ornamental elements into unified design. Prepares sketches of proposed project for client. Writes specifications and prepares scale and full-size drawings and other contract documents for use of building contractors and crafts people.	Architectural drafter Designer Evaluating architect Landscape architect Landscape drafter Marine architect Principal architect Technical architect Urban designer
ARCHITECT (m)	216	1979	40.6	17.7	15.6	See women's sample above. 72% completed BA degree, 15% MA. Areas of specialty included institutional (30%), commercial (27%), housing (16%), and a combination (16%).		
ARMY ENLISTED PERSONNEL (f)	197	1984	30.2	13.5	7.6	Roster of enlistees provided by Defense Manpower Data Center, Department of De-	378. Prepares weapons, equipment, and artillery for movement and combat op-	Armor reconnaissance specialist

Sample/ scale	N	Year tested	Mean age	Mean years educ	Mean years exper	Composition	DOT code and description	Related occupations
						fense. 66% had high school diploma, 8% a degree or certificate from a vocational-technical institution, 17% completed AA degree, 8% BA, 1% MA.	erations. Repairs and maintains overland vehicles. Aids in the transportation of military passengers, mail, and freight. May participate in drills and operations concerned with protecting the nation from enemies. May be trained in any number of jobs paralleling civilian occupations.	Camouflage specialist Cartographer Combat rifle crew member Disaster specialist Drafter Field artillery crew member Infantry unit leader Map editor Tank crew member Topographical drafter
Army Enlisted Personnel (m)	185	1984	34.1	12.9	13.8	See women's sample above. 64% had high school diploma, 13% received a degree or certificate from a vocational-technical institution, 18% completed AA degree, 3% BA.		
Army Officer (f)	285	1979	32.2	16.8	7.9	Roster of commissioned officers provided by Defense Manpower Data Center, Department of Defense. 57% completed BA degree, 35% MA. Rank: warrant officer (4%), lieutenant (19%), captain (59%), major (14%), lt. colonel (3%), colonel (1%).	378. Directs personnel in preparing weapons, equipment, and artillery, for movement and combat operations. Organizes unit operations when deployed in field. Prepares unit reports, correspondence, and schedules. Provides leadership. May take any of a variety of administrative assignments.	Artillery officer Communications officer Infantry officer Intelligence officer Tank officer Transportation officer
Army Officer (m)	309	1979	36.8	16.9	13.5	See women's sample above. 11% had taken courses not leading to a degree, 42% completed BA degree, 44% MA. Rank: warrant officer (12%), lieutenant (3%), captain (31%), major (23%), lt. colonel (23%), colonel (7%), higher (1%).		
Art Teacher (f)	360	1981	39.0	18.0	11.2	Members, National Art Association, secondary division. All were secondary school teachers. 41% completed BA degree, 58% MA. 79% of sample spent a minimum of 50% of time teaching; other activities included lesson preparation, grading, and administrative functions. Main areas of art included general, painting and drawing, sculpture, ceramics, print making, and weaving.	149. Teaches courses such as drawing, color, weaving, crafts, sculpture, water colors. Instructs students through lectures, demonstrations, and audiovisual aids. Prepares teaching outline for course of study. Administers tests to evaluate students' progress. Keeps attendance records and maintains discipline. Participates in faculty and professional meetings, conferences, and teacher-training workshops. Performs related duties such as sponsoring special activities or student organizations.	Art therapist Crafts instructor Design instructor Drawing teacher Graphic arts teacher Industrial design instructor
Art Teacher (m)	303	1978	40.2	19.2	14.9	See women's sample above. All were secondary school teachers. 15% completed BA degree, 64% MA, 19% PhD		
Artist, Commercial (f)	222	1983	33.9	15.5	9.8	Artists working for agencies and studios listed in *The Creative Black Book*, a national directory of art services, as well as national sample of artists listed in *Bell*	141. Designs artwork to promote public consumption of materials, products, or services. Designs artwork for books, magazines, newspapers, television, or packaging.	Art director Cartoonist Cinematographer Clothes designer Color expert

Sample/scale	N	Year tested	Mean age	Mean years educ	Mean years exper	Composition	DOT code and description	Related occupations
						Yellow Pages. 3% had high school diploma, 20% had had some art courses not leading to a degree in art, 8% completed AA degree in art, 54% BA, 8% MA. 33% were freelance artists, 22% were employed by an advertising agency, 19% by a studio. Major activities included illustration (17%), graphic design (13%), administration (8%), keylining (7%), layout (7%), and a combination (38%).	Determines arrangement of material; prepares illustrations and sketches for client; gives instruction to people who prepare final layout. May select type or draw lettering.	Display designer Fashion artist Furniture designer Graphic designer Illustrator Keyliner artist Mechanical artist Photograph retoucher Production artist Publication designer Set designer
ARTIST, COMMERCIAL (m)	206	1979	38.8	16.2	15.6	See women's sample above. 27% had taken art courses not leading to a degree, 47% completed BA degree, 6% MA. 39% were freelance artists, 23% were employed by a studio, 10% by an advertising agency, 15% by a combination of employers.		
ARTIST, FINE (f)	247	1979	44.4	17.6	17.0	Selected from *Who's Who in American Art*. 18% had taken art courses not leading to a degree, 25% completed BA degree, 42% MA. 58% were freelance artists, 15% were employed by educational institutions, 22% by a combination of employers.	**144.** Creates art works whose primary purpose is to be viewed for aesthetic content. Conceives and develops works of art, selects the theme, subject matter, medium, and manner of execution. May paint a variety of original subject material using watercolors, oils, acrylics, tempera, or other paint medium. May create art work on stone, metal, wood or other material, using various tools, procedures, and processes to etch, engrave, carve, paint, or draw. May design and construct three-dimensional artworks, using any combination of mediums, methods, and techniques.	Filmmaker Glassblower Metalsmith Painter Photographer Potter Printmaker Sculptor Weaver
ARTIST, FINE (m)	213	1979	43.5	18.0	20.5	See women's sample above. 13% had taken art courses not leading to a degree, 15% completed BA degree, 55% MA. 39% were freelance artists, 39% were employed by educational institutions, 15% by a combination of employers.		
ATHLETIC TRAINER (f)	242	1983	29.3	18.0	5.9	National sample of certified athletic trainers from National Athletic Trainers Assoc. 25% completed BA degree, 73% MA, 2% PhD. Employers included four-year colleges (59%), high schools (22%), two-year colleges (5%), professional athletic teams (1%), other (12%). 7% specialized in a particular sport. Major activities included evaluation and treatment of injuries (39%), covering practices and games (29%), and a combination (27%).	**153.** Evaluates physical condition and advises and treats professional and amateur athletes to maintain maximum physical fitness for participation in athletic competition. Prescribes routine and corrective exercises to strengthen muscles. Recommends special diets to build up health and reduce overweight athletes. Gives massages to relieve soreness, strains, and bruises. Gives first aid to injured players. Treats chronic minor injuries and related disabilities to maintain athletes' performance. May give heat and	Physical fitness teacher Physical therapist Sports medicine coordinator
ATHLETIC TRAINER (m)	250	1983	32.5	18.0	9.4	See women's sample above. 30% completed BA degree,		

Sample/ scale	N	Year tested	Mean age	Mean years educ	Mean years exper	Composition	DOT code and description	Related occupations
						68% MA, 1% PhD. Employers included four-year colleges (59%), high schools (16%), professional athletic teams (9%), two-year colleges (5%), and a combination (2%). 21% specialized in a particular sport. Major activities included evaluation and treatment of injuries (48%), covering practices and games (24%), and a combination (25%).	diathermy treatments as prescribed by health service.	
BANKER (f)	247	1981	43.8	13.8	18.8	Selected from *Yearbook of the National Association of Bank Women, Inc.* 51% had high school diploma, 12% completed BA degree, 14% MA. 99% were employed by banks, the remainder by trust companies, credit unions, and mortgage companies. Major activities included administration (28%), customer contact (25%), financial planning and development (5%), and a combination (33%).	**186.** Directs bank's monetary programs, transactions, and security measures in accordance with banking principles and legislation. Coordinates program activities and evaluates operating practices to ensure efficient operations. Oversees receipt, disbursement, and expenditure of money. Signs documents approving or effecting monetary transactions. Directs safekeeping and control of assets and securities. Approves loans and participates as member of committees concerned with lending and customer-service functions. Directs accounting for assets and maintains specified legal cash reserve. Reviews financial and operating statements and presents reports and recommendations to bank officials or board committees. Maintains financial and community business affiliations.	Bank controller Bank officer Cashier Credit union manager Loan officer Operations officer Teller Trust officer
BANKER (m)	205	1981	44.8	16.7	18.8	Selected from *Directory of American Bankers Association.* 10% had high school diploma, 5% completed AA degree, 42% BA, 22% MA, 16% a law degree. 92% were employed by banks, 5% by trust companies. Major activities included administration (28%), customer contact (12%), financial planning and development (7%), and a combination (42%).		
BEAUTICIAN (f)	181	1984	35.3	13.1	13.6	From listings of state licensing boards of Alaska, Georgia, Illinois, Iowa, Michigan, Minnesota, South Dakota, Utah, Wisconsin, as well as national sampling from *Bell Telephone Yellow Pages.* 3% had high school diploma, 91% attended a school of cosmetology, 1% completed AA degree, 4% other. Major activities included hairdressing (72%), management (6%), and a combination (20%).	**332.** Provides beauty services for customers. Suggests hair styles according to physical features of patron and current styles, or from instructions of patron. Styles hair using clippers, scissors, and razors. Shampoos hair and scalp and rinses hair with prepared rinses. Massages scalp and gives other hair and scalp-conditioning treatments for hygienic or remedial purposes.	Barber Cosmetologist Hair stylist Make-up artist Salon manager
BEAUTICIAN (m)	195	1984	37.0	13.8	14.6	See women's sample above. 6% had high school diploma, 82% attended a school of cosmetology, 3% completed AA degree, 4% BA. Major ac-		

Sample/ scale	N	Year tested	Mean age	Mean years educ	Mean years exper	Composition	DOT code and description	Related occupations
						tivities included hairdressing (62%), management (17%), teaching (2%), and a combination (15%).		
BIOLOGIST (f)	214	1975	42.5	21.1	12.7	Members, American Institute of Biological Sciences. 34% were in teaching, 24% in research, and 37% in a combination of activities.	**041.** Studies origin, relationship, development, anatomy, functions, and other basic principles of plant and animal life. May specialize in research centering around a particular plant, animal, or aspect of biology. May teach college courses.	Anatomist Aquatic biologist Bacteriologist Biochemist Biomedical researcher Botanist Ecologist Entomologist Geneticist Microbiologist Oceanographer Ornithologist Physiologist Plant pathologist Zoologist
BIOLOGIST (m)	214	1975	43.6	21.6	15.4	See women's sample above. 30% were in teaching, 46% in a combination of teaching, research, and administration.		
BROADCASTER (f)	220	1983	32.4	15.3	7.8	Sample collected from stations listed in *Broadcasting Yearbook* and from responses to ads in *Inside Radio* and *Radio and Records.* Also members of American Women in Radio and Television, Inc. 23% had high school diploma, 57% completed BA degree, 9% MA. 84% were employed by a commercial station, 15% by a public station. 56% were department heads. Major activities included on-the-air broadcasting (28%), programming (13%), sales (9%), research (7%), newsgathering and reporting (6%), a combination (26%), and other (general management, production, and copyrighting functions, 9%).	**159.** Announces radio and television programs to audience. Memorizes script, reads, or ad-libs to identify stations; introduces and closes shows; announces station breaks, commercials, or public service information. Cues worker to transmit program from network central station according to schedule. May describe public event or interview guest or moderate panel or discussion show. May keep daily program log. May be designated according to media or type of program.	Anchor Announcer Assignment editor Continuity director Disc jockey General manager Local announcer Music director Network announcer News director Operations director Promotions director Reporter Sports director Television announcer Traffic director
BROADCASTER (m)	213	1983	34.2	15.5	12.8	Sample collected from stations listed in *Broadcasting Yearbook* and from responses to ads in *Inside Radio* and *Radio and Records.* 26% had high school diploma, 53% completed BA degree, 7% MA. All were radio broadcasters; 85% were employed by a commercial station. 65% were department heads. Major activities included on-the-air broadcasting (30%), programming (21%), management and administration (8%), newsgathering and writing (4%), sales (3%), a combination (25%), and other (3%).		

Sample/ scale	N	Year tested	Mean age	Mean years educ	Mean years exper	Composition	DOT code and description	Related occupations
Bus Driver (f)	117	1984	37.9	12.8	7.3	Members, American Bus Association, which distributed packets to drivers; packets also mailed to bus companies listed in national sampling of telephone directories and to drivers of Metropolitan Transit Commission, Minneapolis, MN. 64% had high school diploma, 16% completed a degree or certificate from a vocational-technical school, 2% completed AA degree, 8% BA. 41% drove bus within a metropolitan area, 6% between cities, 53% a combination. Employers included metropolitan bus company (33%), school bus company (33%), interstate bus company (9%), charter bus company (9%), and a combination (11%). 80% of sample spent a minimum of 75% of work time driving bus. Other activities included inspection of vehicle and preparation of reports.	**913.** Drives bus to transport passengers over specified routes to local or distant points according to time schedule. Assists passengers with baggage and collects tickets or cash fares. Complies with local traffic regulations. Reports delays or accidents. Records cash receipts or ticket fares. May inspect bus and check gas, oil, and water before departure. May load or unload baggage checked by passengers.	Charter bus driver Chauffeur Interstate bus driver Metro bus driver Motor coach driver School bus driver Taxi cab driver Trolley coach driver
Bus Driver (m)	138	1984	39.3	13.7	9.4	See women's sample above. 56% had high school diploma, 16% completed a degree or certificate from a vocational-technical institution, 4% completed AA degree, 18% BA, and 2% MA. 45% drove bus within a metropolitan area, 13% between cities, and 42% a combination. Employers included metropolitan bus company (54%), charter bus company (20%), interstate bus company (12%), school bus company (5%), and a combination (6%). 82% of sample spent a minimum of 75% of work time driving bus. Other activities included inspection of vehicle and preparation of reports.		
Business Education Teacher (f)	420	1978	38.3	18.0	11.4	Members, National Business Education Association; all were secondary school teachers. 31% completed BA degree, 66% MA.	**091.** Instructs students through lectures, demonstrations, and audiovisual aids. Prepares teaching outline for course of study, assigns lessons, and corrects homework. Administers tests to evaluate students' progress. Keeps attendance records and maintains discipline. Participates in faculty and professional meetings, con-	Accounting teacher Bookkeeping instructor Business law teacher Merchandising instructor Typing teacher
Business Education Teacher (m)	232	1978	38.8	18.5	13.2	See women's sample above. 15% completed BA degree, 78% MA, 5% PhD.		

Sample/ scale	N	Year tested	Mean age	Mean years educ	Mean years exper	Composition	DOT code and description	Related occupations
							ferences, and teacher-training workshops. Performs related duties such as sponsoring special activities or student organizations. Teaches courses in typing, business law, bookkeeping, accounting, shorthand, merchandising, word processing, or office management.	
BUYER (f)	214	1983	35.4	14.9	8.8	Names from *Salesmen's Guide to Women's and Children's Wear Buyers* and *Salesmen's Guide to Men's and Boy's Wear Buyers*. 33% had high school diploma, 11% completed AA degree, 48% BA. 46% were employed by department stores, 29% by specialty shops, 10% by chains. 81% bought for more than one department.	**162.** Purchases merchandise for resale. Selects and orders merchandise from showings of manufacturing representatives, basing selection on nature of clientele, demand for specific merchandise, and experience as buyer. Authorizes payment of invoices or return of merchandise. May conduct staff meetings with selling personnel to introduce new merchandise. May price items for resale.	Assistant buyer Children's buyer Men's buyer Women's buyer
BUYER (m)	219	1983	36.9	16.3	10.8	See women's sample above. 25% had high school diploma, 8% completed AA degree, 60% BA, 7% MA. 40% were employed by department stores, 25% by specialty shops, 18% by chains. 96% bought for more than one department.		
CARPENTER (f)	97	1984	31.4	15.1	4.7	Members, United Brotherhood of Carpenters and Joiners of America, and participants in a Women in the Trades Conference. 46% had high school diploma, 6% AA degree, 33% BA, 8% MA. 39% were final-year apprentices, 34% were at journey level. 26% did mainly rough carpentry work, 5% finish, and 64% a combination. 36% of sample specialized in a particular area of carpentry. 91% of sample spent a minimum of 50% of time doing manual labor. Other activities included reading blueprints, communicating with contractors, problem-solving, and administrative functions.	**860.** Constructs, erects, installs, and repairs structures and fixtures of wood, plywood, and wallboard, using carpenter's hand tools and power tools, and conforming to local building codes. Studies blueprints, sketches, or building plans for information pertaining to type of material required, and dimensions of stucture or fixture to be fabricated. Selects specified type of materials, prepares layout, marks cutting and assembly lines on materials, and fastens them together. Verifies trueness of structure, erects framework for structures.	Acoustical carpenter Apprentice carpenter Boatbuilder Cabinet maker Carpentry repairer Contractor Finish carpenter Form builder Joiner Journey carpenter Maintenance carpenter Mold carpenter Rough carpenter
CARPENTER (m)	199	1983	27.3	13.3	4.6	Members, United Brotherhood of Carpenters and Joiners of America. 73% had high school diploma, 7% received AA degree, 8% BA, 2% other. 82% were final-year apprentices, 15% were at journey level. 18% did mainly rough carpentry, 21% finish,		

Sample/scale	N	Year tested	Mean age	Mean years educ	Mean years exper	Composition	DOT code and description	Related occupations
						53% a combination. 30% of sample specialized in a particular area of carpentry. 62% of sample spent a minimum of 75% of time doing manual labor. Other activities included reading blueprints, communicating with contractors, problem-solving, and administrative functions.		
CHAMBER OF COMMERCE EXECUTIVE (f)	217	1979	45.5	13.4	7.3	Members, American Chamber of Commerce Executives (ACCE), and names selected from *Johnson's World Wide Chamber of Commerce Directory*. 67% had high school diploma, 12% completed BA degree.	187. Directs activities of Chamber of Commerce to promote business, industrial development, and civic improvements in community. Administers programs of committees that perform such functions as providing economic and marketing information, promoting economic growth and stability in community, and counseling business organizations and industry on problems affecting local economy. Prepares and submits annual budget to authorized elected officials for approval. Studies government legislation, taxation, and other fiscal matters to determine effect on community interests.	Branch director Community organization director Executive director Executive vice president Program director
CHAMBER OF COMMERCE EXECUTIVE (m)	290	1978	42.7	15.9	12.4	See women's sample above. 9% had high school diploma, 61% completed BA degree, 10% MA.		
CHEF (f)	106	1984	31.8	14.5	6.8	Members, American Culinary Federation, Inc., and graduates of Johnson and Wales College in Providence, RI, and of Culinary Institute, Hyde Park, NY. 6% had high school diploma, 14% attended a trade or vocational school, 58% completed AA degree, 12% BA, 1% MA. 21% were employed by restaurants, 16% by hotels, 11% by private clubs, 6% by catering services, 5% by educational institutions, 25% by a combination, and the remainder by resorts, hospitals, or institutional firms. Major activities included food preparation (42%), supervision and training (15%), planning menus (3%), and a combination (33%).	313. Supervises, coordinates, and participates in activities of cooks and other kitchen personnel engaged in preparing and cooking foods in a hotel, restaurant, or other eating establishment. Estimates food consumption and purchases, or requisitions food stuffs and kitchen supplies. Selects and develops recipes. May employ, train, or discharge workers. May plan menus.	Banquet chef Chef saucer Chef tournant Cook Corporate chef Executive chef Food production manager Garden manager Pantry chef Pastry chef Sous chef
CHEF (m)	296	1983	37.4	13.9	14.0	Members, American Culinary Federation, Inc. 17% had high school diploma, 33% attended a technical or vocational school, 22% had AA degree, 10% BA, 3% MA.		

Sample/ scale	N	Year tested	Mean age	Mean years educ	Mean years exper	Composition	DOT code and description	Related occupations
						25% were employed by restaurants, 21% by private clubs, 15% by hotels, 18% by a combination, and the remainder by resorts, hospitals, educational institutions, caterers, industrial firms, or other. Major activities included supervision and training (30%), food preparation (22%), ordering food (3%), and a combination (40%).		
CHEMIST (f)	260	1978	37.9	20.9	11.0	Members, American Chemical Society, all with PhD degree. 43% were in research, 26% in teaching, and 14% in a combination of activities; 60% were employed by educational institutions, 22% by industry.	022. Performs chemical tests or qualitative and quantitative chemical analyses, or conducts chemical experiments in laboratories for quality or process control or to develop new products or new knowledge. Conducts experiments on substances to develop and improve materials and products and to discover scientific facts. May teach college courses.	Assayer Biochemist Clinical chemist Food chemist Forensic researcher Immunochemist Organic chemist Perfumer Pharmaceutical chemist
CHEMIST (m)	278	1978	41.0	20.6	15.1	See women's sample above. 47% were in research, 18% in administration, 14% in teaching, and 17% in a combination of activities; 52% were employed by industry, 35% by educational institutions.		
CHIROPRACTOR (f)	212	1979	42.8	17.9	14.3	Rosters obtained from American Chiropractic Association, International Chiropractors Association, and *Digest of Chiropractic Economics*. 90% were self-employed or in partnerships; 10% were employed by clinics, educational institutions, or a combination.	079. Adjusts spinal column and other joints of body to prevent disease and correct abnormalities of human body believed to be caused by interference with nervous system. Examines patient to determine nature and extent of disorder using x-ray machines and other instruments. Manipulates spine or other involved areas.	Accupuncturist Chiropractic assistant Osteopath
CHIROPRACTOR (m)	230	1982	38.7	19.2	11.7	Members, American Chiropractic Association. 90% were self-employed or in partnerships; 10% were employed by clinics, educational institutions, or a combination. 88% of sample spent a minimum of 50% of time in diagnosis or treatment of patients.		
COLLEGE PROFESSOR (f)	400	1972	49.0	19.6	17.0	From college-catalog faculty listings; mix sought with respect to academic area, type of institution, and location; criteria of selection included high academic rank and level of education. 1% completed less than MA degree, 22% MA, 77% PhD or equivalent. Academic disciplines included business and law (9%), linguistics (8%), mathematics (7%), physical sciences (12%), biomedical sciences (10%),	090. Conducts college or university classes for undergraduate or graduate students. Prepares and delivers lectures, compiles bibliographies of specialized materials, and stimulates discussions. Compiles, administers, and grades examinations or assigns this work to others. Directs research of others. Conducts research in particular field of knowledge and publishes findings in pro-	Dean Department chair Instructor

Sample/ scale	N	Year tested	Mean age	Mean years educ	Mean years exper	Composition	DOT code and description	Related occupations
						medical services (10%), social services and education (10%), social sciences (10%), art, music, and literature (13%), miscellaneous (12%).	fessional journals. Performs related duties such as advising students and working with student organizations. Serves on faculty committees; provides professional consulting services to government and industry.	
COLLEGE PROFESSOR (m)	229	1983	43.5	20.4	13.2	Nationwide sample from maillist company of college and university professors. 19% completed MA degree, 79% PhD. 42% were employed by public universities, 21% by private universities, 16% by private four-year colleges, 14% by public four-year colleges. Titles included full professor (38%), associate professor (39%), and assistant professor (23%). Academic disciplines included social sciences (23%), physical sciences (16%), biomedical sciences (15%), art and literature (13%), social service and education (11%). Major activities included teaching (23%), research (12%), administration (7%), class preparation (7%), publishing (2%), and a combination (45%). 37% held an administrative as well as an academic appointment.		
COMPUTER PROGRAMMER (f)	243	1975	33.0	15.7	6.9	Rosters provided by Society for Data Processors, and write-in responses to articles in *Computerworld*; those selected for sample spent at least 50% of time programming. 13% had high school diploma, 54% completed BA degree, 14% MA. 71% worked in business-related areas, 14% scientific areas, 5% educational areas.	**020.** Develops and writes natural- and artifical-language computer programs to store, locate, and retrieve specific documents, data, and information. Applies knowledge of advanced mathematics and understanding of computer capabilities and limitations. May confer with supervisor and representatives of departments affected by program to resolve questions, output requirements, input data acquisition, extent of automatic programming and coding use, and modification and inclusion of internal checks and controls. Observes or operates computer during testing or processing runs to analyze and correct programming and coding errors by such methods as altering program steps and sequences. Develops new subroutines for a specific area of application.	Business programmer Computer scientist Data processor Engineering programmer Information scientist Process control programmer Scientific programmer Software manager Systems analyst Technical consultant
COMPUTER PROGRAMMER (m)	214	1979	34.5	15.6	8.7	See women's sample above. 25% had high school diploma, 42% completed BA degree, 12% MA. 76% worked in business-related areas, 7% educational areas, 3% scientific areas.		
CREDIT MANAGER (f)	193	1975	45.6	13.1	11.2	Members, North Central Credit and Financial Manage-	**168.** Manages credit and collection department of com-	Credit analyst Credit counselor

Sample/scale	N	Year tested	Mean age	Mean years educ	Mean years exper	Composition	DOT code and description	Related occupations
CREDIT MANAGER (m)	203	1975	41.9	15.1	12.9	ment Association, and Midwest Credit Managers Association. See women's sample above.	mercial house, department store, hotel, or similar institution. Investigates financial standing and reputation of prospective customer accounts. Supervises collection of bad accounts and worthless checks. Keeps records of collection. May submit delinquent account to agency or attorney for collection.	Finance manager Loan officer
DENTAL ASSISTANT (f)	215	1979	32.8	13.7	8.7	Members, American Dental Association, and write-in responses to articles in *The Explorer*, a publication of National Association of Dental Assistants. 30% had high school diploma, 16% completed associate degree, 45% had certificates in dental assisting. 76% were employed by private clinics, 14% by educational institutions.	079. Performs duties in office of dentist. Obtains and records patients' personal information and medical history and records dental treatment. Arranges dental instruments, materials, and medications and hands them to dentist as required. Keeps oral operating area clear during dental procedures. Measures silver-alloy powder and mercury and operates mechanical amalgamator to prepare dental amalgam. Aids dentist in patient management. Sterilizes and stores instruments. Explains to patients post-operative care, oral hygiene, and importance of preventive dentistry. Receives patients and performs routine maintenance. May expose and process dental x-ray films.	Chairside dental assistant Dental office manager Dental secretary Dental surgical assistant Orthodontics technician
DENTAL HYGIENIST (f)	236	1982	32.6	15.4	9.7	Members, National Dental Hygiene Association. All were licensed hygienists. 56% completed AA degree, 32% BA, 3% MA. 90% worked for a private dental office. 93% spent a minimum of 50% of time working in preventive dentistry.	078. Performs dental prophylactic treatment and instructs groups and individuals in care of teeth and mouth. Removes calcareous deposits, accretions, and stains from teeth by using rotating brush, rubber cup, and cleaning compound. Charts condition of disease and decay for diagnosis and treatment by dentist. Lectures community organizations regarding oral hygiene using various visual aids. May expose and develop x-ray film, apply solutions to aid in arresting dental decay, prepare filling material, and sterilize instruments.	Community health dental hygienist Oral hygienist Public school dental hygienist
DENTIST (f)	240	1979	38.3	20.2	12.2	Members, American Dental Association, and Association of Women Dentists. 68% were in general practice, 29% in a specialty area. 66% were self-employed or in partner-	072. Diagnoses and treats disease, injuries, and malformations of teeth and gums and related oral structures. Examines patient to determine nature of condition, using x-	Endodontist Oral pathologist Oral surgeon Orthodontist Pediatric dentist Periodontist

Sample/ scale	N	Year tested	Mean age	Mean years educ	Mean years exper	Composition	DOT code and description	Related occupations
						ship in a clinic, 8% were in educational institutions, 4% in government agencies, and 15% in a combination.	rays, mirrors, explorers, and other diagnostic procedures and instruments. Cleans, fills, extracts, and replaces teeth using rotary and hand instruments, dental appliances, medications, and surgical implements.	Prosthetic dentist Public health dentist
DENTIST (m)	217	1983	40.8	19.9	14.5	Members, American Dental Association. All were licensed DDS's. 80% were in general practice, 20% in a specialty area. 88% were in private practice, 5% in educational institutions, 1% in government agencies, and 5% in a combination. 94% of sample spent a minimum of 50% of time treating patients.		
DIETITIAN (f)	208	1983	37.9	17.5	11.4	Obtained with assistance of American Dietetic Association; all were practicing, registered dietitians. 51% completed BA degree, 45% MA, 3% PhD. 31% were employed by hospitals, 16% by government, 15% by educational institutions, 14% were self-employed, 5% by business/industry, and 12% a combination. Major activities included administration/ management (28%), teaching (24%), consulting (22%), a combination (17%), and other (8%).	077. Plans and directs food-service program in hospitals, schools, restaurants. Plans menus and diets, providing required food and nutrients to feed individuals and groups. Directs workers engaged in preparation and serving of food. Purchases or requisitions food, equipment, and supplies. Maintains and analyzes food cost-control records to determine improved methods for purchasing and using food, equipment, and supplies. Instructs individuals and groups in the application of principles of nutrition to the selection of food. May prepare educational materials on nutritional value of foods and methods of preparation.	Clinical dietitian Community dietitian Dietetic technician Food scientist Nutrition education coordinator Nutritionist Pediatric dietitian Public health dietitian Renal dietitian Research dietitian Therapeutic dietitian
DIETITIAN (m)	108	1983	34.1	17.9	7.8	See women's sample above. 50% completed BA degree, 33% MA, and 14% PhD. 24% were employed by hospitals, 18% by government, 13% by educational institutions, 7% by military, 5% were self-employed, 2% by business/ industry, 9% other, and 22% a combination. Major activities included administration and management (54%), teaching (16%), consulting (11%), and a combination (16%).		
ELECTED PUBLIC OFFICIAL (f)	224	1978	48.2	15.5	6.3	Selected from rosters provided by National Women's Education Fund, including state legislators, statewide constitutional office holders, and members of House of Representatives; and from a list of city and county officials from *Women in Public Office: A Biographical Directory and Statistical Analysis*. 23% had high school diploma, 39% completed BA degree, 16%	188. Holds elected public office in legislative bodies such as Congress, state legislatures, county commissions, and city councils. Involved in legislative action of the government. Listens to lobbyists; determines budget for the government.	Attorney general City council member County commissioner Governor Legislator Mayor Representative Senator

Sample/ scale	N	Year tested	Mean age	Mean years educ	Mean years exper	Composition	DOT code and description	Related occupations
						MA. 39% were employed in other occupations while they held office.		
ELECTED PUBLIC OFFICIAL (m)	208	1979	46.3	16.4	8.6	Members of 93rd U.S. Congress, tested by R. Willow. Others selected from *State Elective Officials and the Legislatures*, published by Council of State Governments. 20% had high school diploma, 30% completed BA degree, 26% law degree, 13% MA, and 6% PhD. 67% were employed in other occupations while they held office.		
ELECTRICIAN (f)	60	1984	29.2	15.5	4.4	Members, International Brotherhood of Electrical Workers and numerous women's organizations. 33% had high school diploma, 18% completed an electrical apprenticeship, 13% had a certificate from a vocational school, 7% completed AA degree, 25% BA. 77% were employed as construction electricians, 8% maintenance electricians, 8% other, and 7% a combination. 83% of sample spent a minimum of 50% of time doing manual labor. Other activities included reading blueprints, communication with contractors, problem-solving, and administrative functions. 57% of sample were third- or fourth-year apprentices, 32% were at journey level.	**824.** Plans layout, installs and repairs wiring, electrical fixtures, apparatus, and control equipment. Plans new or modified installations to minimize waste of materials, to provide access for future maintenance, and to avoid unsightly, hazardous, and unreliable wiring, consistent with specifications and local electrical codes. Prepares sketches showing location of wiring or follows diagrams and blueprints, ensuring that concealed wiring is in future walls, ceilings, and flooring. Measures, bends, cuts, threads, assembles, and installs electrical conduit. Pulls wire through conduit, splices wires, and connects wiring to lighting fixtures and power equipment. Installs control and distribution apparatus. Connects power cable to equipment and installs grounding leads.	Airplane electrician Apprentice electrician Automotive electrician Electrical installation supervisor Electrical repairer Estimator Inspector Journey electrician Line maintainer Line repairer Powerhouse electrician Street-light supervisor Wireperson
ELECTRICIAN (m)	260	1984	34.6	14.4	13.2	Members, International Brotherhood of Electrical Workers. 22% had high school diploma, 46% completed an electrical apprenticeship, 14% had a certificate from a vocational school, 8% completed AA degree, 7% BA. 88% were employed as construction electricians, 4% maintenance electricians, 5% other, and 4% a combination. 79% of sample spent a minimum of 50% of time doing manual labor. Other activities included reading blueprints, communicating with contractors, problem-solving, and administrative functions. 31% of sam-		

Sample/ scale	N	Year tested	Mean age	Mean years educ	Mean years exper	Composition	DOT code and description	Related occupations
						ple were third- or fourth-year apprentices, 61% were at journey level.		
ELEMENTARY TEACHER (f)	250	1978	36.8	17.5	10.6	From commercially compiled national listing. 62% completed BA degree, 37% MA. 97% were employed in public schools; 27% taught more than one grade.	092. Teaches elementary school students academic, social, and manipulative skills. Lectures, demonstrates, and uses audiovisual teaching aids to present subject matter to class. Prepares, administers, and corrects tests and records results. Assigns lessons, corrects papers, and hears oral presentations. Counsels students when adjustment and academic behavioral problems arise. Discusses problems with parents and suggests remedial action. Keeps attendance and grade records as required by school board.	Children's tutor Daycare worker Kindergarten teacher Nursery school teacher Preschool teacher Remedial teacher Teacher's aide
ELEMENTARY TEACHER (m)	249	1979	35.5	17.9	10.9	From commercially compiled national listing, and members of Minnesota State Board of Education. 52% completed BA degree, 43% MA. 96% were employed in public schools; 22% taught 5th grade, 35% 6th grade, 25% more than one grade.		
EMERGENCY MEDICAL TECHNICIAN (f)	207	1983	37.2	14.1	5.7	Members, National Association of Emergency Medical Technicians. 13% had high school diploma, 6% attended a vocational school, 36% had some college, 8% completed AA degree, 19% BA, 2% MA. Employers included community and municipal services, such as police and fire departments (45%), private ambulance companies (24%), hospitals (20%), a combination (6%), and other (4%). 74% spent a minimum of 50% of time giving emergency medical care; other activities included driving ambulance, determining nature of injuries, and taking training courses.	079. Administers first aid treatment to and transports sick or injured persons to medical facility, working as a member of emergency medical team. Determines nature and extent of illness or injury, or magnitude of catastrophe, to establish first aid procedures to be followed or the need for additional assistance, basing decisions on statements of persons involved, examination of victim, and knowledge of emergency medical practice. Communicates with professional medical personnel at emergency treatment facility to obtain instructions regarding further treatment and to arrange for reception of victims at treatment facility.	Ambulance attendant Paramedic Rescue squad member
EMERGENCY MEDICAL TECHNICIAN (m)	241	1983	33.8	14.8	7.1	See women's sample above. 10% had high school diploma, 16% attended a vocational school, 24% had some college, 15% completed AA degree, 22% BA. Employers included community and municipal services, such as police and fire departments (55%), hospitals (18%), private ambulance companies (17%), a combination (3%), and other (6%). 50% of sample spent a minimum of 50% of time giving emergency medical care; other activities included driving ambulance, determining nature of injuries, and taking training courses.		

Sample/ scale	N	Year tested	Mean age	Mean years educ	Mean years exper	Composition	DOT code and description	Related occupations
ENGINEER (f)	205	1978	33.0	17.5	8.7	From American Institute of Chemical Engineers, Institute of Electrical and Electronics Engineers, American Society of Civil Engineers, and American Society of Mechanical Engineers; names selected in proportion to membership of each organization. 55% completed BA degree, 34% MA, 9% PhD. 32% were employed by industry, 27% by engineering firms, 20% by government; major activities included development and design (43%), administration (10%), and a combination (19%).	003. Electrical engineer: conducts research and developmental activities concerned with electrical components. 005. Civil engineer: plans and designs structures. 007. Mechanical engineer: applies principles of physics and engineering for the use of mechanical power. 008. Chemical engineer: applies principles of chemistry to manufacturing operations. All engineering specialties function in one or more activities, such as research, development, design production, consulting, administration, management, teaching, technical writing or technical sales, or service.	Aeronautical engineer Biomedical engineer Chemical engineer Civil engineer Electrical engineer Geophysicist Industrial engineer Marine engineer Mechanical engineer Metallurgist Mineral engineer Nuclear engineer Product engineer
ENGINEER (m)	233	1978	40.9	17.8	16.4	See women's sample above. 48% completed BA degree, 37% MA, and 17% PhD. 48% were employed by industry, 22% by engineering firms, 12% by government; major activities included development and design (43%), administration (24%), and a combination (18%).		
ENGLISH TEACHER (f)	304	1982	39.1	17.5	11.0	National sample, members of National Council of Teachers of English, Secondary Section. All secondary school English teachers. 39% completed BA degree, 57% MA. 48% taught mainly literature, 35% writing, 12% grammar. 81% spent a minimum of 40% of time teaching; other activities included lesson preparation, grading, and meetings.	091. Teaches courses in composition, literature, grammar, poetry, creative writing, and speech. Instructs students through lectures, demonstrations, and audiovisual aids. Prepares teaching outline for course of study. Assigns lessons and corrects homework. Administers tests to evaluate students' progress. Keeps attendance records and maintains discipline. Participates in faculty and professional meetings, conferences, and teacher-training workshops. Performs related duties such as sponsoring special activities or student organizations.	Literature teacher Publications advisor Speech teacher Writing teacher
ENGLISH TEACHER (m)	222	1982	39.1	18.2	14.6	See women's sample above. 29% completed BA degree, 68% MA, and 3% PhD. 49% taught mainly literature, 29% writing, 16% grammar. 87% spent a minimum of 40% of time teaching; other activities included lesson preparation, grading, and meetings.		
EXECUTIVE HOUSEKEEPER (f)	203	1979	44.7	13.1	8.5	From subscribers to *Executive Housekeeper,* a publication for housekeeping managers of hospitals, hotels/motels, nursing homes, and educational institutions. 43% had high school diploma, 9% completed AA degree, 9% BA. 52% were employed by hospitals, 16% by nursing homes, 13% by hotels/motels; major activities included per-	187. Directs institutional housekeeping program to ensure clean, orderly, and attractive condition of establishment. Establishes standards and procedures for work of housekeeping staff. Inspects and evaluates physical condition of establishment and submits to management recommendations for painting or repairs. Organizes and di-	Athletic equipment custodian Building services manager Caretaker Custodian Home housekeeper Janitorial services manager Laundry ser-

Sample/ scale	N	Year tested	Mean age	Mean years educ	Mean years exper	Composition	DOT code and description	Related occupations
						sonnel management (45%), safety and sanitation (11%), and a combination (36%).	rects departmental training programs, resolves personnel problems, and hires new employees. Writes activities and personnel reports for review by management.	vices manager Property service manager
EXECUTIVE HOUSE-KEEPER (m)	209	1979	42.4	13.8	9.0	See women's sample above. 54% had high school diploma, 18% completed AA degree, 18% BA. 63% were employed by hospitals, 12% by nursing homes, 8% by educational institutions, 4% by hotels/motels; major activities included personnel management (48%), safety and sanitation (11%), and a combination (30%).		
FARMER (f)	212	1977	40.7	13.3	17.7	National sample from write-in responses to articles in rural or farm-directed publications, and with assistance of organizations such as American National Cowbelles, Washington State Dairy Wives, United Farm Wives, Wisconsin State Grange, California Women for Agriculture, and Indiana Women for Agriculture. 58% had high school diploma, 23% completed BA degree. Those selected spent about same amount of time managing their farms (32 hours per week) as managing their homes (37 hours per week), and most of farm-management time was in outdoor work, as opposed to accounting and bookkeeping. Major farm products included dairy (41%), grain (36%), and livestock (18%).	421. Manages a tract of land devoted to production of plants and animals. Raises various kinds of crops and livestock according to market conditions, weather, and size and location of farm. Selects and purchases seed, fertilizer, farm machinery, livestock, and feed, and assumes responsibility for sale of crop and livestock products.	Animal breeder Dairy farmer Field crop farmer Grain farmer Livestock farmer Poultry farmer Rancher Tree farmer Vegetable farmer Vine-fruit farmer
FARMER (m)	204	1979	40.8	13.3	24.3	National sample from names provided by participants in female sample, write-in responses to articles in agricultural magazines, and with assistance of Minnesota Agricultural Extension Service. 59% had high school diploma, 23% completed BA degree. Those selected averaged 65 hours per week in farm management, 8 hours per week in home management; 75% of work time was spent outdoors. Major farm products included grain (33%), dairy (27%), and livestock (24%).		
FLIGHT ATTENDANT (f)	286	1979	30.5	14.4	8.7	From Ozark Air Lines, Trans World Airlines, Western Airlines, Eastern Airlines, Braniff International, and Delta	352. Provides variety of personal services for safety and comfort of airline passengers during flight. Explains use of	Bus attendant Cabin attendant In-flight service coordinator

Sample/ scale	N	Year tested	Mean age	Mean years educ	Mean years exper	Composition	DOT code and description	Related occupations
FLIGHT ATTENDANT (m)	202	1979	28.4	15.4	4.0	Air Lines. 55% had high school diploma, 12% completed AA degree, 29% BA. Flight time averaged 76 hours per month. See women's sample above: also from Association of Flight Attendants. 35% had high school diploma, 48% completed BA degree. Flight time averaged 80 hours per month.	safety equipment such as seatbelts, oxygen masks, and life jackets. Serves previously prepared meals and beverages. Observes passengers to detect signs of discomfort. Answers questions regarding performance of aircraft, stopovers, and flight schedule. Prepares reports showing place of departure and destination, passenger ticket numbers, and meal and beverage inventories.	Passenger service representative Purser Train steward/ stewardess
FLORIST (f)	211	1983	40.4	13.4	11.3	Retail members, Society of American Florists listing in *Who's Who in Floriculture*. 18% had high school diploma, 9% attended vocational school, 35% had some college, 9% completed AA degree, 21% BA. 84% worked in a family-owned florist shop; 91% of the shops employed less than 10 people. 93% were single florist shops, 7% part of a chain. 79% bought all inventory from a supplier, 2% had a greenhouse, 18% obtained inventory from a combination of the two. Major activities included designing arrangements (25%), taking inventory (17%), customer contact (13%), and a combination (44%).	142. Designs and fashions live, cut, dried, or artificial floral arrangements for events. Confers with client regarding price and type of arrangement desired. Plans arrangements according to client's requirements and costs, using knowledge of design and properties of materials, or selects appropriate standard design pattern. Selects and arranges flora and foliage necessary for arrangement. May instruct or direct other workers.	Floral arranger Floral designer Greenhouse florist Retail florist Wholesale florist
FLORIST (m)	207	1983	40.2	14.8	15.8	See women's sample above. 6% had high school diploma, 35% had attended some college, 9% completed AA degree, 36% BA. 84% worked in a family-owned florist shop; 72% of the shops employed less than 10 people. 79% were single florist shops, 21% part of a chain. 63% bought all inventory from a supplier, 6% had a greenhouse, 31% obtained inventory from a combination of the two. Major activities included designing arrangements (23%), taking inventory (18%), customer contact (11%), and a combination (41%).		
FOOD SERVICE MANAGER (f)	180	1984	40.6	13.8	9.9	Members, Hospital, Institution, and Educational Food Service Society. 33% had high school diploma, 27% completed AA degree, 17% BA, 5% MA, 18% other. 88%	187. Coordinates food service activities of hotels, restaurants, or other institutional establishments or at social functions. Estimates food and beverage costs and requisi-	Banquet manager Cafeteria/ lunchroom manager Caterer

Sample/ scale	N	Year tested	Mean age	Mean years educ	Mean years exper	Composition	DOT code and description	Related occupations
						were employed by hospitals or nursing homes, 5% by educational institutions. Major activities included personnel management (23%), customer contact (6%), record keeping and financial planning (5%), and a combination (55%).	tions or purchases supplies. Confers with food preparation and other personnel to plan menus and related activities, such as dining room and banquet operations. Directs hiring and assignment of personnel. Investigates and resolves food quality and service complaints.	Catering manager Coffee shop manager Commissary production supervisor Dietitian Food and beverage manager
FOOD SERVICE MANAGER (m)	116	1984	36.4	15.8	10.7	See women's sample above. 22% had high school diploma, 5% a certificate from a vocational-technical institution, 7% completed AA degree, 30% BA, 32% MA, 1% PhD. 53% were employed by hospitals or nursing homes, 20% by educational institutions, 19% other. Major activities included personnel management (24%), purchasing and inventory (6%), customer contact (3%), record keeping and financial planning (3%), and a combination (56%).		Food production manager Food service supervisor Industrial cafeteria manager
FOREIGN LANGUAGE TEACHER (f)	315	1978	37.5	18.3	11.6	Members, American Council on the Teaching of Foreign Languages. 35% completed BA degree, 64% MA. 91% were employed by secondary schools.	091. Instructs students through lectures, demonstrations, and audiovisual aids. Prepares teaching outline for course of study, assigns lessons, and corrects homework. Administers tests to evaluate students' progress. Keeps attendance records and maintains discipline. Participates in faculty and professional meetings, conferences, and teacher-training workshops. Performs related duties such as sponsoring special activities or student organizations. Teaches courses in grammar, reading, and speaking of various languages plus cultural customs, history, geography, and literature.	Interpreter Translator
FOREIGN LANGUAGE TEACHER (m)	251	1979	38.8	19.2	13.4	See women's sample above. 25% completed BA degree, 71% MA. 92% were employed by secondary schools.		
FORESTER (f)	174	1974	26.6	17.2	3.4	Members, Society of American Foresters. 76% completed BA degree, 22% MA. 57% were employed by government, 26% by industry. Largest area of specialization was timber management (42%); remainder included land and fire management and other.	040. Manages and develops forest lands and their resources for economic and recreational purposes. Maps forest areas, estimates standing timber and future growth, and manages timber sales. Conducts research on cutting and removing timber, with minimum waste and damage, and on methods of processing wood for various uses. Directs suppression of forest fires and conducts fire-prevention programs. Plans	Fire ranger Forest ecologist Forest geneticist Forestry economist Land use manager Range manager Research forester
FORESTER (m)	298	1979	38.9	17.1	14.3	See women's sample above. 67% completed BA degree, 23% MA, 9% PhD. 54% were employed by government, 29% by industry. Largest area		Silviculturist Soil conservationist Timber forester Tree planter

Sample/scale	N	Year tested	Mean age	Mean years educ	Mean years exper	Composition	DOT code and description	Related occupations
						of specialization was timber management (28%); remainder included fire, land, and recreation management.	campsites and recreation centers and directs construction and maintenance of cabins, fences, and roads.	Urban forester
FUNERAL DIRECTOR (f)	138	1984	41.4	15.0	14.2	Roster from ten state licensing boards. 41% had high school diploma, 22% completed AA degree, 23% BA, 11% MA. 32% were employed by funeral homes, 60% owned or managed a funeral service. 50% received on-the-job training only, 32% had college education plus mortuary science schooling, 6% had a maximum of a year of embalming courses. 20% directed less than 50 funerals per year, 45% directed over 100 funerals per year. Major activities included a combination of directing, arranging, and embalming.	**187.** Arranges and directs funeral services, coordinates activities of workers to move body to mortuary for embalming. Interviews family to arrange details, such as preparation of obituary notice, selection of urn or casket, determination of location and time of cremation or burial, selection of pallbearers, procurement of official for religious rites, and transportation of mourners. May prepare body for interment.	Embalmer Funeral attendant Funeral home manager Mortician
FUNERAL DIRECTOR (m)	262	1978	40.1	15.2	18.0	From National Funeral Directors's Association membership directory. 6% had high school diploma, 13% completed AA degree, 27% BA, 2% MA. 65% owned or managed a funeral service, 10% were partners, 18% employees. 82% had had some mortuary science training courses. 63% directed over 100 funerals per year. Major activities included embalming, arranging, and directing.		
GEOGRAPHER (f)	195	1979	38.3	19.3	11.3	Members, Association of American Geographers. 15% completed BA degree, 43% MA, 40% PhD. 54% were employed by educational institutions, 26% by government, 10% by private industry; major activities included teaching (41%), research/field work (22%), administration (11%), and a combination (15%). Areas of specialty included physical/environmental (26%), urban/economic (24%), and cultural (18%).	**029.** Studies nature and use of earth's surface, conducts research on physical and climatic aspects of area or region, making observations of landforms, climates, soils, plants, and animals. Acts as consultant on subjects such as economic exploitation of regions and determination of ethnic and natural boundaries between nations. Uses surveying equipment; constructs maps, graphs, and diagrams. May teach college courses.	Cartographer Community developer Environmental planner Land surveyor Marine surveyor Photogrammetrist Topographical drafter Urban planner
GEOGRAPHER (m)	277	1979	40.7	20.6	14.9	See women's sample above. 3% completed BA degree, 14% MA, 81% PhD. 81% were employed by educational institutions, 11% by government; major activities in-		

Sample/ scale	N	Year tested	Mean age	Mean years educ	Mean years exper	Composition	DOT code and description	Related occupations
						cluded teaching (51%), administration (15%), research/field work (13%), and a combination (20%). Areas of specialty included urban/economic (26%), physical/environmental (24%), and cultural (16%).		
GEOLOGIST (f)	212	1979	35.4	19.2	9.9	From *Geological Society of America Directory*. 23% completed BA degree, 47% MA, 30% PhD. 36% were employed by government, 27% by educational institutions, 26% by private industry; major activities included research and exploration (59%), teaching (13%), and a combination (12%).	**024.** Studies composition, structure, and history of earth's crust; examines rocks, minerals, and fossils to identify sequence of processes affecting development of earth. Helps to locate mineral, geothermal, and petroleum deposits and underwater resources. Studies ocean bottom; prepares reports and maps and interprets research data. May teach college courses.	Earth science teacher Forest geologist Hydrologist Marine geologist Mineralogist Paleontologist Petroleum geologist Prospector Seismologist Soils engineer
GEOLOGIST (m)	242	1979	39.4	19.9	15.0	See women's sample above. 12% completed BA degree, 36% MA, 52% PhD. 39% were employed by educational institutions, 30% by private industry, 24% by government; major activities included research and exploration (41%), teaching (22%), administration (12%), and a combination (18%).		
GUIDANCE COUNSELOR (f)	208	1982	42.3	18.5	10.3	High school guidance counselors, all members of American Association for Counseling and Development. 89% completed MA degree, 1% PhD, 1% EdD. An average of 49% of work day was spent counseling students. Major areas of counseling included crisis and personal counseling (27%), class scheduling (16%), graduation requirements (10%), pre-college/vocational school counseling (7%), career counseling (7%), and a combination (30%).	**045.** Counsels individuals and provides group educational and vocational guidance services. Collects and organizes information about individuals through records, tests, interviews, and professional sources, to appraise their interests, aptitudes, abilities, and personality characteristics for vocational and educational planning. Compiles and studies occupational, educational, and economic information to aid counselees in making and carrying out objectives. Assists individuals to understand and overcome social and emotional problems. Engages in research and follow-up activities to evaluate counseling techniques.	Counseling service director Counselor Dean of guidance Education coordinator School counselor School psychologist Vocational counselor
GUIDANCE COUNSELOR (m)	266	1982	42.3	18.9	12.5	See women's sample above. 2% completed BA degree, 79% MA, 6% PhD, 5% EdD. An average of 48% of work day was spent counseling students. Major areas of counseling included class scheduling (20%), crisis and personal counseling (18%), pre-college/vocational school counseling (11%), career counseling (10%), graduation requirements (8%), and a combination (31%).		

Sample/ scale	N	Year tested	Mean age	Mean years educ	Mean years exper	Composition	DOT code and description	Related occupations
HOME ECONOMICS TEACHER (f)	312	1979	38.3	17.7	12.3	Members, American Home Economist Association. 51% completed BA degree, 47% MA. 86% were employed by elementary or secondary schools.	**096.** Teaches courses in food, textiles, sewing, budget management, child care, and homemaking practices. Instructs students through lectures, demonstrations, and audiovisual aids. Prepares teaching outline for course of study, assigns lessons, and corrects homework. Administers tests to evaluate students' progress. Keeps attendance records and maintains discipline. Participates in faculty and professional meetings, conferences, and teacher-training workshops. Performs related duties such as sponsoring special activities or student organizations.	Consumer services consultant Extension service agent 4-H club agent Home economist Home-extension agent Home-service director
HORTICULTURAL WORKER (f)	155	1983	31.5	14.7	6.7	Nationwide sample from catalog of *American Association of Nurserymen*. 28% had high school diploma, 12% a certificate from a vocational-technical institution, 12% completed AA degree, 36% BA, 4% MA. Employers included retailers and landscapers combined (28%), wholesalers only (25%), wholesalers, retailers, and landscapers combined (19%), retailers only (11%), wholesalers and retailers combined (6%), landscapers only (5%), and other (5%). 44% were in place of employment specializing in an area of horticulture. Major activities included customer service (35%), care of plants (18%), administrative functions (9%), soil preparation (6%), and a combination (26%).	**405.** Plants, cultivates, and harvests horticulture specialties such as flowers and shrubs, and performs related duties in environmental systems. Hauls and spreads topsoil, fertilizer, and peat moss to condition land. Sows seeds and plants cuttings. Determines nutrient and moisture requirements and detects and identifies germ and pest infestations. Applies herbicides, fungicides, and pesticides to destroy undesirable growth and pests. Reads and interprets sensing indicators and regulates humidity, ventilation, and carbon dioxide systems to control environmental conditions. Pollinates, prunes, and transplants plants to ensure development of marketable products.	Horticulturist Greenhouse laborer Greenhouse manager Landscaper Nursery laborer Propagator
HORTICULTURAL WORKER (m)	208	1983	32.9	15.4	10.4	See women's sample above. 17% had high school diploma, 10% certificate from a vocational-technical institution, 9% completed AA degree, 55% BA, and 5% MA. Employers included wholesalers only (29%), retailers and landscapers combined (22%), landscapers only (12%), wholesalers, retailers, and landscapers combined (12%), retailers only (7%), wholesalers and retailers combined (7%), wholesalers and landscapers combined (5%),		

Sample/ scale	N	Year tested	Mean age	Mean years educ	Mean years exper	Composition	DOT code and description	Related occupations
						and other (6%). 53% were in place of employment specializing in an area of horticulture. Major activities included customer service (20%), administrative functions (17%), care of plants (16%), soil preparation (10%), and a combination (30%).		
INTERIOR DECORATOR (f)	222	1982	40.4	16.6	14.9	Names supplied by American Society of Interior Designers. 65% completed BA degree, 9% MA, 13% graduated from a professional school of interior design. 59% were self-employed or in a partnership, 18% were employed by a retail store, 4% by an architectural firm. 34% specialized in residential design. Major activities included preparation of presentations for clients (32%), administrative functions (12%), conferring with clients and contractors (5%), and a combination (45%).	142. Plans and designs artistic interiors for homes, hotels, and commercial and institutional structures. Analyzes functional requirements, moods, and purpose of furnishing interior based on clients' needs and preferences. Devises harmonious color scheme and sketches plans of rooms, showing arrangement of furniture and accessories. Estimates cost. Selects and purchases decorative and functional material and accessories or creates original designs for furnishings to conform with decorative scheme.	Color director Environmental planner Facilities planner Interior architect Interior designer Set decorator Space planner
INTERIOR DECORATOR (m)	214	1982	41.6	15.9	16.5	See women's sample above. 58% completed BA degree, 11% MA degree, 14% graduated from a professional school of interior design. 57% were self-employed or in a partnership, 15% were employed by a retail store, 4% by an architectural firm, 9% worked for more than one employer. 27% specialized in residential designing, 22% in commercial design. Major activities included preparation of presentations for clients (32%), administrative functions (15%), conferring with clients and contractors (6%), and a combination (36%).		
INVESTMENTS MANAGER (f)	212	1982	34.8	17.1	9.7	Members, Financial Analysts Federation. 44% completed BA degree, 46% MA, 1% PhD, 3% other. 47% considered themselves financial analysts, 38% money managers, 15% investment managers. Employers included commercial banks (30%), corporations (19%), money management firms (18%), investment banks (9%), brokerage firms (6%), government (4%), self-employed (4%), and other (8%). Major activities in-	020. Financial analyst: conducts statistical analyses of information affecting investment programs of public, industrial, and financial institutions. 186. Investment fund manager: trades securities and provides securities investment and counseling services for a bank and its customers. 251. Stockbroker: buys and sells stocks and bonds for individuals and organizations as representatives of stock-brokerage firm.	Bond analyst Commodity analyst Financial advisor/ planner Financial analyst Investment analyst Investment fund manager Money manager Portfolio manager Security analyst Stockbroker

Sample/ scale	N	Year tested	Mean age	Mean years educ	Mean years exper	Composition	DOT code and description	Related occupations
						cluded managing funds and portfolios (29%), research and analysis (15%), consulting (12%), investing (11%), a combination (24%), and other (4%).		
INVESTMENTS MAN-AGER (m)	212	1982	40.9	17.6	15.4	See women's sample above. 26% completed BA degree, 68% MA, 4% PhD. 42% considered themselves financial analysts, 38% money managers, 20% investment managers. Employers included commercial banks (26%), corporations (23%), money management firms (21%), brokerage firms (9%), investment banks (8%), and other (7%). Major activities included managing funds and portfolios (29%), investing (12%), research and analysis (10%), consulting (8%), administration (8%), selling (6%), a combination (22%), and other (4%).		
IRS AGENT (f)	300	1976	37.8	14.9	5.4	Three groups: tax auditors, who consult with taxpayers and explain issues that do not involve accounting; revenue officers, who explain to taxpayers their delinquent tax obligations and collect unpaid taxes; and revenue agents, who as professional accountants examine books of individuals or corporations to determine federal tax liability.	**160.** Tax auditor: audits financial records to determine tax liability; reviews information gathered from taxpayer to verify net worth or reported financial status and identify potential tax issues. Evaluates evidence of taxpayer finances to determine tax liability; prepares written explanation of findings.	Pension trust reviewer Revenue agent Revenue officer Tax agent Tax analyst Tax auditor Tax examiner
IRS AGENT (m)	300	1976	37.6	14.9	8.4	See women's sample above.	**160.** Revenue agent: conducts independent field audits and investigations of income-tax returns to verify or amend tax liabilities; examines selected tax returns, analyzes accounting books and records, investigates documents, financial transactions, operation methods, industry practices and legal instruments, and confers with taxpayer to explain issues involved and applicability of pertinent tax laws and regulations.	
							188. Revenue officer: investigates and collects delinquent taxes according to prescribed laws and regulations. Examines and analyzes tax assets and liabilities to determine solution for resolving tax problem. Directs service of legal documents, and rec-	

Sample/ scale	N	Year tested	Mean age	Mean years educ	Mean years exper	Composition	DOT code and description	Related occupations
							ommends criminal prosecutions and civil penalties when necessary. Writes report of actions taken for departmental files.	
LAWYER (f)	273	1977	32.8	19.2	5.9	From *Martindale-Hubbell Law Directory*. Areas of practice included corporate law, criminal law, divorce, work in government agencies, legal research, general practice.	**110.** Conducts criminal and civil lawsuits, draws up legal documents, advises clients of legal rights, and practices other phases of law. Represents clients in court or	Corporate lawyer Criminal lawyer District attorney Government attorney
LAWYER (m)	215	1977	37.1	19.4	10.6	See women's sample above. Areas of practice included corporate law, criminal law, work in government agencies, tax law, general practice.	before quasi-judicial or administrative agencies of government. May act as trustee, guardian, or executor. May teach college courses in law.	Patent lawyer Probate lawyer Real estate lawyer Tax attorney Trial attorney
LIBRARIAN (f)	280	1977	37.6	17.7	9.9	Members, American Library Association. 92% completed MA degree or higher. 43% were employed by community or county, 30% by colleges or universities, 9% by high schools.	**100.** Maintains library collection of books, periodicals, documents, films, recordings, and other materials and helps groups and individuals to locate and obtain materials. Explains use of reference sources. Describes or dem-	Acquisitions librarian Audiovisiual librarian Bibliographer Bookmobile librarian
LIBRARIAN (m)	315	1977	39.1	18.4	11.6	See women's sample above. 98% completed MA degree or higher. 46% were employed by colleges or universities, 37% by community or county.	onstrates procedures for searching catalog files and shelf collections to obtain materials. Performs variety of duties to maintain reference and circulation matter, such as copying author's name and title on catalog cards. May select, order, catalog, or classify materials.	Branch librarian Catalog librarian Children's librarian Circulation librarian Medical librarian Reference librarian
LIFE INSURANCE AGENT (f)	216	1973	45.3	13.8	10.0	National sampling, holders of American College of Life Underwriters certificate. All indicated connection with sales activities.	**250.** Selects and sells all types of life insurance based on client's present insurance and government benefits to establish plan for financial security. Calls on policyhold-	Insurance broker Life insurance underwriter Pension specialist
LIFE INSURANCE AGENT (m)	264	1973	43.6	14.7	14.0	See women's sample above.	ers to keep insurance plan up to date and to advise client concerning life-insurance pensions, taxation, and family financing. Suggests method of premium payments and settlement option. May require knowledge of law, accounting, taxation, or government benefits.	
MARINE CORPS ENLISTED PERSONNEL (f)	191	1984	29.5	13.4	8.3	Roster of enlistees provided by Defense Manpower Data Center, Department of Defense. 64% had high school diploma, 14% a degree or certificate from a vocational-technical institution, 10% completed BA degree, 8% MA.	**378.** Provides technical support for the operation of amphibious military vehicles and equipment. Repairs and maintains vehicles and equipment. May prepare weapons, equipment, and artillery. Follows commands of officers and may participate in unit	Airborne sensor specialist Amphibian crew member Defense fire control systems operator Electronics mechanic

Sample/scale	N	Year tested	Mean age	Mean years educ	Mean years exper	Composition	DOT code and description	Related occupations
MARINE CORPS ENLISTED PERSONNEL (m)	201	1984	32.3	12.7	13.0	See women's sample above. 77% had high school diploma, 11% a degree or certificate from a vocational-technical institution, 8% completed AA degree, 3% BA, 10% MA.	drills and operations concerned with protecting the nation. May be trained in any number of jobs paralleling civilian occupations.	Equipment installer Maintenance inspector Teletype technician
MARKETING EXECUTIVE (f)	215	1979	33.0	17.0	7.6	Members, American Marketing Association. 43% completed BA degree, 45% MA. 52% reported research as major activity; remainder included planning, advertising, administration, and product management.	**050.** Researches market conditions to determine potential sales of products or services; establishes research methodology and designs format for data-gathering such as surveys, polls, or questionnaires. Analyzes data to determine future trends.	Data collection manager Marketing analyst Marketing promotion director Media research director
MARKETING EXECUTIVE (m)	309	1979	37.9	17.8	11.5	See women's sample above. 27% completed BA degree, 66% MA. 40% reported research as major activity; remainder included administration, planning, product management, advertising, and sales.		
MATHEMATICIAN (f)	213	1982	41.1	20.9	14.9	Names from combined membership list of Mathematical Association of America and Society for Industrial and Applied Mathematics. All completed PhD. 93% were employed by colleges or universities, 3% by business/industry, 1% by government. 29% considered themselves theoretical mathematicians, 22% applied, and 48% a combination. 81% identified primary job function as teacher, 8% researcher, 2% statistician, 2% computer scientist. Major activities included teaching (74%), research (5%), and a combination (15%).	**020.** Conducts research in fundamental mathematics and in application of mathematical techniques to science management and other fields or solves or directs solutions to problems by mathematical methods. Conducts research in such branches of mathematics as algebra, geometry, and number theory. Performs computations and applies methods of numerical analysis to solve problems in support of mathematical, scientific, or industrial research activity. May teach college courses.	Actuary Applied mathematician Computer application engineer Engineer analyst Operation research analyst Statistician
MATHEMATICIAN (m)	270	1982	41.7	20.8	16.4	See women's sample above. All completed PhD. 95% were employed by colleges or universities, 2% by business/industry, 1% by government. 32% considered themselves theoretical mathematicians, 23% applied mathematicians, and 44% a combination. 68% identified primary job function as teacher, 14% researcher, 4% computer scientist, 2% statistician. Major activities included teaching (67%), research (10%), and a combination (14%).		
MATHEMATICS TEACHER (f)	245	1982	37.7	17.8	11.9	National sample, *National Science Teachers' Association U.S. Registry*. 40% completed	**091.** Teaches courses such as algebra, geometry, arithmetic, and computer science. In-	Algebra teacher Arithmetic teacher

Sample/ scale	N	Year tested	Mean age	Mean years educ	Mean years exper	Composition	DOT code and description	Related occupations
						BA degree, 59% MA. 43% taught mainly algebra, 20% geometry, 14% basic math; other areas included trigonometry, calculus, computer science, and analytic geometry. All were high school teachers; 98% taught more than one grade. 92% spent a minimum of 40% of time teaching; other activities included lesson preparation, grading, administrative functions. 22% also were involved in advising other school activities relating to math, such as math club.	structs students through lectures, demonstrations, and audiovisual aids. Prepares teaching outline for course of study, assigns lessons, and corrects homework. Administers tests to evaluate students' progress. Keeps attendance records and maintains discipline. Participates in faculty and professional meetings, conferences, and teacher-training workshops. Performs related duties such as sponsoring special activities or student organizations.	Calculus teacher Computer science teacher Geometry teacher Statistics teacher Trigonometry teacher
MATHEMATICS TEACHER (m)	226	1982	39.1	18.1	14.0	See women's sample above. 31% completed BA degree, 64% MA. 42% taught mainly algebra, 19% geometry, 10% basic math, 7% computer science, 4% trigonometry, 4% calculus, and 10% a combination. All were high school teachers; 96% taught more than one grade. 91% spent a minimum of 40% of time teaching; other activities included lesson preparation, grading, administrative functions. 20% also were involved in advising other school activities related to math, such as math club.		
MEDICAL ILLUSTRATOR (f)	99	1984	37.2	18.3	11.0	Members, Association of Medical Illustrators. 40% completed BA degree, 52% MA. 44% were self-employed, 26% were employed by medical centers, 14% by teaching institutions, 5% by other, and 9% a combination. 78% of those not self-employed also did free-lance work. 34% specialized in a particular medical field. 76% spent a minimum of 50% of time illustrating; other activities included consulting, research, and administrative functions.	141. Makes sketches and constructs tridimensional models to illustrate surgical and medical research procedures, anatomical and pathological specimens, and unusual clinical disorders. Develops drawings, paintings, diagrams, and models illustrating medical findings for use in publications, exhibits, consultation, research, or teaching activities. Devises visual aids to assist in interpreting research programs. May specialize in illustrations in a particular medical field.	Audiovisual resource person Biocommunication graphic artist Medical graphic technician Medical sculptor Scientific illustrator
MEDICAL ILLUSTRATOR (m)	61	1984	41.9	19.0	16.2	See women's sample above. 20% completed BA, 63% MA, 12% PhD. 15% were self-employed, 31% were employed by medical centers, 28% by teaching institutions, 20% by other, and 7% by a combination. 83% of those not self-employed also did		

Sample/ scale	N	Year tested	Mean age	Mean years educ	Mean years exper	Composition	DOT code and description	Related occupations
						freelance work. 38% specialized in a particular medical field. 58% spent a minimum of 50% of time illustrating; other activities included consulting, research, and administrative functions.		
MEDICAL TECHNICIAN (f)	259	1982	43.3	12.2	21.2	Certified members, Association of American Medical Technologists. 83% had some college courses and/or training in medical technology; 11% completed BA degree, 2% MA. 50% were employed by a hospital laboratory, 9% by a clinic of 5 physicians or less, 7% by a clinic of more than 5, 7% by an independent clinic lab, 6% by a health agency, 6% by the military, and 14% by other. Specialties included clinical chemistry (8%), hematology (7%), blood bank (6%), a combination (38%), no specialty (25%), and other (8%). Major activities included conducting lab tests (46%), supervisory functions (7%), administrative functions (7%), specimen preparation (4%), and a combination (33%).	078. Performs routine tests in medical laboratory for use in treatment and diagnosis of disease. Prepares tissue samples, takes blood samples, and executes such laboratory tests as urinalysis and blood counts. Makes quantitative and qualitative chemical and biological analyses of body specimens, under supervision of medical technologist.	Blood and plasma laboratory assistant Blood bank technician Cytotechnician Hematology technician Medical technologist Serology technician
MEDICAL TECHNICIAN (m)	233	1982	44.6	14.8	22.1	See women's sample above. 75% had some college and/or training in medical technology, 17% completed BA degree, 5% MA. 54% were employed by a hospital laboratory, 13% by an independent clinic lab, 9% by the military, 5% by a clinic of more than 5 physicians, 4% by a clinic of less than 5, 3% by a health agency, and 13% other. Specialties included clinical chemistry (7%), cystology (5%), hematology (5%), a combination (38%), no specialty (21%), and other (15%). Major activities included conducting lab tests (30%), supervisory functions (16%), administration (18%), and a combination (30%).		
MEDICAL TECHNOLOGIST (f)	266	1984	37.9	17.0	13.7	Members, American Society for Medical Technology. 88% completed BA degree, 12% MA. 68% were employed by a hospital laboratory, 9% by an independent clinic lab, 5% by a clinic, 3% by govern-	078. Performs chemical, microscopic, and bacteriologic tests to provide data for use in treatment and diagnosis of diseases. Receives specimens from laboratory and makes quantitative and qualitative	Bloodbank technologist Chemistry technologist Cytotechnologist Hematology technologist

Sample/ scale	N	Year tested	Mean age	Mean years educ	Mean years exper	Composition	DOT code and description	Related occupations
						ment, 2% by a research institution, 2% by physicians, 10% other, 2% a combination. Specializations included clinical chemistry (18%), hematology (17%), blood bank (10%), microbiology (9%), other (7%), a combination (25%), and no specialization (13%). Major activities included conducting lab tests (44%), administrative functions (11%), supervising lab workers (8%), analyzing results (2%), and a combination (31%).	chemical analyses. Cultivates, isolates, and identifies bacteria, parasites, and other microorganisms. Cuts, stains, and mounts tissue sections for study by pathologist. Performs blood tests and transfusions, studies morphology of blood, prepares vaccines and serums, groups or types blood, and cross-matches that of donor and recipient to ascertain compatibility. May calibrate and use equipment designed to measure glandular or other bodily activities.	Histologist Laboratory technologist Medical technician Nuclear medical technologist Serology technologist Tissue technologist
MEDICAL TECHNOLOGIST (m)	206	1984	37.0	17.2	12.4	See women's sample above. 93% completed BA degree, 7% MA. 68% were employed by a hospital laboratory, 8% by an independent clinic lab, 4% by a clinic, 8% other, and 5% a combination. Specializations included clinical chemistry (18%), hematology (8%), microbiology (6%), blood bank (3%), other (15%), a combination (20%), and no specialty (28%). Major activities included conducting lab tests (41%), administrative functions (22%), supervising lab workers (10%), analyzing results (2%), and a combination (24%).		
MINISTER (f)	250	1977	34.8	19.7	5.8	Collected with cooperation of Midwest Career Development Center. 6% completed Bachelor of Divinity degree, 78% Master of Divinity, 6% Doctor of Divinity. 95% were employed by churches; 90% served as pastors, 4% as chaplains. 42% were Methodist ministers, 25% Presbyterian, 14% Church of Christ, and 19% other.	**120.** Conducts religious worship and performs other spiritual functions associated with beliefs and practices of religious faith. Provides spiritual and moral guidance and assistance to members. Prepares and delivers sermons and other talks. Interprets doctrine of religion. Instructs people who are to become members of the faith. Counsels those in spiritual need and comforts bereaved. Oversees religious education program. May write articles for publication and engage in interfaith, community, civic, educational, or recreational activities sponsored by or related to interests of denomination.	Assistant pastor Campus pastor Chaplain Hospital chaplain Missionary Pastor Youth director
MINISTER (m)	255	1982	41.1	20.1	14.1	See women's sample above. Members, United Presbyterian Church, Episcopalian Church Center, Lutheran Church of America, and American Lutheran Church. 3% completed Bachelor of Divinity degree, 88% Master of Divinity, 8% Doctor of Divinity. 59% were Lutheran ministers, 24% Episcopal, and 17% Presbyterian. 93% were employed by churches; 89% served as pastors, 2% as chaplains. Hours spent equal-		

Sample/scale	N	Year tested	Mean age	Mean years educ	Mean years exper	Composition	DOT code and description	Related occupations
						ly in conducting services, counseling, teaching, and administrative functions.		
Musician (f)	209	1979	35.4	16.7	14.4	Members, musicans' unions in Milwaukee, San Francisco, Fort Worth, Atlanta, St. Louis, Denver, and Minneapolis; and from national write-in response to articles in musicians' publications. Data collected with assistance of L. Harmon. 23% had high school diploma, 40% completed BA degree, 24% MA. 94% had had private instruction averaging 13 years. 22% were employed in other occupations simultaneously.	152. Plays one or more musical instruments in recital, in accompaniments, or as a member of orchestra, band, or other musical group. Plays music either reading score or by memory, manipulating keys, bow, valves, string, or percussion devices. May improvise or transpose music. May compose or arrange music.	Arranger Composer Conductor Music teacher Orchestrator Singer Sound producer Stage manager
Musician (m)	230	1979	34.2	16.0	16.3	See women's sample above. 34% had high school diploma, 30% completed BA degree, 14% MA. 86% had had private instruction averaging 8 years. 31% were employed in other occupations simultaneously.		
Navy Enlisted Personnel (f)	257	1984	29.7	12.9	8.0	Roster of enlistees provided by Defense Manpower Data Center, Department of Defense. 66% had high school diploma, 10% a degree or certificate from a vocational-technical institution, 17% completed AA degree, 5% BA, 1% MA.	378. Provides technical support for the operation of military vessels. Repairs and maintains military vessels and equipment. Aids in the transportation of military passengers, and freight. May aid officer in navigation of vessel; may prepare weapons or artillery; may participate in drills and operations concerned with protecting the nation. May be trained in any number of jobs paralleling civilian occupations.	Boatswain Boiler technician Cryptologic technician Electronics technician Naval gunfire observer Ocean systems technician Ship crew member Sonar operator Weather forecaster Yeoman
Navy Enlisted Personnel (m)	222	1984	33.1	12.9	13.4	See women's sample above. 67% had high school diploma, 14% a degree or certificate from a vocational-technical institution, 13% completed AA degree, 4% BA, 1% MA.		
Navy Officer (f)	282	1979	32.0	16.8	9.2	Roster of commissioned officers provided by Defense Manpower Data Center, Department of Defense. 62% completed BA degree, 33% MA. Rank: lieutenant (67%), lt. commander (21%), commander (9%), captain (3%).	197. Operates and manages vessels; performs technical supervision of marine operations; has administrative and technical responsibility for operation, maintenance, and safety of vessels; pilots vessels; sets courses using navigational aids; supervises and coordinates activities of crew aboard ship. May take any of a variety of administrative assignments.	Captain Commander Communications officer Intelligence officer Military weapons analyst Missile officer Supply officer Surface warfare officer
Navy Officer (m)	298	1979	37.6	17.1	14.4	See women's sample above. 48% completed BA degree, 27% MA. Rank: lieutenant (31%), lt. commander (30%), commander (26%), captain (13%).		
Nurse, Licensed Practical (f)	228	1983	41.4	11.4	11.7	Members, National Federation of Licensed Practical Nurses. 12% had high school diploma, 80% attended a vocational-technical school,	079. Cares for ill, injured, convalescent, and handicapped persons in hospitals, clinics, and similar institutions. Takes and records	Chiropractor assistant Dialysis technician Emergency

Sample/ scale	N	Year tested	Mean age	Mean years educ	Mean years exper	Composition	DOT code and description	Related occupations
						3% had AA degree. 61% were employed by hospitals, 14% by nursing homes, 4% by clinics, 4% by industry, and 5% by a combination. 58% specialized in one area of nursing; specialties included psychiatric nursing, intensive care, orthopedics, pediatrics, and metabolics. 94% spent a minimum of 50% of time doing applied nursing.	temperature, blood pressure, and pulse. Dresses wounds and gives alcohol rubs and massages. Administers specified medications. Assembles and uses such equipment as catheters, tracheotomy tubes, and oxygen suppliers. Performs routine laboratory work such as urinalysis. Sterilizes equipment and supplies. Records food and fluid intake and output. Bathes, dresses, and assists patients in walking and turning.	medical technician Medical record clerk Nurse's aide Optometric assistant Orderly Orthopedic technician Orthoptist Podiatric assistant Practical nurse Psychiatric aide Respiratory therapist Surgical technician
NURSE, LICENSED PRACTICAL (m)	128	1983	38.5	13.9	10.8	Members, National Federation of Licensed Practical Nurses, and names selected from a list of state associations and state boards of examiners. 8% had high school diploma, 88% a certificate from a vocational-technical school, 4% had AA degree. 77% were employed by hospitals, 8% by private homes, 4% by clinics, 4% by nursing homes, 4% by a combination, and 4% other. 62% specialized in a particular area of nursing, including psychiatric nursing, intensive care, pediatrics, orthopedics, and geriatrics. 96% spent a minimum of 50% of time doing applied nursing.		
NURSE, REGISTERED (f)	291	1977	38.9	17.4	14.8	Sample drawn from various state nursing associations, hospitals, medical offices, and individual contacts. 8% completed RN degree, 25% BA, 59% MA, 8% PhD. 44% were employed by schools of nursing, 33% by hospitals; major activities included teaching (41%), administration (35%), and applied areas (14%).	075. Performs acts requiring substantial specialized judgement and skill in observation, care, and counsel of ill, injured, or infirm persons and in promotion of health and prevention of illness. Administers medication; prepares equipment; assists physician; takes temperature, pulse, blood pressure, and other vital signs. May teach nursing courses.	Anesthetic nurse Community health nurse General duty nurse Head nurse Mental health nurse Midwife Nurse practitioner Occupational health nurse Oncology nurse Private duty nurse Psychiatric nurse Public health nurse School nurse Surgical nurse
NURSE, REGISTERED (m)	291	1973	35.8	16+	10.0	Sample drawn from list of registered nurses obtained from state associations and state boards of examiners. All had at least an RN degree. Major activities were anesthesiology, administration, surgery, psychiatry, and teaching; 34% were in the military.		
NURSING HOME ADMINISTRATOR (f)	205	1979	43.6	14.5	9.4	From list of administrators of nursing homes approved by Veterans Administration. 43% had high school diploma, 13% completed AA degree, 17% BA.	187. Directs administration of home; develops programs and services; administers fiscal operations such as budget planning; directs hiring and training of personnel; directs and	Health care administrator Hospital administrator Institution director

Sample/ scale	N	Year tested	Mean age	Mean years educ	Mean years exper	Composition	DOT code and description	Related occupations
NURSING HOME ADMINISTRATOR (m)	300	1979	39.9	15.9	9.1	See women's sample above. 46% completed BA degree, 20% MA.	coordinates activities of medical, nursing, and service staffs. Develops policies and procedures.	Sheltered workshop director
OCCUPATIONAL THERAPIST (f)	301	1978	37.2	17.0	10.5	Members, American Occupational Therapy Association and Minnesota Occupational Therapy Association. 75% completed BA degree, 22% MA. 37% were employed by clinics or hospitals (17% general, 13% psychiatric, 7% children's), 15% by educational institutions, 11% by rehabilitation centers.	**076.** Plans, organizes, and participates in medically oriented occupational programs in hospitals or similar institutions to rehabilitate patients who are physically or mentally ill. Uses creative and manual arts, recreational, educational, and social activities, pre-vocational evaluations, and training in everyday activities such as personal care and homemaking. Consults with other members of rehabilitation team to coordinate therapeutic activities for individual patients.	Art therapist Corrective therapist Music therapist Occupational therapy aide Pediatric therapist Recreational therapist Rehabilitation therapist Vocational evaluator
OCCUPATIONAL THERAPIST (m)	211	1979	36.8	17.8	10.3	See women's sample above. 62% completed BA degree, 36% MA. 44% were employed by clinics or hospitals (18% general, 23% psychiatric, 3% children's), 14% by educational institutions, 10% by rehabilitation centers.		
OPTICIAN (f)	258	1982	36.0	13.6	9.9	Members, Opticians Association of America. 25% had high school diploma, 9% attended a vocational-technical school, 43% had had some college, 12% completed AA degree, 8% BA, 2% MA. 55% learned dispensing skills on the job, 8% in school, 4% as apprentices, and 33% a combination. Employers included retail optical stores (44%), self-owned optical stores (36%), ophthalmologists (10%), and department stores (7%). Major activities included a combination of determining style and size of lens, adjusting glasses, and writing work orders. No one who spent more than 25% of time attending to administrative details was included in sample.	**713.** Designs, fits, and adapts lenses and frames, using written optical prescription. Analyzes prescription in conjunction with client's vocational and avocational visual requirements. Recommends specific lenses for safety and efficiency. Assists clients in selecting frames according to style and color, coordinating frames with facial and eye measurements and optical prescriptions. Measures client's bridge and eye size, temple length, vertex distance, pupillary distance, and optical centers of eyes. Prepares work order and instructions for grinding lenses and fabricating spectacles. Verifies exactness of finished lens spectacles. Adjusts frames and lens position to fit client. Instructs client on adapting and wearing spectacles and procedures for their care. Sells optical goods.	Contact lens molder Contact lens technician Ophthalmic technician Optical model maker Optical technician Plastic eye technician Precision lens technician
OPTICIAN (m)	213	1981	37.8	13.9	15.2	See women's sample above. 19% had high school diploma, 7% attended a vocational-technical school, 43% had had some college, 13% completed AA degree, 15% BA, 1% MA. 52% learned dispensing skills on the job, 10% in school, 4% as apprentices, 2% in the military, and 31% a combination. Employers included retail optical stores (38%), self-owned optical stores (35%), ophthalmologists (16%), hos-		

Sample/ scale	N	Year tested	Mean age	Mean years educ	Mean years exper	Composition	DOT code and description	Related occupations
						pitals (2%), and department stores (2%). Major activities included a combination of determining style and size of lens, fitting and adjusting lens, and analyzing prescriptions. No one who spent more than 25% of time attending to administrative details was included in sample.		
OPTOMETRIST (f)	191	1979	38.0	18.8	11.8	Members, American Optometric Asociation. 60% were self-employed or in a partnership, 11% were employed by clinics or hospitals, 13% a combination. 75% reported private practice as major activity.	**079.** Examines eyes to determine visual efficiency and prescribes protective procedures. Examines patient for visual pathology or ocular manifestations of systemic diseases and refers those with pathological condition to medical practitioner. May specialize in prescribing and fitting contact lens and subnormal visual devices and administering visual training and eye exercises.	Ophthalmologist Optician Optometric assistant Pediatric optometrist
OPTOMETRIST (m)	220	1979	39.7	18.8	14.2	See women's sample above. 83% were self-employed or in a partnership. 93% reported private practice as major activity.		
PERSONNEL DIRECTOR (f)	330	1978	38.3	15.1	9.1	Members, American Society for Personnel Administration. 29% had high school diploma, 39% completed BA degree, 11% MA. Major activities included administration (37%), recruiting and selection (18%), and a combination (32%).	**166.** Plans and carries out policies relating to all phases of personnel activities. Organizes recruitment, selection, and training procedures. Confers with company and union officials to establish pensions and insurance plans, workmen's compensation policies, and similar functions. Studies personnel records and supervisors' reports for information such as educational background to determine personnel suitable for promotions or transfers. May act as liaison between management and labor.	Benefits manager Career development director Compensation manager Director of human resources Director of placement Education and training manager Employee relations manager Employee welfare manager Employment manager Industrial relations director Job analyst Salary and benefits analyst
PERSONNEL DIRECTOR (m)	214	1978	39.1	16.7	10.7	See women's sample above. 1% had high school diploma, 61% completed BA degree, 28% MA. Major activities included administration (38%), recruiting and selection (10%), and a combination (34%).		
PHARMACIST (f)	207	1979	33.6	17.4	10.1	Members, American Pharmaceutical Association, and pharmacists obtained with assistance of University of Minnesota College of Pharmacy. All were registered pharmacists. 83% completed BA degree, 5% MA, 9% PhD. 3% were employed by hospitals, 26% by independent pharmacies, 21% by chain pharmacies. Major activities included dispensing	**074.** Compounds and dispenses medications following prescriptions issued by physician, dentist, or other authorized medical practitioner. Weighs, measures, and mixes drugs and fills bottles or capsules with correct quantity and composition of preparation. Stores and preserves vaccines, serums, and other drugs subject to deterioration. May assay medications to de-	Hospital pharmacist Pharmacy helper Pharmacy manager Research pharmacist

Sample/ scale	N	Year tested	Mean age	Mean years educ	Mean years exper	Composition	DOT code and description	Related occupations
PHARMACIST (m)	226	1976	39.6	17.3	15.9	(60%), management (12%), and a combination (18%). Obtained with assistance of the University of Minnesota College of Pharmacy. All were registered pharmacists. 90% completed BA degree, 4% MA, and 6% PhD.	termine identity, purity, and strength. May participate in store-management activities.	
PHOTOG-RAPHER (f)	249	1978	36.9	15.3	10.9	Members, Professional Photographers of America, National Press Photographers Association, and Society of Photographers in Communication. 21% had high school diploma, 38% completed BA degree, 13% MA; 35% received training on the job, 23% from photography courses not leading to a degree, 14% from degree courses, and 28% a combination. 51% were self-employed or in partnerships; remainder were employed by studios, businesses, newspapers, magazines, or a combination.	**143.** Photographs persons, motion picture sets, merchandise, exteriors and interiors, machinery, and fashions. Arranges equipment such as lighting, screens, and shades and moves objects to obtain desired effects. Sets camera for correct angle and distance, adjusts lens for focus. Mixes solutions and chemicals used in developing films; enlarges and prints pictures.	Audiovisual producer Biological photographer Camera operator Industrial photographer Medical photographer Motion picture photographer Photo editor Photo journalist Portrait photographer Scientific photographer Travel photographer Video technician
PHOTOG-RAPHER (m)	223	1978	38.9	15.1	15.1	See women's sample above. 24% had high school diploma, 10% completed AA degree, 31% BA; 44% received training on the job, 15% from photography courses not leading to a degree, 20% from degree courses, 22% from a combination. 56% were self-employed or in partnerships; 14% were employed by newspapers or magazines, remainder by studios, businesses, or a combination.		
PHYSICAL EDUCATION TEACHER (f)	291	1979	36.6	18.0	13.1	Members, American Alliance for Health, Physical Education, and Recreation. 47% completed BA degree, 52% MA. 84% were employed by secondary schools.	**099.** Instructs students in physical-education activities in educational institutions. Teaches field, court, and combative sports to individuals or groups using knowledge of sports techniques and of physical capabilities of students. Instructs individuals or groups in calisthenics, gymnastics, or corrective exercises, determines type and level of difficulty of exercises, corrections needed, and appropriate movements. Organizes, leads, instructs, and referees indoor and outdoor games.	Aquatic director Athletic director Coach Dance instructor Exercise instructor Recreational therapist Team manager Umpire-referee
PHYSICAL EDUCATION TEACHER (m)	219	1979	38.5	19.0	14.2	See women's sample above. 18% completed BA degree, 76% MA. 84% were employed by secondary schools.		
PHYSICAL THERAPIST (f)	332	1978	34.6	16.8	10.4	Members, American Physical Therapy Association, and a listing of Registered Physical	**076.** Treats patients with disabilities, disorders, and injuries to relieve pain, develop or	Athletic trainer Coordinator, rehabilitation

Sample/ scale	N	Year tested	Mean age	Mean years educ	Mean years exper	Composition	DOT code and description	Related occupations
						Therapists in Minnesota. 82% completed BA degree, 15% MA. 47% were employed by hospitals or clinics, 15% by educational institutions, 6% by rehabilitation centers, 5% by home health agencies, 5% were self-employed or in private practice, and 12% a combination.	restore function, and maintain maximum performance, using physical means such as exercise, massage, heat, water, light, and electricity as prescribed by physician. Applies diagnostic and prognostic muscle, nerve, joint, and functional ability tests. Directs and aids patients in active and passive exercises, muscle reeducation, and in using pulleys and weights, steps, and inclined surfaces. Directs patients in care and use of wheelchairs, braces, canes, crutches, and prosthetic and orthotic devices.	medicine Home health physical therapist Pediatric physical therapist Physical therapy aide Physical therapy assistant Research physical therapist
PHYSICAL THERAPIST (m)	230	1978	37.3	17.3	12.8	See women's sample above. 80% completed BA degree, 17% MA. 46% were employed by hospitals or clinics, 17% were self-employed or in private practice, 5% were employed by rehabilitation centers, 4% by educational institutions, and 17% a combination.		
PHYSICIAN (f)	211	1982	38.8	21.9	9.4	National sample from mail list company, and members, American College of Physicians. 26% practiced medicine in small private clinics (less than 5 physicians), 14% in public hospitals, 11% in private hospitals, 8% in HMO clinics, 6% for government, 3% in large private clinics (more than 5 physicians), 19% other, and 10% a combination. Specialties included general/family practitioner, internist, pediatrician, anesthesiologist, gynecologist/ obstetrician, neurologist, pathologist, radiologist, dermatologist, allergist, medical researcher, and college professor. Major activities included patient consultation and examination (33%), diagnosis and treatment (13%), research (8%), surgery (2%), other (7%), and a combination (31%).	**070.** Diagnoses and treats diseases and disorders of the human body. Examines patients, using all types of medical equipment, instruments, and tests, following standard medical procedures. Performs surgery, prescribes and administers medication, and engages in research to aid in control and cure of disease.	Allergist Anesthesiologist Cardiologist Dermatologist Emergency room physician Family practitioner Internist Neurologist Nurse practitioner Obstetrician Ophthalmologist Pathologist Pediatrician Physician's assistant Psychiatrist Radiologist Research physician Surgeon
PHYSICIAN (m)	272	1982	40.9	20.0	10.8	See women's sample above. 33% practiced medicine in small private clinics (less than 5 physicians), 13% in private hospitals, 12% in large private clinics (more than 5 physicians), 10% in public hospitals, 8% other, and 12% a combination. Specialties included general/family practitioner, cardiologist, internist, pediatrician, urologist, pathologist, radiologist, otolaryngologist, anesthesiolo-		

Sample/ scale	N	Year tested	Mean age	Mean years educ	Mean years exper	Composition	DOT code and description	Related occupations
						gist, gynecologist/obstetrician, dermatologist, surgeon, medical researcher, and college professor. Major activities included patient consultation and examination (32%), diagnosis and treatment (19%), research (9%), surgery (5%), and a combination (26%).		
PHYSICIST (f)	255	1973	38.8	20+	9.0	National sample from roster compiled by Committee on Women in Physics of American Physical Society; all had PhD. 58% were employed by colleges and universities, 16% by government or national laboratories, 12% by industry; major activities included research (52%), teaching (30%), and administration (11%).	**023.** Conducts research into phases of physical phenomena; develops theories and laws on basis of observation and experiments, and develops methods to apply laws and theories of physics to industry, medicine, and other fields. Performs experiments with lasers, betatrons, telescopes, mass spectrometers, electron microscopes, and other equipment to observe structure and properties of matter. May teach college courses.	Astrophysicist Biophysicist Geophysicist Medical physicist Nuclear physicist Plasma physicist Solid-state physicist Theoretical physicist
PHYSICIST (m)	230	1977	40.3	21.1	12.1	Members, American Physical Society; all had PhD. 40% were employed by educational institutions, 27% by government, 27% by industry; major activities included research (47%), administration (13%), teaching (12%), and a combination (20%).		
POLICE OFFICER (f)	207	1979	32.0	14.8	6.1	National sample gathered with assistance of member police departments of Police Executive Research Forum, and from participants in International Association of Women Police training meeting. 41% had high school diploma, 18% completed AA degree, 35% BA. Areas of work included patrol (46%), investigation (14%), and a combination (21%); clerical work averaged 39% of time working.	**375.** Patrols assigned beat to control traffic, prevent crime or disturbance of peace, and arrest violators. Reports to scene of accident, renders first aid to injured, investigates causes and results of accidents. Writes and files daily activity report with superior officer.	Accident-prevention squad Constable Deputy Detective Highway Patrol officer Narcotics investigator Sheriff Special agent Vice detective
POLICE OFFICER (m)	294	1979	33.0	14.7	9.1	National sample gathered with assistance of member police departments of Police Executive Research Forum. 35% had high school diploma, 28% completed AA degree, 28% BA. Areas of work included patrol (55%), investigation (11%), and a combination (14%); clerical work averaged 42% of time working.		
PSYCHOLOGIST (f)	287	1981	40.1	21.2	10.4	National sample of members, American Psychological Association. All completed PhD degree. 46% were employed by educational in-	**045.** Collects, interprets, and applies scientific data to human and animal behavior and mental processes, formulates hypotheses and experimental	Clinical psychologist Counseling psychologist Developmental

Sample/ scale	N	Year tested	Mean age	Mean years educ	Mean years exper	Composition	DOT code and description	Related occupations
						stitutions, 23% were self-employed or in a partnership, 10% were employed by the government, 2% by private industry, 14% a combination, and 5% other. Most frequent specialties included clinical (44%), counseling (10%), developmental (7%), educational (6%), experimental (5%), and social (4%), plus industrial/ organizational.	designs, analyzes results using statistics; writes papers describing research; provides therapy and counseling for groups or individuals. Investigates processes of learning and growth, and human interrelationships. Applies psychological techniques to personnel administration and management. May teach college courses.	psychologist Educational psychologist Engineering psychologist Experimental psychologist Industrial-organizational psychologist School psychologist Social psychologist Vocational psychologist
PSYCHOLOGIST (m)	318	1981	41.0	21.1	13.0	See women's sample above. All completed PhD degree. 51% were employed by educational institutions, 16% were self-employed or in a partnership, 15% were employed by the government, 3% by private industry, 9% a combination, and 6% other. Most frequent specialties included clinical (38%), experimental (9%), counseling (9%), social (4%), industrial/ organizational (4%), and educational (4%), plus developmental and personality.		
PUBLIC ADMINISTRATOR (f)	202	1979	37.7	17.9	9.0	Members, American Society for Public Administration. 22% completed BA degree, 65% MA. 69% were employed by government agencies, 11% by educational institutions.	188. Manages federal, state, local, and international government activities, as well as government-owned and -operated business and educational institutions. Directs and coordinates activities; develops program; prepares and releases reports and studies; represents agency at meetings; evaluates programs.	Affirmative action coordinator City manager Commercial development administrator Community organization director Compliance director Conservation commissioner Consumer affairs director Correctional agency director County administrator District administrator Economic development director Educational program director Employment service director Hospital administrator
PUBLIC ADMINISTRATOR (m)	216	1979	38.0	18.4	11.7	See women's sample above. 17% completed BA degree, 73% MA. 82% were employed by government agencies, 5% by educational institutions.		

Sample/ scale	N	Year tested	Mean age	Mean years educ	Mean years exper	Composition	DOT code and description	Related occupations
								Institution director
								Law enforcement director
								Legislative administrator
								Management analyst
								Medical facilities director
								Program analyst
								Public works commissioner
								Social welfare administrator
								Zoning director
PUBLIC RELATIONS DIRECTOR (f)	298	1979	39.2	16.3	12.1	From membership-register issue of *Public Relations Journal*, a publication of Public Relations Society of America. 63% completed BA degree, 22% MA. 41% were employed by business or industrial counseling firms, 17% by health or welfare agencies, 11% by educational institutions.	**165.** Plans and promotes programs designed to create and maintain favorable public image. Plans and directs development and communication of information designed to inform. Prepares and distributes fact sheets, news releases, photographs, and motion pictures to media representatives. Purchases advertising time and space; promotes goodwill.	Audiovisual communications manager
PUBLIC RELATIONS DIRECTOR (m)	302	1979	45.0	16.7	17.8	See women's sample above. 63% completed BA degree, 29% MA. 71% were employed by business or industrial counseling firms.		Communication specialist
								Community relations director
								Employee communications manager
								Fundraising director
								Information services director
								Lobbyist
								Marketing director
								Media relations director
								Municipal community consultant
								Public affairs manager
								Sales-service promoter
								Sports information director
PURCHASING AGENT (f)	247	1983	38.3	14.1	7.8	Members, National Institute of Governmental Purchasing, members, National Association of Purchasing Management, and write-in responses to articles in purchasing publications. 15% had high school diploma, 50% had attended some college, 7% completed AA degree, 21% BA, 2% MA. 33% saw themselves as senior buyer, 31% as chief purchasing officer, 7% as assistant purchasing officer, 7% as supervisory buyer, 7% as junior	**162.** Purchases machinery, equipment, tools, raw materials, parts, and supplies necessary for operation of an organization such as an industrial establishment, public utility, or government unit. Interviews vendors to obtain information relative to products' price and to determine ability of vendor to produce product or service and to meet delivery date. Keeps records pertaining to costs, delivery, product perform-	Contact specialist
								Field contractor
								Finance and purchasing director
								Subcontract administrator

Sample/ scale	N	Year tested	Mean age	Mean years educ	Mean years exper	Composition	DOT code and description	Related occupations
						buyer. Sample consisted of purchasers and buyers for industrial, commercial, and utility firms, educational institutions, and governmental agencies.	ance, and inventories. Discusses defects of purchased goods with quality-control personnel to determine source of trouble and takes corrective action.	
Purchasing Agent (m)	224	1979	41.2	15.9	11.2	See women's sample above. 27% had some college education, 44% completed BA degree, 18% MA.		
Radiologic Technologist (f)	225	1978	31.8	14.5	9.5	From *American Registry of Radiologic Technologists*; all were registered technologists. 29% had high school diploma, 17% completed AA degree, 6% BA, 36% received certificate or degree in radiologic technology. 78% were employed by hospitals or clinics; 82% reported x-ray technology as specialty; other specialties included nuclear medicine and radiation therapy.	**078.** Applies roentgen rays and radioactive substances to patients for diagnostic and therapeutic purposes. Administers drugs or chemical mixtures orally to render organs opaque. Develops film in accordance with photographic techniques. Assists in treating diseased or affected areas of body under supervision of physician by exposing area to specified concentration of x-rays for prescribed periods of time. May assist in therapy requiring application of radium or radioactive isotopes.	Health physicist Mammography technician Nuclear medical technician Radiation therapist Ultrasound technologist X-ray technician
Radiologic Technologist (m)	239	1978	34.4	14.9	11.1	See women's sample above. 38% had high school diploma, 24% completed AA degree, 19% BA, 14% received certificates or degrees in radiologic technology. 72% were employed by hospitals or clinics; specialty areas included x-ray technology (65%) and nuclear medicine (13%).		
Realtor (f)	209	1977	44.3	13.7	8.3	Members, Women's Council of Realtors. 64% had high school diploma, 26% completed BA degree. 55% were employed by real estate firms; 36% were self-employed or in partnerships. Sales specialty areas included residential (64%) and a combination of residential and commercial (30%).	**250.** Rents, buys, and sells properties for clients on commission basis. Reviews trade journals to keep informed of market conditions and property values. Interviews prospective clients and accompanies prospects to property sites; quotes purchase price and discusses conditions of sale or terms of lease. Draws up real estate contracts such as deeds and negotiates loans on property.	Building consultant Fee appraiser Real estate sales agent Residence leasing agent
Realtor (m)	208	1983	41.7	15.6	8.9	National sample, members of National Association of Realtors. 25% had high school diploma. 11% completed AA degree, 47% BA, 12% MA, 2% PhD. 45% were self-employed or in partnerships, 46% were employed by real estate firms. Sales specialty areas included residential (48%), commercial (5%), and a combination of residential and commercial (40%). Major activities included obtaining listings (9%), learning about properties (6%), showing		

Sample/ scale	N	Year tested	Mean age	Mean years educ	Mean years exper	Composition	DOT code and description	Related occupations
						properties (6%), arranging details of transaction (6%), and a combination (59%).		
RECREATION LEADER (f)	264	1979	36.4	17.3	11.5	Members, National Recreation and Park Association. 49% completed BA degree, 37% MA. 59% were employed by government; major activities included administration (41%), education (10%), program leadership (10%), supervision (10%), and a combination (24%).	**195.** Conducts recreation activities with assigned groups in public department or volunteer agency. Organizes, promotes, and develops interest in activities such as arts and crafts, sports, music, dramatics, camping, and hobbies. Cooperates with other staff members in conducting community-wide events and works with neighborhood groups to determine recreational interests and needs of all ages.	Camp director Community center director Leisure service supervisor Outdoor recreation director Park manager Parks and recreation director Recreational therapist Resort manager Youth activities director
RECREATION LEADER (m)	222	1979	38.6	16.0	13.9	See women's sample above. 45% completed BA degree, 40% MA, 11% PhD. 89% were employed by government; major activities included administration (66%), education (11%), and a combination (15%).		
REPORTER (f)	207	1979	38.0	16.1	10.7	From *Alphabetized Directory of American Journalists*; all those selected indicated "reporter" or "writer" as job title. Also members, National Federation of Press Women. 15% had high school diploma, 69% completed BA degree, 14% MA.	**131.** Collects and analyzes facts about newsworthy events by interview, investigation, or observation, and writes newspaper stories. Takes notes and reads publicity releases, copies of speeches, or similar materials to facilitate organization and writing of stories. Refers stories to supervising editor for approval. Receives and evaluates news tips and suggestions for future stories. Monitors police and fire radio communications to obtain news-story leads.	Bureau chief Business writer City editor Columnist Copy editor Court reporter Critic Editorial writer Entertainment reviewer Fashion editor Food editor Investigative reporter News editor Outdoor writer Political analyst Sports writer
REPORTER (m)	208	1979	35.3	16.2	11.9	See women's sample above; all of those selected indicated "reporter" or "writer" as job title. 14% had high school diploma, 72% completed BA degree, 12% MA.		
RESEARCH AND DEVELOPMENT MANAGER (f)	201	1983	37.7	18.2	5.4	National sample from Hugo Dunhill Mailing Lists, Inc., file on Women R&D managers, and from nine U.S. Navy laboratories. 45% completed BS degree, 30% MS, 25% PhD. Educational background by general area was 45% life sciences, 34% physical sciences, 11% mathematics and computer sciences, 10% engineering. Management level included lower (34%), middle (43%), upper (18%), and vice president (5%). Collected by R. Hill, University of Michigan.	**189.** Directs and coordinates activities concerned with research and development of new concepts, ideas, basic data on, and applications for, organization's products, services, or ideologies. Plans and formulates aspects of research and development proposals, and reviews and analyzes proposals submitted to determine if benefits derived and possible applications justify expenditures.	Director of marketing research and analysis Director of product research Manufacturing engineer Product development manager
RESEARCH AND DEVELOPMENT MANAGER (m)	215	1983	44.8	18.5	10.9	From R&D departments of a broad range of scientific and engineering-based firms. 38% completed BS degree, 31%		

Sample/ scale	N	Year tested	Mean age	Mean years educ	Mean years exper	Composition	DOT code and description	Related occupations
						MS, 31% PhD. Educational background by general area was 57% engineering, 27% physical sciences, 10% life sciences, 6% mathematics and computer science. Management level included lower (11%), middle (45%), upper (39%), and vice president (5%). Collected by R. Hill, University of Michigan.		
RESPIRATORY THERAPIST (f)	216	1983	33.0	15.7	7.1	Members, American Association for Respiratory Therapy. All were staff therapists. 4% had a certificate from a vocational school, 7% had had some college, 56% completed AA degree, 33% BA. 94% were employed by hospitals: 53% in intensive care, 16% in respiratory therapy unit, 22% other. Major activities included implementation of treatment programs (51%), emergency care (11%), giving instruction (5%), pulmonary lab work (4%), and a combination (23%). 88% were registered or certified therapists. 34% specialized in an area of pulmonary care, including newborn intensive care, pulmonary rehabilitation, critical care, and geriatric care.	**079.** Administers respiratory therapy and life support to patients with deficiencies and abnormalities of cardiopulmonary system, under supervision of physician and by prescription. Operates breathing devices, performs bronchopulmonary drainage, and assists patients in breathing exercises. Monitors patient's physiological responses to therapy, as well as equipment function. Maintains patient's chart. Consults with physician in the event of adverse reaction.	Cardiopulmonary technician Home care coordinator Neonatal care coordinator
RESPIRATORY THERAPIST (m)	206	1983	31.8	16.0	7.4	See women's sample above. 3% had a certificate from a vocational school, 9% had had some college, 49% completed AA degree, 34% BA. 86% were employed by hospitals: 54% in intensive care, 15% in respiratory therapy unit, 18% in other. Major activities included implementation of treatment programs (43%), administrative duties (9%), emergency care (7%), pulmonary lab work (6%), giving instruction (4%), and a combination (28%). 92% were registered or certified therapists. 42% specialized in an area of pulmonary care, including newborn intensive care, pulmonary rehabilitation, critical care, and geriatric care.		
RESTAURANT MANAGER (f)	152	1984	37.4	14.6	10.0	Members, National Restaurant Association, and a national sampling from *Bell*	**319.** Supervises employees engaged in serving food; trains workers; oversees kitch-	Cafeteria manager Caterer

Sample/scale	N	Year tested	Mean age	Mean years educ	Mean years exper	Composition	DOT code and description	Related occupations
						Yellow Pages. 24% had high school diploma, 27% had had some college, 9% completed AA degree, 31% BA, 6% MA. 37% were restaurant owners, 63% held management positions. Major activities included customer contact (26%), personnel management (17%), record keeping and financial planning (9%), and a combination (41%).	en; hires personnel; keeps records and requisitions supplies and equipment. May direct preparation of food and beverages and plan menus. Coordinates work of employees to promote efficiency.	Chef Club manager Convention manager Deli manager Fast-food manager Flight kitchen manager Food services director Hotel manager Innkeeper Resort manager
RESTAURANT MANAGER (m)	193	1984	38.8	14.9	14.3	See women's sample above. 18% had a high school diploma, 26% had had some college, 10% completed AA degree, 43% BA, 3% MA. 49% were restaurant owners, 41% held management positions. Major activities included customer contact (25%), personnel management (23%), record keeping and financial planning (11%), and a combination (38%).		
SCHOOL ADMINISTRATOR (f)	204	1979	43.9	19.9	7.8	Members, American Association of School Administrators. 61% completed MA degree, 12% specialist certificate, 9% EdD, 11% PhD. 47% were employed by elementary schools, 27% by junior/senior high schools; major activities included administration (37%), student and faculty interaction (14%), and a combination (49%).	**099.** Administers affairs of city, county, or other school system under direction of board of education. Administers program for selection of school sites, construction of buildings, and provision of education. Directs preparation and presentation of school budget and determines amount of school-bond issues required to finance educational program. Interprets programs and policies of school system to school personnel, individual and community groups, and government agencies. Coordinates work of school system with related activities of other school districts and agencies.	Assistant principal Assistant superintendent Career education director County school administrator Curriculum director Dean of students Principal School district administrator Superintendent Vocational education administrator
SCHOOL ADMINISTRATOR (m)	289	1979	43.3	20.1	12.1	See women's sample above. 55% completed MA degree, 17% specialist certificate, 16% EdD, 9% PhD. 30% were employed by elementary schools, 9% by junior/senior high schools, 27% by school districts, and 15% a combination; major activities included administration (50%) and administration combined with student and faculty interaction and school board responsibilities (38%).		
SCIENCE TEACHER (f)	213	1983	38.7	18.0	12.3	National sample, *National Science Teacher's Association, U.S. Registry.* 32% completed BA degree, 65% MA. All were high school teachers; 84% taught more than one grade. 55% taught primarily biology, 16% chemistry, 9% general science, 5% physics, 14% mixed; other subjects in-	**091.** Instructs students through lectures, demonstrations, and audiovisual aids. Prepares teaching outline for course of study. Assigns and corrects homework. Administers tests to evaluate students' progress. Keeps attendance records and maintains discipline. Partici-	Astronomy teacher Biology teacher Chemistry teacher Earth science teacher General science teacher Geology teacher

Sample/ scale	N	Year tested	Mean age	Mean years educ	Mean years exper	Composition	DOT code and description	Related occupations
						cluded physiology, environmental science, geology, astronomy, and botany. 92% of sample spent a minimum of 40% of time teaching; other activities included lesson preparation, grading, meetings, conferences. 28% were involved in other school activities relating to subject taught.	pates in faculty and professional meetings, conferences, and teacher-training workshops. Performs related duties such as sponsoring special activities or student organizations.	Health teacher Physics teacher Physiology teacher
SCIENCE TEACHER (m)	237	1983	39.5	18.2	14.7	See women's sample above. 30% completed BA, 66% MA, 2% PhD, 3% other. All were high school teachers; 89% taught more than one grade. 45% taught primarily biology, 18% chemistry, 12% general science, 9% physics, 14% mixed; other subjects included physiology, environmental science, geology, astronomy, and botany. 96% of sample spent a minimum of 40% of time teaching; other activities included lesson preparation, grading, meetings, conferences. 17% were involved in other school activities relating to subject taught.		
SECRETARY (f)	269	1983	40.7	13.3	17.0	National sample, members of Professional Secretaries International. 52% had high school diploma, 12% attended secretarial school, 16% business school, 8% completed AA degree, 8% BA. 33% were employed by manufacturing firms, 9% by private business, 6% by hospitals, 51% other (casinos, trade associations, publishers, chemical research industries). Specialties included corporate secretary (15%), medical (6%), public relations (3%), education (3%), technical (2%), legal (2%), other (7%), no specialty (45%), and a combination (18%). 75% spent less than 50% of time typing (the mode was 25%). Other activities included dictation, transcription, filing, maintenance of records, correspondence, supervisory functions, and research.	**201.** Schedules appointments, gives information to callers, take dictation, and otherwise relieves officials of clerical work and administrative and business detail. Composes and types routine correspondence. Schedules appointments. Greets visitors, ascertains nature of business, and conducts visitors to appropriate person. May arrange travel schedule and reservations. May compile and type statistical reports.	Administrative assistant Clerk-typist Executive secretary Financial secretary Legal secretary Medical secretary Office manager Personal secretary Receptionist School secretary Social secretary Stenographer
SOCIAL SCIENCE TEACHER (f)	230	1983	39.8	17.9	11.9	National sample, *National Science Teachers' Association, U.S. Registry*. 39% completed BA degree, 58% MA, 1%	**091.** Teaches courses such as American studies, career exploration, economics, geography, government, civics, his-	American studies teacher Career development teacher

Sample/ scale	N	Year tested	Mean age	Mean years educ	Mean years exper	Composition	DOT code and description	Related occupations
						PhD. All were high school teachers; 86% taught more than one grade. 54% taught primarily history, 12% government/civics, 6% psychology, 4% geography, 3% economics, 10% mixed; other areas included marriage and family, area studies, energy/ecology, and ethics. 86% spent a minimum of 40% of time teaching; other activities included lesson preparation, grading, and meetings/conferences. 22% were involved in other school activities relating to subject taught.	tory, and political science. Instructs students through lectures, demonstrations, and audiovisual aids. Prepares teaching outline for course of study. Assigns lessons and corrects homework. Administers tests to evaluate student's progress. Keeps attendance records and maintains discipline. Participates in faculty and professional meetings. Performs related duties such as sponsoring special activities or student organizations.	Criminology teacher Economics teacher European studies teacher Geography teacher Government/ civics teacher History teacher Political science teacher Psychology teacher Sociology teacher
SOCIAL SCIENCE TEACHER (m)	224	1983	39.2	18.0	14.1	See women's sample above. 27% completed BA degree, 68% MA, and 4% PhD. All were high school teachers; 81% taught more than one grade. 56% taught primarily history, 16% government/civics, 5% economics, 4% psychology, 3% geography, 10% mixed; other areas included marriage and family, area studies, energy/ecology, ethics. 91% spent a minimum of 40% of time teaching; other activities included lesson preparation, grading, and meetings/conferences. 9% were involved in other school activities relating to subject taught.		
SOCIAL WORKER (f)	208	1975	42.8	18.5	14.7	Members, American Association of Social Workers. 96% completed MA degree. Major activities included casework (35%), administration (27%), and a combination (18%).	195. Performs social-service functions in a public or volunteer social-welfare agency. Counsels and aids individuals and families requesting assistance of social-service agency. Interviews clients with problems such as personal and family adjustment, finances, or physical or mental impairments to determine nature and degree of problem. Counsels clients individually or in groups regarding plans for meeting needs and assists clients to mobilize their inner capacities and environmental resources to improve social functioning. Helps clients to modify attitudes and patterns of behavior by increasing understanding.	Camp director Case aide Caseworker Child welfare caseworker Community organization worker Family caseworker Field director Group worker Management aide Marriage counselor Medical social worker Parole officer Probation officer Program aide Psychiatric social worker School social worker
SOCIAL WORKER (m)	234	1975	41.8	18.7	15.1	See women's sample above. 95% completed MA degree. Major activities included administration (46%), casework (27%), and a combination (12%).		

Sample/ scale	N	Year tested	Mean age	Mean years educ	Mean years exper	Composition	DOT code and description	Related occupations
								Social welfare administrator
SOCIOLOGIST (f)	210	1974	42.2	21.4	11.2	Members, American Sociological Association; all had PhD degree. Major activities included teaching (48%), research (15%), administration (9%), and a combination (24%).	**054.** Conducts research into development, structure, and behavior of groups of people and patterns of culture and social organization that have arisen out of group life in society. Collects and analyzes data concerning social phenomena. May teach college courses.	Criminologist Demographer Industrial sociologist Medical sociologist Research sociologist
SOCIOLOGIST (m)	212	1974	40.3	21.1	11.4	See women's sample above. Major activities included teaching (45%), research (17%), administration (15%), and a combination (21%).		Rural sociologist Social research analyst Urban sociologist
SPECIAL EDUCATION TEACHER (f)	209	1979	35.5	17.9	6.4	From a commercially compiled national listing. 46% completed BA degree, 54% MA. 63% were employed in elementary schools; specialty areas included mental retardation (44%), learning disabilities (23%), and a combination including physically disabled (28%).	**094.** Teaches disabled students, adapting techniques and methods of instruction to meet individual needs of students. Plans curriculum and prepares other materials, considering factors such as individual needs, abilities, learning levels, and physical disabilities. Devises special teaching tools and techniques. Confers with other members of staff to develop programs that maximize students' potentials. Instructs students through lectures, demonstrations, and audiovisual aids. Prepares teaching outline for course of study, assigns lessons, and corrects homework. Administers tests to evaluate students' progress. Keeps attendance records and maintains discipline. Participates in faculty and professional meetings, conferences, and teacher-training workshops. Performs related duties such as sponsoring special activities and student organizations.	Educational therapist Teacher, blind Teacher, deaf Teacher, emotionally disturbed Teacher, gifted Teacher, learning disabled Teacher, mentally disabled Teacher, physically disabled
SPECIAL EDUCATION TEACHER (m)	250	1979	34.7	18.7	7.9	See women's sample above. 40% completed BA degree, 56% MA. 28% were employed in elementary schools; specialty areas included mental retardation (36%), learning disabilities (15%), and a combination including physically disabled (29%).		
SPEECH PATHOLOGIST (f)	230	1978	36.3	18.2	10.1	From directory of The American Speech and Hearing Association. 96% completed MA degree or higher. 41% were employed by elementary or secondary schools, 14% by colleges or universities, 10% by hospitals, and 10% were self-employed or in partnerships. Major activities included therapy (67%), teaching (9%), administration (6%), and a combination (10%).	**076.** Diagnoses, treats, and performs research related to speech and language problems. Treats language and speech impairments such as aphasia, stuttering, and articulatory problems of organic and nonorganic etiology. Plans, directs, or conducts remedial programs designed to restore or improve communicative efficiency. Provides counseling and guidance to speech- and language-handicapped individuals.	Audiologist Hearing-test technician Interpreter for deaf Oral myologist Speech clinician Speech consultant Speech correctionist Speech and hearing specialist Speech therapist

Sample/ scale	N	Year tested	Mean age	Mean years educ	Mean years exper	Composition	DOT code and description	Related occupations
SPEECH PATH-OLOGIST (m)	336	1973	40.3	18.8	13.0	See women's sample above. All held advanced clinical certification; 50% completed MA degree, 36% PhD. Major activities included therapy (27%), administration (16%), teaching (13%), and a combination (44%).		
STORE MANA-GER (f)	176	1984	36.8	14.4	9.8	Obtained with assistance of National Retail Merchants Association, Minnesota Retail Merchants Association, and through national *Bell Yellow Pages*. 50% had high school diploma, 3% a vocational-technical certificate, 9% completed AA degree, 33% BA, 2% MA. Types of merchandise included clothing (32%), jewelry (7%), and a combination (57%, including food, hardware, and other). Major activities included financial records and planning (15%), personnel management (13%), inventory control (9%), customer service (8%), merchandise presentation (5%), other (12%), and a combination (34%).	**189.** Directs and coordinates activities of stores. Develops and implements policies and procedures for store. Negotiates or approves contracts with suppliers of merchandise, security, or maintenance. Reviews operating and financial statements. Confers with administrative personnel. Conducts supervisory staff meetings. Prepares budgets, reports on operations. Supervises and trains workers.	Advertising manager Buyer/ purchasing director Credit manager General merchandiser Personnel manager Retail sales manager
STORE MANA-GER (m)	238	1984	39.1	15.1	15.5	See women's sample above. 23% had high school diploma, 16% had had some college, 7% completed AA degree, 46% BA, and 4% MA. Types of merchandise included clothing (36%) and a combination (54%, including jewelry, hardware, food, and other). Major activities included financial records and planning (13%), inventory control (11%), personnel management (9%), administrative functions (6%), merchandise presentation (5%), customer service (5%), and a combination (47%).		
SYSTEMS AN-ALYST (f)	258	1975	32.9	15.9	7.9	From rosters provided by Society for Data Processors, and from write-in responses to articles in *Computeworld*; all spent at least 50% of time in systems analysis. 16% had high school diploma, 59% completed BA degree, 16% MA. 67% worked in business-related areas, 14% in educational areas, 9% in scientific areas.	**012.** Analyzes business procedures and problems to refine data and convert it to programmable form for electronic data processing. Evaluates system effectiveness; develops new systems; specifies in detail the logical and/or mathematical operations to be performed. Plans and prepares technical reports and instructional manuals.	Computer programmer Computing applications specialist Data control analyst Electronic data analyst Information scientist Management methods analyst
SYSTEMS AN-ALYST (m)	361	1975	39.4	16.3	12.9	See women's sample above. 10% had high school diploma,		

Sample/ scale	N	Year tested	Mean age	Mean years educ	Mean years exper	Composition	DOT code and description	Related occupations
						49% completed BA degree, 28% MA. 79% worked in business-related areas, the remainder in educational, scientific, and other areas.		Project analyst Systems development director Systems research officer Technical analyst Technical support analyst
TRAVEL AGENT (f)	264	1983	41.4	14.7	11.7	Members, American Society of Travel Agents. 30% had high school diploma, 15% a certificate from a travel school, 5% a certificate from a vocational school not related to travel, 9% completed AA degree, 34% BA, 3% MA. 9% made primarily commercial bookings, 23% leisure, 68% a combination. 32% were members of Institute of Certified Travel Agents. Major activities included administrative functions (25%), reservations (16%), advising clients (11%), traveling (3%), and a combination (42%).	**252.** Plans itineraries, and arranges accommodations and other travel services for customers of travel agency. Converses with customer to determine destination, mode of transportation, travel dates, financial considerations, and accommodations required. Plans or describes and sells itinerary package tour. Gives customer brochures concerning travel. Computes cost of travel and accommodations, books customer on transportation carrier, makes hotel reservations. Tickets passenger and collects payment. May specialize in foreign or domestic service, may act as wholesaler and assemble tour packages.	Airline reservation agent Travel clerk Travel counselor Ticket agent Traffic agent Tour operator
TRAVEL AGENT (m)	214	1983	41.8	15.7	13.4	See women's sample above. 16% had high school diploma, 8% a certificate from a travel school, 2% a certificate from a vocational school not related to travel, 6% completed AA degree, 49% BA, 13% MA, 5% other. 11% made primarily commercial bookings, 20% leisure, 69% a combination. 20% were members of Institute of Certified Travel Agents. Major activities included administrative functions (37%), reservations (12%), advising clients (10%), traveling (2%), and a combination (38%).		
VETERINARIAN (f)	308	1973	36.2	20.0	11.0	Members, Women's Veterinary Medical Association; minimum educational level was DVM degree. 79% were in private practice, the majority specializing in small animals; 13% were in research or teaching.	**073.** Diagnoses and treats diseases and disorders of animals. Inoculates animals against disease. Performs autopsies to determine cause of death. Advises on care and breeding of animals. Engages either in general practice, treating various animal species, or in specialty, restricting practice to pets or to a single species.	Equine veterinarian Feline veterinarian Food-animal veterinarian Laboratory animal veterinarian Large-animal veterinarian Livestock inspector Poultry veterinarian
VETERINARIAN (m)	210	1973	37.7	19.9	11.0	National sample from *American Veterinary Medical Association Directory*; minimum educational level was DVM degree. 82% were in private practice, 13% in research or teaching.		

Sample/scale	N	Year tested	Mean age	Mean years educ	Mean years exper	Composition	DOT code and description	Related occupations
								Research veterinarian
								Small-animal veterinarian
								Veterinary anesthesiologist
								Veterinary assistant
								Veterinary microbiologist
								Veterinary pathologist
								Zoo veterinarian
VOCATIONAL AGRICULTURE TEACHER (f)	135	1982	31.1	17.2	5.8	Collected with assistance of National Vocational Agriculture Teacher's Association, Inc., and names from *Agriculture Teachers' Directory*. 3% completed AA degree, 53% BA, 36% MA, 7% other. 59% were employed by high schools, 14% by vocational-technical institutions, 8% by junior or community colleges, 4% by colleges or universities. 76% spent a minimum of 40% of time in classroom instruction; other activities included lesson preparation, assignment evaluation, administrative functions, and outdoor instruction.	**091.** Teaches courses in agriculture, horticulture, farm management, equipment maintenance and repair, crop judging, production, agricultural supplies, and services. Prepares teaching outline for course of study, assigns lessons, and corrects homework. Administers tests to evaluate students' progress. Keeps attendance records and maintains discipline. Participates in faculty and professional meetings, conferences, and teacher-training workshops. Performs related duties such as sponsoring special activities and student organizations.	Agribusiness teacher
VOCATIONAL AGRICULTURE TEACHER (m)	239	1982	37.6	17.9	11.7	See women's sample above. 38% completed BA degree, 49% MA. 69% were employed by high schools, 10% by colleges or universities, 9% by vocational institutions, 7% by junior or community colleges. 75% spent a minimum of 40% of time in classroom instruction; other activities included lesson preparation, assignment evaluation, administrative functions, and outdoor instruction.		Agricultural education instructor
								Agricultural mechanics teacher
								Animal husbandry teacher
								Farm management instructor
								Forestry instructor
								Horticulture instructor
								Landscaping instructor
								Vocational training teacher
YWCA DIRECTOR (f)	216	1978	37.2	16.1	7.5	Obtained with assistance of Professional Directors of YWCAs in the United States. 12% had high school diploma, 60% completed BA degree, 18% MA.	**187.** Directs activities of organization to coordinate functions of various programs; organizes and develops programs; reviews and prepares budgets; prepares reports; recruits and trains volunteer workers; represents organization in community.	Camp director
								Child care director
								Community education director
YMCA DIRECTOR (m)	313	1978	38.4	17.0	13.6	Obtained with assistance of Professional Directors of YMCAs in the United States. 68% completed BA degree, 27% MA.		Extension director
								Girl/Boy Scout professional
								Girl's/Boy's club director
								Program coordinator

Sample/ scale	N	Year tested	Mean age	Mean years educ	Mean years exper	Composition	DOT code and description	Related occupations
								Senior program director
								Social projects director
								Sports director
								Volunteer services supervisor
								Women's/Men's center director

Occupations and Their Code Types

The list of occupations that follows—it includes all of the occupations on the Strong profile and many others—is designed for use with the six General Occupational Theme scales scored on the profile of the SVIB-SCII. Each occupation has been assigned a code type indicating the Theme or Themes that most strongly characterize it. For example, the occupation "machine shop supervisor" has been given the code type RCS, indicating that the three Themes REALISTIC, CONVENTIONAL, and SOCIAL, in that order, are descriptive of that occupation. The occupations are ordered in the list according to their code types.

The code type for each occupation was derived either by testing people in that occupation to see on which of the Themes they scored highest or by asking people of known code types which occupations they liked. Thus, the list includes only those occupations for which empirical data are available.

Because the samples were classified by sex, and because the sexes sometimes showed substantial differences on these Themes, an "f" or "m" is given after each occupation to indicate the sex that the code type is based on: "(f,m)" when the two sexes in a given occupation are of the same code type, and "(f)" or "(m)" when data are available on only one sex. When the two sexes in an occupation are of different code types, each is listed at its appropriate code location, and at each location a cross-reference to the code type for the other sex is given—for example, "(f; m = SEI)."

These code types should be seen only as guidelines: they were assigned on the basis of the best available statistics, and they usually accord well with common sense; but they are based only on averages and should be treated as such. Occasionally, quirks appear, and the user must understand that not all of the problems of occupational classification have been solved. In particular, not all people in any one occupation are alike; though the code types of people working together usually are similar, many people (even many who are contentedly employed) have code types other than the one listed for their occupation.

When working with an individual profile, it is useful to focus on those sections of the list that correspond to the respondent's highest scores on the General Occupational Themes. For example, if the respondent scored highest on the ENTERPRISING, SOCIAL, and CONVENTIONAL themes, those sections of the list dealing with the E, S, and C themes in all of their various combinations—ESC, ECS, SEC, CES, ES, CE, SE, and so forth—should be scanned for ideas. The list thus identifies areas and particular occupations that deserve more attention.

RC	Army officer	(f,m)
RC	Drafting technician	(m; f = AR)
RC	Farmer	(f; m = R)
RC	Instrument assembler	(f,m)
RC	Marine Corps enlisted personnel	(m; f = CRS)
RC	Navy enlisted personnel	(f,m)
RC	Prison warden	(m)
RCS	Machine shop supervisor	(m)
RCS	Vocational agriculture teacher	(m; f = R)
RCE	Highway Patrol officer	(f; m = RSE)
RCE	Interstate bus driver	(m; f = R)
RSE	Athletic director	(f; m = E)
RSE	County sheriff	(m)
RSE	Highway Patrol officer	(m; f = RCE)
RSE	Marine Corps officer	(m; f = RSI)
RE	Baker	(m; f = CE)
RE	Building contractor	(m)
RE	Professional athlete	(f; m = ER)
RE	Secret Service agent	(m; f = ER)
RSC	City or state employee	(m; f = SC)
RSI	Cabinetmaker	(m)
RSI	Marine Corps officer	(f; m = RSE)

RS	Emergency medical technician	(f; m = R)
RS	Industrial arts teacher	(m)
R	Air Force enlisted personnel	(m; f = C)
R	Air Force officer	(f,m)
R	Bus driver	(f,m)
R	Carpenter	(m; f = RI)
R	Charter bus driver	(f,m)
R	Corrections officer	(f,m)
R	Electrician	(m; f = RI)
R	Emergency medical technician	(m; f = RS)
R	Farmer	(m; f = RC)
R	Forest ranger	(m)
R	Forester	(m; f = RI)
R	Horticultural worker	(f,m)
R	Interstate bus driver	(f; m = RCE)
R	Metro bus driver	(f,m)
R	Painter	(f,m)
R	Police officer	(f,m)
R	Rancher	(m)
R	School bus driver	(m; f = CR)
R	Telephone technician	(m)
R	Tool-and-die maker	(m)

Code	Occupation	
R	Union leader	(m)
R	Vocational agriculture teacher	(f; m = RCS)
RI	Auto mechanic	(m)
RI	Carpenter	(f; m = R)
RI	Cartographer	(f,m)
RI	Civil engineer	(f,m)
RI	Electrician	(f; m = R)
RI	Engineer	(f,m)
RI	Forester	(f; m = R)
RI	Machinist	(m)
RI	Mechanical engineer	(f,m)
RI	Merchant Marine officer	(m)
RI	Navy officer	(f; m = RIC)
RI	Petroleum engineer	(m)
RI	Pilot	(m; f = ERI)
RI	Radiologic technologist	(f,m)
RI	Veterinarian	(m; f = IR)
RIA	Architect	(f; m = ARI)
RIC	Navy officer	(m; f = RI)
RIS	Athletic trainer	(f; m = SR)
IR	Animal husbandry professor	(m)
IR	Astronaut	(m)
IR	Biologist	(f; m = I)
IR	Chemical engineer	(f,m)
IR	Chemist	(f,m)
IR	Chiropractor	(f; m = I)
IR	Dentist	(f,m)
IR	Electrical engineer	(f,m)
IR	Electronics technician	(m; f = I)
IR	Experimental psychologist	(f; m = IA)
IR	Geographer	(f; m = I)
IR	Geologist	(f,m)
IR	Inventor	(m; f = IA)
IR	Laboratory technician	(f,m)
IR	Medical researcher	(f; m = IA)
IR	Medical technician	(m; f = IC)
IR	Medical technologist	(m; f = IRC)
IR	NASA scientist	(m)
IR	Obstetrician	(f,m)
IR	Optometrist	(f,m)
IR	Pathologist	(f,m)
IR	Physicist	(f,m)
IR	Research and development manager	(f,m)
IR	Respiratory therapist	(f; m = IRS)
IR	Science teacher	(m; f = IRS)
IR	Surgeon	(f,m)
IR	Urologist	(m)
IR	Veterinarian	(f; m = RI)
IRS	Osteopath	(m)
IRS	Physical therapist	(f,m)
IRS	Respiratory therapist	(m; f = IR)
IRS	Science teacher	(f; m = IR)
ISR	Dietitian	(f; m = CSE)
ISR	Registered nurse	(m; f = SI)
IRE	Food scientist	(m)
IE	Pharmacist	(m; f = IC)
IC	Computer operator	(m; f = C)
IC	Medical technician	(f; m = IR)
IC	Pharmacist	(f; m = IE)
IRC	Computer programmer	(f,m)
IRC	Dental hygienist	(m; f = SCI)
IRC	Medical technologist	(f; m = IR)
IRC	Systems analyst	(f,m)
I	Biologist	(m; f = IR)
I	Chiropractor	(m; f = IR)
I	College professor	(f,m)
I	Electronics designer	(m)
I	Electronics technician	(f; m = IR)
I	Geographer	(m; f = IR)
I	Internist	(f,m)
I	Mathematician	(f,m)
I	Physician	(f; m = IA)
I	Scientific researcher	(f,m)
I	Social scientist	(m; f = AI)
I	Statistician	(f,m)
I	Technical writer	(f,m)
IS	Educational psychologist	(m; f = ISA)
IS	Hospital supervisor	(m)
IS	Pediatrician	(f; m = IAS)
ISA	Educational psychologist	(f; m = IS)
IA	Astronomer	(m)
IA	Clinical psychologist	(f,m)
IA	Economist	(m)
IA	Experimental psychologist	(m; f = IR)
IA	Inventor	(f; m = IR)
IA	Language interpreter	(f,m)
IA	Medical researcher	(m; f = IR)
IA	Physician	(m; f = I)
IA	Psychologist	(f,m)
IA	Scientific illustrator	(f)
IA	Sociologist	(f,m)
IAS	Counseling psychologist	(f,m)
IAS	Pediatrician	(m; f = IS)
IAS	Psychiatrist	(f,m)
AIS	Orchestra conductor	(m)
AI	Social scientist	(f; m = I)
AI	Anthropologist	(m)
AI	Ballet dancer	(f; m = AE)
AI	Landscape gardener	(f; m = AR)
AI	Medical illustrator	(f,m)
AIR	Sculptor	(m; f = AER)
ARI	Architect	(m; f = RIA)
AR	Chef	(f; m = EA)
AR	Drafting technician	(f; m = RC)
AR	Landscape gardener	(m; f = AI)
A	Advertising executive	(f,m)
A	Art museum director	(f,m)
A	Art teacher	(f,m)
A	Author	(f,m)
A	Broadcaster	(f,m)
A	Commercial artist	(f,m)
A	Entertainer	(f,m)
A	Fine artist	(f,m)
A	Flight attendant	(m; f = AE)
A	Interior decorator	(m; f = AE)
A	Lawyer	(f,m)
A	Librarian	(f,m)
A	Musician	(f,m)
A	Opera singer	(f,m)
A	Photographer	(f,m)
A	Poet	(f,m)
A	Public administrator	(f; m = AS)
A	Public relations director	(f,m)
A	Reporter	(f,m)
AE	Ballet dancer	(f; m = AI)
AE	Beautician	(m; f = E)
AE	Children's clothes designer	(f)
AE	Costume designer	(f)
AE	Fashion model	(f)
AE	Flight attendant	(f; m = A)
AE	Illustrator	(f)
AE	Interior decorator	(f; m = A)

AER	Sculptor	(f; m = AIR)	EI	Computer salesperson	(m; f = ES)
AS	English teacher	(f,m)	EI	Marketing executive	(f,m)
AS	Foreign language teacher	(m; f = SA)	EIC	Investments manager	(f; m = ECI)
AS	Music teacher	(m; f = SA)	ECI	Investments manager	(m; f = EIC)
AS	Public administrator	(m; f = A)	EA	Chef	(m; f = AR)
AS	Writing teacher	(f,m)	EA	Professional dancer	(f)
SA	Foreign language teacher	(f; m = AS)	E	Athletic director	(m; f = RSE)
SA	Grammar teacher	(f,m)	E	Beautician	(f; m = AE)
SA	Mental health worker	(m; f = SE)	E	Buyer	(m; f = EC)
SA	Minister	(f,m)	E	Chamber of Commerce executive	(m; f = EC)
SA	Music teacher	(f; m = AS)	E	Elected public official	(m; f = ES)
SA	Social worker	(f,m)	E	Florist	(f,m)
SA	Writer, children's books	(f)	E	Foreign correspondent	(f)
SAI	Speech pathologist	(m; f = SIA)	E	Funeral director	(m; f = ECS)
SIA	School psychologist	(f,m)	E	Personnel director	(f; m = ES)
SIA	Speech pathologist	(f; m = SAI)	E	Realtor	(f,m)
SI	Registered nurse	(f; m = ISR)	E	Restaurant manager	(m; f = EC)
SI	Student personnel worker	(m)	E	Retailer	(f,m)
S	Director, Christian education	(f)	E	Sports reporter	(m)
S	Elementary teacher	(f,m)	E	Travel agent	(m; f = EC)
S	Guidance counselor	(f,m)	E	Traveling salesperson	(m)
S	Playground director	(m; f = SRE)	E	Waitress	(f)
S	Priest	(m)	E	Women's style shop manager	(f)
S	Public health nurse	(f,m)	ER	Auctioneer	(m)
S	Social science teacher	(f,m)	ER	Dancing teacher	(f)
S	Special education teacher	(f,m)	ER	Nursery manager	(m)
SAR	Occupational therapist	(m; f = SRI)	ER	Optician	(m; f = EC)
SRI	Occupational therapist	(f; m = SAR)	ER	Pest controller	(m; f = CE)
SR	Athletic trainer	(m; f = RIS)	ER	Professional athlete	(m; f = RE)
SR	Physical education teacher	(f,m)	ER	Secret Service agent	(f; m = RE)
SRE	Agricultural extension agent	(m)	ERA	Stockbroker	(f; m = EC)
SRE	Playground director	(f; m = S)	ERI	Pilot	(f; m = RI)
SRE	Recreation leader	(f; m = SE)	ECR	Agribusiness manager	(m; f = CES)
SE	Football coach	(m)	ECR	Factory manager	(m)
SE	Juvenile parole officer	(m)	ECR	Farm implement manager	(m)
SE	Labor arbitrator	(m)	ECR	Farm supply manager	(m)
SE	Manager, child care center	(m)	ECR	Ready-to-wear salesperson	(m; f = EC)
SE	Mental health worker	(f; m = SA)	ECS	Auto sales dealer	(m)
SE	Recreation leader	(m; f = SRE)	ECS	Funeral director	(f; m = E)
SE	Vocational counselor	(f)	ECS	Hotel manager	(f,m)
SE	YMCA director	(m)	ECS	Retail clerk	(m; f = EC)
SE	YWCA director	(f)	ECS	Travel bureau manager	(f; m = ESC)
SCI	Dental hygienist	(f; m = IRC)	EC	Appliance salesperson	(m)
SC	Airline ticket agent	(m)	EC	Buyer	(f; m = E)
SC	City or state employee	(f; m = RSC)	EC	Chamber of Commerce executive	(f; m = E)
SC	Licensed practical nurse	(f,m)	EC	Corporation executive	(m)
SC	Teaching nun	(f)	EC	Launderer	(m)
SCE	Home economics teacher	(f; m = SEC)	EC	Manufacturer	(m)
SCE	Rehabilitation counselor	(m)	EC	Office manager	(m; f = C)
SCE	School administrator	(m; f = SEC)	EC	Optician	(f; m = ER)
SEC	Home economics teacher	(m; f = SCE)	EC	Purchasing agent	(f,m)
SEC	School administrator	(f; m = SCE)	EC	Ready-to-wear salesperson	(f; m = ECR)
ESC	Employment manager	(m; f = CSE)	EC	Restaurant manager	(f; m = E)
ESC	Nursing home administrator	(m; f = CSE)	EC	Retail clerk	(f; m = ECS)
ESC	Receptionist	(f)	EC	Stockbroker	(m; f = ERA)
ESC	Travel bureau manager	(m; f = ECS)	EC	Store manager	(f,m)
ES	Computer salesperson	(f; m = EI)	EC	Travel agent	(f; m = E)
ES	County extension agent	(m)	EC	Wholesaler	(m)
ES	Elected public official	(f; m = E)	CE	Administrative assistant	(f)
ES	Encyclopedia salesperson	(m)	CE	Baker	(f; m = RE)
ES	Industrial salesperson	(m)	CE	Certified public accountant	(f,m)
ES	Life insurance agent	(f,m)	CE	Courtroom stenographer	(f)
ES	Occupational health nurse	(f)	CE	Department store clerk	(f,m)
ES	Personnel director	(m; f = E)	CE	IRS agent	(f,m)
ES	Sales manager	(f,m)	CE	IRS revenue officer	(m; f = CSE)
ES	TV announcer	(f,m)	CE	Office worker	(f)

CE	Pest controller	(f; m = ER)		C	Hospital records clerk	(f)
CES	Agribusiness manager	(f; m = ECR)		C	Hospital secretary	(f)
CES	Business education teacher	(f,m)		C	IRS revenue agent	(m; f = CEI)
CES	Credit manager	(f,m)		C	IRS tax auditor	(f,m)
CES	Food service manager	(m; f = CS)		C	Office clerk	(f,m)
CSE	County welfare worker	(m)		C	Office manager	(f; m = EC)
CSE	Dietitian	(m; f = ISR)		C	Printer	(m)
CSE	Employment manager	(f; m = ESC)		C	Production manager	(m)
CSE	Executive housekeeper	(f,m)		C	Proofreader	(f)
CSE	IRS revenue officer	(f; m = CE)		C	Secretary	(f; m = CSA)
CSE	Nursing home administrator	(f; m = ESC)		CR	Army enlisted personnel	(m; f = CRS)
CS	Bank cashier	(m; f = C)		CR	School bus driver	(f; m = R)
CS	Dental assistant	(f)		CR	Sewing machine operator	(f,m)
CS	Dietary assistant	(f)		CR	Telephone operator	(f; m = CER)
CS	Food service manager	(f; m = CES)		CRS	Army enlisted personnel	(f; m = CR)
CSA	Secretary	(m; f = C)		CRS	Marine Corps enlisted personnel	(f; m = RC)
C	Accountant	(m,f)		CRE	Army noncommissioned officer	(f,m)
C	Air Force enlisted personnel	(f; m = R)		CER	Dairy processing manager	(m)
C	Bank cashier	(f; m = CS)		CER	Grain elevator manager	(m)
C	Banker	(f,m)		CER	Telephone operator	(m; f = CR)
C	Bookkeeper	(f,m)		CEI	IRS revenue agent	(f; m = C)
C	Computer operator	(f; m = IC)		CIR	Mathematics teacher	(f,m)

Mean Strong Profiles for Female Agribusiness Managers and Male Dental Hygienists and Secretaries

Every effort has been made to provide both female- and male-normed Occupational Scales for every occupation presented on the 1985 Strong profile. All but five of the 207 Occupational Scales are in matched pairs; for each of 101 occupations there is a scale based on a female-normed Criterion Sample and a scale based on a male-normed sample. In fact, every new occupation added to the profile in this revision is represented by a female- and a male- normed scale.

However, for five occupations that have been represented on the profile since 1974, it proved impossible to collect samples for both genders that were large enough for valid scale construction. Four of the occupations are represented only by female-normed scales—DENTAL AS-SISTANT, DENTAL HYGIENIST, HOME ECONOMICS TEACH-ER, and SECRETARY; one is represented only by a male-normed scale—AGRIBUSINESS MANAGER. These five scales have proved useful for occupational exploration, and have therefore been retained on the profile to augment the Strong's representation of the world of work.

To help guide profile interpretation for the un-represented gender, mean profiles (based on samples that are smaller than necessary for scale construction) are presented in the following pages for female agribusiness managers and male dental hygienists and secretaries. Unfortunately, the effort to obtain even small samples of male dental assistants and home economics teachers was unsuccessful, and therefore no mean profiles are presented for those occupations.

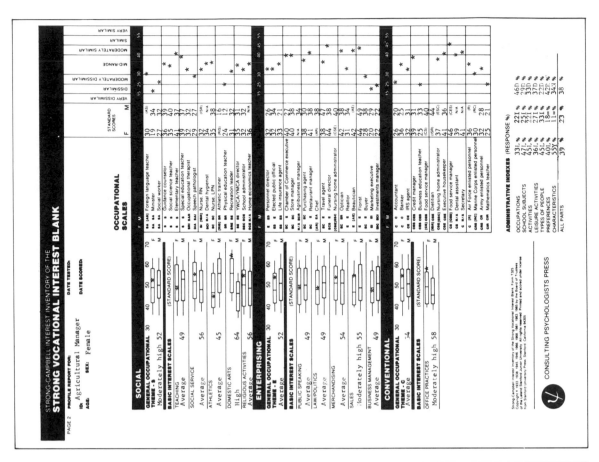

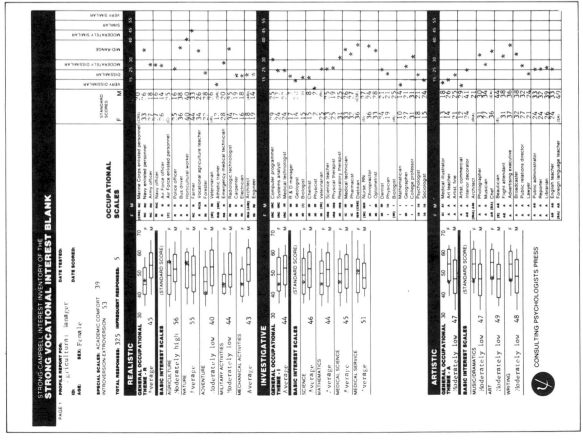

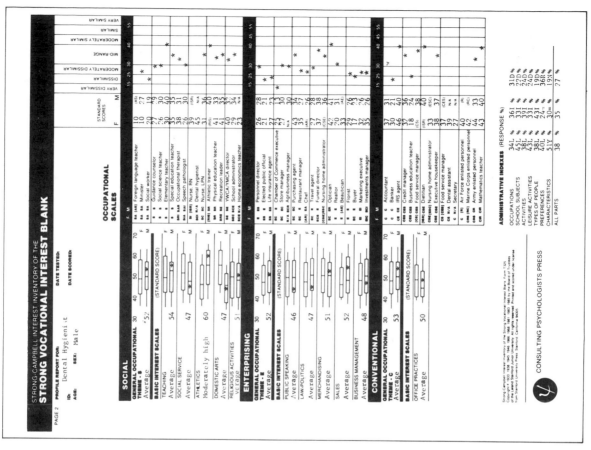

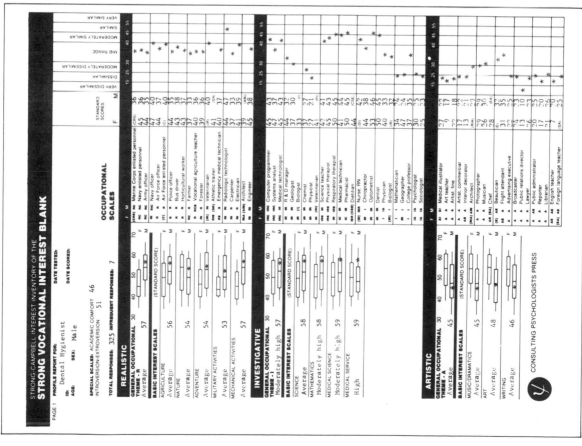

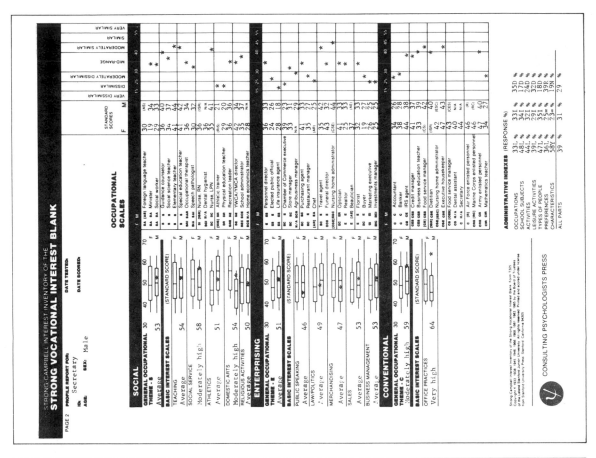

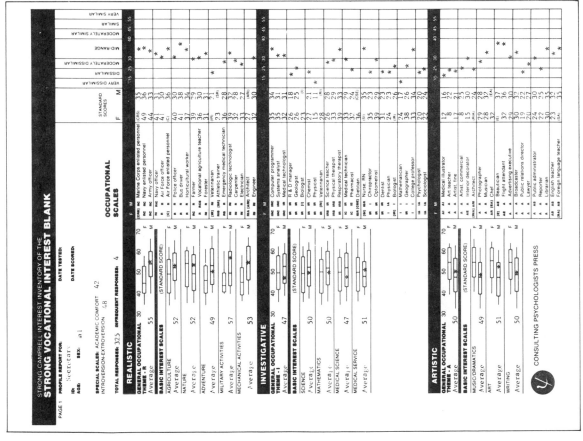

Mean Strong Profiles for Female and Male Bakers, Cartographers, Office Managers, Painters, Pest Controllers, and Retail Clerks

One of the major objectives of the research done for the 1985 Strong was to expand the number of vocational-technical and nonprofessional Occupational Scales offered by the profile. However, in a few cases, occupations with good employment outlooks did not have a sufficient representation of one gender or the other to allow collection of a sample large enough for valid scale construction. In keeping with the intent of expanding the usefulness of the Strong with non-college-bound clients, small samples were nonetheless collected for these occupations, and their mean profiles are presented in the following pages. The 12 samples, smaller than those needed for scale construction but large enough to

provide reliable mean profiles, were collected using the same method used to collect Criterion Samples. (See Chapter 6 for a detailed explanation of sample collection.) The occupations, listed below, also were assigned General Occupation Theme codes to aid in understanding how the occupations fit into the world of work.

Code	Female samples	Code	Male samples
CE	Bakers	RE	Bakers
RI	Cartographers	RI	Cartographers
C	Office managers	EC	Office managers
R	Painters	R	Painters
CE	Pest controllers	ER	Pest controllers
EC	Retail clerks	ECS	Retail clerks

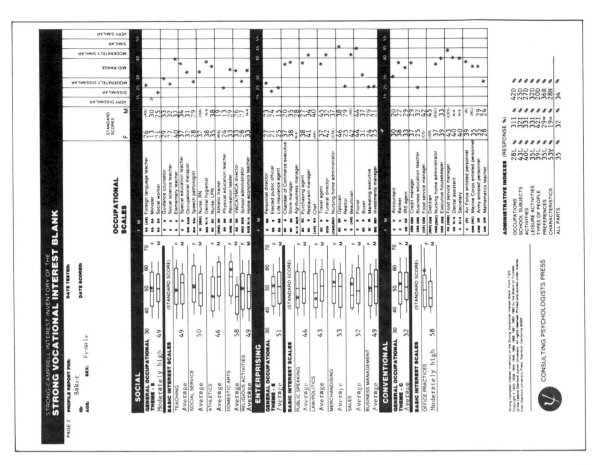

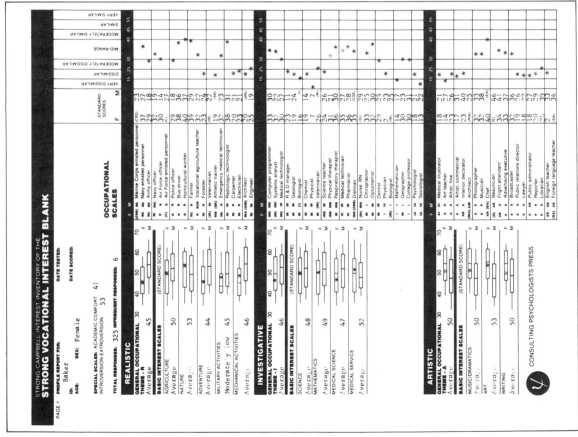

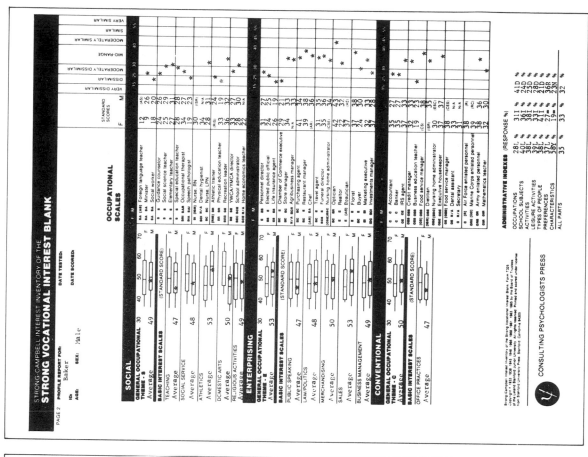

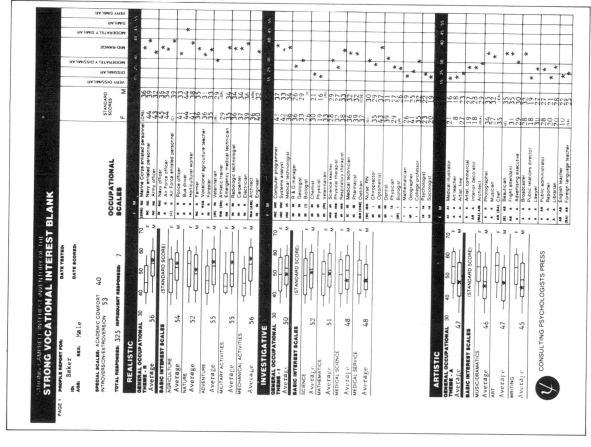

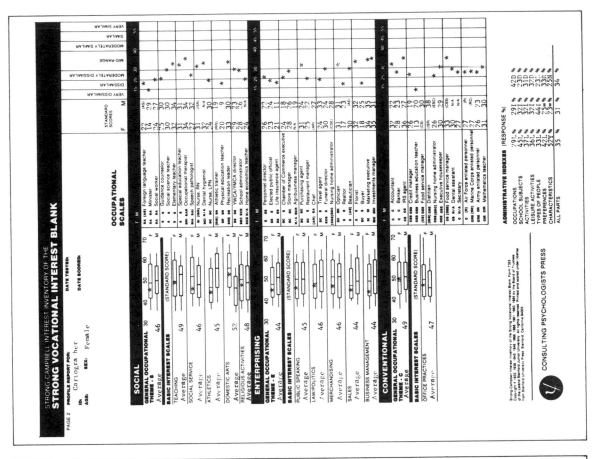

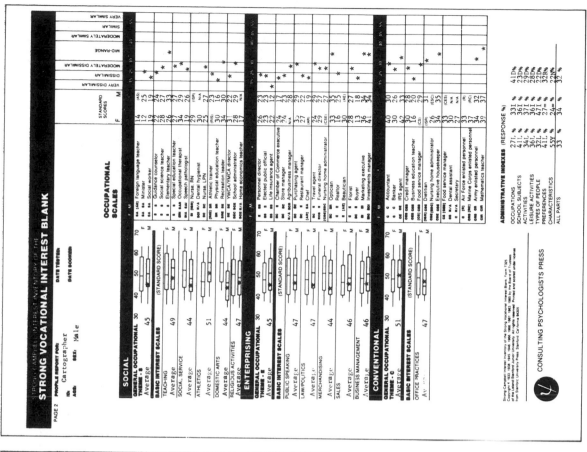

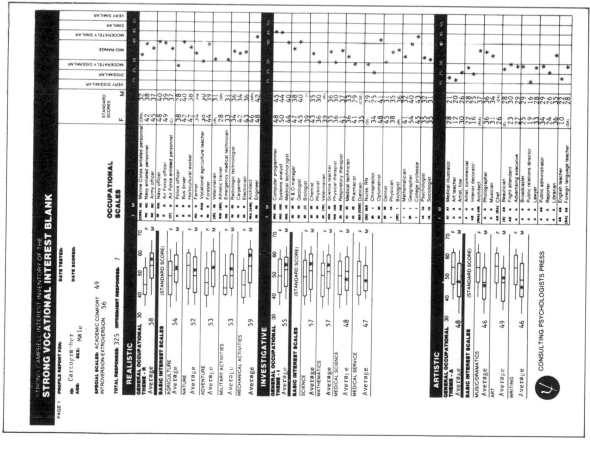

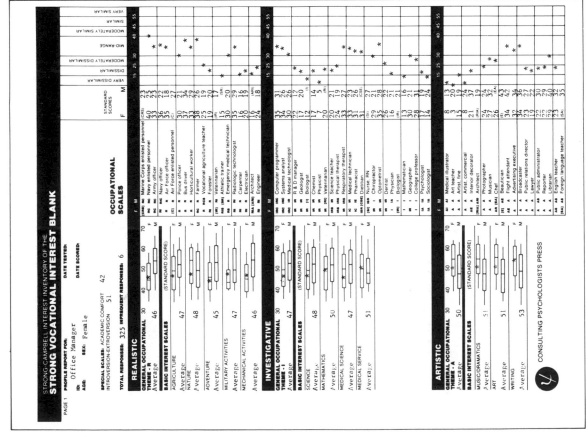

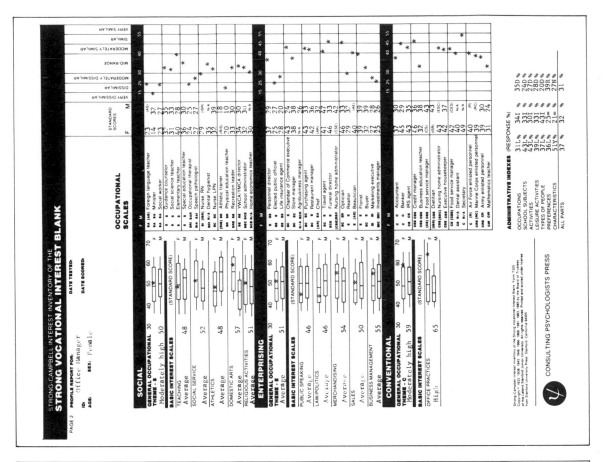

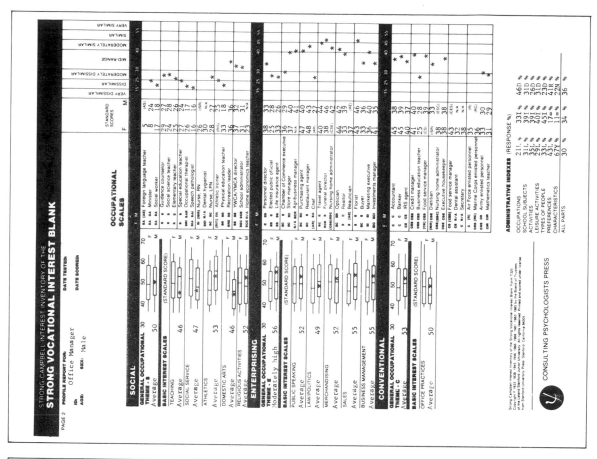

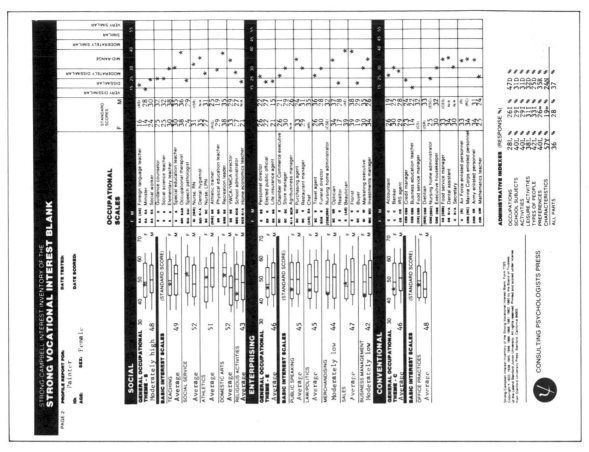

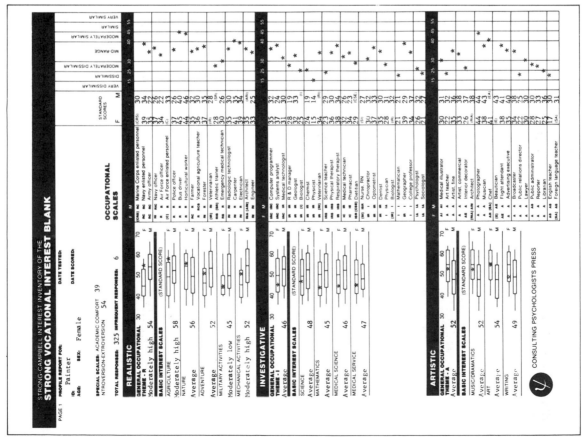

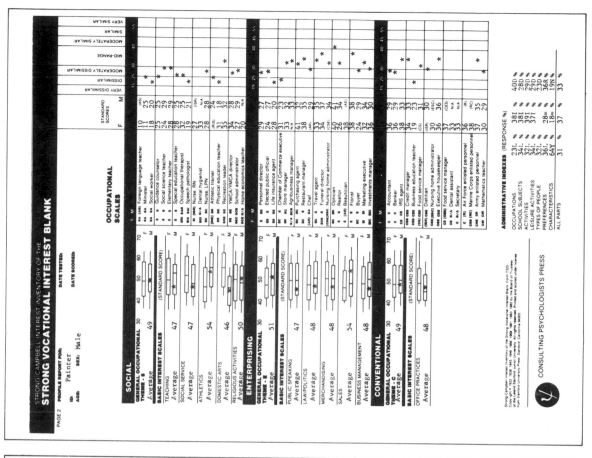

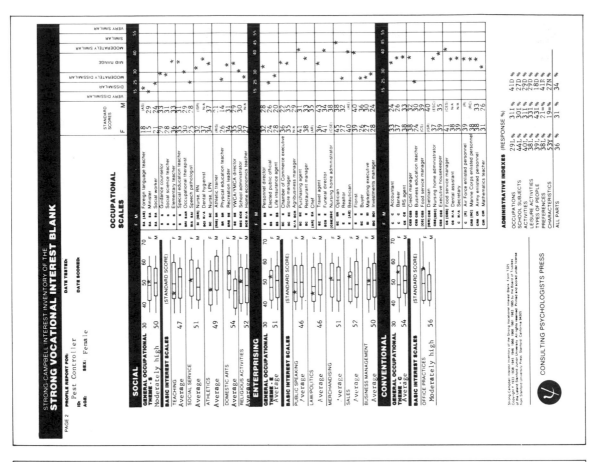

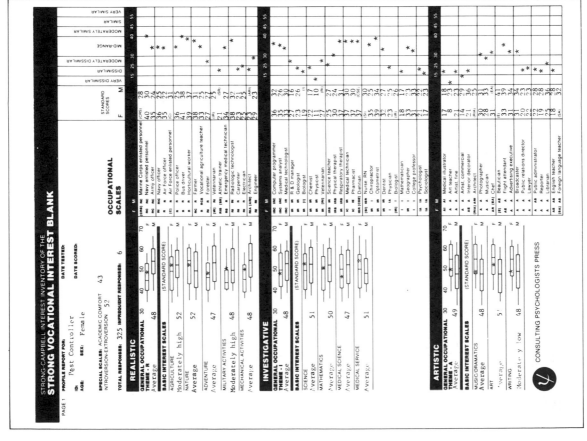

STRONG-CAMPBELL INTEREST INVENTORY OF THE
STRONG VOCATIONAL INTEREST BLANK

PAGE 1

PROFILE REPORT FOR: Pest Controller
ID:
AGE: SEX: Male

DATE TESTED:
DATE SCORED:

SPECIAL SCALES: ACADEMIC COMFORT 37
INTROVERSION-EXTROVERSION 52

TOTAL RESPONSES: 375   INFREQUENT RESPONSES: 7

OCCUPATIONAL SCALES

REALISTIC

	F	M
GENERAL OCCUPATIONAL THEME - R	56	

INVESTIGATIVE

ARTISTIC

CONSULTING PSYCHOLOGISTS PRESS

STRONG-CAMPBELL INTEREST INVENTORY OF THE
STRONG VOCATIONAL INTEREST BLANK

PAGE 2

PROFILE REPORT FOR: Pest Controller
ID: SEX: Male
AGE:

DATE TESTED:
DATE SCORER:

OCCUPATIONAL SCALES

SOCIAL

ENTERPRISING

CONVENTIONAL

ADMINISTRATIVE INDEXES (RESPONSE %)

CONSULTING PSYCHOLOGISTS PRESS

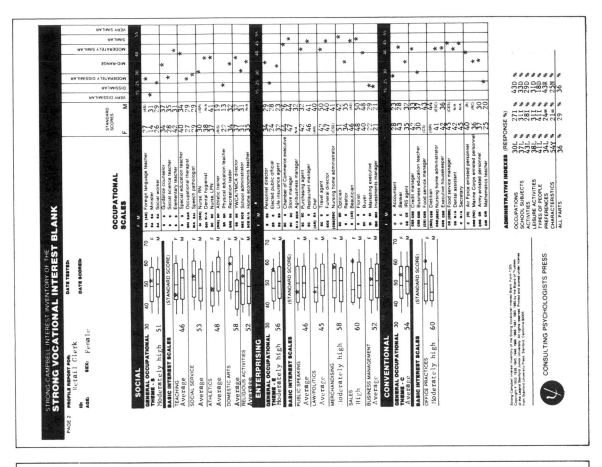

PAGE 2

STRONG-CAMPBELL INTEREST INVENTORY OF THE
STRONG VOCATIONAL INTEREST BLANK

PROFILE REPORT FOR:
ID: Retail Clerk DATE TESTED:
AGE: SEX: Male DATE SCORED:

OCCUPATIONAL SCALES

SOCIAL

GENERAL OCCUPATIONAL THEME - S
Average 53

BASIC INTEREST SCALES
TEACHING Average 48
SOCIAL SERVICE Average 52
ATHLETICS Average 57
DOMESTIC ARTS Average 49
RELIGIOUS ACTIVITIES Average 51

	F	M
Foreign language teacher	19	(AB)
Minister	14	32
Social worker	27	30
Guidance counselor	33	38
Social science teacher	33	33
Elementary teacher	33	30
Special education teacher	29	25
Occupational therapist	29	27
Speech pathologist	27	
Nurse, RN	31	
Dental hygienist	32	N/A
Nurse, LPN	25	33
Athletic trainer	27	19
Physical education teacher	41	39
Recreation leader	43	36
YWCA/YMCA director	43	38
School administrator	25	
Home economics teacher		

ENTERPRISING

GENERAL OCCUPATIONAL THEME - E
Moderately high 61

BASIC INTEREST SCALES
PUBLIC SPEAKING Average 54
LAW/POLITICS Average 54
MERCHANDISING High 60
SALES High 62
BUSINESS MANAGEMENT Average 56

	F	M
Personnel director	42	37
Elected public official	35	35
Life insurance agent	38	31
Chamber of Commerce executive	39	32
Store manager	38	46
Agribusiness manager	N/A	33
Purchasing agent	50	40
Restaurant manager	50	43
Chef	42	
Travel agent	41	40
Funeral director	46	43
Nursing home administrator	44	42
Optician	44	44
Realtor	36	43
Beautician	36	43
Florist	36	34
Buyer	35	26
Marketing executive		
Investments manager		

CONVENTIONAL

GENERAL OCCUPATIONAL THEME - C
Moderately high 55

BASIC INTEREST SCALES
OFFICE PRACTICES Average 51

	F	M
Accountant	35	33
Banker	37	33
IRS agent	45	40
Credit manager	35	
Business education teacher	23	39
Food service manager	40	
Dietitian	35	
Nursing home administrator	38	40
Executive housekeeper	37	
Food service manager	35	
Dental assistant	35	N/A
Secretary	35	N/A
Air Force enlisted personnel	35	
Marine Corps enlisted personnel	40	32
Army enlisted personnel		24
Mathematics teacher		

ADMINISTRATIVE INDEXES (RESPONSE %)

OCCUPATIONS	33 L %	35 I % 33 D %
SCHOOL SUBJECTS	41 L %	34 I % 26 D %
ACTIVITIES	45 L %	31 I % 23 D %
LEISURE ACTIVITIES	45 L %	33 I % 23 D %
TYPES OF PEOPLE	45 L %	39 I % 17 D %
PREFERENCES	32 L %	27 = % 41 R %
CHARACTERISTICS	57 Y %	21 = % 2 N %
ALL PARTS	39 %	33 % 28 %

CONSULTING PSYCHOLOGISTS PRESS

PAGE 1

STRONG-CAMPBELL INTEREST INVENTORY OF THE
STRONG VOCATIONAL INTEREST BLANK

PROFILE REPORT FOR:
ID: Retail Clerk DATE TESTED:
AGE: SEX: Male DATE SCORED:

SPECIAL SCALES: ACADEMIC COMFORT 39
INTROVERSION-EXTROVERSION 45

TOTAL RESPONSES: 325 INFREQUENT RESPONSES: 7

OCCUPATIONAL SCALES

REALISTIC

GENERAL OCCUPATIONAL THEME - R
Average 53

BASIC INTEREST SCALES
AGRICULTURE Average 51
NATURE Average 49
ADVENTURE Average 54
MILITARY ACTIVITIES Average 49
MECHANICAL ACTIVITIES Average 53

	F	M
Marine Corps enlisted personnel	41	32
Navy enlisted personnel	41	32
Army officer	43	30
Navy officer	42	33
Air Force officer	40	31
Air Force enlisted personnel	33	32
Police officer	39	29
Bus driver	39	39
Horticultural worker	33	30
Farmer	34	29
Vocational agriculture teacher	28	24
Forester	25	19
Veterinarian	23	18
Athletic trainer	29	26
Emergency medical technician	30	26
Radiologic technologist	28	26
Carpenter	32	28
Electrician	33	23
Architect		

INVESTIGATIVE

GENERAL OCCUPATIONAL THEME - I
Average 48

BASIC INTEREST SCALES
SCIENCE Average 48
MATHEMATICS Average 50
MEDICAL SCIENCE Average 47
MEDICAL SERVICE Average 48

	F	M
Computer programmer	34	28
Systems analyst	36	28
Medical technologist	29	29
R & D manager	21	20
Geologist	11	9
Chemist	21	
Physicist	21	
Veterinarian		
Science teacher	22	21
Physical therapist	25	28
Respiratory therapist	28	32
Medical technician	32	
Pharmacist	30	27
Nurse, RN	29	22
Chiropractor	38	28
Optometrist	16	16
Dentist	15	19
Physician	35	18
Mathematician	16	17
Geographer		
College professor		
Psychologist		
Sociologist		

ARTISTIC

GENERAL OCCUPATIONAL THEME - A
Average 49

BASIC INTEREST SCALES
MUSIC/DRAMATICS Average 50
ART Average 48
WRITING Average 48

	F	M
Medical illustrator	10	10
Art teacher	16	18
Artist, fine	18	16
Artist, commercial	15	21
Interior decorator	25	32
Architect	21	21
Photographer	31	30
Musician	26	30
Chef		
Beautician	37	40
Flight attendant	35	35
Advertising executive	28	28
Broadcaster	28	28
Public relations director	32	30
Lawyer		
Reporter	34	34
Librarian	25	23
English teacher	17	30
Foreign language teacher	17	29

CONSULTING PSYCHOLOGISTS PRESS

References Cited

Only those works cited in the text are listed here. The most complete bibliography of the Strong inventory is in O. K. Buros, *The Mental Measurements Yearbook*, Vols. 1–8, 1933–78 (Highland Park, N.J.: The Gryphon Press), where 1,521 entries are listed.

Barnette, W. L., Jr., and J. N. McCall. 1964. Validation of the Minnesota Vocational Interest Inventory for vocational high school boys. *Journal of Applied Psychology*, 48: 378–82.

Borgen, F. H., and G. T. Harper. 1973. Predictive validity of measured vocational interests with black and white college men. *Measurement and Evaluation in Guidance*, 6: 19–27.

Bouchard, T. J., Jr., J. C. Hansen, S. Scarr, and R. A. Weinberg. 1983. Family resemblance for psychological interests. Paper presented at meetings of International Congress on Twins Research, London, June.

Bouchard, T. J., Jr., L. L. Heston, E. D. Eckert, M. Keyes, and S. Resnick. 1981. The Minnesota Study of Twins Reared Apart: Project description and sample results in the developmental domain. *Twin Research 3: Intelligence, Personality and Development*, 227–33.

Brandt, J. E., and A. B. Hood. 1968. Effect of personality adjustment on the predictive validity of the Strong Vocational Interest Blank. *Journal of Counseling Psychology*, 15: 547–51.

Cairo, P. C. 1979. The validity of the Holland and Basic Interest Scales of the Strong Vocational Interest Blank: Leisure activities versus occupational membership as criteria. *Journal of Vocational Behavior*, 15: 68–77.

Campbell, D. P. 1966a. Occupations ten years later of high school seniors with high scores on the SVIB life insurance salesman scale. *Journal of Applied Psychology*, 50: 369–72.

———— 1966b. The stability of vocational interests within occupations over long time spans. *Personnel and Guidance Journal*, 44: 1012–19.

———— 1969. The vocational interests of Dartmouth College freshmen: 1947–67. *Personnel and Guidance Journal*, 47: 527–30.

———— 1971. *Handbook for the Strong Vocational Interest Blank*. Stanford, Calif.: Stanford University Press.

Campbell, D. P., F. H. Borgen, S. Eastes, C. B. Johansson, and R. A. Peterson. 1968. A set of Basic Interest Scales for the Strong Vocational Interest Blank for men. *Journal of Applied Psychology Monographs*, 52, no. 6, part 2.

Campbell, D. P., and J.C. Hansen. 1981. *Manual for the SVIB–SCII*, 3rd Ed. Stanford, Calif.: Stanford University Press.

Campbell, D. P., and J. L. Holland. 1972. A merger in vocational interest research: Applying Holland's theory to Strong's data. *Journal of Vocational Behavior*, 2: 353–76.

Chevrier, J. M. transl. and ed. 1979. Test de préférences professionnelles Strong-Campbell manuel. French translation of D. P. Campbell, *Manual for the Strong-Campbell Interest Inventory*. Montreal: Institut de Recherches Psychologiques, Inc.

Clark, K. E. 1961. *Vocational Interests of Non-professional Men*. Minneapolis: University of Minnesota Press.

Clark, K. E., and D. P. Campbell. 1965. *Minnesota Vocational Interest Inventory*. New York: Psychological Corporation.

Crites, J. O. Career counseling: A review of major approaches. *The Counseling Psychologist*, 1974, 4: 3–23.

Darley, J. G. 1941. *Clinical Aspects and Interpretation of the Strong Vocational Interest Blank*. New York: Psychological Corporation.

Dolliver, R. H., J. A. Irvin, and S. E. Bigley. 1972. Twelve-year follow-up of the Strong Vocational Interest Blank. *Journal of Counseling Psychology*, 19: 212–17.

Dolliver, R. H., and J. E. Kunce. 1973. Who drops out of an SVIB follow-up study? *Journal of Counseling Psychology*, 20: 188–89.

Douce, L. C. 1978. Career aspirations and career development of women in relation to Adventure scale scores on the Strong-Campbell Interest Inventory. *Dissertation Abstracts International*, 38 (10-B): 5091.

Fouad, N. A. 1984. Comparison of interests across cultures. *Dissertation Abstracts International*, 4503A (84-13): 777.

Fouad, N. A., R. Cudeck, and J. C. Hansen. 1984. Convergent validity of the Spanish and English forms of the SCII for bilingual Hispanic high school students. *Journal of Counseling Psychology*, 31: 339–48.

Hanlon, R. J. 1971. Validation of the Strong Vocational

Interest Blank for use in the Irish Republic. Unpublished Ph.D. dissertation, Social Science Research Centre, University College Galway, Ireland.

Hansen, J. C. 1976. Exploring new directions for SCII occupational scale construction. *Journal of Vocational Behavior*, 9: 147–60.

—— 1978. Age differences and empirical scale construction. *Measurement and Evaluation in Guidance*, 11: 78–87.

—— 1981. *Changing interests: Myth or reality?* Paper presented at meetings of American Psychological Association, Los Angeles, August.

—— 1982. The effect of history on the vocational interests of women. Paper presented at meetings of International Congress of Applied Psychology, Edinburgh, Scotland, July.

—— 1984. *User's Guide for the SVIB-SCII.* Stanford, Calif.: Stanford University Press.

Hansen, J. C., and N. A. Fouad. 1984. Translation and validation of the Spanish form of the Strong-Campbell Interest Inventory. *Measurement and Evaluation in Guidance*, 16: 192–97.

Hansen, J. C., and C. B. Johansson. 1972. The application of Holland's vocational model to the Strong Vocational Interest Blank for Women. *Journal of Vocational Behavior*, 2: 479–93.

Hansen, J. C., and J. Stocco. 1980. Stability of vocational interests of adolescents and young adults. *Measurement and Evaluation in Guidance*, 13: 173–78.

Hansen, J. C., and J. L. Swanson. 1983. Stability of interests and the predictive and concurrent validity of the 1981 Strong-Campbell Interest Inventory for college majors. *Journal of Counseling Psychology*, 30: 194–201.

Harmon, L. W. 1969. The predictive power over 10 years of measured social service and scientific interests among college women. *Journal of Applied Psychology*, 53: 193–98.

Holland, J. L. 1959. A theory of vocational choice. *Journal of Counseling Psychology*, 6: 35–45.

—— 1965. *Manual for the Vocational Preference Inventory.* Palo Alto, Calif.: Consulting Psychologists Press.

—— 1966. *The Psychology of Vocational Choice.* Waltham, Mass.: Blaisdell.

—— 1973. *Making Vocational Choices: A Theory of Careers.* Englewood Cliffs, N.J.: Prentice-Hall.

Hutchins, E. B. 1964. The AAMC longitudinal study: Implications for medical education. *Journal of Medical Education*, 39: 265–77.

Johansson, C. B., and D. P. Campbell. 1971. Stability of the Strong Vocational Interest Blank for Men. *Journal of Applied Psychology*, 55: 34–36.

Johansson, C. B., and L. W. Harmon. 1972. Strong Vocational Interest Blank: One form or two? *Journal of Counseling Psychology*, 19: 404–10.

Johnson, R. W. 1972. Contradictory scores on the Strong Vocational Interest Blank. *Journal of Counseling Psychology*, 19: 487–90.

Johnson, R. W., and C. B. Johansson. 1972. Moderating effect of basic interests on predictive validity of SVIB occupational scales. *Proceedings, 80th Annual Convention, American Psychological Association*, pp. 589–90.

Johnson, W. F., T. A. Korn, and D. J. Dunn. 1975. Comparing three methods of presenting occupational information. *Vocational Guidance Quarterly*, 24: 62–65.

Kivlighan, D. M., Jr., J. A. Hageseth, R. M. Tipton, and T. V. McGovern. 1981. Effects of matching treatment approaches and personality types in group vocational counseling. *Journal of Counseling Psychology*, 28: 315–20.

Lonner, W. J. 1968. The SVIB visits German, Austrian, and Swiss psychologists. *American Psychologist*, 23: 164–79.

—— 1969. Bericht ueber Untersuchungen mit der deutschen Fassung des Strong Vocational Interest Blank for Men (SVIB). *Psychologische Rundschau*, 20: 151–56.

Lonner, W. J., and H. L. Adams. 1972. Interest patterns of psychologists in nine western nations. *Journal of Applied Psychology*, 56: 146–51.

Maola, J., and G. Kane. 1976. Comparison of computer-based versus counselor-based occupational information systems with disadvantaged vocational students. *Journal of Counseling Psychology*, 23: 163–65.

McArthur, C. 1954. Long term validity of the Strong Interest Test in two subcultures. *Journal of Applied Psychology*, 38: 346–54.

Miller, M. J., and J. R. Cochran. 1979. Evaluating the use of technology in reporting SCII results to students. *Measurement and Evaluation in Guidance*, 12: 166–73.

Oliver, L. W. 1977. Evaluating career counseling outcome for three modes of test interpretation. *Measurement and Evaluation in Guidance*, 10: 153–61.

Rayman, J. R. 1976. Sex and the single interest inventory: The empirical validation of sex-balanced interest inventory items. *Journal of Counseling Psychology*, 23: 239–46.

Shah, I. 1971. A cross-cultural comparative study of vocational interests. *Dissertation Abstracts International*, 31 (8-B), 5049.

Spokane, A. R. 1979. Occupational preference and the validity of the Strong-Campbell Interest Inventory for college women and men. *Journal of Counseling Psychology*, 26: 312–18.

Stauffer, E., transl. and ed. 1973. [E. K. Strong, Jr., and D. P. Campbell.] Questionnaire d'intérets vocationnels: Manuel d'instructions. Issy-les-Moulineaux, France.

Strong, E. K., Jr. 1927. *Vocational Interest Blank.* Stanford, Calif.: Stanford University Press.

—— 1935. Predictive value of the Vocational Interest Test. *Journal of Educational Psychology*, 26: 332.

—— 1938. *Vocational Interest Blank for Men* (revised). Stanford, Calif.: Stanford University Press.

_____ 1943. *Vocational Interests of Men and Women.* Stanford, Calif.: Stanford University Press.

_____ 1955. *Vocational Interests 18 Years After College.* Minneapolis: University of Minnesota Press.

Swanson, J. L., and J. C. Hansen. 1985. The relationship of the construct of academic comfort to educational level, performance, aspiration, and prediction of college major choice. *Journal of Vocational Behavior*, 26: 1–12.

Tilton, J. W. 1937. The measurement of over-lapping. *Journal of Educational Psychology*, 28: 656–62.

Utz, P., and D. Korben. 1976. The construct validity of the Occupational Themes on the Strong-Campbell Interest Inventory. *Journal of Vocational Behavior*, 9: 31–42.

Varca, P. E., and G. S. Shaffer. 1982. Holland's theory: Stability of avocational interests. *Journal of Vocational Behavior*, 21: 288–98.

Webber, P. L., and L. W. Harmon. 1978. The reliability and concurrent validity of three types of occupational scales for two occupational groups: Some evidence bearing on handling sex differences in interest scale construction. Chapter in *Sex-Fair Interest Measurement: Research and Implications.* C. K. Tittle, and D. G. Zytowski eds., Washington, D.C.: NIE, Department of Health, Education and Welfare.